THE COMMUNITY OF RIGHTS

ALAN GEWIRTH

THE
COMMUNITY
OF
RIGHTS

THE UNIVERSITY OF CHICAGO PRESS
CHICAGO & LONDON

ALAN GEWIRTH is the Edward Carson Waller Distinguished Service Professor at the University of Chicago. His books include *Reason and Morality; Human Rights: Essays on Justification and Applications;* and *Marsilius of Padua and Medieval Political Philosophy.*

The University of Chicago Press, Chicago 60637
The University of Chicago Press, Ltd., London
©1996 by The University of Chicago
All rights reserved. Published 1996
Printed in the United States of America
05 04 03 02 01 00 99 98 97 96   1 2 3 4 5

ISBN: 0-226- 28880-3 (cloth)
ISBN: 978-0-226-28881-9 (paper)

Library of Congress Cataloging-in-Publication Data

Gewirth, Alan.
The community of rights / Alan Gewirth.
    p.   cm.
Includes bibliographical references (p.   ) and index.
    1. Human rights. 2. Mutualism. I. Title.
    JC571.G437 1996   95-33026
                               CIP

⊗ The paper used in this publication meets the minimum requirements of the American National Standard for Information Sciences—Permanence of Paper for Printed Library Materials, ANSI Z39.48-1984.

To the Memory of Marcella

and

to Susela, Andy, Dan, and Letty

CONTENTS

Preface   xi

CHAPTER ONE
ACTION AND HUMAN RIGHTS

1.1.   The Opposition between Rights and Community   1

1.2.   The Initial Conciliation of Rights and Community   6

1.3.   Are There Any Moral or Human Rights?   8

1.4.   Human Action as the Basis of Human Rights   13

1.5.   The Argument for Human Rights   16

1.6.   Some Objections to the Argument   20

1.7.   Comparisons to Some Other Doctrines   26

CHAPTER TWO
POSITIVE RIGHTS

2.1.   The Importance of Positive Rights   31

2.2.   The Distinction between Negative and Positive Rights   33

2.3.   The Argument for Positive Rights   38

2.4.   Objections to Positive Rights: Freedom and Degrees
        of Needfulness for Action   44

2.5.   Objections to Positive Rights: Overload of Duties   54

2.6.   Objections to Positive Rights: Universality   62

CHAPTER THREE
MUTUALITY AND COMMUNITY

3.1.   Justice and Equality   71

3.2.   Mutuality and Reciprocity   75

3.3. Rights, Charity, and Humanity 79

3.4. The Idea of Community and the Social Contribution Thesis 81

3.5. Further Replies to the Adversarial Conception 87

3.6. Community and Conceptions of the Self 91

3.7. Ethical Individualism, Socialism, and the Economic
      Constitution 96

3.8. The Problems of Rights Inflation and Specification 101

CHAPTER FOUR
THE RIGHT TO PRODUCTIVE AGENCY

4.1. The Right to Welfare and the Deprivation Focus 106

4.2. The Welfare System and Autonomy 114

4.3. Welfare Dependence, Autonomy, and Mutuality 118

4.4. Organicist Relations and Welfare Recipience 125

4.5. Workfare and Its Problems 127

4.6. Productive Agency and Productivist Welfarism 131

4.7. Human Capital as a Form of Productive Agency 136

4.8. Productive and Unproductive Labor 141

4.9. Education for Productive Agency 149

4.10. Early Education and Equality of Self-Actualization 155

4.11. The Nonneutrality of the Community of Rights 162

CHAPTER FIVE
THE RIGHT TO PRIVATE PROPERTY

5.1. Productive Agency and Two Justifications of Property Rights 166

5.2. Consequentialist Justification of Property Rights 170

5.3. Antecedentalist Justification of Property Rights 181

5.4. Primordialist Objections to the Purposive-Labor Thesis:
      Self-Ownership 188

5.5. Primordialist Objections to the Purposive-Labor Thesis:
      World Ownership 194

5.6. Relations between the Two Justifications 198

5.7. The Contribution Principle and Economic Inequality 203

CHAPTER SIX
THE RIGHT TO EMPLOYMENT

6.1. The Argument from Productive Agency and Basic Well-Being 214

6.2. The Argument from Self-Respect and Self-Esteem 223

6.3. Is There No Need for Work? 229

6.4. Is There a Duty to Work? When Do Right-Holders Have
     Corresponding Duties? 231

6.5. Is All Unemployment Voluntary? 236

6.6. Full Employment and Inflation 242

6.7. Wage Costs of Full Employment 246

6.8. Full Employment and Shirking 249

6.9. Employment at Will and Property Rights in Jobs 252

CHAPTER SEVEN
THE RIGHT TO ECONOMIC DEMOCRACY

7.1. Economic Democracy as Workers' Control 257

7.2. Economic Democracy and the Right to Freedom 266

7.3. Analogies between Economic and Political Democracy 273

7.4. Economic Democracy and the Right To Well-Being 278

7.5. Disanalogies between Economic and Political Democracy 288

7.6. The Universalization of Economic Democracy 294

7.7. Competition and Solidarity 301

7.8. Economic Democracy and Social Democracy 308

CHAPTER EIGHT
THE RIGHT TO POLITICAL DEMOCRACY

8.1. Political Democracy as the Method of Consent 311

8.2. Should Economic Rights Be Subject to Political Democracy? 318

8.3. Should Basic Rights and Political Rights Be Subject to Political
     Democracy? 324

8.4. Will Economic Rights Be Supported by Political Democracy? 327

8.5. Civil Liberties as Effective Powers 335

8.6. Civil Liberties as Positive Rights 341

8.7. Some Concluding Reflections 348

Index 359

PREFACE

This book is a sequel to *Reason and Morality*, which was first published by the University of Chicago Press in 1978.[1] In that book I undertook to show that morality, far from being based on variable personal preferences or social conventions, has a firm rational foundation in the necessary conditions of human action. My central argument was that by virtue of having an indispensable need for freedom and well-being as the necessary goods of action, every actual or prospective agent logically must hold that he or she has rights to these goods and that all other actual or prospective agents also have these rights. The argument thus eventuates in a principle of equal and universal human rights, which I also called the Principle of Generic Consistency (PGC) because it combines the formal consideration of consistency with the material consideration of the generic features and rights of action. That argument has received a large amount of critical discussion, including not only some 150 articles, book sections, and reviews but also three full-length books, two in English and one in German.[2] I am very grateful for this outpouring of (still continuing) scrutiny, from which I have learned much. An at least partial culmination of this scrutiny was achieved by the publication in 1991 of Deryck Beyleveld's massive book, which presented, besides a very acute analysis of my argument, cogent replies to most of the objections that had appeared to 1990.[3] In chapter 1 of the present book I offer a very abbreviated recapitulation of the

1. *Reason and Morality* will usually be referred to in the text and notes as *RM*, followed by page number.
2. Edward Regis Jr., ed., *Gewirth's Ethical Rationalism: Critical Essays with a Reply by Alan Gewirth* (Chicago: University of Chicago Press, 1984); Deryck Beyleveld, *The Dialectical Necessity of Morality: An Analysis and Defense of Alan Gewirth's Argument to the Principle of Generic Consistency* (Chicago: University of Chicago Press, 1991); Klaus Steigleder, *Die Begründung des moralischen Sollens* (Tübingen: Attempto Verlag, 1992).
3. See above, n. 2.

argument for the PGC as a way of setting the stage for the subsequent developments.

The last two chapters of *Reason and Morality* are taken up with what I called "direct" and "indirect" applications of the PGC. In the indirect applications the PGC's justificatory requirements of equal rights are imposed in the first instance on the social rules of four kinds of institutions—voluntary associations, the minimal state, the democratic state, and the supportive state—and the requirements of these institutions are then in turn imposed on the actions of individuals. The main function of the supportive state is the instrumental dynamic one of promoting certain important equalities of the effective rights to freedom and well-being where these equalities have institutional sources. And the central project of the present book is to give an extensive development of the requirements of the supportive state, which I also call "the community of rights" for reasons indicated in chapters 1, 2, and 3.

Like most other workers in political philosophy, I have been strongly influenced by the institutional developments of our time. The dramatic downfall of the Soviet Union has confirmed the moral bankruptcy of political dictatorship and central planning. But all is far from well in the liberal democracies and market economies of the United States and Western Europe. Their democratic structures are vital bases of political morality—and here I want to pay special tribute to my own country for its continuing and almost unparalleled efforts to accommodate within a single society, on a constitutional basis of equal rights, the large varieties of racial, ethnic, cultural, and other diversities that make up its population. But the liberal democracies with their capitalist market economies are also plagued by deeply rooted social ills, including massive poverty, unemployment, crime, homelessness, and other pathologies that show no signs of diminishing. For these reasons the Western societies, including the United States, are in important respects far from serving as adequate models for development either in Eastern Europe or in the so-called Third World. Predictions are, of course, precarious and causal diagnoses only slightly less so. But, amid the univeralist pretensions that I, like other writers in political philosophy, have tried to maintain (epitomized in part in the Universal Declaration of Human Rights promulgated by the United Nations in 1948), it has been the severe social and economic afflictions undergone by so many members both of the Western democracies and other parts of the world that have served as a special stimulus to the project I have undertaken in this book. For reasons presented in detail below I have characterized these afflictions as violations of the human rights to freedom and well-being, and I have sought in various applications of the principle of human rights, especially as specified in economic and social rights, to show how the root causes of the afflictions should be removed and a greater effective equalization of human rights achieved. It is to this task that the community of rights is dedicated.

In the last five chapters of this book I have tried to work out a sequence of "economic biography" and "economic constitution" whereby this achievement can be progressively realized. In so doing I have sought to avoid the vices not only of unrealism and utopianism but also of witting or unwitting acceptance of the status quo as mired in permanent, unchanging verities. In this regard the present book may be regarded as an attempt to give a philosophical elucidation and specification of some of the main economic and social rights set forth in the Universal Declaration of Human Rights by showing how they can be derived, by various modes of argument, from a single rationally justified moral principle that serves to ground their more specific contents. It is on this moral principle, with the mutuality of rights and duties that it embodies, that the community of rights is based.

It may be helpful to call attention to certain ways in which my endeavor here bridges various familiar social and political divides in addition to the antithesis between rights and community to which the first three chapters are addressed. Like many so-called "conservatives" I place great stress on individual responsibility and autonomy. But like many so-called "liberals" I emphasize that these values are not already possessed by large groups in our societies, especially those who are most deprived; on the contrary, these values must be achieved by helping persons to develop their abilities of productive agency. In a parallel way, large groups in our societies are in drastic need of help; this help, however, must emphasize not the continuation of passive recipience and dependence but rather the abilities whereby each person can be a productive agent on his or her own behalf, while at the same time taking positive account of the mutual rights of others. It is, indeed, the need for mutuality on the part of all members of society that constitutes the moral structure of the community of rights, and this need is a central theme of the present book.

Especially controversial among the divides just mentioned is the question of the role of government in the securing of economic and social rights. What is at issue here is both whether the goods or interests that are their objects are matters of rights in the first place, and also whether the means of promoting or fulfilling them should be through governmental provision or through private or voluntary arrangements. Libertarians and others have argued vehemently for the latter course. In upholding a certain modified governmental or political role in this regard, I have had to take account of the value of freedom, including the "free market," but I have also emphasized that the necessities of the objects of rights for human action entail that the means of attaining these objects cannot be left to optional choices. This divide figures prominently in many of the analyses and arguments presented here.

I have in this book gone into the specifics of economic and social problems in perhaps more detail than is customary in treatises of political philosophy. My justification for this is that the empirical understanding of these problems is of crucial importance for the philosophical task of evaluating proposed solutions through the norms of human rights. In this connection it may be helpful if I briefly indicate the more general philosophical context within which the present work falls. Beginning at least with Aristotle, Western political philosophers have worked on three different levels of analysis, which may be called the empirical, the moral or ethical, and the metaphysical. At the first, empirical level (represented in bks. 4, 5, and 6 of Aristotle's *Politics*), the ongoing problems of contemporary and other societies are set forth and specific solutions are evaluated. In the present book, similarly, the problems of the deprived masses of persons in contemporary societies are examined and specific solutions are proposed. At the second, moral level, the focus is on the general moral principles that are used to evaluate the problems and proposed solutions, and hence on the applications of the principles. This level is represented in Aristotle's *Politics* in book 3, with its analysis of justice as the "common good." In the present book, in a parallel way, the PGC as the moral principle of human rights is applied to justify the community of rights and thereby the more specific economic and social rights whose effectuation would help to rectify the problems of severe deprivation in modern societies. At the third, metaphysical level, the concern is with the still more general ontological and justificatory context of the moral principle adduced on the second level; this context is invoked to elucidate the foundations of the moral principle. In Aristotle's *Politics,* book 1, this task is fulfilled by his appeals to "nature," in such famous theses as that "the state exists by nature" and "man is by nature a political animal." In the present book, the metaphysical level is provided by the concept of human action as the ontological and justificatory context of the principle of human rights. I have elsewhere presented arguments in criticism of the Aristotelian naturalistic foundations and in support of the context of human action.[4]

It is the requirements of human action, both in its general possibility and as generally successful, that ground the human rights to freedom and

4. See my essays "The Ontological Basis of Natural Law: A Critique and an Alternative," *American Journal of Jurisprudence* 29 (1984): 95–121, and "The Constitutive Metaphysics of Ethics," *Revue de Métaphysique et de Morale* 98, no. 4 (Oct.–Dec. 1993): 489–504.

well-being which serve in turn to ground the economic and social rights upheld and elucidated in this book as essential parts of the community of rights.

Amid my concentration here on economic needs and problems, it is important to keep in mind that my whole project has an important spiritual dimension. This spirituality is directly reflective of the moral concern that all humans, as actual or prospective agents, be enabled to live lives of dignity, self-fulfillment, and mutuality of respect. This may be a secular spirituality, but it is none the worse for that. The theses I present in this book, epitomized in the community of rights, can indeed be viewed as arguing not only for a caring society but also, in a parallel way, for an institutionalization of love. If it is held that love as a personal emotion cannot be institutionalized, it can nevertheless be embodied in a system of policies motivated by a concern for the fulfillment of all persons' needs for dignity, self-respect, and more generally for the necessary conditions of action and generally successful action. In this regard the "moral" emphasis on the rights of others and duties toward others goes hand in hand with the "ethical" emphasis on living a good life, a life of flourishing, autonomy, and fruitful association with others. The concept of the community of rights which I invoke throughout this book is intended to fix this unity of social and personal emphases at the heart of political philosophy in a normatively cogent way.

During this book's long gestation period I have published many articles that have incorporated parts or aspects of its central theses. I may here refer especially to my articles on economic justice[5] and economic rights;[6] in addition, I have presented papers bearing this book's title as invited lectures at the Eighteenth World Congress of Philosophy held in 1988 in Brighton, England, and at the Twelfth Interamerican Congress of Philosophy held in 1989 in Buenos Aires. The latter paper has been published in Spanish translation.[7] My Bar-Hillel Lectures delivered at Tel Aviv University, Israel, in 1987 also incorporated segments of the theses of this book. I am grateful for the helpful comments I have received on all these occasions as well as at many other public presentations, including guest lectures at the annual meetings of the History of Economics Society in 1986 and the Society for Business Ethics in 1984.

I also wish to acknowledge other important debts. The National En-

5. "Economic Justice: Concepts and Criteria," in Kenneth Kipnis and Diana T. Meyers, eds., *Economic Justice: Private Rights and Public Responsibilities* (Totowa, N.J.: Rowman and Allanheld, 1985), pp. 7–32.

6. "Economic Rights," *Philosophical Topics* 14 (1986): 169–93.

7. "La Comunidad de Derechos," trans. Cristina Gonzalez and Eduardo Rabossi, *Analisis Filosofico* 10, no. 2 (1990): 105–22.

dowment for the Humanities, by awarding me a second fellowship, greatly facilitated my work on this book. Dean Philip Gossett of the Division of the Humanities at the University of Chicago gave me a special research fund to support my work. I also wish to thank two of my other Chicago colleagues who were especially helpful. Theodore W. Schultz, Nobel Laureate in economic science, discussed with me at length his important concept of human capital; he was very generous in taking time to answer my queries and sending me some of his unpublished writings on education. Laurence E. Lynn, Jr., contributed greatly to my understanding of the welfare system. Of course, neither of these scholars is responsible for the use I have made of their ideas. Many other persons have given me help of various kinds in my work on this book, by commenting on my lectures and articles, by sending me their books and papers, by suggesting important lines of inquiry, by supporting my grant applications, and in other ways. In these connections I wish to thank Timothy Brennan, Jeanne Cumming, Robert D. Cumming, David Ellerman, Jon Elster, Georges Enderle, the late William K. Frankena, Harry G. Frankfurt, Nancy Fraser, N. L. Gage, John Johannes, Derek Jones, Jean Laves, Don Lavoie, Robert E. Lucas Jr., William L. McBride, Carlos S. Nino, John T. Noonan Jr., Onora O'Neill, Alex Orden, Roger Pilon, Adam Przeworski, Louis Putterman, Eduardo Rabossi, David D. Raphael, Eugene Rotwein, Richard Sabot, Justin Schwartz, David Schweickart, Tony Smith, James P. Sterha, the late George J. Stigler, Cass Sunstein, Brian Tierney, the late Gregory Vlastos, and Patricia H. Werhane. I am greatly indebted to Kathy Cochran for her very fine competence and cooperativeness in word processing my manuscript. For invaluable help of a different kind I am deeply grateful to Bernie Brown, Dotty and Dick Carlin, Lil and Joe Cropsey, Maryal Stone Dale, and Phyllis and the late Manley Thompson. I dedicate this book to the memory of my beloved Marcella and to our children.

ONE

ACTION AND HUMAN RIGHTS

1.1. THE OPPOSITION BETWEEN RIGHTS AND COMMUNITY

This book has two chief aims. One is to show that rights and community, far from being antithetical to one another, have a relation of mutual support. The other, to which the first is ancillary, is to develop in some detail how this relation can serve to fulfill the economic and other rights of the most deprived members of society and thereby lead to greater economic and political equality. The argument I shall present is thus concerned with the moral justification of economic and social policies and institutions, especially as they help to relieve human suffering. Such policies and institutions, when they are embodied in the state or political society, constitute what I call the community of rights.

The issue of the relation between rights and community is of more than merely conceptual interest. It bears on a whole host of problems, not only moral and political but also ontological. A central difficulty of getting at these problems is that they are interpreted in different ways by opposed protagonists of the values and ideas in question. In one of the main modes of interpretation, to focus on rights in moral and political philosophy entails giving primary consideration to individuals conceived as atomic entities existing independent of social ties, while to focus instead on community is to regard persons as having inherent affective social relations to one another—relations in groups ranging from one's family through one's ethnic and other clusters to one's country. A direct consequence of this contrast is that the phrase "community of rights" is viewed as an oxymoron by many thinkers, going back at least to Bentham and Marx.[1] According to these views, rights presuppose competition and conflict, since rights are intended as guarantees that self-seeking individuals will not be trampled in

---

1. Jeremy Bentham, *A Critical Examination of the Declaration of Rights*, in B. Parekh, ed., *Bentham's Political Thought* (New York: Barnes and Noble, 1973), pp. 261, 263 ff.; Karl Marx, *On the Jewish Question*, in R. C. Tucker, ed., *The Marx-Engels Reader*, 2d ed. (New York: W. W. Norton, 1978), p. 43.

I

their adversarial relations with one another. Community, on the other hand, connotes the absence of such conflicts: it signifies common interests and cooperation, mutual sympathy and fellow-feeling. Since a right involves a claim that a person makes for the protection of his or her interests, the focus on rights is held to evince an exclusive individualistic preoccupation with fulfillment of one's own desires or needs regardless of broader social goals; hence, it submerges the values of community and obscures or annuls the moral responsibilities that one has to other persons and to society at large. As a result, it is charged that the rights doctrine atomizes society and alienates persons from one another. But when persons maintain the ties of community that make for social harmony, there is no need for rights. The claiming of rights, then, is egoistic and antithetical to morality and community. I shall call this the *adversarial conception* of the relation between community and rights.[2] In this view, one must reject not only the thesis that rights and community have a relation of mutual support but also my project of showing how the community of rights can fulfill the rights of persons.

A more affirmative relation between rights and community has indeed been upheld by some thinkers. They have said that community provides the justifying basis or at least the essential background of rights, in that right-claims presuppose the existence of a community to which the claims are addressed and which understands and accepts the claims and the common rules that serve to justify them.[3] It has also been held that communities themselves have rights, such as the rights to self-determination, to a common language and culture, to development, and so forth.[4]

2. See Charles Taylor, "Atomism," in Taylor, *Philosophy and the Human Sciences* (Cambridge: Cambridge University Press, 1985), vol. 2, pp. 187–210, and "Cross-Purposes: The Liberal-Communitarian Debate," in Nancy L. Rosenblum, ed., *Liberalism and the Moral Life* (Cambridge, Mass.: Harvard University Press, 1989), pp. 159–82; Michael J. Sandel, *Liberalism and the Limits of Justice* (Cambridge: Cambridge University Press, 1982), and "The Procedural Republic and the Unencumbered Self," *Political Theory* 12 (1984): 81–96; Richard E. Flathman, *The Practice of Rights* (Cambridge: Cambridge University Press, 1976); John Charvet, "A Critique of Human Rights," in J. Roland Pennock and J. W. Chapman, eds., *Nomos XXIII: Human Rights* (New York: New York University Press, 1981), pp. 31–51; Alasdair MacIntyre, *After Virtue* (Notre Dame, Ind.: University of Notre Dame Press, 1981); Michael Walzer, *Spheres of Justice* (New York: Basic Books, 1983: Judith J. Thomson, *The Realm of Rights* (Cambridge, Mass.: Harvard University Press, 1990), pp. 222–23; Mary Ann Glendon, *Rights Talk: The Impoverishment of Political Discourse* (New York: Free Press, 1991), pp. 110–11, 175.

3. See Martin P. Golding, "Towards a Theory of Human Rights," *The Monist* 52 (Oct. 1968): 521–49; R. E. Ewin, *Liberty, Community, and Justice* (Totowa, N.J.: Rowman and Littlefield, 1987), chaps. 3–5; MacIntyre, *After Virtue*, p. 65. I have given a detailed reply to MacIntyre in "Rights and Virtues," *Review of Metaphysics* 38, no. 4 (June 1985): 739–62.

4. See Vernon Van Dyke, "The Individual, the State, and Ethnic Communities in Political Theory," in D. P. Kommers and G. D. Loescher, eds., *Human Rights and American For-

The bearing of these views on the adversarial conception outlined above is doubtful, however, because there is no assurance that they interpret "community" in the extensively cooperative, mutualist sense that underlies the asserted opposition between community and rights. But even apart from this, the first of the views just cited is largely mistaken. It is true that persons who claim rights assume that their addressees can understand their claims and can comply with them. But the addressees need not constitute a community in the sense of a group that upholds or recognizes rules on which the right-claims are based, let alone rules that are solidaristic and cooperative. Such a view is unduly conservative; it ignores that the persons addressed may not accept the right-claims and may even reject the rules that underlie them. The claims of the abolitionists and the opponents of apartheid are familiar examples. So the claiming of rights does not assume the existence of a justificatory community even in this attenuated sense.

As for the view that communities or groups themselves have rights, even if this is granted, important grounds may remain for not assimilating the communities in question to the strong sense of "community" in which it has been opposed to rights. For one thing, there is the perennial question of whether the community's rights can be reduced to the rights of individuals. If they can, the adversarial relation between rights and community could still be maintained if the rights in question have the self-seeking character outlined above. If, moreover, the rights are held to belong to the community as a corporate entity distinct from its individual members, this may raise the question of whether the community respects the rights of its individual members and does so equally—which would again leave open at least one segment of the adversarial relation between rights and community. Persons may, indeed, rebel against their community in the name of their individual rights.

A chief aim of this book is to provide a detailed reply to the adversarial conception of the relation between rights and community. The importance of this conciliatory project hardly needs emphasis. A perennial problem of moral and political philosophy has concerned the proper relation of self-seeking individuals both to one another and to their wider society. In attempting to justify their diverse solutions to this problem, philosophers

eign Policy (Notre Dame, Ind.: University of Notre Dame Press, 1979), pp. 36–62; Jeremy Waldron, "Can Communal Goods Be Human Rights?" in Waldron, *Liberal Rights* (Cambridge: Cambridge University Press, 1993), pp. 339–69; A. J. M. Milne, *Human Rights and Human Diversity* (Albany: State University of New York Press, 1986), p. 4; Jack Donnelly, *Universal Human Rights in Theory and Practice* (Ithaca, N.Y.: Cornell University Press, 1989), chap. 8; Joseph Raz, "Right-Based Moralities," in Jeremy Waldron, ed., *Theories of Rights* (Oxford: Oxford University Press, 1984), pp. 182–200; Jean-Bernard Marie, "Relations between People's Rights and Human Rights: Semantic and Methodological Distinctions," *Human Rights Law Journal* 7 (1986): 195–204.

have invoked contrasting ideals of freedom and equality, individualism and solidarity, competition and cooperation, self-reliance and mutual aid, particularism and universalism, changes in individuals and changes in systems, market incentives and moral motivations, and many more. It has often been assumed that these contrasts are so strong and enduring that no viable reconciliations can be found. It is in this context that the antithesis between rights and community has been held to be both centrally significant and unbridgeable.

The project of conciliating rights and community, then, is important not merely as a conceptual exercise but because it bears directly on the necessity of tying the protection of persons' most vital interests to the justified functioning of social institutions. Thus the antithesis between rights and community also has a close connection with the second chief aim of this book: to show how the relation between rights and community can serve to fulfill the economic and other rights of the most deprived members of society. Libertarians, various conservatives, and other thinkers, unlike many communitarians, do indeed ascribe prime value to the rights of individuals; but they hold that these rights preclude using some persons as means to fulfill the needs or interests of other persons. Insofar as the idea of community is held to support such fulfillment, especially through governmental provision or coercion, the idea, according to these views, must be rejected as morally vicious and tyrannical. What must be relied on instead is the free market, which respects persons' rights to freedom and derives other rights from the voluntary contracts that individuals make with one another through their own conceptions of their respective interests. Thus the conceptual antithesis between rights and community now eventuates in strong opposition to governmental intervention in economic affairs, except to prevent force and fraud and perhaps to secure a stable supply of money for the economy as a whole.

This book attempts to provide reasoned arguments against this political —or perhaps rather antipolitical—rejection of an affirmative relation between rights and community. I shall try to show that rights—especially the human rights that equally belong to all humans as such—are positive as well as negative, and that as positive they warrant serious and active governmental concern for protecting and promoting the freedom and well-being of all humans, especially those who are most deprived. A government violates human rights when its hands-off policy lets the most vulnerable members of its society suffer harms and injuries like poverty, disease, illiteracy, or unemployment when it can take measures to prevent or alleviate such ills and when the persons affected cannot ward them off by their own efforts. The governmental policies here upheld do not preclude individual initiatives or remedies; on the contrary, a main aim must be to enable persons to be productive agents on their own behalf. But it is a serious error to confuse the desirability of this aim with the belief that it is already fully within the powers or abilities of the persons or groups in question.

The community of rights, then, as it will be delineated in the following chapters, is a society whose government actively seeks to help fulfill the needs of its members, especially those who are most vulnerable, for the freedom and well-being that are the necessary goods of human agency, when persons cannot attain this fulfillment by their own efforts. This governmental activity will be justified on the basis of the very concept—rights—to which the antigovernmental theorists have appealed; but, as I have said, the rights in question will be shown to be positive as well as negative, so that they entail on the part of their respondents—who include governments acting as representatives of their citizens—duties not only of noninterference in certain contexts but also of active assistance in vitally important economic and social contexts. I shall undertake to show how the justificatory argument can take full account of the freedom rights of persons who are called upon to support such active governmental policies.

The idea of the community of rights, as it will be developed in this book, thus takes sides on what is perhaps the most controversial issue of modern political theory and practice. In the United States alone, to go back no further than the last century, there have been the various policies and programs of populism, progressivism, the New Deal, the Great Society, and related currents, each of which has met vehement opposition from individualists and libertarians who have invoked the negative rights of freedom (construed solely as noninterference) to reject the governmental interventions into economy and society. These interventions have been depicted as totalitarian oppressions; but those who so depict them have ignored the oppressions endured by masses of persons whose ability to compete in the economic marketplace has been seriously weakened by forces beyond their control. The aim of this treatise on the community of rights is to provide detailed justifications and elucidations of the governmental policies and institutions that are designed to ward off such oppressions and to enable all persons to develop their own abilities of productive agency. Thereby important moral steps will be taken toward a certain valuable kind of self-fulfillment for all persons. To show that rights and community have a relation of mutual support will thus enable us to understand not only how the libertarian and related individualist doctrines are to be answered but also how this relation can justify a kind of liberal democratic welfare state that enables all persons to be or become productive agents who help to fulfill the needs and interests both of themselves and of other persons.

1.2. THE INITIAL CONCILIATION
OF RIGHTS AND COMMUNITY

Because the issues of the community of rights are so complex and controversial, great care must be taken that the stages of the argument be laid out
as clearly and carefully as possible. I shall now begin this process by presenting an initial conciliation of the previously adumbrated antithesis between rights and community. As against this antithesis, I shall here argue
that when rights are properly understood, they entail a communitarian
conception of human relations, relations of mutual assistance, social solidarity, and important kinds of equality.

A brief statement of the argument to this effect can be given as follows.
The rights in question are human rights, rights that are had by every human
being simply insofar as he or she is human. But while the rights involve
claims to the protection of individual interests, they also require of each
person that she act with due regard for other persons' interests as well as
her own. For, as human rights, they are not only had by all humans; they
are also rights against all humans. In other words, each human being is
both the subject or right-holder and the respondent or duty-bearer. The
objects of these rights, what they are rights to, are freedom and well-being,
which are the necessary conditions of action and generally successful action (this will be shown below). It follows that, with regard to human
rights, every human has rights to freedom and well-being against all other
humans, but every other human also has these rights against him, so that he
has correlative duties toward them. The concept of human rights thus entails a mutualist and egalitarian universality: each human must respect the
rights of all the others while having his rights respected by all the others, so
that there must be a mutual sharing of the benefits of rights and the burdens
of duties. In this way, each individual's personal claim to and protected
property in the necessary goods of action are combined with a required
concern for interests shared in common with all other persons. Because
this principle of human rights entails the requirement of mutual respect
(and of mutual aid when needed and practicable), it is a principle of social
solidarity, as against exclusive preoccupation with personal interest. This
solidarity requires institutions whereby hitherto deprived groups can be
brought nearer to equality. By the effective recognition of the mutuality entailed by human rights, the society becomes a community. So the antithesis
between rights and community is bridged.

This brief conceptual argument, which will receive extensive explication and specification in what follows, provides an at least partial answer to
the familiar charge that an emphasis on rights leads to a neglect of duties.
For in the case of human rights, as also in more specific contexts, right-

holders logically must acknowledge that they have correlative duties (see also 6.4). But now we must confront the question of just how the argument bears on the adversarial conception of the relation between rights and community. If, as the conception assumes, individuals as claimants of rights are entirely or at least largely self-interested, then why will they heed an argument, even if based on the concept of human rights, that purports to impose duties that may be contrary to their self-interest? Isn't it question-begging to appeal to this concept if its acceptance entails at least modifying the self-interest whose preponderant force is precisely the issue? What motivation do people have to accept the concept of human rights in the first place, let alone abide by its implications? Just as Kant pointed out that to derive the existence of God from the concept of God is a mere verbal exercise, so it may be held that to derive communitarian obligations from the concept of human rights is similarly verbal. It may also be contended that the universal mutuality of rights here envisaged is utterly impractical.

It will be noticed that this objection in effect repeats the adversarial conception of the relation between rights and community, simply replacing the relata, respectively, by self-interest and human rights. So the objection retains that aspect of the concept of rights whereby it was held to characterize exclusively self-seeking individuals.

At least part of the objection can be dismissed at the outset. Since the initial question concerned the relation between the concepts of rights and community, including their implications for persons' actual conduct and social institutions, no question is so far begged when these concepts are analyzed and their implications are brought out. Doubts may also be raised about the objection's imputation of exclusive self-interest to the individuals in question.[5] It is perhaps safest to remain with this at least for the present in order to avoid begging some questions. As for the charge of impracticality, this will be dealt with in the next chapter (2.5). There are at least two other major ways, however, in which the objection can still be pressed. First, it may be held that self-seeking individuals need have no concern with rights or any other moral or normative concepts; they will pursue their own interests but will not regard them, or their protection, as rights. Second, it may be held further that even if an individual does accept that

5. Arguments against the thesis of exclusive self-interest can be traced back at least to Butler and Hume; see David Hume, *Enquiry Concerning the Principles of Morals*, Appendix II: "Of Self-Love," ed. L. A. Selby-Bigge (Oxford: Clarendon Press, 1962), pp. 295–302, including his striking condemnation of the "philosophical chymistry" whereby all passions are reduced to self-love (p. 297). For recent discussions, see Amartya Sen, "Rational Fools," *Philosophy and Public Affairs* 6, no. 4 (Summer 1977), pp. 317–42; Howard Margolis, *Selfishness, Altruism, and Rationality* (Chicago: University of Chicago Press, 1984); Jane J. Mansbridge, ed., *Beyond Self-Interest* (Chicago: University of Chicago Press, 1990).

she herself has rights, she need not extend this to the much more far-reaching thesis that all humans have rights, so that there are human rights. Hence, on either or both of these grounds she will reject the conceptual argument that ties human rights to community.

The first of these two points shifts the argument from the question of the relation between rights and community to the prior question of the justification for being concerned with rights or making right-claims in the first place. To deal with the objection in this more extensive form, then, requires consideration of the two following questions: First, what logical or rational justification is there for attributing to self-interested individuals a concern for their own having rights or making right-claims? Second, what logical or rational justification is there for a self-interested individual's moving, or having to move, from an acceptance that she herself has rights to the much broader moral judgment that every individual has rights, so that there are human rights and correlative duties? To answer these questions requires that we look more deeply into the concept of rights and the argument for human rights. The conciliation of rights and community is quite incomplete without this additional inquiry, which concerns, indeed, the rational foundation of morality. The analyses and arguments to be presented in the next four sections will largely recapitulate, although in much briefer form, the discussions set forth in the first three chapters of *Reason and Morality*. Although the reader who is sufficiently familiar with those discussions may skip directly to section 1.7 below, it may be helpful in the present context to give the following summary of my answers to the above questions.

1.3. ARE THERE ANY MORAL OR HUMAN RIGHTS?

Let us begin with an initial depiction of the concept of a right, which will also indicate in a preliminary way why even exclusively self-interested and amoral individuals must claim rights for themselves. As was suggested in the argument given in the preceding section, the rights that are here in question are primarily claim-rights, that is, rights that entail correlative duties at least to refrain from interfering with persons' having the objects of their rights and, in certain circumstances, to help persons to have these objects.

The general structure of a claim-right is given by the following formula:

A has a right to X against B by virtue of Y.

There are five main elements here: first, the *subject* (A) of the right, the right-holder; second, the *nature* of the right, what being a right consists in; third, the *object* (X) of the right, what it is a right to; fourth, the *respondent*

(B) of the right, the person or group that has the correlative duty; and fifth, the *justifying basis* (Y) of the right. When the rights in question are human rights, both the subjects and the respondents comprise all human beings equally; the objects are certain essential interests of human beings as prospective purposive agents; and the justifying basis is a stringently rational supreme principle of morality.

What, then, is the nature of a right? In briefest compass, a right is an individual's interest that ought to be respected and protected; and this 'ought' involves, on the one side, that the interest in question is something that is due or owed to the subject or right-holder as her personal property, as what she is personally entitled to have and control for her own sake; and, on the other side, that other persons, as respondents, have a mandatory duty at least not to infringe this property. The importance of rights stems from the need for and value of such protection, from the claim that this protection is justified as being owed to persons for their own sakes (so that rights go beyond mere interests as such), from the mandatoriness of this protection as thus owed and as grounding strict duties, and, especially when they are human rights, from the great value of the objects or interests that need to be protected: interests ranging from life, physical integrity, and economic security to self-esteem and education.

It should be noted that although claim-rights and duties are correlative, this does not mean that they are identical. Instead, they have different normative contents and a different valuational status, in that rights are to duties as benefits are to burdens. For rights are justified claims to certain benefits, the support or protection of certain interests of the right-holder. Duties, on the other hand, are justified burdens on the part of the respondent or duty-bearer: they restrict his freedom by requiring that he conduct himself in ways that directly benefit not himself but rather the right-holder. But burdens are for the sake of benefits, and not vice versa. Hence, duties, which are burdens, are for the sake of rights, whose objects are benefits. Rights, then, are prior to duties in the order of justifying purpose or final cause, in that respondents have correlative duties *because* subjects have certain rights. This justificatory priority of rights over duties is not antithetical to their being correlative to one another; and it still leaves open that some duties may have grounds other than rights.[6]

This brief analysis already suggests why even exclusively self-interested individuals must be concerned with their own having rights. For, as self-interested, they have interests and they want them to be protected for their own sakes, or at least not harmed or infringed. An especially strong way to provide this protection is for other persons to be placed un-

6. For fuller explication of these points, see my essay "Why Rights Are Indispensable," *Mind* 95 (1986): 329–44.

der strict duties not to interfere with the interests, and even in certain circumstances to help fulfill the interests. But this still leaves open important questions about each of the last three of the elements of a claim-right listed above. Do any and all interests of persons serve to ground their having rights or making right-claims? How does the interest of some person A, including the need for its protection, serve to ground the duties of other persons B, C, and so forth to protect A's interest? What justifying basis is there for attributing to self-interested or any other persons, who may be amoralists or adeonticists, the use of normative concepts like 'ought,' especially when they themselves may have to shoulder the burdens of the 'oughts' or duties? In addition, there is the question of whether rights are so mandatory that they can under no circumstances be overridden. Let us now attack these questions systematically, with a view to reaching a rationally justified conclusion about the human rights whose mutualist relation to community provided the initial answer to the adversarial conception of the relation between rights and community.

Are there any human rights? Or, more generally, since human rights are a species of moral rights, are there any moral rights at all? Or, to put it still more generally, do humans have any rights? We must first note that the words "are" and "have" are here ambiguous; they may refer to at least two different kinds of justifying basis: on the one hand, to social recognition and legal enforcement; on the other hand, to moral justification. Legal rights may not be morally justified, such as the past legal right to own slaves; and morally justified rights may not be socially recognized and legally enforced, such as, in the past, the rights of women to vote and own property. In the face of this potential conflict between legal and moral rights, one's tendency may be to say that the latter, and with them human rights, have normative priority over the former, since moral rights are invoked in criticism or evaluation of legal rights. But may not the reverse relation also obtain? And how do we know that there are any moral rights? In the case of legal rights, the epistemological question is readily answered: one consults the statute books and the empirical data of effective enforcement. But where does one look to ascertain the existence of moral rights or human rights?

Some philosophers have rejected the very idea of such a justificatory or epistemological question. They have declared that what they call "human rights foundationalism" is "outmoded and irrelevant," and that "the most philosophy can hope to do is summarize our culturally influenced intuitions about the right thing to do in various situations."[7] This intuitionism,

---

7. Richard Rorty, "Human Rights, Rationality, and Sentimentality," in Stephen Shute and Susan Hurley, eds., *On Human Rights: The Oxford Amnesty Lectures, 1993* (New York:

however, incurs familiar difficulties. Intuitions vary from group to group, so to rely on the intuitions of one group, even one dedicated to "our own culture—the human rights culture"—does not, as such, show why they should be preferred to the intuitions of other groups, including groups that reject human rights or any kind of rights talk.

Many attempted answers to the justificatory question about moral or human rights are at best inconclusive. To say that all that is needed to have moral or human rights is that one be human raises the question of just how "A is human" serves to ground "A has rights." The connection between these is not analytic; one can, without contradiction, affirm the antecedent and deny the consequent. A similar disconnection arises if one puts the antecedent as "A has needs or interests" or even "important (or imperative) needs or interests": Why should A's having needs justify the imposition of duties on B, C, and other persons to respect or fulfill A's needs? It may well be true that B, C, and so forth want their own needs to be respected. But if they can achieve this without respecting A's needs—and such asymmetry has surely characterized much of human history—why should they nonetheless respect A's needs?

If it is said, further, that special moral rights like the right to have promises kept arise from the institution of promising,[8] this raises the question of how that institution is itself to be justified. After all, there may be morally wrong institutions, such as slavery; hence, the fact of being based on an "institution" does not serve to establish morally legitimate rights and duties. The attempt to justify a given rights-generating institution would presumably involve the justification of rights themselves.

The appeal to "rational choice" to answer the justificatory question might appear more promising. If a rational individual is one who chooses the most efficient means to achieve his ends, whatever they may be, the self-interested person A may well decide that claiming rights for himself is at least an efficient way of protecting his interests. To make such claims is in his self-interest.

I think this is a promising line of attack. But, taken alone, it incurs questions like those considered above, especially about respondents. Why should other persons respect A's right-claim? And in what way, if at all, does A's claiming rights for himself logically commit him to respecting the rights of other persons?[9] As for utilitarianism, it has well-known difficulties

---

Basic Books, 1993), pp. 116, 117. In the first passage Rorty is quoting Eduardo Rabossi's article, "Human Rights Naturalized."

8. See H. L. A. Hart, "Are There Any Natural Rights?" *Philosophical Review* 64 (1955): 185 ff.

9. These difficulties are not overcome in David Gauthier's important version of a rational choice–contract justification of morality (*Morals by Agreement* [Oxford: Clarendon Press,

in accommodating the distributive concerns of individual rights to its aggregative emphasis on the maximizing of utility overall.[10] In particular, as we saw above in the nature of a right, when an individual A has a right to X, this entails that she is to be protected in having X for her own sake, not for the sake of maximizing utility for society as a whole. As we shall see below, however, this does not militate against the general thesis that human rights are not only consistent with but require community.

I have elsewhere examined in some detail many other attempts to justify the ascription of moral rights, and have indicated that a successful justificatory argument must satisfy at least twelve conditions.[11] For present purposes, two of these conditions require special emphasis. First, because of the stringency of the 'oughts' or duties entailed by claim-rights, the rights justified by the argument must emerge as categorically obligatory or normatively necessary, in that their requirements cannot be rightly evaded by any actual or prospective agents regardless of their self-interested inclinations or their variable ideals, institutional affiliations, or social conventions. Hence, the antecedent of the argument must itself also be necessary, not contingent, in that it must logically impose itself on all the protagonists who figure in the argument. Second, the rights-principle that emerges from the argument must be determinate in that it does not serve to justify mutually conflicting duties based on conflicting interests or different cultural or

---

1986]). It is a great merit of Gauthier's theory that it begins with a realistic recognition of unequal power among the protagonists, who comprise both masters and slaves (chap. 7); it is largely this inequality that sets the problem of justification for rational choice–contract theories. But from this unequal starting point, Gauthier is unable to secure the egalitarian moral outcome of impartiality that he intends. Why should the masters, being stronger than the slaves, undertake to "bargain" with them in the first place? Gauthier's answer is that the masters do this because they want to remove their costs of coercion. But, as he candidly recognizes, this then leads the quondam slaves to refuse to work voluntarily for the masters, so that the latter have to make further concessions, against their interests. But surely the masters, if they had used even crude empirical (cause-effect) rationality, could have foreseen this result. So in Gauthier's rational choice–contract theory no adequate answer is given to the authoritative question of why one should accept the constraints of morality, including respect for the rights of other persons.

10. See my "Can Utilitarianism Justify Any Moral Rights?" in J. R. Pennock and J. W. Chapman, eds., *Nomos XXIV: Ethics, Economics, and the Law* (New York: New York University Press, 1982), pp. 158–93; reprinted in Alan Gewirth, *Human Rights: Essays on Justification and Applications* (Chicago: University of Chicago Press, 1982), pp. 143–62. For recent attempts to give utilitarian justifications of rights, see Allan Gibbard, "Utilitarianism and Human Rights," *Social Philosophy and Policy* 1, no. 2 (spring 1984): 92–102; Richard B. Brandt, "Utilitarianism and Moral Rights," *Canadian Journal of Philosophy* 14 (1984): 1–20; Russell Hardin, *Morality within the Limits of Reason* (Chicago: University of Chicago Press, 1988), chaps. 3, 4.

11. See my "The Epistemology of Human Rights," *Social Philosophy and Policy* 1, no. 2 (1984): 1–24.

other norms. In view of the conciliation here envisaged between rights and community, this is an especially pressing requirement.

1.4. HUMAN ACTION AS THE BASIS OF HUMAN RIGHTS

I have elsewhere worked out in great detail an argument for a moral rights principle that I consider to meet these and other conditions (*RM,* chaps. 1–3). In the present context I shall select from that argument only the minimal apparatus that is needed to ground the main theses of this book.

As was suggested by my reference to institutions, the justification of rights requires the delineation of a basis from which rights can be logically generated. Institutions as such are too indeterminate to provide such a basis; moreover, they do not correspond to the whole range of morality. Since moral rights may be noninstitutional as well as institutional, the relevant basis must be one that is at least as extensive as that of morality itself; and it must be a basis that is necessary or inescapable for all humans as actual or prospective agents. Only from such a basis can the normative necessity of moral rights be established.

The relevant basis is *human action.* For it is with actions that all moralities or moral precepts deal, directly or indirectly. All moral precepts tell human beings how they ought to act, especially toward one another, whether within or outside of institutions; or, as in the case of the virtues, they tell what kind of person one ought to be. Since to have a virtue is, among other things, to be disposed to act in certain ways, actions figure at least indirectly in moral precepts focused on virtues. The context of action also has the necessity indicated above, since all humans, at least insofar as they are relevant to right-claims, are actual, prospective, or potential agents. No human, then, can evade the context of action, except perhaps by committing suicide; and even then the steps he takes for this purpose are themselves actions.

Now when moral precepts are addressed to persons as actual or prospective agents, two assumptions are made about the proximate generic features of the actions they prescribe. One feature is *voluntariness* or *freedom:* it is assumed that the persons addressed can control their behavior by their unforced choice while having knowledge of relevant circumstances. The other feature is *purposiveness* or *intentionality:* it is assumed that agents aim to attain some end or goal which constitutes their reason for acting; this goal may consist either in the action itself or in something to be achieved by the action. Since, moreover, the aim of acting is to succeed in fulfilling one's purposes, when purposiveness is extended to the general conditions required for such success, it becomes the more general feature which I shall call *well-being.* Viewed from the standpoint of action, then, well-being consists in having the various substantive conditions and abilities that are proximately required either for acting at all or for having general chances of success in achieving one's purposes through one's action. Such well-being falls into a hierarchy of three different levels. *Basic well-being* consists in having the essential preconditions of action, such as life, physical integrity, mental equilibrium. *Nonsubtractive well-being* consists in having the general abilities and conditions needed for maintaining undiminished one's general level of purpose-fulfillment and one's capabilities for particular actions; examples are not being lied to or stolen from. *Additive well-being* consists in having the general abilities and conditions needed for increasing one's level of purpose-fulfillment and one's capabilities for particular actions; examples are education, self-esteem, and opportunities for acquiring wealth and income.

In delineating these components of well-being, we must take account of historical variability. What Marx, for example, says about the worker applies to all humans: "the number and extent of his so-called necessary wants, as also the modes of satisfying them, are themselves the product of historical development, and depend therefore to a great extent on the degree of civilization of a country, more particularly on the conditions under which, and consequently on the habits and degree of comfort in which, the class of free laborers has been formed."[12] This variability, however, applies less to the components of basic and nonsubtractive well-being than to additive well-being. And even with regard to the latter we must distinguish between its more specific and its more general components. Modes of education, work, communication, transportation, and so forth are far different in the era of computers, telephones, automobiles, and the like than in earlier times. But the general point remains that persons need some kind of education and other additive goods in order to be successful agents.[13]

In these ways, then, freedom and well-being are the proximate necessary conditions and generic features of action and of generally successful action. They are distinguished from one another as being, respectively, the

12. Karl Marx, *Capital* (New York: International Publishers, 1967), vol. 1, p. 171. See ibid., pp. 232, 514, 519. The partial relativity of "necessaries" to "the custom of the country" is also stressed by Adam Smith, *Wealth of Nations*, bk. 5, chap. 2, art. 4 (New York: Modern Library, 1937), pp. 821–22. See also the discussion of "concepts of poverty" in Amartya Sen, *Poverty and Famines* (Oxford: Clarendon Press, 1982), chap. 2. Cf. Christopher Jencks, *Rethinking Social Policy* (Cambridge, Mass.: Harvard University Press, 1992), pp. 7, 210. From an Aristotelian standpoint Henry B. Veatch has emphasized that "the bare necessities of life" are to be supplemented by specifically human social, intellectual, and other needs (*Human Rights: Fact or Fancy?* [Baton Rouge: Louisiana State University Press, 1985], pp. 79–80). These needs are included in what I have called "additive well-being."

13. See below, 4.1, on the "absolute" concept of poverty.

procedural and the substantive conditions of action, or, again respectively, as involving the efficient causes and the final causes of action. The freedom that is here in question comprises both negative and positive freedom: negative, in that when one controls one's behavior by one's unforced choice one is not obstructed or interfered with by other persons; positive, in that one then has the power or ability to act as one chooses.[14] As we shall see, freedom, like well-being, is a complex notion. It has different aspects relevant to action, including autonomy and the distinction between occurrent and dispositional freedom, which will be discussed below (2.4; 4.2, 3; 8.5). Although actions have initially been delineated as the general objects of all moral precepts, they constitute the objects of all other practical precepts as well. The status of all these actions, moreover, is not only conceptual but also real. Although their generic features have been elicited from the assumptions of moral and other practical precepts, the contents of these assumptions conform to the realities of human conduct or behavior.

One of the important components of additive well-being, and indeed of well-being generally, is community, in two respects. The first is instrumental: being a member of a supportive community helps one to be more effective in achieving one's purposes. Indeed, it is through being born into and nurtured by a sheltering community that one acquires the abilities and conditions needed for achieving one's purposes. In this way community is a means toward the fulfillment of self-interest (see 3.4). A second respect is constitutive: this is epitomized in the Aristotelian doctrine that "man is by nature a social animal." This "by nature" applies not only at a primitive level but also at a finalistic one: one can develop one's full humanity only by and in association with other humans in a stably regulated order. Such association involves an awareness of and concern for other persons' interests. As we shall see, this general idea requires qualifications about kinds of community (3.8, 9). But it also points toward important respects in which

14. Even Isaiah Berlin's famous concept of "negative liberty" includes this positive component: "Political liberty in this sense is simply the area within which a man *can act* unobstructed by others" (*Four Essays on Liberty* [London: Oxford University Press, 1968], p. 122; emphasis added). See also Berlin's further elucidation: "the absence of obstructions along which a man *can decide* to walk" (ibid., p. 123; emphasis added). See my essay, "Civil Liberties as Effective Powers," in Gewirth, *Human Rights*, pp. 311–17. See also John Locke, *Essay Concerning Human Understanding* 2.21.8: "So far as a man has power to think or not to think, to move or not to move, according to the preference or direction of his own mind, so far is a man *free*" (emphasis in original). The point made here is not the same as Gerald C. MacCallum, Jr.'s thesis that all freedom involves both "freedom from" and "freedom to" ("Negative and Positive Freedom," *Philosophical Review* 36 [1967]: 312 ff.). MacCallum does not define "freedom" in the course of using it; for these and other reasons, the basis of the combination he asserts of negative and positive freedom is left unclear.

community is itself protective of the individual interests that are the objects of rights. This provides an important basis (to be developed below) for the community of rights and the conciliation of rights and community.

1.5. THE ARGUMENT FOR HUMAN RIGHTS

How are moral or human rights derived from the context and generic features of action? It is surely not the case that when one acts, one thereby acquires a right to act, let alone to succeed in achieving one's purposes. As against such an assertoric method, what must be used here is a *dialectically necessary method*. The method is *dialectical* (as against assertoric) in that it begins not from statements made by the writer or speaker himself but rather from statements presented as being made or accepted by a purposive agent, and it examines what they logically imply. The method is dialectically *necessary* (as against dialectically contingent) in that the statements in question logically must be made or accepted by every agent because they derive from the generic features of purposive action, including the conative standpoint common to all agents. The reason for using the dialectically necessary method is at least twofold. Only through its necessary aspect can the argument achieve the normative necessity or categoricalness that was seen to be required for the grounding of rights. And only through its dialectical aspect can the argument for rights surmount certain familiar logical difficulties about the transition from 'is' to 'ought.' For the argument's antecedents logically incorporate the conativeness that figures essentially in right-claims. Moreover, only through its dialectical aspect can the argument show how, from the agent's standpoint, her claiming of rights entails duties of other persons to respect her rights.

It must be emphasized, then, that the argument for rights, as dialectically necessary, is presented as being relative to what every agent logically must accept for herself. This relativity to agents does not go counter to the argument's categoricalness because the whole relevant context is that of action or agency.

The central point of the argument is that rights and rights-claims arise logically and fundamentally out of the concern of all human beings, as prospective purposive agents, that the proximate necessary conditions of their action and generally successful action be protected. This concern corresponds both to the general definition of rights given above and to the primary occasions on which they are claimed. It is in this way that action serves as the basis of human rights: persons must have and claim these rights because their objects are needed for the very possibility of action and generally successful action.

I shall now give a brief outline of the dialectically necessary argument from the generic features of action to the ascription of human rights and thereby to the supreme principle of morality. The argument undertakes to establish two main theses, each of which we saw above (1.2) has to be established if self-interested individuals are to accept the idea of human rights. The first thesis is that every agent logically must accept that *he or she* has rights to freedom and well-being. The second is that the agent logically must also accept that *all other agents* also have these rights equally with his or her own, so that in this way the existence of universal moral rights, and thus of human rights, must be accepted within the whole context of action or practice.

Reduced to its barest essentials, the argument for the first main thesis is as follows. Since the agent has at least a minimum of self-awareness, when he acts for some purpose there can be attributed to him a statement of the form (1) "I do X for end or purpose E." This is a statement form that logically must be accepted by every agent for himself, so that it serves to ground the categoricalness of the rights-principle generated by the argument. From (1), the agent logically must accept (2) "E is good." For while the goodness in question need not be moral, and the ascription of goodness need not be definitive, it involves the agent's acceptance that the purpose for which he acts has for him at least some value sufficient to merit his trying to attain it. Now since freedom and well-being are the proximate necessary conditions of the agent's acting to attain any of his purposes and thus any goods, the agent, on the basis of his accepting (2), must also accept (3) "My freedom and well-being are necessary goods." Hence he must also accept (4) "I must have freedom and well-being," where this 'must' is practical-prescriptive in that it signifies the agent's advocacy or endorsement of his having the conditions he needs to have in order to act and to act successfully in general.

The next step is an especially crucial one. On the basis of his accepting (4), the agent logically must also accept (5) "I have rights to freedom and well-being." It is at this step that the normative (though not necessarily moral) concept of rights (in the strong sense of claim-rights) is introduced, as an essential element in the thinking of every rational agent. That the agent logically must accept (5) on the basis of accepting (4) can be shown as follows. Suppose he rejects (5). Then, because of the correlativity of claim-rights and strict 'oughts,' he also has to reject (6) "All other persons ought at least to refrain from removing or interfering with my freedom and well-being." By rejecting (6), he has to accept (7) "Other persons may (i.e., It is permissible that other persons) remove or interfere with my freedom and well-being." And by accepting (7), he also has to accept (8) "I may not (i.e., It is permissible that I not) have freedom and well-being." But (8) contradicts (4). Since every agent must accept (4), he must reject (8). And since

(8) follows from the denial of (5), every agent must reject that denial, so that he must accept (5) "I have rights to freedom and well-being." I call them *generic rights* because they are rights to have the generic features of action and successful action characterize one's behavior.

The argument for the first main thesis has thus established that all action is necessarily connected with the concept of rights. For every agent logically must hold or accept that he has rights to the necessary conditions of action and successful action in general.

It will have been noted that this dialectical argument applies to even completely self-interested agents. Their self-interested purposes generate the prudential right-claim of step (5), because their rejection of this claim would entail their acquiescing in removal from them of the necessary conditions of their action. Objections, including those about the amoralist or adeonticist, will be considered in the next section.

Let us now turn to the argument for the second main thesis. This is also of special importance because it involves the transition from prudential to moral rights. On the basis of his having to accept that he has the generic rights, every agent logically must accept that all other actual or prospective agents have these rights equally with his own. This generalization is an application of the logical principle of universalizability: if some predicate P belongs to some subject S because S has a certain quality Q (where the 'because' is that of sufficient condition), then P logically must belong to all other subjects S_1 to S_n that also have Q. Thus, if any agent holds that he has the generic rights because he is a prospective purposive agent, then he also logically must hold that every prospective purposive agent has the generic rights.

Now every agent logically must accept (9) "I have rights to freedom and well-being because I am a prospective purposive agent." For suppose some agent A were to object that the necessary and sufficient justifying condition of his having the generic rights is his having some property R that is more restrictive than simply being a prospective purposive agent. Examples of R might include his being a wage-earner or an entrepreneur or a banker or a landlord or an American or white or black or male or being named "Wordsworth Donisthorpe," and so forth. From this it would follow that A would logically have to hold that it is only his having R that justifies his having the generic rights, so that if he were to lack R, then he would not have the generic rights.

But such an agent would contradict himself. For we saw above that, as an agent, he logically must hold that he has the generic rights, since otherwise he would be in the position of accepting that he normatively *need not* have what he has accepted that he normatively *must* have, namely, the freedom and well-being that are the necessary conditions of action and successful action in general. Hence, since no agent, including A, can consistently hold that he does not have the generic rights, he must give up the idea that any such restrictive property R can be the necessary as well as sufficient justifying condition of his having these rights. From this it follows that every agent logically must acknowledge that, simply by virtue of being a prospective purposive agent, he has the generic rights, so that he also logically must accept (10) "All prospective purposive agents have rights to freedom and well-being." At this point the rights in question become moral rights, because the agent is now committed to taking favorable account of the interests of other persons as well as of himself. The argument has thus shown that it is no longer rational for any agent to be exclusively self-interested, where 'rational' signifies conformity to the principle of noncontradiction as the fundamental principle of reason.

Since the universalized judgment (10) sets a prescriptive requirement for the action of every agent toward all other prospective purposive agents, who are or may be the recipients of his action, every agent logically must also accept for himself a moral principle which may be formulated as follows: (11) *Act in accord with the generic rights of your recipients as well as of yourself.* I call this the *Principle of Generic Consistency* (PGC), because it combines the formal consideration of logical consistency with the material consideration of the generic features and rights of action. This concludes the argument for the second main thesis. Since the generic rights are rights had equally by all agents, and since all humans are actual, prospective, or potential agents, the generic rights are now seen to be human rights. So the PGC is the principle of human rights. Underlying this argument is the more general point that human rights are based on persons' equal dignity as having the abilities of rational and volitional agency (see 2.6(b)).

The argument for the PGC has thus dialectically established that the human rights have as their objects the necessary conditions of action and successful action in general and that all humans equally have these rights. This, then, completes the argument for the existence of human rights. One way to epitomize the whole argument is that a person is generically inconsistent, or inconsistent at a fundamental level, if, while exercising his own capacities of agency, he rejects, either in thought or in action, the possession or exercise of those capacities on the part of other persons.

We must now connect the principle of human rights as thus established with our initial attempt to conciliate rights and community (1.2). This attempt emphasized the mutuality whereby human rights require that each person both respect the freedom and well-being of all other persons and have her freedom and well-being respected by all other persons. We halted the development of this relation of mutuality in order to take account of skeptical objections against the whole idea that human rights are relevant to the endeavors of self-seeking agents. We have now seen that human rights are indeed thus relevant, because no actual or prospective agent can rationally evade the context of action and the moral principle of human rights entailed by it. To this extent, then, the conciliation of rights and community has been established, and with it the refutation of the adversarial conception.

Before this conclusion can be accepted, however, three important lines of inquiry must be pursued. First, the above argument for the principle of human rights raises many questions of adequacy; and although I have dealt with these rather fully elsewhere, some notice must be taken of them here. Second, the rights that are conciliated with community must be primarily positive rights, not only negative ones; so we must provide an analysis of positive rights, including their existence and the problems they raise. This whole topic will be taken up in chapter 2. Third, the formal feature of mutuality that figures crucially in the conciliation of rights and community must be discussed on its own account, and its connection with community must be explicitly examined. Only then can the concept of the community of rights be sufficiently understood. This will occupy us in chapter 3. In chapter 4 I shall begin to pursue the other chief aim of this book: to develop in some detail how the mutualist idea of the community of rights, buttressed by the rational analyses and arguments of the first three chapters, serves to establish the economic and social rights that are of vital importance especially to the most deprived members of the society. This will involve us in the formation of both an economic biography for the individuals and an economic constitution for the society.

1.6. SOME OBJECTIONS TO THE ARGUMENT

The above argument for the PGC as the principle of human rights has received a very large amount of critical discussion. I have replied to many of the criticisms, and in a recent book Deryck Beyleveld has presented a very acute and comprehensive battery of responses to just about all of the criticisms that have appeared through 1990.[15] I refer the interested reader to Beyleveld's book for a thorough analysis and defense of the argument to the PGC. For the sake of some completeness in the present context, I shall here briefly cite and reply to some of the main criticisms.

Two of the standard objections have overlooked the dialectically necessary character of the argument.

---

15. Deryck Beyleveld, *The Dialectical Necessity of Morality: An Analysis and Defense of Alan Gewirth's Argument to the Principle of Generic Consistency* (Chicago: University of Chicago Press, 1991).

(a) Its *dialectical* character is overlooked by the objection that from "A needs freedom and well-being" it does not follow that "A has rights to freedom and well-being." But what does follow is "A *holds* or *thinks* that she has rights to freedom and well-being." The whole argument proceeds from within the conative purview of the purposive agent.

(b) The argument's *necessary* character is overlooked by the objection that the argument commits one to the thesis that whenever some person wants something or insists on having it, she also has to hold that she has a right to it. For wants do not, as such, give rise to rights or right-claims.[16] The reply is that the argument, with its 'must' in step (4), is restricted to the truly necessary goods of action; it is only concerning these that necessary right-claims are made. Contingent, dispensable goods do not meet the conditions of this 'must.'

(c) A related objection is that persons have a great need for love and indeed for a loving spouse, so that without these they are not likely to be successful agents. Hence, on the premise upheld here, they have claim-rights to receive love and to have a loving spouse.[17] But this is absurd.

This objection seems to construe the claim-right in question as a legal one, so that it trades on the contrast between the external or 'objective' mandates of law and the internal feelings of love and intimacy. But if the right is interpreted as a moral one, having a moral justification, the picture is more complex. For one thing, on some interpretations of 'love' the objection can be denied; love as a deeply spiritual rapport and commitment, while highly valuable, is not a necessary condition of successful action. On the other hand, love as a protective, nurturing parental feeling and corresponding conduct may well be a necessary condition for the growth of children into successful agency, and at least some modicum of this is a right of each child, although its legal enforceability raises many problems. Nevertheless, the state has an appropriate concern to prevent the kind of neglect that signals the absence of such effective love. Even with regard to adults, persons have a right to an effective appreciation for their human dignity, and a corresponding right not to be subjected to the kinds of con-

16. See R. M. Hare, "Do Agents Have to Be Moralists?" and W. D. Hudson, "The 'Is-Ought' Problem Resolved?" both in Edward Regis, Jr., ed., *Gewirth's Ethical Rationalism* (Chicago: University of Chicago Press, 1984), pp. 54, 127. See also Alasdair MacIntyre, *After Virtue*, pp. 64–65. I have given an extensive reply to MacIntyre on this point in my article "Rights and Virtues," *Review of Metaphysics* 38, no. 4 (June 1985): 739–62, at pp. 745–46.

17. This objection was not raised specifically against my argument, but it is relevant to it. It is found in Jon Elster, "Is There (or Should There Be) a Right to Work?" in Amy Gutmann, ed., *Democracy and the Welfare State* (Princeton, N.J.: Princeton University Press, 1988), pp. 62, 74, and in David Braybrooke, *Meeting Needs* (Princeton, N.J.: Princeton University Press, 1987), pp. 48, 135.

tempt or blazing hatred that signal the absence of such appreciation. None of this, however, entails the positive legal claim-right to a loving spouse, because, among other things, the condition in question is too deeply spiritual and personal to be an object of legislation.

(d) A further objection is that the agent cannot be claiming rights against other persons, because claim-rights entail correlative 'oughts' on the part of respondents or duty-bearers; but persons are not subject to 'oughts' unless they have reason to do what the 'oughts' require, and the argument has not shown that the persons addressed by the agent have any reason to refrain from interfering with his freedom and well-being.[18] The reply is that the expression "A has reason to do X" when addressed to some person is ambiguous: it can refer either to the addressee's reason or to the speaker's reason. Now when the agent addresses her right-claim and correlative 'ought'-judgment to other persons, it is sufficient that the agent has *her* reasons for making the judgment; it is not required that her addressees also have *their own* reasons for complying with it. What the addressees must have, at this stage of the argument, is an understanding of what the agent is saying, as well as a general acceptance of the canons of deductive and inductive logic. Given this acceptance, however, the addressees can understand the rational basis of the agent's right-claim as deriving from within the agent's point of view; and when this claim is universalized to entail the generic rights of all prospective purposive agents, the addressees come to see that they also have their own reasons for accepting the agent's right-claim.[19] These reasons are not primarily self-interested; they derive rather from the logical consistency that every person must accept insofar as he or she fulfills the minimal conditions of rationality.

(e) A related objection is that the argument does not establish that anyone has or claims rights, because an agent may accept the 'ought' of step (6) above without accepting the 'rights' of step (5). For 'oughts' may be upheld for many reasons other than their being correlative with rights, as on utilitarian grounds. The reply is that any such other grounds for the 'ought' would remove from it the directly personal, prudential basis which the argument shows it must have because of its exclusive initial concern with the agent's own needs of agency. Thus the 'ought' is not upheld on general utilitarian grounds or on other grounds not primarily related to its beneficiary, but rather as something which he must hold is due or owed to himself by

18.   See Loren E. Lomasky, "Gewirth's Generation of Rights," *Philosophical Quarterly* 31 (1981): 248–53; Christopher McMahon, "Gewirth's Justification of Morality," *Philosophical Studies* 50 (1986): 261–81.

19.   I have developed this point more fully in "The Justification of Morality," *Philosophical Studies* 53 (1988): 245–62. See also James Scheuermann, "Gewirth's Concept of Prudential Rights," *Philosophical Quarterly* 37 (1987): 291–304.

virtue of its being required for all his purposive actions. Such an 'ought' is correlative with a claim-right.

(*f*) It has also been objected that, since freedom and well-being are the necessary conditions of action, every agent, as engaging in action, already has these conditions, so that there is no point in his claiming rights to them. It has been further objected that having these rights cannot be necessary conditions of action because many agents throughout the world lack these rights (insofar as they involve social recognition and legal enforcement).[20] The answer to these interrelated objections is twofold. First, a person who is presently an agent may subsequently come to lack freedom and well-being; hence, he claims the right to freedom and well-being not only as a present agent but as a prospective or future agent. Thus he is not in the position of claiming a right to something he necessarily has already. Second, the objects of human rights are the necessary conditions not only of action but also of generally successful action. Especially pertinent here is the distinction indicated above of the different levels of well-being (*RM*, 68). When it is said that many persons throughout the world are agents and yet do not have human rights, this involves not the moral but rather the legally effective meaning of "have." What the objection says about such persons is not that they cannot act at all or achieve any of their purposes but rather that they do not have the abilities and conditions required for generally successful action: such abilities and conditions as adequate health, education, income, and freedom from torture and other oppression. The objects of human rights include such abilities and conditions of nonsubtractive and additive well-being as well as of basic well-being. Hence, the effective having of these rights is required not only for action per se but also for generally successful action.[21]

(*g*) Another objection is that the agent may be an amoralist or 'adeonticist' who rejects all deontic concepts, so that his rejection of the 'ought'-judgment (6) would not commit him to accept any of the ensuing 'may'-judgments about what is permissible.[22] The reply is that no agent can rationally reject either a self-directed or an other-directed 'ought'-judgment if he is conatively normal (see *RM*, 90).[23] For if his life or some

20. See Douglas N. Husak, "Why There Are No Human Rights," *Social Theory and Practice* 10 (1984): 132.

21. See my "Why There Are Human Rights," *Social Theory and Practice* 11 (1985): 235–48.

22. See Edward Regis, Jr., "Gewirth on Rights," *Journal of Philosophy* 78 (1981): 786–94; Martin P. Golding, "From Prudence to Rights: A Critique," in J. R. Pennock and J. W. Chapman, eds., *Nomos XXII: Human Rights* (New York: New York University Press, 1981), pp. 165–74.

23. See also Beyleveld, *Dialectical Necessity*, pp. 163–66.

other aspect of his basic well-being is threatened, and he thinks the only way he can ward off this threat is by doing X, which is in his power, then he will say or think "I ought to do X." This 'ought' is, of course, self-interested. Hence, he must also accept "I ought to be free to do X," which is equivalent to the other-directed 'ought'-judgment "Other persons ought to refrain from interfering with my doing X." At this stage the quondam adeonticist still uses a self-interested criterion of 'ought.' Thus, even an adeonticist or amoralist must accept 'ought'-judgments and their correlative rights-judgments, as well as judgments about what is permissible, so that the argument applies to all agents regardless of whether they initially accept moral or other normative judgments or concepts (see *RM*, 89–95, for a much fuller presentation of this argument).

(*h*) It may be objected that the argument for the PGC does not establish that all humans have *equal* rights, because some humans, such as the very ill and the mentally handicapped, as well as children, do not have the proximate capacity to be full-fledged voluntary and purposive agents.[24] The answer to this objection requires reference to a Principle of Proportionality: humans who are less than normal agents have the generic rights to the degree to which they approach being normal agents. This point is discussed more fully below in connection with the universality of positive human rights (2.5), and still more fully in *Reason and Morality* (120–25).[25]

(*i*) The appeal to consistency in ethics—the thesis that the immoral person contradicts himself and thus is inherently irrational—goes back to Kant and indeed to Plato. It may be and has been objected, however, that such an appeal goes beyond what ethical argument needs and is capable of, and that it reflects a kind of rationalistic or intellectual fallacy, in that it reduces moral evil to logical error.[26] There are two replies. First, the modality of logical necessity is the only way of accounting for, and doing justice to, the categorical obligatoriness of moral judgments, especially those concerning human rights, whereby compliance with them is rationally mandatory for all actual or prospective agents regardless of their personal inclinations or institutional affiliations. Second, since the general sphere of morality is one of great dissensus, its competing claims and counterclaims can be rationally adjudicated in a nonquestion-begging way if we can show that one principle is such that logical inconsistency results from rejecting it,

24. See Arval A. Morris, "A Differential Theory of Human Rights," in Pennock and Chapman, *Nomos XXIII*, pp. 158–64.

25. See also my "Why There Are Human Rights." (above, n. 21).

26. See E. J. Bond, "Gewirth on Reason and Morality," *Metaphilosophy* 11 (1980): 36–53; Jeffrey Reiman, *Justice and Modern Moral Philosophy* (New Haven, Conn.: Yale University Press, 1990), pp. 109–11, 127, 181.

while this is not so with the other principles. For this provides a conclusive argument in favor of the first principle, since a proposition whose denial is self-contradictory is itself necessarily true. This, then, is the point of emphasizing the criterion of logical consistency: not that of superseding moral criteria that use specifically moral concepts of persons and their interests, but rather that of providing a culminating structural argument where other arguments fail of conclusiveness.

(*j*) The objection about rationalism may be directly supplemented by an objection about motivation. Even if someone contradicts himself in thinking or arguing about human rights, how or why should this motivate a self-interested agent to care about the human rights of other persons? He may say, "So I contradict myself," and go about violating other persons' rights for his own criminal purposes.

I have dealt with this objection in some detail in *Reason and Morality* (190–98). It must be kept in mind that the whole argument for the principle of human rights begins from the purposes of the self-interested agent. By the argument, the agent is brought to see that he cannot consistently maintain an exclusively self-interested position. This does not mean, however, that he must surrender all concern for his self-interest, for the principle of human rights requires that he act in accord with the generic rights of his recipients *as well as of himself.* The argument thus eventuates in what may be called a moderate altruism. There may, of course, be conflicts between the agent's rights and those of other persons; these will be discussed below. But by the fact that the argument has required that the agent move from interests (or purposes) to necessary goods and rights, it has shown that the rational agent cannot dwell solely on whatever interests he may happen to have; he must first take account of the necessary conditions for his pursuit of any of his interests, so that these, and the generalized right-claims in which they logically eventuate, must have a kind of controlling influence on his thinking as an agent, and accordingly on his modes of action.

Insofar as motivation is an empirical matter, there is no surefire way of motivating persons to act with respect for the human rights of other persons. The arguments philosophers have devised based on various versions of self-interest, from Plato's conception of mental health to Hobbesian and contemporary theories of social contracts and rational choice, have fallen prey to objections about healthy tyrants, free riders, and other "defectors" from moral cooperation. The logical argument presented above escapes these empirical difficulties. For the reason it gives for the agent's having to act in other than purely self-interested ways is not the Hobbesian prudential or contingent one that if he violates other persons' rights he may probably expect them to violate his own rights, but rather the logically necessary reason that the rights he necessarily claims for himself rest on grounds that also apply to all other prospective purposive agents.

Persons can be motivated to act from considerations other than exclusive self-interest. They can be motivated to act as reason requires—that is, to be consistent in their treatment of other persons in such a way that the rules they necessarily want to have applied to themselves they also apply to other persons. They can also be motivated to modify this self-interest out of respect for the moral rights of others.[27]

Education and laws based on the principle of human rights are important helps toward motivating persons to act rationally and morally. But so too are the very ideas of reason and rights. When someone is aware of other persons' rights, and hence of what is the right thing to do—and this awareness is in large part a function of reason (and it can be a function of feeling as well)—he can be strongly motivated to act accordingly. The awareness of moral rights can be a strong buttress against the exclusive influence of self-interest. But in any case, the conclusiveness of the justificatory argument for human rights is not affected by, although it should take account of, the contingencies of human motivation.

1.7. COMPARISONS TO SOME OTHER DOCTRINES

It may help to further elucidate some of the matters just discussed if I contrast the above argument for the PGC as the principle of human rights with some other contemporary dialectical arguments that seek to establish the foundations of morality, including justice or equal rights. Let us begin with the famous argument of John Rawls for his two principles of justice.[28] Rawls's argument is dialectical in that he does not proceed directly or assertorically by arguing in his own person for certain moral or political principles; rather, he proceeds by asking what kinds of choices rational, self-interested persons would make if they were choosing the basic constitutional structure of their society. And, as is well known, the choice is to be made from an "original position" behind a "veil of ignorance" whereby the persons do not know any of their individual qualities or characteristics. From these premises Rawls argues that his protagonists will choose certain principles of justice.

27. See Amartya Sen, *Of Ethics and Economics* (Oxford: Basil Blackwell, 1989), p. 57: "Moral acceptance of rights (and especially rights that are valued and supported and not just respected in the form of constraints) may call for systematic departures from self-interested behaviors."

28. John Rawls, *A Theory of Justice* (Cambridge, Mass.: Harvard University Press, 1971), chaps. 1–3. I here deal only with Rawls's monumental treatise, not with his subsequent writings that have introduced emendations in response to various criticisms.

Rawls's argument, then, is dialectically *contingent* because there is no necessity that any chooser, even one who is fully rational, proceed in this way, that is, choose from behind a veil of ignorance. Hence, Rawls's procedure is incapable of establishing any categorical moral judgments or principles. For why should any actual rational persons, who know about their individual characteristics, accept moral principles that are based on the contrarational assumption of their total ignorance of those characteristics? If the answer is that this assumption is a guarantee of fairness because it serves to remove self-partiality, this shows that the argument is question-begging because it assumes the very moral principle, of impartiality and equal consideration, that the argument is supposed to establish. The argument for the PGC culminates in a categorical moral principle because it proceeds from within a context—the necessary conditions of action—that no agent can rationally or consistently reject, and it shows what judgments agents are logically committed to accept within that context. But Rawls's context of the original position and the veil of ignorance has no such rational necessity, so that his argument provides no conclusive reason why his principles must be accepted.

In addition, the argument for the PGC is not based, as with Rawls, on an artificial stripping away of all particularizing properties of human selves. The argument takes humans as they actually are. What is required is that the features of human selves that are permitted to enter the argument be only those that no agent can consistently reject. The reason for this confinement to the generic features of agency, moreover, is that, as we have seen, action is the universal relevant context of all otherwise divergent moral principles and other practical precepts. Hence, the restriction to the generic features of action, far from being arbitrary, is instead based upon the necessary connection of morality with action, and thus upon reason in the most stringent sense.[29]

Two other modes of dialectical argument avoid some of the contingency found in Rawls's doctrine. But they still incur important difficulties, because the necessary aspects of knowledge and language on which they focus provide only formal, not substantive, criteria for evaluating moral principles. Richard Brandt invokes "cognitive psychotherapy" as a way of attaining "rational criticism" of desires on the basis of "facts and logic." He holds that the desires that survive such criticism will have as their objects what is morally right and just.[30] This procedure avoids the contrara-

29. For related ways of contrasting my argument with Rawls's, to the advantage of the former, see Derek L. Phillips, *Toward a Just Social Order* (Princeton, N.J.: Princeton University Press, 1986), pp. 53–66, 88–101.

30. Richard B. Brandt, *A Theory of the Good and the Right* (Oxford: Clarendon Press, 1979), chaps. 6, 7, 10.

tional features of Rawls's appeal to the "veil of ignorance." But while the procedure may be an excellent device for the achievement of prudential ends, it does not suffice for the ascertainment of what is morally right insofar as this involves the egalitarian ends upheld by Brandt. For inegalitarian ideals that appeal to certain exalted intellectual or aesthetic values (as in Aristotle or Nietzsche) can survive all the tests of "facts and logic."[31] What is missing here is the material consideration of the universalist necessity provided by the generic features of human action.

A similar lack is found in Jürgen Habermas's attempt to derive principles of justice from what would be agreed upon in an "ideal speech situation," a situation characterized by firm dedication to truth, rejection of force, deception, and all irrelevant emotional factors, unrestricted inclusion of all participants, and the like.[32] This approach incorporates in an important social dimension the "facts and logic" upheld by Brandt. Nevertheless, Habermas's doctrine has serious weaknesses. By taking as its context a whole society, the approach raises questions of realism and feasibility. How can it be ascertained whether all the members of a society fulfill the requirements of the ideal speech situation? Even if they do fulfill the requirements, what assurance is there that they will agree on the same policies or institutions? As with Brandt's doctrine, persons may satisfy all the standards of the ideal speech situation and still uphold various conflicting elitist ideals or egalitarian norms. There is a yawning gap between the formal lineaments of the ideal speech situation and substantive requirements of morality, including justice; or, to put it otherwise, the principles of morality, including justice, are left severely underdetermined by the discursive norms of the ideal speech situation. In the absence of more specific substantive criteria, such as those provided by the generic features of action, it would be difficult and perhaps impossible to adjudicate among different moral ends or ideals of justice, on the basis of the very abstract and formal criteria embodied in the ideal speech situation.[33] More generally, even if those criteria set moral norms for the rightness of conduct within speech situations, this, as such, provides no reason for extrapolating from lin-

31. For a fuller presentation of this criticism, see Alan Gewirth, "The Future of Ethics: The Moral Powers of Reason," *Noûs* 15 (1981): 15–30 (reprinted in Gewirth, *Human Rights,* pp. 163–78).

32. Jürgen Habermas, *Legitimation Crisis,* trans. Thomas McCarthy (Boston: Beacon Press, 1975), pp. 107–14; Habermas, *Theory and Practice,* trans. John Viertel (Boston: Beacon Press, 1973), pp. 12–23.

33. See the valuable critique of Habermas's doctrine in Derek L. Phillips, *Toward a Just Social Order,* pp. 84–88. For a critical comparison of my doctrine and that of Habermas, favoring the latter, see Stephen K. White, "On the Normative Structure of Action: Gewirth and Habermas," *Review of Politics* 44 (1982): 282–301. White's critique has been answered by Deryck Beyleveld, *Dialectical Necessity,* pp. 196–201.

guistic conduct to the rightness of extralinguistic social policies and institutions.[34]

So while each of the dialectical approaches just considered has some significant merits, they do not remove the need for the justification of human rights by the dialectically necessary argument from the generic features of action.

For the reasons I have given, the generic rights are human rights. It may be helpful to see how they are related to the rights famously enumerated in the Universal Declaration of Human Rights promulgated by the United Nations in 1948.[35] In general, the above analysis of the generic rights to freedom and well-being in its three levels can be construed as a rational reconstruction of the UN's list of rights. The preamble to the Universal Declaration refers to "the inherent dignity . . . of all members of the human family" and the concern "to promote social progress and better standards of life in larger freedom." In grounding human rights in the necessary conditions of human action I have sought to provide a clearer, more thorough, and more firmly rooted foundation for the declaration's human rights.

For the most part, the generic rights based on the PGC coincide extensionally with the UN declaration's human rights, including its social and economic rights as well as its political and civil rights. But two interrelated differences should be noted. First, the objects of the PGC's rights bear not only on social institutional arrangements but also on individual interpersonal transactions, such as the rights not to be lied to or to have promises to oneself broken, which are cases of nonsubtractive well-being. The reason for these additional contents is that the PGC's aim is that all persons possess the abilities and conditions required for action and generally successful action; and this aim applies to the individual sphere as well as to the social one. Second, where the UN's rights are addressed primarily and even perhaps exclusively to governments as their respondents, the PGC's rights are addressed primarily to each individual person insofar as he or she has the relevant abilities; secondarily, their respondents also include govern-

34. Habermas's thesis is similar, both structurally and in content, to John Dewey's doctrine of "the potential alliance between scientific and democratic method. . . . Freedom of inquiry, toleration of diverse views, freedom of communication, the distribution of what is found out to every individual as the ultimate intellectual consumer, are involved in the democratic as in the scientific method" (*Freedom and Culture* [New York: G. P. Putnam's Sons, 1939], pp. 101–2). I have presented a brief critique of Dewey's doctrine in my article "Ethics," *Encyclopedia Britannica*, 15th ed. (1974), vol. 6, p. 986.

35. The Universal Declaration of Human Rights has been reprinted in many places, including Ian Brownlie, ed., *Basic Documents on Human Rights,* 2d ed. (Oxford: Clarendon Press, 1981), pp. 21–27.

ments as representatives of their individual citizens. Thus the PGC's human rights are universal in that both their subjects and their respondents are all human beings. (This will be discussed more fully below, 2.6.) But not all of these rights are or should be legally enforceable.

Although the legal, institutional context is the most famous area of discussion of human rights, it must be emphasized that these rights also figure centrally in individual interpersonal transactions. A person's rights to freedom and well-being are violated just as surely, although perhaps less powerfully and irrevocably, if she is kidnapped and held for ransom by a private person as if she is subjected to unjust imprisonment by the government; and torture by a private person is just as much an infringement of one's human rights as torture by an agent of the state. So, too, refusal to give food to a starving person violates his human rights regardless of whether it comes from an affluent, appropriately situated private person or from a representative of the government. Similarly, although in lesser degree, a person's human rights are violated when he is lied to, discriminated against, or made to work for starvation wages when better conditions could be made available. Moreover, a large part, although not the whole, of the human rights that should be legally enforced consist in the legal protection of individuals from suffering violations of their most important human rights to just treatment on the part of individuals or groups other than those representing the state. So the concept of rights, including human rights, applies to the sphere of personal ethics as well as of social ethics, although it is the latter that is the primary concern of this book.

In order to bring the PGC into line not only with the UN declaration's rights but also, and especially, with the requirements of community, the argument as so far presented must be supplemented by an explicit consideration of positive rights to freedom and well-being. That is the purpose of the next chapter.

Two

POSITIVE RIGHTS

2.1. THE IMPORTANCE OF POSITIVE RIGHTS

We are now ready to resume the argument for the conciliation of rights and community, the thesis that rights and community have a relation of mutual support. In chapter 1 that conciliation received an initial confirmation through the argument for the thesis that the human rights require, on the part of each person, a concern for interests shared in common with all other persons. This common sharing involves the solidaristic regard of community just as, conversely, that regard requires the mutual protection of individual interests. The conciliation thus attained between rights and community was only an initial one, however, because, among other reasons, it rested on a principle of human rights that required independent proof. The proof has now been given through the dialectically necessary argument for the PGC.

We must now take another major step toward the conciliation. For, so far as the argument for the PGC has gone, the human rights it upholds could be solely negative, in that the correlative duties of their respondents would require only that each person refrain from interfering with other persons' freedom and well-being. I now want to show that the justified rights are also positive, in that in certain circumstances they require active assistance whereby one helps persons to have freedom and well-being.

This positivity of human rights is of first importance for establishing the connection between rights and community. When rights are viewed solely as negative, in that their correlative duties require only noninterference with persons' having the objects of their rights, the adversarial conception of the relation between rights and community is given ready entry. For persons can then fulfill their duties by simply not interfering with or intervening in one another's actions or projects; or, to put it in another way, the having of negative rights entails the warding off of interference from other persons. Although such noninterference is itself valuable as an essential part of freedom and of noninfliction of suffering, when it is the sole conception of rights it may lead to a view of society as consisting of atomized, mutually disregarding, alienated individuals with no positive consideration for cooperation in helping to fulfill one another's needs or interests or for rectifying the extreme inequalities of wealth and power that characterize most societies.

The case is otherwise, however, when it is recognized that human rights are positive as well as negative. For, as positive, they entail mutual obligations to help persons to fulfill their essential agency-needs and thereby move closer to equality. As a result, a human society based on positive human rights requires not only that persons refrain from coercing or harming one another but also that they help one another. This requirement of help is not, however, indiscriminate or open-ended; it is concerned rather to enable all persons equally to become and to function as productive agents who can provide for their own needs, while also making effective contributions to the fulfillment of other persons' needs and desires on a basis of mutual respect and cooperation. Thus positive rights serve to relate persons to one another through mutual awareness of important needs and, as a consequence, affirmative ties of equality and mutual aid. Hence, if there are indeed positive human rights that must be acknowledged as such by every rational agent, then this provides a rational and mandatory basis for the conciliation of rights and community and thus for the mutuality and solidarity of the community of rights.

The conception I have just outlined bears explicitly on familiar contemporary polemics: not only between "liberal individualists" and "communitarians" but also between both of these and central strands of feminist thought. Like communitarians, many feminists have objected to the "atomistic," "formalistic," and "adversarial" emphases they have attributed to the concern of moral and political philosophers with rights and justice; in addition, feminists have objected to the historicist, traditionalist theses of many communitarians with their implicit support of the patriarchal domination of women and also to male neglect of caring relationships of compassion. In this connection, however, it is significant to note that when communitarians seek to separate "rights" from community, they uniformly confine themselves to negative rights. Thus, for example, Charles Taylor says: "To ascribe the natural (not just legal) right of X to agent A is to affirm that A commands our respect, such that we are morally bound *not to interfere* with A's doing or enjoying of X. . . . But to affirm the right is to say that a creature such as A lays a moral claim on us *not to interfere*."[1] The

---

1. Charles Taylor, "Atomism," in his *Philosophical Papers* (Cambridge: Cambridge University Press, 1985), vol. 2, p. 195 (emphasis added); see also p. 194. Feminist writers

separation of rights from community becomes far more difficult, however, when it is seen that positive rights entail positive, mutual responsibilities to help one another on an equal basis.

One of this book's main theses is that the communitarian and feminist contentions, insofar as they are sound, can be properly accommodated by the concept of the community of rights, and that when this concept is appropriately developed to include positive rights, it can enable us to see what is sound and what unsound in the respective positions.

2.2. THE DISTINCTION BETWEEN NEGATIVE AND POSITIVE RIGHTS

To develop these theses, we must first look more closely at the distinction between negative and positive rights. This distinction has been criticized on both conceptual and moral grounds. The distinction turns mainly on the duties of the respondent: whether they consist only in refraining from interference (and so not doing something) or in active assistance (and so in doing something). But an argument against the reality of this distinction may be drawn from an analogy to the more general distinction between letting something happen (which is like noninterference) and bringing something

---

who distinguish "rights" from "caring" also depict rights as solely negative. See, e.g., Carol Gilligan, *In a Different Voice* (Cambridge, Mass.: Harvard University Press, 1982), p. 149: "an injunction not to hurt others": and see p. 22: "Thus it becomes clear why a morality of rights and noninterference may appear frightening to women in its potential justification of indifference and unconcern." See also Annette Baier, "The Need for More Than Justice," in Marsha Hanen and Kai Nielsen, eds., *Science, Morality, and Feminist Theory* (Calgary: University of Calgary Press, 1987), p. 47: "For the main complaint about the Kantian version of a society with its first virtue justice, construed as equal rights to formal goods . . . is that none of these goods do much to ensure that the people who have and mutually respect such rights will have any other relationships to one another than the minimal relationship needed to keep such a 'civil society' going. . . . Their rights, and respect for rights, are quite compatible with very great misery." See also John Hardwig, "Should Women Think in Terms of Rights?" *Ethics* 94 (April 1984). For valuable correctives, see Marilyn Friedman, "Beyond Caring: The Demoralization of Gender," pp. 87–110, and Virginia Held, "Non-contractual Society: A Feminist View," p. 129, both in Hanen and Nielsen, *Science, Morality, and Feminist Theory;* Carol C. Gould, "Feminism and Democratic Community Revisited," in J. W. Chapman and I. Shapiro, eds., *Nomos XXXV: Democratic Community* (New York: New York University Press, 1993), pp. 400–401; Rebecca J. Cook, ed., *Human Rights of Women: National and International Perspectives* (Philadelphia: University of Pennsylvania Press, 1994); Susan Deller Ross et al., *The Rights of Women: The Basic ACLU Guide to Women's Rights* (Carbondale: Southern Illinois University Press, 1993). See also, with emphasis on race as well as gender, Patricia J. Williams, *The Alchemy of Race and Rights* (Cambridge, Mass.: Harvard University Press, 1991), pp. 148–65.

about. For this latter distinction may make no moral difference in certain circumstances, such as when one lets someone die by not interfering with his dying (as against killing him) when one could have saved him.[2] Hence it may be similarly held that the distinction between the duty to refrain from interfering and the duty to provide active assistance also makes no moral difference.

It is important, however, not to confuse the two distinctions. It is indeed true that when one actively assists persons to have freedom and well-being, one brings something about. But such active assistance carries a connotation of beneficence which merely bringing something about lacks, and which is at opposite poles from the killing or other harms standardly adduced in the other distinction. In addition, noninterference may not "let happen" something as diffuse as someone's having freedom and well-being, when these necessary goods of action are confronted by severe social obstacles. When it is said that X lets Y happen, this suggests that Y is already present or in the immediate offing, and X's letting Y happen involves simply that Y comes about regardless of anything that X does. But B's not interfering with A's having freedom and well-being need not involve that A already has freedom and well-being or that A will have them regardless of what B does. On the contrary, such noninterference may permit a situation to continue wherein A remains deprived of freedom or well-being or both.

Even if in some situations the upshots of noninterference and active assistance may be the same, in that freedom and well-being may be promoted by refraining from interfering as well as by assisting, in many other situations, especially in large-scale modern societies, the fulfillment of freedom and well-being may require active assistance, not merely inaction. So the distinction between such assistance and noninterference may make a very great moral difference. The distinction between the negative duty to refrain from interfering with persons' freedom and well-being and the positive duty to assist persons to have these goods is not, then, removed by the complexities and possible moral coalescence of the more general distinction between letting something happen and bringing it about.

The distinction between negative and positive rights has been further challenged on the ground that the negative rights also require positive assistance from government or from other persons. For example, the negative right not to be murdered or mugged calls for an active police force that provides protection for persons who need it, and the negative right not to

2. See Bonnie Steinbock, ed., *Killing and Letting Die* (Englewood Cliffs, N.J.: Prentice-Hall, 1980), pp. 1–19; Henry Shue, "Rights in the Light of Duties," in Peter G. Brown and Douglas MacLean, eds., *Human Rights and U.S. Foreign Policy* (Lexington, Mass.: D. C. Heath, 1979), pp. 71–75; Judith Lichtenberg, "The Moral Equivalence of Action and Omission," *Canadian Journal of Philosophy*, suppl. vol. 8 (1982): 19–36.

be run over by a motorist entails the positive duties to drive carefully and to help disabled pedestrians.[3]

This criticism makes an important point, but it does not remove the distinction between negative and positive rights. For the criticism overlooks that the ground or justification for the positive assistance in question is to see to it that potential offenders *refrain from* the prohibited actions. Thus the correlative duty that provides the ground for the positive assistance is itself still negative. The police, in this example, exist for the sake of assuring or facilitating that the negative duty is fulfilled. Hence, the primary duty here is simply the negative one of refraining from murder, mugging, or running over pedestrians, so that the correlative right is negative. This point also applies more generally to the "positive obligation to protect negative freedoms."[4] The right to freedom that is thus protected is negative because what the obligation aims to achieve is that persons' control of their behavior not be interfered with.

The positive rights to freedom and well-being may not have such negative duties as their primary ground. What they primarily require is not that persons refrain from certain kinds of actions but rather that persons and groups perform certain kinds of actions that provide economic assistance and other helps for persons who cannot attain basic and other action-related goods by their own efforts. It may indeed be the case that the causes of the need for this assistance include that governments and other institutions or groups have performed certain kinds of positive, subsistence-threatening actions, so that the economic rights in question require that the institutions refrain from such actions. Nevertheless, even in these cases the duty of directly alleviating the resulting needs involves giving positive assistance, not simply refraining from action, as in the case of negative rights. Moreover, while many cases of economic deprivation have such positive actions as part of their direct causal background, some may not.

These considerations suggest that rights, so far as concerns their correlative duties, may be divided into three kinds. One kind is purely negative, where the duties to refrain do not have a background where prohibited actions or policies are actually being engaged in and require active inter-

---

3. See Henry Shue, *Basic Rights* (Princeton, N.J.: Princeton University Press, 1980), pp. 37–40, 51; Jack Donnelly, *Universal Human Rights in Theory and Practice* (Ithaca, N.Y.: Cornell University Press, 1989), pp. 33–34. See also Carlos Santiago Nino, *The Ethics of Human Rights* (Oxford: Clarendon Press, 1991), pp. 195–221. See more generally the essays collected in Eric Mack, ed., *Positive and Negative Duties* (*Tulane Studies in Philosophy*, vol. 33, 1985).

4. Amartya Sen, "Rights and Capabilities," in Sen, *Resources, Values, and Development* (Cambridge, Mass.: Harvard University Press, 1984), p. 314. See also Amartya Sen, *On Ethics and Economics* (Oxford: Basil Blackwell, 1987), pp. 56–57.

vention to prevent or rectify them. The right not to be killed or otherwise physically harmed is normally of this sort. A second kind is mixed: certain prohibited actions and policies are actually being engaged in and require active intervention to prevent or rectify them. So, for example, the right not to be killed becomes a mixed right when the active intervention of the police or bystanders is directly required to prevent someone's being killed. A third kind is purely positive, where the positive duties to assist do not have prohibited actions or policies as the background that evokes them, but they are still needed for the positive development of freedom and well-being. The right to education is an example.

Although many of the rights to be discussed in this book are of the kind I have called mixed, I shall continue to refer to them as positive rights in order to bring out their contrast with purely negative rights. It is this pure negativity that is stressed by communitarians and feminists who invoke the adversarial conception to protest using the language of rights. In any case, it is the need for positive assistance, both with and without the rights-threatening backgrounds referred to above, that underlies the policies and institutions that will be discussed in this book as constituting the community of rights.

Freedom may be construed negatively as not being interfered with or coerced, so that the right to freedom would entail both the duty to refrain from interfering with or coercing someone and the duty to prevent such interference or coercion. But since freedom consists more generally in controlling one's behavior by one's unforced choice, the positive right to freedom also entails the positive duty to help persons to have or attain such control on a continuing basis and as matters of personal responsibility, and not only to refrain from interfering with such control. As for the positive right to well-being, this entails that persons be helped to have food, housing, education, income, health care, and other components of basic and additive well-being when they cannot obtain these by their own efforts. As we shall see, the correlative duties bear not only on individuals as recipients but also on the economic and political structures of whole societies.

A further objection to the distinction between negative and positive rights is that there can be no positive rights because all rights are "side-constraints" on the actions of persons other than the right-holders.[5] To have a right is for it to be the case that other persons are debarred from interfering with one's having the object of one's right. Thus the right to life is the right not to be killed, the right to property is the right not to be stolen from, and so forth. There are two variants on or additions to this objection.

5. See Robert Nozick, *Anarchy, State, and Utopia* (New York: Basic Books, 1974), pp. 28–35.

One is that if A has a positive right to X, this may violate the rights of B, the respondent or duty-bearer, for it may interfere with B's own freedom. I shall deal with this below (2.4).

The other addition is that the idea of positive rights confuses rights with consequences. The objection is that to have a positive right is for other persons to have a duty to bring about certain consequences. But consequences are utilitarian considerations, not considerations of rights. Rights consist purely in side-constraints, let the consequences be what they may. One may, indeed, take account of consequences, but then one is no longer considering rights as such. So there are no positive rights.

A large part of this objection is purely verbal. As we shall see, there is wide recognition and support of certain positive rights. They are rights in that they entail correlative duties for the sake of the subject or right-holder, and they are positive because the duties consist in giving active assistance. But the objection about consequences adds a more complex conceptual consideration. Suppose A has a right to food, and that this entails that when he cannot get food by his own efforts other persons have the positive duty to give him food. Is his being given food a consequence of his right, or is it the very object or content of the right? Each answer is plausible, but in different respects. The object of his right to food, what it is a right to, is his being given food; in this respect his being given food is a conceptual constituent of his right to food and not a consequence of his right. On the other hand, the empirical fact of his actually being given food is conceptually distinct from his having the right to food; for his having this right is, of itself, no guarantee that he will in fact be given the food. In this respect, then, his actually being given the food may be regarded as a consequence of his having the right to food, in that, when other persons become aware of his right and need for food, they may well see to it that he is given food. In this respect, then, his actually being given food is a fact that is separate from his having the right.

Consequences are indeed important for positive rights. But, first, they need not be utilitarian, for they may affect the freedom and well-being only of some persons, not of all. And, second, positive rights are still distinct from consequences. The rights have certain objects, consisting ultimately in freedom and well-being. That the rights have these objects is an important part of the rights' value. But the value of the rights cannot be completely reduced to the value of the interests that are their objects, or even to the value of the right-holders' having these interests fulfilled, for at least three reasons that derive from the nature of moral rights. First, in A's having a right to X, A is justified in having X, as against his merely having X without any justification. Second, this justification is of a special kind in that X is A's due, something that belongs to him and that he is entitled to have for his own sake and not for the sake of maximizing utility. Third, A's right to X involves that he can rightly control X and can rightly control the conduct of other persons insofar as it bears on his having X. This third point, however, does not apply to all rights; the right to basic well-being is mandatory and thus not subject to optional choices on the right-holder's part (see 6.4). But the control feature does apply to other rights.

What these considerations show is that the objects or contents of positive rights are distinct from the rights' consequences. The objects are important constituents of the rights and of their value. In upholding positive rights, including their objects, we are not, then, confusing rights with consequences.

2.3. THE ARGUMENT FOR POSITIVE RIGHTS

Even if there is a distinction between negative and positive rights, as I have argued in the preceding section, there remains the question whether there are indeed any positive rights. Since I have held that it is primarily through positive human rights that the community of rights is to be established, this question must be seriously considered before any further progress can be made.

As was noted above in discussing the existence of human rights (1.3), the question of whether there "are" any positive rights may be interpreted and answered in several different ways. The idea of positive rights is not a recent invention; it can be found in late medieval jurisprudence,[6] in Locke,[7] in Paine,[8] and in other writers before and during the French Revolution.[9] Moreover, it is clear that there are positive legal rights, that is, rights that receive social recognition and legal enforcement and that require providing certain kinds of assistance. They include the rights to education, to social security, and to other benefits.

These answers do not, however, go deeply enough. In past eras there were also positive legal rights: to have one's fugitive slaves returned, to sleep with one's vassals' brides (*jus primae noctis*), and so forth. The legal

6. See Brian Tierney, "Origins of Natural Rights Language: Texts and Contexts, 1150–1250," *History of Political Thought* 10, no. 4 (winter 1989): 639–44.

7. John Locke, *Two Treatises of Government*, 1.42.

8. Thomas Paine, *The Rights of Man* (1791–92; Harmondsworth, England: Penguin, 1969), chap. 5, esp. p. 265. Paine regarded monetary support for "aged persons" as "not of the nature of a charity, but of a right," as justified in part by their previously having paid taxes. See also D. D. Raphael, "Human Rights: Old and New," in Raphael, ed., *Political Theory and the Rights of Man* (London: Macmillan, 1967), p. 62.

9. See Carl J. Friedrich, "Rights, Liberties, Freedoms: A Reappraisal," *American Political Science Review* 57, no. 4 (Dec. 1963): 843.

rights reflected the existing distributions of power in the respective societies. It could be and has been argued that the more egalitarian positive rights of our present era likewise reflect the more egalitarian distributions of power, but have no genuine moral or rational arguments in their favor. If, then, one wants to uphold positive rights on other than a contingent legal or conventional basis, one needs a stronger rational or moral argument. The need for such argument is especially pressing because positive rights make far greater demands on their respondents than do negative rights.[10]

We must ask, then, whether there is any rational argument for the existence of positive moral rights, that is, positive rights that are grounded in a rationally justified moral principle. What must be stressed in reply is that the positive human rights have the same originative foundation as the negative ones: the concern of all human beings, as prospective purposive agents, that the proximate necessary conditions of their action and generally successful action be protected. On many occasions such protection may require only noninterference; but on other occasions, especially when persons cannot secure their freedom and well-being by their own efforts, it requires the active assistance of other persons, either as individuals or as groups or as social institutions. Thus the PGC as the principle of human rights, with the argument that justifies it, serves to ground positive as well as negative moral rights to freedom and well-being.

The argument for there being such positive rights is parallel to the dialectically necessary argument outlined above (1.5) for a negative right to freedom and well-being. I shall present a summary of the positive-rights argument, using numbers followed by "a" that match the steps given in the previous argument.

Since freedom and well-being are necessary conditions of action and successful action in general, every actual or prospective agent has a general need for their components. Hence, every agent has to accept (4a) "I must have freedom and well-being." This 'must' is practical-prescriptive in that it signifies the agent's advocacy of his having what he needs in order to act either at all or with general chances of success. Now, by virtue of accepting (4a), the agent also has to accept (5a) "I have positive rights to freedom and well-being." For, if he rejects (5a), then, because of the correlativity of positive rights and strict positive 'oughts,' he also has to reject (6a) "Other persons ought to help me to have freedom and well-being when I cannot have them by my own efforts." By rejecting (6a), he has to accept (7a) "Other persons may (i.e., It is permissible that other persons) refrain from helping

10. For some mitigating considerations, see James W. Nickel, *Making Sense of Human Rights* (Berkeley, and Los Angeles: University of California Press, 1987), pp. 88–89.

me to have freedom and well-being when I cannot have them by my own efforts." And by accepting (7a), he also has to accept (8a) "I may not (i.e., It is permissible that I not) have freedom and well-being." But (8a) contradicts (4a). Since every agent must accept (4a), he must reject (8a). And since (8a) follows from the denial of (5a), every agent must reject that denial, so that he must accept (5a) "I have positive rights to freedom and well-being."

The further steps of this argument are also parallel to the argument for negative rights. Each agent logically must admit that the sufficient reason or ground on which he claims positive rights for himself is that he is a prospective purposive agent, so that he must accept the generalization that all prospective purposive agents equally have positive rights to freedom and well-being. Hence, he must also accept that he has positive duties to help other persons to attain or maintain freedom and well-being when they cannot do so by their own efforts and when he can give such help without comparable cost to himself. When such help is needed by large numbers of persons, and especially when their needs have institutional roots, such help requires a context of institutional rules, including the supportive state as the community of rights.

What the above argument shows is that, on the basis of the necessity of freedom and well-being for action and successful action in general, no actual or prospective agent can rationally deny that she has a positive right to these necessary goods and that she has a duty to provide for others when they need such help and she is in a position to give it without comparable cost. As rational, she has especially to recognize that there may be times, more or less extensive, when phases of her own freedom and well-being may be threatened so that she may then need the help of others, because she cannot have or maintain these necessary goods by her own efforts. This point applies even against the kind of rugged individualist whom Sidgwick described as "a man in whom the spirit of independence and the distaste for incurring obligations would be so strong that he would choose to endure any privations rather than receive aid from others." Sidgwick himself presented the qualification that "every one, in the actual moment of distress, *must necessarily* wish for the assistance of others."[11] In any case, the point at issue here depends not on contingent psychological attitudes but rather on what is logically involved in rational purposive agency, where

11. Henry Sidgwick, *The Methods of Ethics,* 7th ed. (London: Macmillan, 1907), p. 389n; emphasis added. For a valuable reply to Sidgwick, see Marcus G. Singer, *Generalization in Ethics* (New York: Alfred A. Knopf, 1961), pp. 272–74. See also Jeremy Waldron, *Liberal Rights* (Cambridge: Cambridge University Press, 1993), p. 242; Onora O'Neill, *Constructions of Reason* (Cambridge: Cambridge University Press, 1989), pp. 229–30. For complications that may overlook the necessities involved in this argument, see James D. Wallace, "The Duty to Help People in Distress," *Analysis* 29 (Dec. 1968): 33–38.

such agency is defined in terms of the common contents of all moral and other practical precepts. Such agency aims at the fulfillment of a wide range of purposes and hence aims, at least dispositionally, at having the general necessary conditions of such fulfillment. It is for this reason that the implicit claim to positive rights to freedom and well-being is logically attributable to every actual or prospective agent. And these rights entail correlative positive duties to fulfill such rights.

It must also be noted that the rational agent's recognition and support of other persons' positive rights does not have as its ground merely, or even primarily, a kind of "rational," strategic, self-centered calculation of how according these rights to others may probably help him to receive such help himself when he needs it or may otherwise benefit himself. The ground is primarily not one of reciprocity but rather of mutuality (see 3.2). It is not a contingent matter of quid pro quo but rather a necessary matter of persons' common humanity as purposive agents. The agent recognizes that other persons are similar to her in being prospective purposive agents and having the needs of agency, and on this ground she rationally accepts that they have the same positive rights she necessarily claims for herself. Thus a kind of community, a common status of having needs that require for their fulfillment the positive help of others, lies in the background of the argument for positive rights, so that rights and community are in this way also brought together.[12]

As I have already suggested, the argument for positive rights applies also to situations where threats to freedom and well-being arise from social or institutional contexts, such as where economic or political conditions make for unemployment, homelessness, or persecution. Secure and affluent persons, even when they are confident that they will not personally face such threats, must at least concede that if they were threatened by such socially based misfortunes, they would then need and, as rational, would want to be helped. Such cases are close to the point noted above (2.2) that the need for positive assistance may arise from the requirement to refrain from certain kinds of actions or policies so that the rights in question are "mixed." The need for positive rights, however, occurs not only in the case of threats but also to promote the affirmative development of freedom and well-being as necessary goods of successful action, and as reflecting the mutuality of concern for one another's needs that is required by the principle

---

12. For a sensitive discussion of the distinction indicated here (but with partly different terminology), see Kristen R. Monroe, Michael C. Barton, and Ute Klingmann, "Altruism and the Theory of Rational Action: Rescuers of Jews in Nazi Europe," *Ethics* 101, no. 1 (Oct. 1990): 103–22. See also the acute restatement of my argument for positive rights, together with replies to objections, in Deryck Beyleveld, *The Dialectical Necessity of Morality* (Chicago: University of Chicago Press, 1991) chap. 10.

of human rights. In these ways, the human rights also bear on social structures that affect and reflect the comparative degrees to which different groups or classes attain these necessary goods. The positive duties correlative with positive rights can also be seen to pertain in important respects not only to actions and institutions but also to attitudes and motivations.

In the above argument, unlike the argument given earlier for negative rights to freedom and well-being, there is included an important addition, namely the qualification, in steps (6a) and (7a), that the agent cannot attain some phase of freedom and well-being "by his own efforts." This means that in the 'ought'-judgment (6a) he cannot rationally demand of other persons that they help him to have freedom and well-being unless his own efforts to have them are unavailing. For without this qualification there would not follow (8a) "I may not (i.e., It is permissible that I not) have freedom and well-being." In this way, the positive rights require personal responsibility on the part of would-be recipients of help: the responsibility to provide for themselves if at all possible, prior to seeking the help of others.

This effort qualification raises complex problems about what efforts are realistically available to persons and what their efforts can actually accomplish. In view of the preceding argument for the PGC, there are negative moral limitations on the efforts persons may justifiably exert in order to attain their own well-being; for example, they may not kill other innocent persons for this purpose, although, if conditions become sufficiently desperate, they may steal from them. But from the other side, there are questions about what degrees of effort may be justifiably demanded of persons within the context of available resources. For example, may persons be asked, within an economy of abundance, to work for very low, close-to-starvation wages in order to avert their actual starvation? I shall consider this question below in connection with welfare (4.5). More generally, it must be recognized that for many persons long-standing conditions of poverty may generate feelings of hopelessness that derogate from having an effective sense of personal responsibility. A prime objective of social policy must be to provide the conditions for the development of such personal responsibility. But it is an essential part of social realism to recognize the past conditions that may militate against it.

In considering such questions, it is important to keep in mind that basic well-being includes more than mere life; it also involves such necessary goods as the maintenance of health, which requires adequate levels of food, clothing, shelter, and other necessities, including a physically healthful environment. Within the limits of available resources, there must also be a secure assurance of continued supplies of such goods. Hence, persons have positive rights to the help of others if by their own efforts, including their own abilities of personal responsibility, they are incapable of maintaining this assurance while other persons are able to provide it out of their surplus. There are also additive goods, such as education, which directly are helpful not for basic well-being but for enabling persons to increase their levels of purpose-fulfillment. Since, however, education is a prime means of helping persons to maintain their basic well-being by their own efforts, including their acquisition of productive skills, the positive rights extend also to such means so far as they are available (see 4.9, 10).

Two further aspects of the effort qualification need special emphasis. Effort is an essential part of agency, directly related both to the conativeness that figures in one's pursuit of one's purposes and to the freedom that consists in controlling one's behavior by one's unforced choice. When it is held that a person's right to be helped by others is contingent on the insufficiency of his own efforts, this serves to bring out an important limitation on the duty to help and also the direct connection of the human rights with the needs of agency. Far from advocating an open-ended dependence on the help of others, the PGC's requirement of positive rights aims to develop and maintain for each person the freedom and well-being whereby he can have and use, as matters of personal responsibility, his own productive abilities, with the efforts they involve.

It must also be noted that when it is said of someone that she cannot attain some phase of freedom and well-being by her own efforts, this "cannot" may have different bases. Some may be natural, such as age or illness; but others may be institutional or structural, such as poverty or involuntary unemployment. The institutional bases may also affect quite seriously how the natural bases are dealt with, ranging from the negative extreme of complete social noninterference and indifference to various positive social measures of assistance. For this and other reasons, the primary emphasis of this book falls on the institutional effectuation of positive rights, including the greater approach to equality that they serve to promote.

These considerations serve to bring out an important respect in which the human rights doctrine of the PGC is different from both libertarianism and some variants of socialism. The human rights doctrine agrees with libertarianism about the importance of having personal responsibility for using one's freedom to support oneself by one's own efforts. But the libertarian typically confuses his ideal with actualities; he overlooks that many persons do not have and cannot use their freedom in the ways he exalts, and that these negative facts derive from, or are vitally affected by, the structural inequalities of existing institutional arrangements. The PGC requires that there be social institutions whereby persons are helped to achieve such uses of their freedom so that they can then attain, or at least come appreciably closer to, the ideal of productive agency and self-reliance exalted by libertarians. Some variants of socialism strongly endorse such institutional help, but they may tend to overlook that the aim should be not to maintain an all-encompassing dependence on state action but rather that each person achieve independence or autonomy through her own productive abilities and efforts. The cooperativeness required for such achievement is, however, a strong ideal of socialism, and, as we shall see, it is embodied in the mutuality required by the community of rights (3.2, 4, 7).

2.4. OBJECTIONS TO POSITIVE RIGHTS: FREEDOM AND DEGREES OF NEEDFULNESS FOR ACTION

In the preceding section, using the dialectically necessary method, I have argued that there are positive human rights to freedom and well-being as the necessary conditions of action and generally successful action. Before this conclusion can be used to develop the contents of the community of rights, we must take note of certain formidable conceptual and moral objections that have been raised against the existence of positive human rights. The objections have held that there cannot be such rights for at least three reasons: first, they are inconsistent with the human right to freedom; second, they are utterly impracticable because of the "overload" of duties they entail; third, they fail various tests of universality. These objections are sufficiently important, both in themselves and for the project of the community of rights, to warrant detailed scrutiny.

To grasp the first objection, we must note that the positive rights to freedom and well-being as delineated above are in at least potential conflict with the respondents' own right to freedom. For while the latter right involves that one control one's behavior by one's own unforced choice, the positive rights impose obligations on respondents that restrict their freedom. For example, affluent persons must give up some of their property or the money equivalents thereof to provide for the basic well-being of needy persons, as well as fulfilling many other duties. As libertarians have pointed out, such requirements, especially when they are enforced by law, are restrictions on the right to freedom, since they impose on respondents legal as well as moral obligations they may not want to accept and thereby remove from them some of their control over their behavior. But why is it justified to coerce some persons, to infringe their right to freedom, in order to fulfill the rights to freedom and well-being of other persons? Isn't this to use the former persons as mere means for the latter?[13]

---

13. See Nozick, *Anarchy, State, and Utopia*, pp. 30–33, 170, 179n, 238; Tibor Machan and Douglas Den Uyl, "Gewirth and the Supportive State," in Edward Regis Jr., ed., *Gewirth's Ethical Rationalism* (Chicago: University of Chicago Press, 1984), p. 268.

It is only a partial answer to say that negative rights also limit persons' freedom. My right not to be killed or assaulted serves to invalidate your freedom to kill or assault me.[14] This answer does not, however, fully cope with the objection about freedom for at least two reasons. First, there is no right to kill or assault persons at will; hence the freedom to kill or assault which is removed by one's negative right does not remove a freedom to which one has a right. Second, one can comply with the negative right simply by refraining from acting in the prohibited ways. Hence, the negative rights do not impose the same degree of burdens or make the same kind of interference with freedom that are set by positive rights which require that persons interrupt or limit their freedom by engaging in positive actions of assistance or rescue, including giving up some of their income from work that provides such assistance.

To see how the above questions about positive rights are to be answered more fully, we must recur to the justificatory basis of the human rights. As we have seen, these rights have as their objects the necessary conditions of action and of successful action in general. From this derives one of the main bases of the resolution of conflicts of rights, which I shall call the *criterion of degrees of needfulness for action*.[15] In an initial characterization, this criterion may be stated as follows: When two rights are in conflict with one another, that right takes precedence whose object is more needed for action. This is why, for example, the rights not to be stolen from or lied to are overridden by the rights not to starve or be murdered if the latter rights can be fulfilled only by infringing the former.[16] As I noted

14. See Henry Shue, "Subsistence Rights: Shall We Serve *These* Rights?" in Robert A. Goldwin and William A. Schambra, eds., *How Does the Constitution Secure Rights?* (Washington, D.C.: American Enterprise Institute, 1985), pp. 78–80.

15. In *RM,* 343–44, I referred to "degrees of *necessity* for action." Partly under the stimulus of Douglas Husak's objection that necessity cannot admit of degrees ("Why There Are No Human Rights," *Social Theory and Practice* 10 [1984]: 140 n. 15), I switched to "needfulness." But, as Deryck Beyleveld has acutely pointed out, when I talk of "'degrees of necessity,' the alleged variation is not in the relation of necessity itself, but in the range of effect of the necessary condition on the possibility of action and what can be achieved by it" (*Dialectical Necessity,* p. 89). Joel Feinberg has said: "Rights . . . do not differ in degree; no one right is more of a right than another" (*Social Philosophy* [Englewood Cliffs, N.J.: Prentice-Hall, 1973], p. 66). This still leaves it open that some rights are more important than others because of the greater importance of their objects.

16. This point can also be put in terms of a moral interpretation of cost-benefit analysis: the costs of infringing the rights of property and of truthfulness are outweighed by the benefits of fulfilling the rights to life and health, although in some circumstances compensation may be required. See my chapter "Two Types of Cost-Benefit Analysis," in Donald Scherer, ed., *Upstream/Downstream: Issues in Environmental Ethics* (Philadelphia: Temple University Press, 1990), pp. 205–32.

above in connection with the right to well-being, its components of basic, nonsubtractive, and additive rights fall into a hierarchy of progressively less needed conditions of action (1.4).

Now the kinds of freedom also fall into such a hierarchy. 'Freedom' should not be used as a global, undifferentiated concept. There are distinctions between occurrent or particular freedom and dispositional or long-range freedom, and also between different objects of freedom. A temporary interference with a relatively minor freedom, such as a traffic light, is morally less important than a long-range interference with the freedom to perform some highly valued action. Hence, if the more affluent persons are taxed so that a relatively small part of their wealth is removed in order to prevent the destitute from starving, this is a far less significant interference with their freedom than would be the case if they were forced to surrender most of their wealth or were prohibited from supporting political parties, religions, or universities of their choice. So to refer to such taxation as imposing "forced labor"[17] (with its evocation of the cruelties inflicted in totalitarian concentration camps) is to utter an exaggeration that debases the currency of political discourse. Thus, it is not freedom in general that positive rights restrict. By the same token, the right to freedom in the use of one's surplus property is not absolute; it may be overridden by other rights such as the basic rights to life, health, or subsistence, since the objects of the latter rights are more pressing because more needed for action. This overriding is not, indeed, "efficient" according to Pareto optimality because, while making the deprived group of persons better off, it makes the affluent who are taxed worse off in economic terms. On the other hand, it may be held that the affluent are not made worse off because they gain civil peace by deflecting the anger that the deprived persons would otherwise evince (see 4.3). This point indicates some of the many ways in which the Pareto criterion is both vague and inadequate to the requirements of morality.

As these considerations suggest, the criterion of degrees of needfulness for action applies not only to the right to freedom but also to the various components of the right to well-being. In particular, the right to basic well-being takes precedence over the rights to other levels of well-being. (Some necessary qualifications will be indicated below.)

Persons are not treated as mere means, nor is their rationally justifiable freedom violated, when they are taxed in order to support the positive rights to basic well-being of other persons who are suffering from economic privation. For the principle underlying the taxation of the affluent to help others is concerned with protecting equally the rights of all persons, includ-

17. Nozick, *Anarchy, State, and Utopia*, p. 169.

ing the affluent. The PGC's mutualist requirement that agents act in accord with the generic rights of their recipients entails that all prospective purposive agents must refrain from harming one another (according to the principle's criteria of harm) and also that in certain circumstances they must help one another if they can. Hence, limitations on their freedom to abstain from such help are rationally justified. As we shall see more fully below, the facts that only some persons may actually be threatened with harm or need help at a particular time, and that only some other persons may be in a position to inflict harm or to give help, do not alter the universality of the PGC's provision for the protection of rights (2.6). Such protection is not only occurrent but also dispositional and a matter of principle; it manifests an equal and impartial concern for any and all persons whose rights may need protection. Hence, the PGC's requirement for taxing the affluent involves treating all persons as ends, not merely as means. It also involves, as an essential part of this relation, that those who are taxed recognize their rationally grounded obligations on behalf of the needy and the society that helps to fulfill all persons' human rights, and that they support the legislation that effectuates these obligations.

This thesis incurs two sets of objections, both bearing on utilitarianism. The first set concerns the right to freedom. It has been contended that there is no *general* right to freedom because some freedoms, such as the freedom to drive the wrong way on a one-way street, may be justifiably prohibited by the government on utilitarian grounds; and since rights, to be genuine rights, must override utilitarian considerations, freedom in general cannot be the object of a right.[18]

Three points must be made in reply. First, few if any rights are absolute.[19] There cannot be universal or completely unrestricted freedom because the freedom of potential interferers with freedom must be restricted if the freedom of noninterferers is to be preserved (see 5.2). More generally, the freedom to harm other persons must be prohibited, where "harm" is construed according to the requirements of the PGC. On the personal level, harm consists in removing or threatening the basic, nonsubtractive, or additive goods to which all persons have equal rights of well-being. In this context, however, the degrees of needfulness are relevant. On the socio-

---

18. Ronald Dworkin, *Taking Rights Seriously* (Cambridge, Mass.: Harvard University Press, 1977), pp. 268 ff.; Charles Fried, *Right and Wrong* (Cambridge, Mass.: Harvard University Press, 1978), p. 132; Jeremy Waldron, *The Right to Private Property* (Oxford: Clarendon Press, 1988), p. 292. For a good discussion, see Joseph Raz, *The Morality of Freedom* (Oxford: Clarendon Press, 1986), pp. 6–19.

19. See my article "Are There Any Absolute Rights?" *Philosophical Quarterly* 31 (1981): 1–16.

political level, harm consists in violating laws that provide for these goods, including the public goods whose benefits necessarily accrue to each and all the members of a society.

Second, these public goods are close to the utilitarian grounds of collective benefit or general interest, but they can also be construed in terms of the principle of human rights as given in the PGC. Thus traffic regulations, like those which prohibit driving the wrong way on a one-way street, are a justifiable interference with freedom on the PGC's grounds of helping to secure each person's equal right to well-being as embodied in a physically safe and predictable environment. This right is a collective one insofar as its object is a whole system or institution that cannot be parceled out among individuals.[20] But it is also an individual right insofar as its subjects or right-holders are individuals each of whom the system is designed to benefit (see also 7.1; 8.1). The criterion of degrees of needfulness for action shows why the collective and individual rights here indicated override the freedom to drive in the wrong direction.

Although collective rights are similar to utilitarian benefits in their aggregative aspect, the two kinds of value nevertheless differ in at least four ways. First, as we have seen, collective rights have a distributive aspect so that they can also be construed as individual rights, since their objects are designed to benefit individuals as such, and not only a collective entity. Moreover, when the collective rights are in accord with the PGC as the principle of human rights, this distributive aspect requires that the system or institution in question treat equally the individuals affected by it. As we shall see, the community of rights also has this individualist aspect (3.4, 7). Second, utilitarian benefits are not segmented, as are collective rights, according to specific and distinct kinds of goods; on the contrary, in utilitarian calculation the aim is to maximize "utility" overall regardless of the kinds of benefits that enter into the calculus. Thus, to take a familiar example, the collective right to have a system of criminal law requires specific punitive provisions for various crimes; but it does not countenance, as does utilitarian calculation, the flouting of these provisions when overall utility might be increased thereby. Third, where utilitarian benefits may be any kinds of goods associated with persons' desires or preferences, the objects of collective rights are especially important kinds of goods, identified both with individuals' needs of agency and with institutional arrangements that help the society to fulfill its individual members' rights of agency. Fourth, just as interests or benefits as such are not rights unless further factors are present, so for collective benefits to be collective rights they must be due or

20.   See the discussion of collective rights in Raz, *Morality of Freedom*, pp. 207–9.

owed to and controlled by the group or society for its own sake and not simply as a means of maximizing overall utility.

A third point must also be noted with regard to the objection against a general right to freedom. As was mentioned above in discussing the interference of positive rights with freedom, a distinction must be drawn between the freedoms that are essential for action in general and those that pertain to particular actions whose performance or nonperformance does not affect the general necessary conditions of action. In part, this is the distinction between dispositional and occurrent freedom, between having the continuing long-range effective ability to exercise control over one's behavior by one's unforced choice and exercising such control in particular situations. But the distinction also applies to particular exercises of freedom or control, in that the unrestricted ability to perform certain actions is much more important for one's general and equal status and dignity as a rational agent than is the ability to perform other actions. Prime examples of the former type, in each of these two distinctions, are the civil liberties, freedom of movement in general, and choices of ways of life. Utilitarian grounds, where these cannot be shown to coincide extensionally with criteria based on the rights needed for action and generally successful action, may not override any of these freedoms. Hence, there remains a general right to freedom as one of the necessary goods of action. The protection of this general right is essential not only for action and generally successful action but also for the moral legitimacy of governments (see 8.1). But it is not such freedom that is in conflict with or restricted by the positive rights to freedom and well-being, to which the objection about positive rights interfering with freedom referred. The criterion of degrees of needfulness for action thus shows which freedoms may be restricted by positive rights or by utilitarian considerations and which may not.

Let us now turn to a second set of objections to my reply to the contention that positive rights interfere with the right to freedom. This set bears directly on the criterion of degrees of needfulness for action in its relation to utilitarianism. It may be held that this criterion amounts to a "utilitarianism of rights" according to which the minimization of infringements of rights is a desirable end-state to be achieved by infringing less important rights in order to prevent the infringement of more important rights.[21] Such a calculus might be held to justify various gruesome freedom-infringing policies as ways of securing positive rights to basic well-being:

21. See Nozick, *Anarchy, State, and Utopia*, pp. 28–30. See also Jeremy Waldron, *Liberal Rights* (Cambridge: Cambridge University Press, 1993), pp. 222–23, and Waldron, *Right to Private Property*, p. 75.

policies like removing one of a healthy person's kidneys or eyes in order to preserve the life or sight of another person.[22] For, after all, not being dead or blind is more needed for action than is having two kidneys or eyes. Or, to take a different kind of example, since driving automobiles, which may lead to deaths, is less needed for action than is life, the criterion might be held to justify infringing the right to drive automobiles. In addition, the criterion may also be held to suffer from another problem that also dogs utilitarianism: the impossibility of interpersonal comparisons of utility or well-being.[23] For the criterion assumes the possibility of such comparisons when it holds that one person's freedom to do X is less important for action than another person's freedom to do Y or to have some well-being component Z.

A related objection to the criterion of degrees of needfulness for action is that, like some forms of utilitarianism, it eventuates in complete economic equality without regard for persons' differential contributions of work. At least since Hume it has been pointed out that because of the diminishing marginal utility of money, the sum-total of utility is increased the closer one comes to an equal distribution of wealth. Hence, at least in principle, utilitarians are committed to complete equalization of wealth.[24]

The criterion of degrees of needfulness may seem to entail a similar result. Since persons with little or no money have a greater need for money in relation to their agency than do persons with large amounts of money, the right of the latter to retain all their wealth would be overridden by the right of the former to be helped through having some of that wealth transferred to them. And since the comparative degrees of need for money would persist until equality in money holdings was achieved or at least closely approached, the result would be a drastic equalization of financial resources.

To see how these objections are to be answered, four points must be

22. See the discussion of the "survival lottery" in John Harris, *Violence and Responsibility* (London: Routledge and Kegan Paul, 1980), pp. 66–84.

23. See Lionel Robbins, *An Essay on the Nature and Significance of Economic Science* (London: Macmillan, 1952), pp. 136–43. For more recent discussions, see James Griffin, "Are There Incommensurable Values?" *Philosophy and Public Affairs* 7 (1977): 39 ff.; Russell Hardin, *Morality within the Limits of Reason* (Chicago: University of Chicago Press, 1988), pp. 170–78; Jon Elster and John E. Roemer, eds., *Interpersonal Comparisons of Well-Being* (Cambridge: Cambridge University Press, 1991); Jon Elster and Aarund Hylland, eds., *Foundations of Social Choice Theory* (Cambridge: Cambridge University Press, 1986), essays by Allan Gibbard and Donald Davidson, pp. 165–211.

24. See David Hume, *Enquiry concerning the Principles of Morals*, sec. 3, pt. 2, ed. L. A. Selby-Bigge (Oxford: Clarendon Press, 1962), pp. 193 ff.; Jeremy Bentham, *Theory of Legislation*, ed. C. K. Ogden (London: Routledge and Kegan Paul, 1928), p. 104; Henry Sidgwick, *Principles of Political Economy* (London: Macmillan, 1901), pp. 519 ff., and *Elements of Politics* (London: Macmillan, 1919), pp. 160 ff.; Richard B. Brandt, *A Theory of the Good and the Right* (Oxford: Clarendon Press, 1979), chap. 16.

kept in mind about the criterion of degrees of needfulness for action. First, the objects that are compared according to their degrees are not, as with the utilitarians, such vague entities as "utilities" construed as "desires" or "preferences," whose difficulties of interpersonal comparison, while not insurmountable, may nevertheless be severe. The objects compared in the degrees of needfulness for action are precisely those: needs for agency; the goods that must be had either for the very possibility of action or for having general chances of success in action. These goods are objective and not relative to particular, possibly idiosyncratic standards set by preferences or desires. As was indicated above in the demarcation of three levels of well-being (1.4), their degrees of needfulness can be compared in an objective way. At the same time, the criterion can take account of human diversities in the differing extents to which persons can fulfill these needs.

A second point requires emphasis on the action which is the context of the criterion of degrees of needfulness for action. The phrase "utilitarianism of rights" seems to imply a restless calculus reflecting a constant readiness to interfere with rights in order to come out with a weighted minimum of rights-infringements. Such interference could make action, with its need for stability of purposive planning, difficult or impossible. The context of action, on the other hand, requires only comparisons restricted to wide and readily ascertainable disparities in degrees of importance between the objects of rights. The aim is not to cripple some persons' actions in order to facilitate the actions of others, but rather to make the necessary conditions of action available to all prospective agents. Thus, for the most part, the criterion is restricted to areas where the basic well-being of some persons requires infringing the additive well-being of others or the freedom associated with the latter well-being, as in my above examples of lying to prevent murder or stealing to prevent starvation. The criterion thus militates against absolutist interpretations of rights without falling into the morass of trying to set up intricate calculi of the relative strength of desires or preferences.

A third, closely related point concerns the limits of the application of the criterion of degrees of needfulness. These limits are especially set by the physical integrity which is an essential part of basic well-being. The policies cited above, removing healthy persons' kidneys or eyes to prevent the death or blindness of other persons, are attacks on the former persons' physical integrity. As such, they pose serious threats to their continued agency. Persons can indeed survive with one kidney or one eye; but, apart from their voluntary consent, the criterion of degrees of needfulness cannot justify such inflictions of basic harms. It is a serious category mistake to assimilate such sacrifices to the taxation whereby transfers are made from persons who can well afford them to help relieve the misery of others.

The case is different, however, in certain kinds of political contexts where a society that embodies the whole system of human rights can be defended against external aggression only through military conscription.[25] But here it is not diffuse utilitarian calculations either of maximizing utility or of minimizing disutility or rights-infringements that justify the conscription policy; it is rather the defense of the whole system of the rights to freedom and well-being, to which there are both collective and individual rights in the ways indicated above.

A fourth point involves another aspect of the context of agency. The criterion of degrees of needfulness for action bears on each person's needs of *agency;* hence, it is quite different from a policy that encourages passive recipience or dependence on the agency of others. This point bears both on the equalization of wealth to which utilitarianism seems to lead and on the argument whereby the criterion was held to disjustify automobile driving.

As was indicated above, the criterion of degrees of needfulness does justify certain monetary transfers. Nevertheless, it does not go so far as complete equality. The utilitarians halted the movement to equality, based on the diminishing marginal utility of money, through the need for incentives: if wealth is equalized, the incentive to work, let alone to work hard, is removed; hence, redistribution must stop very far short of complete equality.[26] The principle of human rights, while also taking account of the incentive factor, has a related but distinct emphasis. The rational autonomy which is the aim of the human rights involves that each person is to be a self-controlling, self-developing agent, in contrast to being a dependent, passive recipient of the agency of others. Even when the rights require positive assistance from other persons, their point is not to reinforce or increase dependence but rather to give support that enables persons to be agents, that is, to control their own lives and effectively pursue and sustain their own purposes without being subjected to domination and harms from others. For this reason, the criterion of degrees of needfulness for action justifies only such monetary transfers as enable persons to acquire and exercise the abilities for being productive agents on their own behalf. Thus, once basic well-being is equally assured for all either by persons' own efforts or from outside sources, further transfers are justified only insofar as they serve to advance the additive well-being which consists in having the abilities of productive agency. As we shall see, however, there are also important grounds for upholding more extensive kinds of economic redistribution (5.2).

---

25. See my "Individual Rights and Political-Military Obligations," in Gewirth, *Human Rights*, pp. 234–55.

26. See above, n. 24.

This point also bears more generally on the disputed issue of the justification of property rights. The criterion of degrees of needfulness directly upholds a consequentialist justification, bearing on the final cause or purpose subserved by property rights: the securing of freedom and well-being for all. The concern for autonomy and productive agency, on the other hand, directly invokes an antecedentalist justification of property rights, in terms of the efficient cause: the work that has been done to produce the things to which the rights attach. I take up this conflict in chapter 5. But in the present context it can be seen that the conflict is resolved by first making the efficient-cause justification ancillary to the final-cause justification at the level of basic well-being, and then, within certain limits to be spelled out below (5.1, 6), giving the efficient-cause justification relatively free rein.

The criterion of degrees of needfulness for action also enters into the disputed question of the relative importance of political-civil rights and economic-social rights within the whole sphere of human rights. It might be contended that the criterion upholds the primacy of economic rights to subsistence, because subsistence is more needed for agency than are the civil liberties and other objects of political and civil rights. If one is starving, one is hardly interested in the goods of democratic polity.

This thesis, while plausible, takes too narrow a view of the kinds of rights in relation to agency, in at least three ways. First, torture, summary execution, and other violations of political and civil rights are at least as destructive of the proximate conditions of agency as is starvation.[27] Thus the protections of the rule of law to curb otherwise unbridled political power are as much needed to secure the elemental conditions of human life as are assurances of economic subsistence. Second, political rights require the equal distribution of the civil liberties, and these liberties enable persons to determine the holders of political power (see 8.1). Such determination may well be needed to control the distribution of economic resources in ways that do not threaten the subsistence needs of sizable numbers of persons. Third, the political and civil rights are essential for the equal human dignity that, as we saw above, is based on humans' abilities as rational and volitional agents and that serves to ground human rights.

Let us now look briefly at the other example adduced above, where it was contended that on the criterion of degrees of needfulness for agency the right to drive automobiles could be infringed, because the object of this

27. See Rhoda Howard, "The Full-Belly Thesis: Should Economic Rights Take Priority over Civil and Political Rights? Evidence from Sub-Saharan Africa," *Human Rights Quarterly* 5 (1983): 467–90; Louis Henkin, "Human Rights: Reappraisal and Readjustment," in David Sidorsky, ed., *Essays on Human Rights* (Philadelphia: Jewish Publication Society, 1979), p. 83; Thomas Donaldson, *The Ethics of International Business* (New York: Oxford University Press, 1989), pp. 78–80.

right is less needed for action than is life, which is threatened by automobile accidents. This example is also to be dealt with by reference to the right to freedom. Persons' freedom of action normally involves that they can control how they drive and hence their degree of risk in driving. The driver can markedly lower this risk by driving carefully and defensively and by abstaining from liquor and drugs. Since it is the driver who mainly controls whether and to what extent her life will be endangered, she is still enabled to give primary weight to the right to life, despite the statistical possibility of mortal accidents. Thus the hierarchic priority of the right to life over the right to drive automobiles, which reflects the criterion of degrees of needfulness for action, is not refuted by the lethal possibilities of the latter right. This consideration can also be extended to the passengers who entrust their lives to the driver, since they are in a position to ascertain how much the driver can be trusted to protect their rights to life. To a lesser degree, and with special reference to various statistical considerations, a similar point applies to airplane passengers. Thus, when morality and law secure positive rights to basic well-being by imposing positive duties to drive carefully, this is not in conflict with the equal right to freedom as a characteristic of rational agency.[28]

2.5. Objections to Positive Rights: Overload of Duties

A second objection against the thesis that there are positive rights to freedom and well-being concerns the general extent and limits of the duties they impose. In view of the millions of persons who are starving in various parts of the world or who are otherwise threatened in their basic well-being by disease, torture, homelessness, and other severe harms or suffering, doesn't the thesis that persons have positive rights to basic well-being entail

---

28. The problems dealt with by the degrees of needfulness for action are similar to those discussed by Judith Jarvis Thomson, *The Realm of Rights* (Cambridge, Mass.: Harvard University Press, 1990), chap. 8, "Tradeoffs." She presents "The Tradeoff Idea: It is permissible to infringe a claim if and only if infringing it would be sufficiently much better for those for whom infringing it would be good than not infringing it would be for the claim holder" (p. 153). Unlike my invocation of the degrees of needfulness for action, Thomson, after asking, "How much better is sufficiently much better?" says, "The answer is that there is no answer. There is no one size such that for any claim you choose, the claim is permissibly infringeable if and only if infringing it would generate an increment of good of that size" (p. 153). Thomson goes on to adduce the notion of "the stringency of a claim" (pp. 153 ff.). Her generally acute discussion of the difficulties of the "tradeoff idea" might have been strengthened if she had invoked the specific kinds of measurability provided by the criterion of degrees of needfulness for action, instead of (or in addition to) relying on various intuitions.

that other persons who are more affluent or fortunate have correlative strict duties to engage ceaselessly in acts of succor or rescue? The thesis seems to entail that there should be no room for optional ordinary activities; instead it imposes an "overload": unlimited, open-ended positive obligations that require a drastic, indeed a revolutionary, change in whole ways of life.[29] This objection is reinforced by the criterion of degrees of needfulness for action; for since food, shelter, and physical safety are more needed for action than are watching television or playing golf, the liberty-rights to the latter would be overridden by the claim-rights to the former.

This objection points in the right direction insofar as it calls attention to the vast structural inequalities found within and between different societies and the greater degree of responsibility incumbent on those who can help to fulfill the positive rights in question. But in view of the vastness of unfulfilled rights to basic well-being and the societal bases of these unfulfilled needs, the correlative duties belong in the first instance to governments that can command the relevant resources. This point supplies an important clarifying consideration for the thesis presented above (1.2) about the mutualist universality of human rights and duties. The universality of the rights must take account of the empirical conditions of their possible effectuation. How can the resident of Chicago help to fulfill the pressing agency needs that the residents of Bosnia or Afghanistan or Somalia or Ecuador cannot fulfill for themselves by their own efforts? Here the direct respondents of the rights are various governmental institutions. But these institutions function as representatives of individuals, who are in this way jointly responsible for providing the needed assistance. This responsibility, so far as it bears on each individual, requires enlightened, persistent advocacy and related activities that can be carried on by groups of individuals organized for the purposes of removing the structural and other evils that constitute violations of human rights. In these and related ways, the practically primary status of governments as respondents of the positive human rights must be seen to rest on their being representatives

29. See James S. Fishkin, *The Limits of Obligation* (New Haven, Conn.: Yale University Press, 1982); Peter Singer, "Famine, Affluence, and Morality," *Philosophy and Public Affairs* 1 (spring 1972): 229–43; Martin C. McGuire, "The Calculus of Moral Obligation," *Ethics* 95 (Jan. 1985): 199–223; John Harris, *Violence and Responsibility*, chap. 9; Henry Shue, "The Burdens of Justice," *Journal of Philosophy* 80 (Oct. 1983): 600–608; Shelly Kagan, "Does Consequentialism Demand Too Much? Recent Work on the Limits of Obligation," *Philosophy and Public Affairs* 13 (1984): 239–54. For a useful survey of other recent attempts to deal with the problems of overload and scarce resources, see Carl Wellman, "Bibliographic Essay: Welfare Rights," in Kenneth Kipnis and Diana T. Meyers, eds., *Economic Justice: Private Rights and Public Responsibilities* (Totowa, N.J.: Rowman and Allanheld, 1985), pp. 232–39.

of the individuals who are, in principle, the ultimate respondents of the rights.

There is no contradiction, then, between rights' being universal human rights and their implementation's being left largely to the governments of the particular countries in which affected persons and groups reside. This is because 'ought' implies 'can'; more specifically, implementation of the rights requires respondents who can effectively secure them; and these are usually governments rather than private individuals. By the same token, when a government violates its own residents' human rights, effective expressions of concern by other governments, including calls for remediation, are permitted and indeed required.

It is important, then, to take account of the causal background of the kinds of deprivations mentioned in the above objection. Just as 'ought' is limited by 'can,' so it is also limited by the causal factors that both generate these sufferings and affect the attainability of what ought to be done to relieve them. Without adequate awareness of this background, attempts to render assistance may be misguided or futile. Thus one must distinguish, to begin with, between isolated, individual acts of rescue, like throwing a rope to a drowning person, and large-scale evils like genocide, famine, or homelessness, to which the above contention primarily refers. The latter are not merely individual phenomena to be coped with, let alone solved, by individual actions. To be sure, individuals can make a contribution by offering money or shelter and organizing groups for these purposes; and the value, both real and symbolic, of such individual and group actions should not be underestimated. But in the case of large-scale deprivations like famines, their underlying causes include political and other structural factors involving the legally sanctioned unequal distribution of economic and other forms of power. This can be seen from the fact that when famines occur, it is often not the case that sufficient food is unavailable in the countries affected; rather, the poor lack sufficient "entitlements" or effective ownership rights to the food. It is ultimately the existing, drastically unequal distribution of wealth and income, and thus of property, that generates this lack. And it is in large part the use of political power to protect this distribution that enables the evils to persist. Hence, if the positive rights of the deprived persons to basic well-being are to be secured, means must be found for so affecting or restraining the power structure that such access is provided for those who need it. Often this problem is aggravated by wars between contending power-seekers. Even when sufficient food is not available in the countries affected, for example because of drought, populations can obtain food either as gifts or as purchases from other countries if their ruling elites permit this. The distribution of political power is thus a decisive factor. Accordingly, the means of response must be primarily political and institutional rather than individual, although an important kind of individual responsibility must also be recognized.[30]

I shall briefly illustrate these considerations through a recent Oxfam report about the recurrent famines in the Sahel countries. As summarized in the *New York Times,* the report points out that the "standard response to famine" has been "for donor countries and local governments to rush in food for the dying." The report continues: "But it is seldom that there is an actual shortage of food in a country during a famine. The crisis is primarily one of marketing and maldistribution of food crops, not simply one of insufficient agricultural production." An important cause of this maldistribution (in the *Times*'s summary of the Oxfam report) is that "all the millions spent by local governments and the United Nations to expand commercial export crops such as peanuts, cotton and rice has [*sic*] decreased food production without boosting incomes enough for people to buy imported staples. These programs . . . have been driving smaller farmers off better lands and onto marginal fields. . . . These hardships are made worse by the low food prices set by the Sahel governments to aid urban residents. Such prices not only discourage farmers from producing food crops but also leave them without enough cash to fertilize fields or maintain equipment."

The solution to this problem, according to the Oxfam report as summarized in the *Times,* lies in "directing most technical aid to small farmers. And the best means of using this aid . . . is through the formation of village and regional cooperatives, in which these producers jointly protect their lands, share water supplies and, more important, gain a fair price for grains and animals by marketing them as a group."[31]

---

30. For extensive discussion, evidence, and argument on these causal factors, see especially Jean Drèze and Amartya Sen, *Hunger and Public Action* (Oxford: Clarendon Press, 1989). On "entitlements" see Amartya Sen, *Poverty and Famines: An Essay on Entitlement and Deprivation* (Oxford: Clarendon Press, 1982). See also Gunnar Myrdal, *Asian Drama: An Inquiry in the Poverty of Nations* (New York: Twentieth Century Fund, 1969), vol. 2, pp. 895–99; S. Reutlinger and M. Selowsky, *Malnutrition and Poverty* (Baltimore: Johns Hopkins University Press, 1976); John W. Warnock, *The Politics of Hunger* (London: Methuen, 1987). On the legal-political background, see Paul Sieghart, *The Lawful Rights of Mankind: An Introduction to the International Legal Code of Human Rights* (Oxford: Oxford University Press, 1985): "Since Hitler's and Stalin's time there has been a change in international law so profound that it can properly be called a revolution. Today, for the first time in history, how a sovereign state treats its citizens is no longer a matter for its own exclusive determination, but a matter of *legitimate* concern for all other states, and for their inhabitants" (p. vii; emphasis in original).

31. Seth S. King, "In Africa, A Natural Disaster Made Worse by Man," *New York Times,* June 17, 1984, sec. E, p. 8. For similar analyses, see Thomas T. Poleman, "World Food: A Perspective," *Science* 188 (May 19, 1975): 515 ff.; Pierre R. Crosson, "Institutional Ob-

The policy proposals of the Oxfam report may underemphasize the specifically political difficulties of effecting the needed changes, including the indifference and even hostility of ruling elites to the basic needs of suppressed classes in the respective countries. But the appropriate remedies, in any case, including the ability of farmers to "jointly protect their lands," are a far cry from the near-impoverishment endorsed for individual rescuers by the "overload" conception of positive obligations. As a political project, the positive rights of the persons threatened by starvation require certain political changes, including more control by local farmers over their producing and marketing activities. These changes are a matter first for indigenous forces within each nation and, second, for the enlightened support of other nations and of international organizations. The positive duties to work for such changes are a specific institutional response to the institutional causal factors adduced by the Oxfam report, including the vast amounts of money spent by local governments to expand commercial export crops and the low prices set by these same governments for the food produced by the farmers within each country.[32]

These considerations are reinforced by the grounding of human rights in the needs of agency. As I have indicated elsewhere,[33] transfers of food and other basic necessities to starving persons in other nations are indeed morally required in cases of emergencies. But, apart from emergencies, what is also needed is greater democratization within each country so that governments will be more responsive to the needs of all their citizens and hence less prone to impose or accept enormous sacrifices of some for the sake of other, wealthier segments of the population. Insistence on and help toward such democratization is a vital human-rights obligation of democratic governments. So far as concerns their giving aid, this should proceed not by maintaining a relation of recipience and dependence on the part of the nations that are helped but rather by enabling them to develop and use their own resources, personal, political, and environmental, including, so far as possible on the part of each person, an effective implementation of the sense of personal responsibility. The point of such a policy, in keeping with the PGC's concern for the conditions of agency, is to give support that

stacles to World Food Production," *Science* 188 (May 19, 1975): 522–23; Harry T. Walters, "Difficult Issues Underlying Food Problems," *Science* 188 (May 19, 1975): 530; Shue, *Basic Rights,* pp. 41 ff.

32.   See Theodore W. Schultz, *Investing in People* (Berkeley and Los Angeles: University of California Press, 1981), pp. 8–10.

33.   See my "Starvation and Human Rights," in Gewirth, *Human Rights,* pp. 197–217. See also William Aiken and Hugh LaFollette, eds., *World Hunger and Moral Obligation* (Englewood Cliffs, N.J.: Prentice-Hall, 1977); Onora O'Neill, *Faces of Hunger: An Essay on Poverty, Justice, and Development* (London: Allen and Unwin, 1986).

enables persons to maintain these conditions for themselves. On the national level, similarly, welfare assistance must be aimed not only at alleviating the immediate hardships and shortages of poverty and other handicaps but also at helping the poor and other disadvantaged persons to develop for themselves the ability to procure goods and services by their own efforts and thus to improve their capabilities for successful, productive agency (see 4.6).

It is important, then, to reject a purview that assumes a permanent class of welfare dependents (whether domestic or international), with a permanent division between affluent agents or rescuers and poor, dependent recipients. Instead, the PGC's emphasis on the rights of agency requires that all persons have the necessary conditions of action, including property, and that welfare programs (whether domestic or international) aim at fostering for all persons their acquisition of the conditions and abilities needed for successful agency and hence a cessation of exclusive dependence on others for basic goods. Such an aim requires not the kind of open-ended self-sacrifice envisaged in the "overload" conception of positive duties, but rather a more finite set of institutional policies that are based on an analysis of the specific static and dynamic steps that can fulfill the positive rights in question.

The strict duties correlative with the positive rights stressed above might be fulfilled in different ways. Markets cannot be relied on for this purpose, because the persons in need of help do not have the economic resources to compete for the needed commodities. In addition to the considerations about effectiveness presented above, there are at least three reasons why the state, as a community of rights, should be the primary, even if not the only, respondent of these rights, within the indicated limits and aims of personal responsibility and development of productive agency. First, the basic goods and opportunities in question must be securely provided as needed; hence, if they are left to the optional decisions of charity on the part of willing private persons or groups, sufficient funds may not be given. Second, the benefits of these arrangements must be equitably and impartially distributed to the persons who need them, without discrimination based on the variable preferences of potential providers. Third, the duty to contribute to such arrangements through taxes must also be equitably distributed to all the persons who have the required economic resources, in proportion to their ability. To leave the fulfillment of this duty solely to voluntary groups would allow many persons, as "free riders," to shirk their duty. Thus the positive moral rights to basic well-being should also be positive legal rights, to be enforced by the state, so that in this way the state functions as a community of rights. But the legality of the rights rests on the moral rightness of subjecting property rights to the more imperative rights that are concerned with basic well-being. This still leaves open the possibility, and indeed the strong value, of private associations formed for purposes of mutual aid.

As a community of rights, the state's relation to the positive rights to basic well-being should not be one of mere coercion whereby the required taxes are exacted by law; it should also involve civic education and the wide use of civil liberties whereby persons can discuss and appraise their obligations on behalf of deprived groups and thereby recognize the justice of the laws that enforce these obligations. The main justification of the state (and hence of political obligation) is, indeed, that it serves to secure persons' generic rights to both freedom and well-being. The whole question of the overload of positive duties will be further considered when we come to the political effectuation of the economic and social rights in chapter 8.

There are kinds of extreme crisis situations where the joint efforts of governments and individuals are required. When tyrannical regimes set out to murder parts of their populations, as in the Nazis' Holocaust and the "ethnic cleansing" perpetrated in the former Yugoslavia in 1993, it is a human-rights obligation of governments to condemn such policies and to take whatever steps they can to protect the oppressed groups. Here the community of rights requires an overstepping of national boundaries and an effective recognition and enforcement of the universality of human rights.

The ability of individuals to protect or rescue in such situations is usually quite limited. But it is their duty, correlative with the violated rights, to press their governments to take appropriate measures. Where, within the limits set by geographic and other factors, including comparable costs to agents, individual actions of rescue are possible, the principle of human rights prescribes the moral duty to perform them.[34] In any case, indifference in the face of such evils is entirely unacceptable morally.

We must look more closely at the question of how far rights extend in such extreme situations, including the rights both of the threatened persons and of their possible individual rescuers. According to the criterion of degrees of needfulness for action, acts of rescue are morally required of persons if they are in a position to effect the rescues without comparable costs to themselves. The threatened persons have rights to be rescued in such circumstances. But their rights to life do not extend to the lives of any other

34. For the motivation by "the principle of justice" in rescuers of Jews from the Nazis, see Samuel P. Oliner and Pearl M. Oliner, *The Altruistic Personality: Rescuers of Jews in Nazi Germany* (New York: Free Press, 1988), p. 209. The "principle of justice" is stated by the Oliners as "the right of innocent people to be free from persecution." They also state what they call "the principle of care" as "the obligation to help the needy." This obligation can also be construed as the correlative of the positive right to be helped.

innocent persons. In general, if a person has a right to X, then she has a right to anything else Y that may be necessary for her having X, *unless* someone else already has a right to that X *and* Y is as needed for action as is X. For example, if Jones is starving and cannot obtain food by her own efforts, while Smith has abundant food, then Jones has a right to as much of Smith's food as she needs to prevent starvation even though Smith has a property right in the food. But if Smith has only enough food to prevent his own starvation, then Jones has no right to it because Smith's not starving is as needed for his action as Jones's not starving is for hers. In such a case, the correct description of the situation may be put in either of two ways: (*a*) Jones's right not to starve or her right to Smith's food is overridden; (*b*) Jones does not have a right not to starve when her nonstarvation requires the infringement of Smith's equal right.

It is for this reason that the rights to life of the persons who are threatened by murder do not include the right to have their possible rescuers murdered. The lives of the possible rescuers are as needed for their action as the lives of the threatened persons are for theirs. But by the same token, when acts of rescue are possible, with the realistic expectation that the rescuers are not risking their own lives, those acts are morally mandatory positive duties. Obviously in such tragic situations the results of miscalculation can be terrible. But the risks can be and have been shouldered by persons who have sufficiently strong convictions about the community of rights.

There remain further questions about how far this requirement of individual responsibility extends, beyond the governmental provision emphasized above. The questions concern especially the rightness of persons' living their own lives while confronted by other persons whose extreme hardships and sufferings prevent them from having the freedom and well-being needed for living theirs.[35] I want to suggest that a sound answer to these questions is provided by recourse to the full context of human purposive agency. We have duties to help persons to fulfill their generic rights of agency when they cannot do so by their own efforts. Through such fulfillment, persons are enabled to act, with general chances of success, in pursuit of their own purposes, whatever they may be, so long as they do not violate the generic rights of other persons. But by the same token, the helpers, the respondents of the duties, should also be able to act in pursuit of *their* own purposes, in accordance with their own rights to freedom and well-being. An accommodation must, then, be reached between persons' duties to help others and their rights to be free purposive agents on their

---

35. For forceful posing of these questions, with somewhat opposed answers, see Susan Wolf, "Moral Saints," *Journal of Philosophy* 79 (Aug. 1982): 419–38, and Larry May, *Sharing Responsibility* (Chicago: University of Chicago Press, 1992), chap. 6. May's response to the "overload" problem (pp. 118–19) seems to me to be too restrictive.

own behalf. This accommodation is indicated in the PGC's injunction to act in accord with the generic rights of one's recipients *as well as of oneself*. It would be morally wrong to emphasize either of these poles to the exclusion of the other. But since, and insofar as, the duties to help may more readily be undersupported, there is required vigorous advocacy on the part of individuals and groups, together with action by the state as indicated above.

2.6. OBJECTIONS TO POSITIVE RIGHTS: UNIVERSALITY

Let us now consider a third objection, or rather set of objections, against the thesis of positive rights: that they cannot be human rights because they do not meet the test of universality. This test is invoked in at least four different contexts of comparison: (*a*) comparisons between individual persons as both agents and recipients of the actions required by the rights; (*b*) comparisons between "normal" humans and "deficient" humans; (*c*) comparisons between different cultures; and (*d*) comparisons between more general and more specific objects of rights. Some of these contexts do not apply solely to positive rights; but it is convenient to consider them together in the present section because they all concern modes of universality.

(*a*) One objection begins from the correct observation that human rights must be mutual rights of all humans against all humans: all humans must be both the subjects or right-holders and the respondents or duty-bearers of the rights, so that all persons must have the strict right to be treated in the appropriate way and all persons must have the strict duty of acting in accord with the right (1.2). Thus all persons must be both the agents and the recipients of the modes of action required by the human rights. This mutualist requirement is passed by the negative rights, such as the rights to life and to freedom of movement or speech: everyone has the rights not to be killed and not to have her movements or speech interfered with, and everyone has the correlative duties to refrain from killing other persons and from interfering with their movements or speech. But in the case of positive rights, such as the right to be relieved from starvation or from severe economic deprivation, it is objected that there cannot be such universality or mutuality: only some persons have the right: those who are threatened by starvation or deprivation; and only some other persons have the duty: those who are able to prevent or relieve this starvation or deprivation by giving aid.[36] For persons cannot both be starving and at the same

36. See Maurice Cranston, *What Are Human Rights?* (London: Bodley Head, 1973), pp. 66 ff. See also his contribution to D. D. Raphael, ed., *Political Theory and the Rights of Man* (London: Macmillan, 1967), pp. 96 ff.

time have the positive duty to relieve the starvation of others. Hence, not all persons can have the positive duties that are correlative with positive rights. But since the correlativity of rights and duties is essential to claim-rights, not all persons can have the positive right to be relieved from starvation that is correlative with the positive duty to relieve starvation. Hence, positive rights cannot be rights of all persons against all persons, so that they fail the test of universality for human rights.

The answer to this objection need not concede that these rights, like other positive economic and social rights, are universal only in a "weaker" sense, in that while all persons have the right to be rescued from starvation or deprivation, only some persons have the correlative duty.[37] Within the limits of practicability, all persons equally have the right and all equally have the duty. For all persons come under the protection and the requirements of the PGC as the principle of human rights insofar as they are prospective purposive agents. Hence, all the generic rights upheld by the PGC have the universality required for being human rights.

It is, indeed, logically impossible that each person be at the same time both the rescuer and the rescued, both the affluent provider and the deprived pauper. Nevertheless, the fact that some prospective purposive agent may not at some time need to be rescued from deprivation or be able to rescue others from deprivation does not remove the facts that she has the right to be rescued when she has the need and that she has the duty to rescue when she has the ability and when other relevant conditions are met. The universality of a positive right is not a matter of everyone's actually having the related need, nor is it a matter of everyone's actually fulfilling the correlative duty, let alone of her doing so at all times. Nor is it a matter of everyone's always being able to fulfill the duty. It is, rather, a matter of everyone's always having, as a matter of principle, the right to be treated in the appropriate way when he has the need, and the duty to act in accord with the right when the circumstances arise that require such action and when he then has the ability to do so, this ability including consideration of cost to himself.[38] In this way, the universality of the positive human rights is

37. D. D. Raphael, in Raphael, *Political Theory*, pp. 65 ff., 112. See also Andrew Melnyk, "Is There a Formal Argument against Positive Rights?" *Philosophical Studies* 55 (Feb. 1989): 205–9, at 206.

38. This may be what is meant by Melnyk when he says that "we can conditionalise positive rights—formulate them so that they are had only if some condition is satisfied—and thus make them in the appropriate sense universal, i.e. had by all" ("Formal Argument," p. 206). I think, however, that my reference to "principle" is also needed here. Melnyk also provides (pp. 206–7) a sufficient reply to the assertion by Tibor Machan and Douglas Den Uyl ("Gewirth and the Supportive State," above, n. 13) that for a right to be a human right it must be the case that it can be exercised by each and every individual at any and all times and irrespective of contingent technological and economic conditions.

dispositional even if not always occurrent; or, to put it in a related way, even if the rights are not always universally exercised, they are always universally had. So the mutuality of human rights remains.

When it is said that the right to be relieved from economic deprivation and the correlative duty pertain to all persons insofar as they are prospective purposive agents, this does not violate the condition that for human rights to be had one must only be human, as against fulfilling some more restrictive description. As was indicated earlier (1.5), all normal humans are prospective purposive agents; the point of introducing this description is only to call attention to the aspect of being human that most directly generates the human rights to freedom and well-being. In this regard the right in question differs from rights that pertain to persons not simply by virtue of being prospective purposive agents but only in some more restricted capacity, such as being teachers as against students or judges as against defendants. The universality of human rights derives from their direct connection with the necessary conditions of action as against more restrictive objects with which nongeneric rights are connected. And since both the affluent and the economically deprived are prospective purposive agents, the latter's right to be helped by the former is a human right.

It is important to clarify some further considerations about the universality of human rights. Many of the provisions for human rights in the United Nations Universal Declaration of Human Rights (1948) are directly addressed to governments as their respondents. Examples are the rights to a fair trial (art. 10, 11), to a nationality (art. 15), to participate in government (art. 21), to social security (art. 22), and to education (art. 26).[39] These references to governments do not, however, conflict with the thesis that all humans are the respondents of the human rights. For, as was noted in the preceding section, governments function here as the representatives of their citizens. The sequence from the necessary conditions of human action to the functions of social institutions is a complex one which I have discussed in some detail elsewhere (*RM*, chap. 5). But, in general, political institutions are morally justified insofar as they are instrumental to the protection of the rights of individual persons to have the necessary conditions of action and generally successful action. By virtue of this instrumentality, persons have political and civil rights against governments. But that governments are thus the respondents of the rights derives in final analysis from the requirement that governments must enable individual persons both to effectively enjoy the rights and to be the respondents of the correlative duties. Insofar as individuals are in this way the beneficiaries of govern-

---

39. See Rex Martin, *A System of Rights* (Oxford: Clarendon Press, 1993), pp. 87–92. See also Nickel, *Making Sense of Human Rights*, pp. 41–43.

ment, they have the duty to support its morally justified institutions, such as fair trials and education. Thus individuals are at least indirectly the respondents of such political rights (see also 3.4; 8.1).

(b) A second objection about the universality of positive human rights bears on their distribution to physically or mentally handicapped humans. It may be held that the argument for positive rights has not established that the rights belong to *all* humans or to all humans *equally.* For some humans, such as those in a perpetual coma, are not capable of action and hence lack the generic rights, so that they cannot be the agents of positive rights. And other humans, while being agents, vary in their abilities of agency and thus are unequal as agents of positive rights.[40]

There are two main answers to this objection (see also above, 1.6). The first is the Principle of Proportionality: when humans or other entities are less than normal agents (such as mentally deficient persons, persons in a coma, and so forth), they have the generic rights to the degree to which they approach being normal agents (*RM,* 120–25). To be a normal human agent, one must have only the minimal rationality that enters into the practical abilities of the generic features of action: the abilities to control one's behavior by one's unforced choice, to have knowledge of relevant circumstances, and to reflect on one's purposes. Now the less humans have these minimal practical abilities, the less they are able to fulfill their purposes without endangering themselves and others, and this is why their generic rights must be correspondingly reduced.

Nevertheless, these inequalities of having the generic rights are still based on a more fundamental equality of human rights. For the unequal extents to which subnormal humans should have the objects of various rights are grounded in an equal concern for the abilities of agency of all humans. Just as the equality of human rights is compatible with some humans' being given more food or protection than other humans when the former have a greater need for such objects in order to sustain their basic well-being, so too the lesser freedom allowed to some mentally deficient humans is justified by an equal concern for the basic well-being of them and of all other humans. In the limiting case of humans who have no abilities of agency at all, they still have rights to life and to any other goods of agency which they are capable of having; and insofar as they may recover to the extent of being physically capable of action, they have rights that such potential abilities of their agency be protected and fostered. More gener-

40.   See Arval A. Morris, "A Differential Theory of Human Rights," in J. R. Pennock and J. W. Chapman, eds., *Nomos XXIII: Human Rights* (New York: New York University Press, 1981), pp. 158–64; Douglas N. Husak, "Why There Are No Human Rights," *Social Theory and Practice* 10 (1984): 132.

ally, humans who are incapacitated mentally or physically have rights to additional medical and other resources that may enable them, at least in some degree, to overcome their handicaps and thereby come closer to the abilities of normal human agency.[41]

These considerations have a direct bearing on the idea of human dignity. Although human dignity is often held to be the basis of human rights,[42] the above derivations of rights have appealed to dignity only implicitly. That appeal can now be made explicit following the dialectical mode of argument used above. As we have seen, all agents attribute value or worth to the purposes for which they act. But since the agents are the sources or loci of this attribution of worth, they must also attribute worth to themselves. Their purposes are conceived as having worth or value because the agents themselves have worth. This attribution of worth to the agents encompasses not only their purposiveness as such but also the abilities of reason and will that enter into their agency. For in acting for their purposes agents use both will and reason: will in their freedom as controlling their behavior by their unforced choice and in their endeavors to achieve their purposes; reason in ascertaining the means to their ends, in attributing to themselves rights to the necessary conditions of their agency, and in accepting that all other agents also have these rights. Even if they reason incorrectly or will what is wrong, each agent must recognize in herself and others the general abilities that give worth to human life and action and that ground her attribution of the rights of agency. Human dignity consists in having and at least potentially using these abilities, and human rights are derived from human dignity thus conceived. In the case of comatose and other subnormal humans, it is their underlying similarity to normal human agents that grounds the attribution of dignity and rights to them.

(c) A further objection against the universality of positive human rights bears on universality across cultures. It is contended that many Third World countries are too poor to be able to provide the objects of such

41. These considerations raise profound and controversial issues of medical ethics, into which I cannot enter here. For discussions of one important segment of these issues, see J. Gay-Williams, "The Wrongfulness of Euthanasia," in Ronald Munson, ed., *Intervention and Reflection: Basic Issues in Medical Ethics* (Belmont, Calif.: Wadsworth, 1979), pp. 141–43; Gregory E. Pence, *Ethical Options in Medicine* (Oradell, N.J.: Medical Economics Company, 1980), chap. 3, "Euthanasia, Death, and Dying"; James Rachels, *The End of Life: Euthanasia and Morality* (Oxford: Oxford University Press, 1986); A. B. Downing and Barbara Smoker, eds., *Voluntary Euthanasia* (London: Peter Owen, 1986); Daniel Callahan, *Setting Limits: Medical Goals in an Aging Society* (New York: Simon and Schuster, 1988).

42. See my chapter "Human Dignity as the Basis of Rights," in Michael J. Meyer and William Parent, eds., *The Constitution of Rights* (Ithaca, N.Y.: Cornell University Press, 1992), pp. 10–28.

rights, including not only education and medical care but even food.[43] This objection, which is closely related to the "overload" problem considered above, is extended to political and civil rights as well as economic rights. It is held that the wide diversities of traditions in different parts of the world render inapplicable the kinds of positive institutional arrangements required by alleged positive human rights, and that the invocation of these rights is therefore based on an ethnocentric ignoring of the realities of non-Western culture. One version of this objection may reflect a certain communitarian outlook: "Western standards of justice and fairness do not necessarily apply to other cultures,"[44] so that "any definition of human rights should take account of 'national and regional particularities and various historical, cultural, and religious backgrounds.'"[45] A main idea behind this objection is that Third World countries should not be held to the same standards of political and legal rightness, including democratic procedures and the rule of law, as are upheld by positive institutions of Western countries; that the requirements of economic development, while they are far more pressing in underdeveloped countries than are those standards, have not yet been met to the point where positive rights can be fulfilled.

This objection is to be answered on the same grounds as the considerations about freedom and overload considered above (2.4, 5). The universality of human rights, as including political as well as economic rights, is a direct consequence of the universality of the needs of agency among all human beings. Insofar as those needs cannot be fulfilled in some countries, they are to be helped by others; but the political bases of these inabilities must be given special attention. Thus the principle that 'ought' implies 'can' should not be used in such a way as to exempt governments from compliance with the requirements of either positive or negative human rights. Even if, because of economic or cultural factors, complete compliance cannot be achieved at once, palpable, progressive steps in the direc-

43. See David Sidorsky, "Contemporary Reinterpretations of the Concept of Human Rights," in Sidorsky, ed., *Essays on Human Rights: Contemporary Issues and Jewish Perspectives* (Philadelphia: Jewish Publication Society of America, 1979), pp. 105–6. See also Nickel, *Making Sense of Human Rights*, pp. 127–30, 164–65.

44. *New York Times*, June 6, 1993, sec. 1, p. 1.

45. *New York Times*, June 14, 1993, national edition, p. A3. The quoted passage is from a document submitted by some Third World countries to the World Congress on Human Rights held in Vienna, June 1993. This relativist thesis is also upheld by Adamantia Pollis and Peter Schwab, *Human Rights: Cultural and Ideological Perspectives* (New York: Praeger, 1979), chap. 1: "Human Rights: A Western Construct with Limited Applicability," pp. 1 ff. See also A. J. M. Milne, *Human Rights and Human Diversity* (Albany: State University of New York Press, 1968), pp. 2–4. On the historical relativity of human rights, see also Abraham Edel, "Some Reflections on the Concept of Human Rights," in Ervin H. Pollack, ed., *Human Rights* (Buffalo, N.Y.: Jay Stewart Publications, 1971), pp. 1–23, at pp. 6–11.

tion of such compliance are required. Cultural traditions that discriminate against some humans on grounds of race, gender, religion, or other partly interpenetrating variables cannot be permitted to restrict the universal application of human rights.

More generally, viewed in both historical and geographic perspective, the concept of rights can be found in all cultures, ancient as well as modern. The fact that there is often not a specific word for rights does not militate against the further fact that the *concept* of rights can nonetheless be attributed to the ideas and practices of different cultures, in their provisions for property, against criminal assault (however variously interpreted), and in other contexts.[46]

(d) A closely related objection to positive human rights on grounds of universality bears in a different way on the alleged objects of the rights. For something to be a human right, its object—what it is a right to—must be relevant and applicable to all human beings in all places and at all times. Such objects as life, physical integrity, and certain forms of cooperation fulfill this requirement. But many of the objects of alleged positive human rights, including some that figure in the Universal Declaration of Human Rights, are conditions that are far more localized both spatially and temporally. For example, the rights to vote and to have employment seem to have as their necessary backgrounds certain particular political and economic circumstances, so that they cannot be human rights.

This objection would remove from the sphere of human rights not only most economic and social rights but also political and civil rights. It can be countered by noting that the general human rights receive specification in their application to strategic areas of human life. For example, the right to vote is a specification of the generic right to freedom, for it consists in participation in controlling the policies of governmental officials and hence also one's own behavior insofar as it is affected by those policies (see 8.1). Similarly, the right to employment is a specification of the rights to basic and additive well-being (see 6.1).[47] Such specifications of the positive human rights thus provide protections of the kinds of interests that constitute the necessary conditions of action and generally successful action (see also 3.8).

A further fundamental consideration here bears on the relation between human rights and civil rights. An important shift has occurred from the 1789 French Declaration of the Rights of Man and the Citizen to the 1948 United Nations Universal Declaration of Human Rights. The French

46. For a more detailed argument for this universality of the use of the concept of rights, see *RM*, 98–102.

47. See James W. Nickel, "Is There a Human Right to Employment?" *Philosophical Forum* 10 (winter-summer 1978–79): 149–70, at pp. 165–67.

declaration's title suggests a distinction between rights that persons have qua humans and qua citizens, and thus between human rights and civil rights.[48] In the United Nations declaration, on the other hand, civil rights, as well as political, social, and economic rights, are all subsumed under human rights.

This difference is not merely terminological. The reason for the broader view of human rights as including civil rights can be traced back at least as far as Aristotle's insistence that to be fully human is to be a member of a *polis,* a *civitas,* a political community, and thus to be a citizen, a *civis:* "man is by nature a political animal."[49] Hence, the rights of humans include the rights of the citizen; the two are not to be separated. This is an important basis of the unification of rights and community: human rights include one's right to be a member of a political community and to be helped thereby to develop one's full humanity as an agent. The recent subsumption, in the United States, of social and economic rights under "civil rights laws" carries on this recognition. For to be a citizen, and thus to have civil rights, requires not only the political and legal rights of expression, political participation, freedom from arbitrary arrest, and other traditional "civil" liberties; it requires also the economic and social goods without which the former rights lack an essential material and cultural basis. Conversely, to be a fully human agent requires not only possession of economic and social goods but the various political and civil rights and liberties that are indispensable for human security and dignity. This is why human rights include civil rights and why both of these include social and economic rights as well as, more specifically, political rights. Thus even if rights like voting and employment can be interpreted as applying only in particular times and places, this does not remove the normative universality of such conditions, in more general form, as objects of positive human rights.

Parallel considerations apply to various other special rights in the sphere of personal relations. For example, the positive right to have a promise to oneself kept is a right of the particular promisee, and the correlative duty to keep the promise has as its respondent the particular promiser. On this ground it may be held that this positive right is not a human right, but a "special" right.

48.   The *Déclaration des droits de l'homme et du citoyen* is reprinted in David G. Ritchie, *Natural Rights,* 3d ed. (London: George Allen and Unwin, 1916), pp. 290–94. The text of the declaration does not explicitly distinguish between rights *de l'homme* and *du citoyen,* but at a few points (e.g., art. 11) seems to suggest that the latter are derived from the former. See also D. D. Raphael, "The Rights of Man and the Rights of the Citizen," in Raphael, ed., *Political Theory and the Rights of Man* (London: Macmillan, 1967), pp. 101–18, at pp. 106–16.

49.   Aristotle, *Politics,* 1.2.1253 ff. I have discussed this point more fully in "Moral Foundations of Civil Rights Law," *Modern Schoolman* 64 (1987): 235–55.

We must here distinguish, however, between particular transactions and the general institution that provides their ground. The institution of promise-keeping generates a general and, indeed, a human right whose subjects and respondents are all (capable) human beings. For the right that promises be kept is a right that one's general level of purpose-fulfillment and one's general capabilities of action not be lowered by other persons' actions, and that the benefits of having promises kept be maintained. Since all persons are capable of being affected by such an institution, the associated rights and duties are human rights. And the duty to keep one's promises is a positive duty to which there corresponds a positive right (see also *RM*, 230–40).

What has emerged from this chapter is that the human rights which all persons have as prospective purposive agents are positive as well as negative, and that as positive they involve that all humans have rights to active assistance when they cannot attain by their own efforts the freedom and well-being that are the necessary goods of action and generally successful action. This result has advanced the conciliation of rights and community because the rights are now seen to require a context of active mutuality and solidarity, especially as these are provided for in appropriate institutions. The objections about freedom, overload, and universality have been answered in ways that uphold this validation of positive human rights. An important step has thereby been taken toward understanding the community of rights.

THREE

MUTUALITY AND COMMUNITY

3.1. JUSTICE AND EQUALITY

In examining the objections against the idea of positive human rights in chapter 2, I dealt mainly with the objects and contents of the rights as imposing correlative positive duties on their respondents. In order to understand how the positive rights provide the underlying grounds for the community of rights, we must supplement these material factors by certain formal considerations, especially about mutuality, but also about related formal concepts of justice, equality, and reciprocity. It will be recalled that it is the mutuality of human rights that serves to conciliate rights with community (1.2). The principle of human rights requires corresponding mutualist structural patterns of society that affect the comparative possession of freedom and well-being among different social groups or classes. For if rights are the contents of justice, equality and mutuality set the formal framework which determines how those contents are to be distributed. The formal consideration of mutuality, with its related concepts of justice and equality, has an essential bearing on how the community of rights is a just society in which right-holders are related in certain crucially important ways both to one another and, correlatively, to their duty-bearers. I shall begin with certain familiar points about justice.

The PGC as the principle of human rights is a principle of both material or contentual justice and of formal or comparative justice. It is a principle of material justice in that it requires that each person be given what he has a right to (as in the traditional formula that justice consists in giving to each person his due). It is a principle of formal or comparative justice in that it requires that all persons be treated similarly by virtue of being prospective purposive agents so that there must be an equality of generic rights (as in the traditional formula that justice consists in treating similar cases similarly).[1] This latter, formal component of the PGC makes an indispens-

1. I first presented the distinction between material or "substantive" justice and formal or comparative justice in "Political Justice," in R. B. Brandt, ed., *Social Justice* (Englewood

able addition to its contents of freedom and well-being. The addition is comprised in two main relational concepts: equality and mutuality.

It might be thought that the idea of rights should not only be kept separate from the idea of equality but can even dispense with it. The proposal would be that if a person's rights are fulfilled, then there need not be any distinct concern about equality, since, by definition, in the fulfillment of one's rights one already has one's due, what one is entitled to or can justifiably claim for oneself. So what valid basis is there for caring about equality, about how one's resources or holdings, one's freedom and well-being, compare with those of other persons? Or, to put it otherwise, why, in the bearing of justice on rights, do we need the formal or comparative as well as the material or contentual concept of justice? This question is buttressed by the consideration that many arguments that purport to advocate equality, or comparative justice generally, are directly concerned rather with rights to basic goods, that is, with the material concept of justice. This is the case, for example, when it is pointed out that millions of human beings are starving or seriously undernourished while some humans have an overabundance of food and other basic goods. While this view registers a justified moral revulsion against such extreme inequalities of the human condition, the primary concern is nonetheless not with the inequality per se but rather with the overwhelming need to relieve extreme deprivation, that is, with the fulfillment of rights to basic well-being, the material concept of justice.

It must nevertheless be recognized that the idea of equality, which entered into the final, universalization step of the argument for the PGC (1.5), makes an indispensable contribution of its own. Although some philosophers who have tried to explain the value of rights have implicitly assumed that they are had by all humans and by all humans equally,[2] such egalitarian universality is not a part of the concept of a right as such. There have been many societies that effectively provided recognition and legal enforcement of rights, but the rights they acknowledged were had by, or were distributed among, only a small group of persons, so that they were not universal. And even when legal rights have been universally distributed,

Cliffs, N.J.: Prentice Hall, 1962), pp. 124–26. See also my discussion in "Economic Justice: Concepts and Criteria," in Kenneth Kipnis and Diana T. Meyers, eds., Economic Justice: Private Rights and Public Responsibilities (Totowa, N.J.: Rowman and Allanheld, 1985), pp. 9–12. For a fuller discussion of the distinction, but with somewhat different emphases, see Joel Feinberg, "Noncomparative Justice," in Rights, Justice, and the Bounds of Liberty (Princeton, N.J.: Princeton University Press, 1980), pp. 265 ff.

2. See, e.g., Ronald Dworkin, Taking Rights Seriously (Cambridge, Mass.: Harvard University Press, 1977), pp. 272–73; Richard Wasserstrom, "Rights, Human Rights, and Racial Discrimination," pp. 46–57, and Joel Feinberg, "The Nature and Value of Rights," pp. 78–91, both in David Lyons, ed., Rights (Belmont, Calif.: Wadsworth, 1979).

they have often not been had equally. In the feudal era, for example, both lords and vassals had rights, but they were not equal, because the lords' rights were superior to those of their vassals both as to their objects and as to their nature or protection, in that the lords could enforce their rights in ways that were closed to the vassals.

The PGC, on the other hand, is a principle of universal and equal rights. The direct basis of this, as we have seen, is the dialectically necessary argument, to which every agent is logically committed, whose conclusion is that every prospective purposive agent has equal rights to freedom and well-being, so that each agent must also mutually respect these rights in all other prospective agents. A direct corollary of this argument, as we have also seen (2.6), is that inherent dignity or worth pertains equally to all human beings by virtue of their being actual or prospective purposive agents, despite their varying specific abilities of agency. Hence, whatever other rights persons may have, they all have a right to a fundamental equality of positive consideration for their dignity, so that in this way the material and the comparative concepts of justice are brought directly together. The institutions of the society must reflect this equality, and insofar as its social structures fail to do so, the state as the community of rights must take the steps needed to establish it. The solidarity and mutuality that are essential to the idea of community thus rest on the universality and equality of human rights, and this provides a further basis for the conciliation of rights and community.

This point is reinforced by other considerations that argue for combining the comparative and the material concepts of justice. Persons often learn what morally justified rights they have to some X only by comparing their treatment or holdings as to X with how other persons are treated or have holdings of X.[3] This was and is true of the American civil rights movements with regard to race, gender, and other qualities. Moreover, inequalities with regard to certain goods, such as wealth and income, can lead to a loss of even those goods to which persons have rights. In particular, those who live on a much narrower margin of economic security are often unable to compete for such important goods as housing or medical care with persons of greater wealth. Hence, the inequality (with which the comparative concept is concerned) may result in a reduction of the level of goods to which impoverished persons have rights (with which the material concept is concerned). More generally, drastic inequalities of wealth and power enable some persons to dominate others and hence to infringe their rights to both freedom and well-being (see 5.2). This is a main context where equal-

3. See W. C. Runciman, *Relative Deprivation and Social Justice* (London: Routledge and Kegan Paul, 1966).

ity, far from being in conflict with freedom, is a necessary condition of protecting the freedom of those who are especially vulnerable to domination. In addition, such inequalities can generate justified resentments and loss of a sense of community, including the community of rights itself.

The upshot of these considerations is that the principle of human rights requires that to the material consideration of rights to freedom and well-being there be added the formal consideration of equality. There must, then, be equality of these rights. The contents of this equality will be spelled out in the sequel. But, as has already been noted at various points above, their orientation in the necessary conditions of action and generally successful action involves equal protection for persons' procedural and substantive abilities of agency. The equal protection of the procedural abilities bears on such issues as whether persons can control their own lives and behavior without being dominated by other persons and whether they have effective use of the civil liberties. The equal protection of the substantive abilities bears on such issues as whether persons have an adequate supply of basic goods and whether they can develop their productive agency so as to attain secure livelihoods for themselves and their families. These protections are in important part functions of the state as the community of rights.

More generally, because what is at issue here is not bare equality but rather equality of rights to the necessary conditions of successful action in general, the requirements of such equality cannot be satisfied by leveling down; rather, the required direction is upward, in accordance with the conative purposiveness of action. It is to the fulfillment of this equality of rights, both among individuals and among classes, that the community of rights is dedicated.

The context of action, however, also sets certain limits to these egalitarian considerations. This point bears on the disputed issue of whether what is justified is equality of opportunity or equality of outcomes. Because the generic rights are rights to the necessary conditions of *action*, their equality requires the equal protection of these conditions. But once basic goods are assured, the conditions bear on the actions themselves, not on what may be aimed at by the actions. All persons have an equal right that their abilities of action and successful action be developed and protected. But what they then do with these abilities is up to them, as matters of their own personal responsibility, and they are to be rewarded (or punished) accordingly. Thus the equality of generic rights—that all persons have equal rights to freedom and well-being—is distinct from the thesis that all persons have rights to equal amounts of the goods that they may aim to achieve through using their freedom and well-being. In these and other ways, the equality of generic rights takes due account of the differences among human beings. As we shall also see, however, the principle of human rights justifies an intermediate equality of self-actualization as the process whereby persons develop their abilities of productive agency (4.10). And the principle requires special consideration of the structural inequalities, both economic and political, that affect the attainment of equality among individuals.

3.2. Mutuality and Reciprocity

The PGC, with the community it justifies, is a principle not only of equal rights but also of mutual rights. In view of the central significance of this mutuality as constitutive of the community of rights, it is important to grasp its meaning as precisely as possible.

Mutuality entails equality, but not conversely. Both equality and mutuality are symmetrical relations. But whereas equality may be confined to static, noninteractive relations between persons, mutuality is a dynamic, interactive relation. A and B may have equal amounts of some X without interacting with one another. But in a mutual relation, A gives some valued X to B and B gives some other kind of valued X to A. This relation is exemplified in, but is not confined to, some forms of economic exchange. Thus A and B are equal as participating in this interactive relation, and, so far as practicable, the respective amounts of X are also equal. It is this mutuality that figures in the principle of human rights where, in principle, all humans are both the subjects and the respondents of the rights, in that each human respects and protects each other human's interests in freedom and well-being. Here, as above, the qualifications about practicability and governments must be kept in mind, but they do not remove the mutualist principle, with its import for the community of rights.

It must be emphasized that, just as justice has a formal as well as a material component, so mutuality, to be a genuine moral value according to the principle of human rights, must have a material as well as a formal component. It is not merely that A must do some X to B and B must do some X to A; the nature of the 'X' is vitally important. For example, in the policy of "mutual assured destruction" (MAD) that was followed by both the United States and the Soviet Union in their nuclear competition during the Cold War, there was indeed a formal relation of mutuality in that each side threatened death to the other. But this policy was a violation rather than a fulfillment of the principle of human rights.[4] The mutuality that figures in the community of rights, then, must have a content that is in accord with human rights.

4. See Alan Gewirth, "Reason and Nuclear Deterrence," in David Copp, ed., *Nuclear Weapons, Deterrence, and Disarmament, Canadian Journal of Philosophy,* suppl. vol. 12 (1986): 141.

The better to understand this mutuality, let us compare it with reciprocity. Although each of these may vary in certain ways, I shall here confine reciprocity to the returning of good for good received,[5] and mutuality to the relation intrinsic to the PGC as the principle of human rights whereby all persons have generic rights against one another and hence also correlative duties to one another. It may be difficult to distinguish reciprocity from mutuality in certain contexts, for each is a dynamic symmetrical relation. In reciprocity, if A does good for B, then B does good for A. In the mutuality of human rights, A has rights against B and B has rights against A.

There are, nevertheless, at least four important differences that can generally be used to separate them. One is temporal. Reciprocity involves a temporally prior benefit; once A has received a benefit from B, A then should return some comparable benefit to B. Thus, reciprocity is reactive or responsive. The relation involved in the mutuality of human rights, on the other hand, is one of simultaneity. A and B directly have against one another such rights as not being physically injured or lied to and being helped when in dire need, and these rights do not require some prior benefit given to B by A or to A by B. Just as they are simultaneously right-holders against one another, so they are also duty-bearers or respondents to one another. Of course, in the case of positive rights to help they may not be able to fulfill these rights simultaneously. If A is in dire need, B's ability to help may require that B not also then be in dire need; for example, as was noted above, B cannot at the same time be a homeless beggar and an affluent provider (2.5). Nevertheless, the rights and duties here are in principle simultaneous mutual ones. The mutuality of the principle of human rights involves that everyone always has, as a matter of principle, the right to be treated in the appropriate way when one has the need, and the duty to act in accord with the right when circumstances arise that require such action and when one has the ability to do so, this ability including consideration of cost to oneself. Thus mutuality does not prohibit some persons' taking helpful initiatives toward others. The circumstances affecting the feasibility of exercising a relationship should not be confused with the justificatory conditions of the relationship. If, however, the helping abilities of some groups are markedly inferior to those of others, the actual relation of the former group to the latter may be one of receiving unilateral help rather than mutuality.

From this temporal difference there directly follow two other differences between reciprocity and mutuality. The beneficiaries of reciprocity, the persons to whom benefits are owed, are limited to one's prior benefactors. Because A has benefited B, B should benefit A. Thus persons are

---

5. See Lawrence C. Becker, *Reciprocity* (London: Routledge and Kegan Paul, 1986), chap. 3.

excluded from the benefits of reciprocity if they do not, or are not in a position to, confer prior benefits on other persons. This can have severely adverse effects on disadvantaged persons.[6] In the mutuality of human rights, on the other hand, the beneficiaries, the right-holders to whom duties are owed, are not thus limited. The benefits of human rights are universal; they are owed to all persons as actual or prospective agents, regardless of whether some have antecedently conveyed benefits to other persons. There is, indeed, a certain proportionality in the having of human rights, but this bears only on the inherent capacities for being agents and for benefiting from fulfillment of the rights. Thus, as we have seen (2.6), children, severely injured or mentally deficient persons, and animals lack in varying degrees some of the practical abilities of the generic features of action: the abilities to control one's behavior by one's unforced choice, to have knowledge of relevant circumstances, and to reflect rationally on one's purposes. Members of such groups do not have the generic rights in the full way that they are had by normal human adults—those who have the aforementioned abilities. But the human entities in question approach having the generic rights to the degree to which they have the requisite abilities; and they have rights to be helped to attain these abilities. This is a quite different kind of restriction from the prior, optional conferring of benefits that sets limits to the beneficiaries of reciprocity.

A parallel difference bears on the persons who owe benefits. In reciprocity the giving of benefits is an obligation only of those who have previously received benefits. But the mutuality of human rights involves that all persons are in principle the duty-bearers or respondents; the duties correlative with the rights are owed by all persons, not only by those who have been prior beneficiaries of others' actions. By this mutuality, all persons are directly members of the community of rights, and the state through its taxing and other powers must embody it.

A fourth difference concerns modality, in two respects. First, the antecedent of the reciprocity relation is a contingent one: *if* A has received some good X from B (this receipt being contingent on an optional decision by B), *then* A owes a fitting response to B. This contingency is also found in contractualist theories, where the rendering of benefits is contingent on persons' prior agreements or contracts. In the mutuality of human rights, by contrast, the antecedent is itself necessary: *Because* other persons have human rights against you (these rights not being contingent for their generation or validity on some prior optional beneficent actions on their part), *it necessarily follows that* you have correlative duties to them. Their having

6. See Allen Buchanan, "Justice as Reciprocity versus Subject-Centered Justice," *Philosophy and Public Affairs* 19, no. 3 (summer 1990): 227–52.

the human rights in question, as we have seen, arises from the necessary needs of human action and generally successful action; it is not contingent on optional prior decisions to confer benefits. Second, the objects or benefits themselves also differ in a parallel way. The benefits given and owed in relations of reciprocity may be various contingent goods. But the objects of the mutual human rights are necessary goods: what is needed either for the very possibility of action or for having general chances of success in fulfilling one's purposes. Moreover, where in reciprocity the amount of goods that are owed varies with or is proportional to the amount of goods that were initially bestowed, in the mutuality of human rights the amount of goods owed is relatively constant (but see 4.1). All persons have rights to the necessary goods of action and generally successful action. And it is to the fulfillment of these rights that the community of rights is dedicated.

The rights to receive these goods may indeed be restricted or varied in several ways. In voluntary associations (whose moral justification derives from the freedom component of the PGC: *RM*, 282–90), persons may consent to have their freedom restricted according to certain rules; for example, when the umpire in a baseball game declares the batter out, he is out. In the minimal state governed by the criminal law persons may lose some of their rights to freedom and well-being because they have violated the rights of others (*RM*, 290–304). In cases of conflicts of rights, as we have seen, a right whose object is less needed for action may be overridden by a right whose object is more needed for action (2.4). In all such cases, however, the restrictions or variations in the fulfillment of rights are themselves justified by the PGC as the principle of human rights.

The mutuality of human rights is exempt from the kind of "loop" or circularity that may be found in situations of "mutual benevolence," where A's only desire is for B's happiness while B's only desire is for A's happiness. It has been plausibly argued that such desires can never be satisfied, since the satisfaction of each one would require the satisfaction of the other in an endless loop.[7] There are at least two differences between such an apparently self-defeating kind of mutuality and the mutuality of human rights. First, in the mutuality of human rights A wants that his own rights be fulfilled as well as that B's rights be fulfilled, and conversely; and the fulfillment of each person's rights has a content that is independent of the fulfillment of the other's rights. So A is not in the position of wanting only the fulfillment of the rights of B who in turn wants only the fulfillment of the

---

7. See David M. Estlund, "Mutual Benevolence and the Theory of Happiness," *Journal of Philosophy* 87, no. 4 (Apr. 1990): 187–204, and the cogent response by William N. Nelson, "Mutual Benevolence and Happiness," *Journal of Philosophy* 90, no. 1 (Jan. 1994): 50–51.

rights of A. Second, the concept of human rights does not have an all-inclusive valuational content as does happiness construed as fulfillment of any and every desire; on the contrary, the contents or objects of human rights are restricted to the freedom and well-being that are the necessary goods of action. Hence, A in acting to fulfill B's human rights is not confronted by a global, open-ended task.

The mutuality of human rights is an important ground of persons' self-respect. For in recognizing that they are both the subjects and the respondents of rights, persons see that they fulfill essential moral requirements. There is an important difference in this regard between self-respect and self-esteem. Persons' self-esteem is based on their conviction about the value of the purposes they pursue in their actions and on their ability to fulfill these purposes. But self-respect adds the vital moral considerations that persons fulfill their obligation to help other persons to secure their rights to the necessary conditions of their actions and that they themselves have the correlative rights (see 6.2).

The mutuality of human rights has an essential role in the conciliation of rights and community and in the community of rights reflected therein. For, as we have seen (2.1), the fact that humans have positive duties to one another by virtue of having human rights entails the kind of required mutuality of consideration that figures directly in social solidarity and thus in the community of rights. The moral requirement that governments enforce rights and thereby enable all humans to have the necessary goods of action is a direct consequence of the mutuality of human rights. And this governmental provision is an important part of what constitutes a morally justified state as a community of rights.

3.3. RIGHTS, CHARITY, AND HUMANITY

Before going on to connect the mutuality of human rights more fully and explicitly with the idea of community, we must briefly examine some theses that would replace the central role here assigned to rights by alternative concepts of charity and humanity. It is important to see why these theses, amid their suggestive emphases, have certain significant limitations.

The argument for positive human rights, with its modal orientation of "must" in step 5a above (2.3), brings out why the assistance to have freedom and well-being must be a matter of rights and not, or at least not only, of charity or private beneficence. Since freedom and well-being are necessary goods of agency, their provision should not be made contingent on the optional choices of persons or groups. Because without freedom and well-being one cannot be either an agent at all or a generally successful agent, one must have an assurance, so far as possible, that these goods will be securely possessed. Positive rights with their correlative strict 'oughts' provide the normative grounds for such effective assurance. These 'oughts' are directly translatable into legal enforcement, in a way that the looser 'oughts' of charity are not. So charity, while very valuable, cannot do the normative work accomplished by rights.[8] By the same token, this assurance cannot be provided by a utilitarian calculus, not only because such a calculus may have negative results for some persons but also because it would obscure what is brought out by the primary emphasis on rights: that the goods in question should be the personal property of each prospective agent, under her control and due to her for her own sake and not merely as a means of maximizing utility.

It has been contended that assistance for freedom and well-being can have such obligatory stringency without being made a matter of rights, that the emphasis on rights is an example of that overuse to which many critics have objected. Thus a distinction has been drawn between rights (or justice) and "humanity," with the latter being upheld as the appropriate value-concept for the distribution of economic goods and especially for the relief of distress. Like justice, humanity is "an obligation that it would be wrong not to carry out."[9] But while two interrelated contrasts have been adduced to show the normative superiority of considerations of humanity over considerations of justice, each contrast has overlooked a salient aspect of justice and rights as they have been presented here.

According to one contrast, humanity is concerned with protecting basic well-being while justice is concerned with fairness in the sense of treating similar cases similarly. On the basis of this contrast it is contended that "humanity in certain cases overrides justice. Sometimes it is more important to relieve distress than to be fair."[10] This view overlooks, however, that justice is material as well as formal or comparative, and that, as material, it

8.   I find somewhat unconvincing Allen Buchanan's thesis that "duties of charity" may be enforced, partly because he has not made out that "a system of aid for the needy" (which he calls a "collective good") is properly classified as charity rather than as justice. See his "Justice and Charity," *Ethics* 97, no. 3 (Apr. 1987): 564. If my above arguments are sound, the needy have a right to be helped. In addition, Buchanan bases the enforceability of charity not on its being owed to individuals as such but rather as a "collective good." Hence there remains the contrast between the needy person's right to be helped for her own sake as against its promoting a collective end. For another important but I think ultimately unsuccessful attempt to render "charity" as obligatory as "justice" (but as a matter of "imperfect" rather than "perfect" duty), see Onora O'Neill, "The Great Maxims of Justice and Charity," in her collection *Constructions of Reason* (Cambridge: Cambridge University Press, 1989), pp. 219–33.

9.   Brian Barry, *Liberty and Justice* (Oxford: Clarendon Press, 1991), p. 188; and see T. D. Campbell, "Humanity before Justice," *British Journal of Political Science* 4 (1974): 1–16.

10.   Campbell, "Humanity before Justice," p. 14.

is concerned with securing persons' rights, especially to basic well-being
(3.1). Hence, the principle of human rights as given by the PGC incorporates the norm that is here ascribed to humanity. And while justice as upheld by the PGC is also concerned with fairness or equality of rights, the
criterion of degrees of needfulness for action accords superior weight to the
relief of distress conceived as loss of basic well-being.

In a second contrast, humanity is held to be "goal-based" while justice
is "rights-based," and this involves that whereas justice is concerned with
"how control over resources should be allocated," humanity is concerned
rather with getting resources to the persons who lack them, regardless of
what they may have done or not done and regardless also of what control
they may have over them.[11] In this contrast rights are confined to what I
have called freedom in the sense of control over one's behavior. The contrast overlooks that the various levels of well-being ("resources") are also
the objects of human rights. In separating control from possession of resources, or freedom from well-being, the contrast blurs the important
point that freedom, consisting as it does in control of one's behavior by
one's unforced choice, bears also on one's control of the things or resources
that impinge on one's behavior. In this regard there is no sharp separation
between "goal-based" and "rights-based" theories, so long as it is recognized that the goals in question are primarily individual or distributive
rather than collective or aggregative: they involve that each person have
freedom and well-being, not that these goods be maximized without regard for their individual distribution. The centrality of human rights derives from the necessity for each prospective agent both that she have the
necessary goods of agency and that, so far as possible, these goods be under
her own control.

3.4. THE IDEA OF COMMUNITY AND THE SOCIAL
CONTRIBUTION THESIS

Thus far in this chapter and the preceding one I have focused on the general
idea of positive human rights, both on their general objects or contents and
on their formal features of equality and mutuality. We must now turn to the
idea of community to see more fully how it coalesces with rights to become
the community of rights. The society based on the PGC as the principle of
human rights, with its mutualist sharing of rights and duties, is a genuine
community. Before developing this point, let us look at the general notion
of community.

In many of its uses, "community" is an honorific word. It connotes a

11. Barry, *Liberty and Justice*, p. 204.

morally superior mode of human association characterized by social harmony, mutual support, and fellow-feeling that overcome the divisiveness
and alienation of individualism. Phrases like "real community" and "genuine community" are often employed to connect these favored modes of
relationship with kinds of groupings upheld by the writers. In this regard,
"community" is also sometimes used to hearken back to a presumably
idyllic, small-scale town or village as it is imagined to have existed before
the Industrial Revolution. Considerable anachronism and unrealism can
therefore be charged to some communitarian writers who wish to assimilate such a premodern conception to the complexities of large-scale modern societies.[12]

The ideas of harmony and solidarity associated with community are,
nevertheless, important values that are still worthy of support. With appropriate modifications they can be realistically attributed to relationships and
institutions that can, and to some extent do, exist in the contemporary era
in liberal democratic welfare states. In trying to show that the society of
human rights justified by the PGC is a genuine community, I shall gradually introduce these modifications. In significant respects they do not so
much depart from but rather build upon moral values that are implicit in
the principle of human rights. The principle will serve as a guide to the
kinds of extensions of modern social and economic institutions that can
fulfill these values. Even if the modifications I present depart at certain
points from descriptive contents upheld by some communitarian writers,
this need not require withdrawing the attribution of "community" itself. In
significant respects, "community" is too important to be left to such communitarians.

There are two main bases for calling the PGC's society of human rights
a genuine community of rights. First, the society provides for equal and
mutual assistance to secure persons' human rights. It does so by equally
protecting and promoting the freedom and well-being of all its members. In
the first instance, this is a matter of institutional arrangements focused in

12. See Raymond Plant, "Community: Concept, Conception and Ideology," *Politics
and Society* 8 (1978): 79–107; Ira Katznelson, "Community, Capitalist Development, and
the Emergence of Class," *Politics and Society* 9 (1979): 203–37; Derek L. Phillips, *Looking
Backward* (Princeton, N.J.: Princeton University Press, 1993), Introduction and *passim*.
Michael Taylor, noting that 'community' is "an open-textured concept," lists three attributes
of the communities he discusses: first, that persons "have beliefs or values in common";
second, that "relations between members be direct and many-sided"; third, that they involve
"reciprocity." The second attribute excludes groups that pursue "common ends not by dealing directly with one another but through the agency of the state" (*Community, Anarchy, and
Liberty* [Cambridge: Cambridge University Press, 1982], pp. 25–33). This attribute, however, could remove the issue of community from many of the debates in political philosophy
between communitarians and those they oppose.

the society's legally enforced policies, so that they serve to secure legal rights. But these arrangements already mark a departure from egoism and individualism, because the positive obligations they require through taxation and other means involve that persons must mutually further the agency-related needs and interests of other persons besides themselves, especially those who are more deprived. In these ways the society through its institutional arrangements makes indispensable contributions to its members' education, health, safety, and various other social and economic goods that comprise the necessary conditions of action and of generally successful action, and thereby it helps them to attain a position of personal responsibility.

These arrangements already reflect what may be called an institutional harmony among the society's members, in that they mutually share in the related benefits. But the harmony is also psychological insofar as the members are aware of the rightness of the arrangements as deriving from the rationally justified principle of human rights. Indeed, in a significant respect these arrangements represent an institutionalization of love as a deep concern for the freedom and well-being of all the members of the society.

These contributions indicate a second, closely related basis for calling the PGC's society a community of rights. Where the first basis consisted in the society's contributions to effectuating the human rights of its members, the second basis goes in the reverse direction: by virtue of these contributions, the members have, recognize, and accept obligations to the society. Because of the society's contributions all persons are to some extent "social products": the nurturing they receive from their social context, beginning with the family but continuing on to the wider society, is a necessary condition of their being successful purposive agents. I shall call this the *social contribution thesis*. This thesis may not apply in its full scope to persons who are born into conditions of extreme deprivation that, unless they are helped by the community of rights, may hinder them from becoming productive agents. But, by virtue of the social contributions they receive, all other persons have obligations both of reciprocity and of mutuality. Because the society has given them the benefits of having the necessary goods of action, they owe it correlative benefits of support and allegiance. In this way the community has a collective right to an institutionalized system of support from those it has benefited (see 2.4). This relation can also be construed as one of mutuality: the community does indispensable good for its members by helping to fulfill their human rights, and they do indispensable good for the community by helping to fulfill its collective right of support. And because for the society to provide these benefits its members must cooperate in mutually respecting one another's human rights of agency, the society thereby becomes a genuinely moral community of rights.

The community of rights, then, means not only that the community supports the rights of its members but also that those rights support the community insofar as its support of its members' rights both enables and obligates them to support the community. The members' contribution to the society as a community of rights may range from the work they do in providing exchange values whence they derive income, through paying taxes to support the community, to much more heroic contributions in military service and other ways of protecting the society. But in all such modes of action the relation of mutuality is paramount whereby persons fulfill one another's needs and rights. They have obligations to the society as enabling the development of this mutuality.

Against the social contribution thesis it has been objected that its principle could generate many kinds of clearly unwarranted social obligations. My neighbors could institute on their own a public-address system whose rules would require me to give up a day to participate in the system, even if I have not consented to it. The general premise of this objection is that if one is confronted by a cooperative project that has been established without one's consent, one has no obligation to participate in it or to contribute to it.[13]

This objection does not count against the social contribution thesis, however, because it overlooks a crucial point both about the nature of the project and about one's participation in it. There is a difference between contingent and necessary projects, between projects that are set up at the option of various persons and projects that are so pervasive and necessary in their beneficial impact on human agency that they cannot be rationally rejected, either at all or without great sacrifice of well-being. The system of social and political support and economic production is such a project. Although it can vary in its specific forms, the whole general social and economic system of the maintenance of law and order, education, and the production of goods and services is so virtually inescapable if the needs of human agency are to be fulfilled that participation in it, or in its results, is also rationally inescapable. Persons cannot reject it or its results except at a prohibitive price. Hence, on the principle of reciprocity according to which persons who benefit from a project and its constituent rules are obligated to reciprocate for those benefits, productive agents must accept that part of what they produce is owed to the whole social context that enables them to

---

13. For this objection, see Robert Nozick, *Anarchy, State, and Utopia* (New York: Basic Books, 1974), pp. 93–95. It is concurred in by Ronald Dworkin, *Law's Empire* (Cambridge, Mass.: Harvard University Press, 1986), pp. 193–95, and by G. A. Cohen, "Self-Ownership, World-Ownership, and Equality, Part II," *Social Philosophy and Policy* 3.2 (spring 1986): 89, n. 16.

produce it.[14] This thesis can also be assimilated in important part to the mutuality of the principle of human rights: each person has a right against all other persons to the goods he needs for his freedom and well-being, and each person has duties to all other persons to respect these goods. As we shall see, this principle becomes specified in various ways in different contexts not only by the intervention of governments (2.5, 6) but also by the rights and duties of productive agency; but its general point remains invariant. It can thus withstand the kind of trivializing objection that assimilates the practically indispensable social and economic process, and persons' inescapable participation in it, to an optional "scheme" or project.

The obligations generated according to the social contribution thesis indicate a further way in which the PGC's society is a community of rights. Because the society functions to fulfill their human rights of agency, its members develop psychological attitudes of gratitude and loyalty to it, so that it becomes a community of cooperativeness and fellow feeling.

Against the interpretation I have just given of the social contribution thesis, it may be held that the human-rights society is at bottom egoistic, and thus not a genuine community, because its members value the society simply as means to their own self-interested ends whereby they are enabled to be effective agents. It may be further held that the equal distribution of such means, whereby all persons are helped to develop their abilities of agency, is regarded by each individual simply as the price she must pay to fulfill these personal rights for herself, so that the underlying motivation is still egoistic.

Even if we accept this interpretation, the society is so structured institutionally that it promotes equal rights and mutuality. The institutional structure, therefore, is mutualist, not egoistic, while at the same time it

---

14. This principle is close to the "principle of fair play" or "fairness" set forth by H. L. A. Hart, "Are There Any Natural Rights?" *Philosophical Review* 64 (1955): 175–91, and by John Rawls, "Legal Obligation and the Duty of Fair Play," in Sidney Hook, ed., *Law and Philosophy* (New York: New York University Press, 1964), pp. 3–18. Hart's and Rawls's theses are vulnerable to Nozick's criticisms because they do not take account of the distinction presented in my text. Richard J. Arneson presents a revised version of the principle that *almost* recognizes the distinction; thus in his revision "a scheme of cooperation is established that supplies a collective benefit that is worth its cost to each recipient . . . and where the collective benefit is either voluntarily accepted or such that voluntary acceptance of it is impossible" ("The Principle of Fairness and Free-Ride Problems," *Ethics* 92, no. 4 [July 1982]: 616–33, at p. 623). Arneson's revision, however, is still open to objections about arbitrary imposition of benefits, since he does not recognize the importance of the distinction between necessary goods of action and contingent goods. See also Lawrence C. Becker, *Reciprocity* (London: Routledge and Kegan Paul, 1986), pp. 361–62; and Brian Barry, "Justice as Reciprocity," in Eugene Kamenka and Alice Ehr-Soon Tay, eds., *Justice* (London: Edward Arnold, 1979), pp. 55–57.

helps to move the poorer members of society closer to equality. But in addition, the persons who participate in this structure can come to see, as rational, that the society is a just and genuine community because of its mutual sharing of benefits and burdens, and thereby its upholding of equal rights for all. The rights are thus moral as well as legal, and it is their morality that underlies and justifies their legality. This psychological element of awareness, of understanding and rational and emotional acceptance and support, accompanies the institutional structure and makes it a community not only of institutions but also of fellow feeling. The institutional arrangements thus derive from, and are reflected in, the individual members' rational awareness of the need for and the rightness of such mutuality of assistance. The society does not, then, consist of "bare" individuals who are unaware of and indifferent to one another's fates. On the contrary, as rational, they can grasp at least the rudiments of the argument for the PGC as the principle of human rights: just as I, as a prospective purposive agent, have a right to the fulfillment of my own agency-needs for freedom and well-being, so too is it with all other prospective purposive agents. The universality here envisaged may be restricted, for reasons of practical convenience of effectuation, to members of societies geographically demarcated as countries or nation-states; but in principle it applies internationally as well. At the same time, this universality does not militate against the particularism whereby persons give special consideration to the members of their own families and other partial groups of friends or colleagues. Such particularism not only is consistent with but is justified by the universal principle of human rights.[15]

Because the society in this way fulfills rational criteria of moral rightness, its members can also come to value it for itself, as an end in itself. They can identify themselves with their society because it embodies an ideal of social-moral excellence whose value and requiredness they can understand and support.

Great importance attaches to the justificatory sequence I have just outlined for the community of rights, with its primary basis in the community's protection of each individual's rights and its secondary basis of a more general affective outlook whereby persons have obligations to the community. This sequence stands in contrast to the views of some communitarians who impose no such restrictions of the primary basis in the fulfillment of individual moral rights on the communities they uphold as valuable. But such writers are thereby committed to regarding as worthy of support even unjust societies that do not give equal protection to each person's vital inter-

---

15. See Alan Gewirth, "Ethical Universalism and Particularism," *Journal of Philosophy* 85 (1988): 283–302.

ests. This is an important reason why the society of the PGC must be a community *of rights*. It is the aspect of the obligatory fulfillment of each person's agency-needs for his or her own sake that makes the society a community of rights. And it is the aspect of mutuality and social solidarity that figures in this fulfillment that makes the society a community. Thus, just as human rights, through their mutuality, entail community, so community, in order to be morally justified, requires human rights. The relation of rights and community, then, is one of mutual support.

3.5. FURTHER REPLIES TO THE ADVERSARIAL CONCEPTION

At this point the project of conciliating rights and community is almost completed. To bring it closer to completion, we must confront anew the thesis of the adversarial conception of the relation between rights and community that I presented at the beginning of this book (1.1). According to this thesis, the function of rights and right-claims is to protect one's interests against actual or potential adversaries. But in a genuine community there are no adversaries, because there are only common interests. Hence, if rights and right-claims are needed in some society, then it is not a genuine community; while if it is a genuine community, then there is no place for rights and right-claims. In particular, the mutual assistance that was here stressed as the object of positive rights can be attained, if there is a genuine community, without the claiming of rights, because by the harmony of interests that characterizes a genuine community the assistance will be forthcoming as a matter of spontaneous cooperation and good will.

This thesis can be attacked on at least three points. First, its idealistic conception of community removes it from all, or nearly all, relevance to actual political societies. One need not go so far as to hold, with Marx, that all history is the scene of class struggles to recognize that the very stuff of politics is the management of conflicts of interests. The completely peaceable community may indeed be upheld as an ideal for actual societies to aim at, but it is a mistake to confuse the ideal with the actual. Just as Aristotle criticized Plato for trying to reduce the unity of the state to the unity of the family,[16] so some contemporary communitarians seek to make good their thesis about the dispensability of rights and justice by invoking the benevolent, sympathetic feelings characteristic of families at their best as well as of other relatively small human friendship groups. In such groups there may indeed be common interests and goals in the strong, collective sense whereby 'common' signifies that it is the group as such, the collective or communal entity, that is the object of loyalty. But it is a mistake to ex-

16. Aristotle, *Politics*, 2.2.

trapolate from such small ideal groupings to large-scale political societies in which justified loyalty requires the protection of rights. Insofar as communitarians insist on tying community to a certain "concrete" particularism of partial groups, in contrast to the "abstract" universalism of human rights, it must be said both that even in partial groups the members' human rights must be protected and that, for the reasons already given, societies that provide such protection have crucially important attributes of community.

It must also be noted that although community as an ideal may have an all-or-nothing character, in that idyllic mutuality and harmony are contrasted in an absolute fashion with individualist and adversarial relations, the actual attainment of community is a matter of degree. Through the fulfillment of rights, this attainment is more fully approached. But a mistake in analysis arises when communitarian philosophers, confusing the ideal with the actual, view "community" in an absolute fashion and contrast it with some of the manifestations of rights, especially property rights as they actually function in adversarial societies. This mistake is parallel to the one committed by libertarians when they uncompromisingly absolutize "freedom" and attribute to all actual human protagonists the abilities and conditions that characterize the maximally effective use of freedom, while rejecting governmental protections of freedom and well-being.

As used here, the word "community," in its bearing on persons' interests and psychological relations, refers neither to such an ideal nor to all aspects of actual societies. It signifies rather the institutionalized social bond that unites persons by virtue of their society's fulfillment of important needs of agency and persons' mutual contributions thereto. This fulfillment is not conceived as already present in its full scope either in actual societies (including modern welfare states) or in an ideal human grouping devoid of conflicts. Instead, it is the object of mutual obligations that derive from the rational awareness that the fulfillments in question are owed to persons by virtue of their imperative needs of agency. The argument for the PGC sketched above (1.5) provides the outline of this owing or due that is central to rights and right-claims.

A second response to the thesis that genuine communities can dispense with rights is the following. Even if there is a community in the extreme form of a society of universal benevolence, there would still be a need for rights. For insofar as the benevolence is to be practically effective it involves mutual contributions by the members, and there would be a need for systematization to ascertain where the contributions are most needed, including agreement on relevant criteria, amounts, methods of implementation, and so forth. This systematization would take the form of allocating duties

or responsibilities, and thus of correlative positive rights of recipients demarcated according to the indicated criteria. Such an idealized society
would be a community of rights.[17] The fact that the rights are positive
would hence merge the idea of mutual assistance with the organized aspects of community.[18]

This consideration brings us to a third reply to the thesis that a genuine
community can dispense with rights. Even as claim-rights, rights need not
be explicitly claimed or demanded in order to be rights. We must distinguish between the contents of rights and the claiming of them. Or, to put it
in other terms, when one utters a sentence of the form "A has a right to X,"
the locutionary act (whereby one says it with a certain sense and a certain
reference) is distinct both from the illocutionary act (whereby one says it
with a certain intention, such as demanding that A have X) and from the
perlocutionary act (whereby one achieves a certain effect by saying it, such
as the demand's being granted).[19] Thus rights may be understood, recognized, and fulfilled without having to be demanded as rights. What makes
them rights in their primary form is that they are important interests whose
fulfillment or protection is owed or due to persons for their own sakes, with
correlative duties of respondents. If this fulfillment is not contested by
others, the primary aspect of their being rights is not thereby removed. Persons have rights to freedom and well-being even if these necessary goods
are not threatened or endangered by other persons. Such endangerment
may be potentially in the offing, and correspondingly the claiming of the
rights may be potential. But it need not be actual. Hence, even if there is a
community in the strong sense of fully harmonized interests, there is still a

17. See Steven Lukes, *Marxism and Morality* (Oxford: Clarendon Press, 1985), pp. 65–
66, 94. Lukes cites from Joseph Raz, *Practical Reason and Norms* (London: Hutchinson,
1975) the idea that "Even a society of angels may have a need for legislative authority to ensure co-ordination" (p. 159). This position can be traced back at least to Thomas Aquinas's
thesis that even in the "condition of innocence" before the fall of man there would have been a
need for government that "would aim at the common good: for many persons by themselves
aim at many different things" (*Summa Theologica* 1.96.4).

18. There is also sociological evidence that the caring and compassion emphasized by
both communitarian and feminist thinkers require a concern for the rights of the persons
cared for. See Robert Wuthnow, *Acts of Compassion* (Princeton, N.J.: Princeton University
Press, 1991), p. 251: "But the testimony about compassion that we have examined thus far
belies this distinction. It suggests that compassion in our society is also rooted in a respect for
individual rights . . . that one's compassion implies a strong sense of the rights and needs of
others."

19. See J. L. Austin, *How to Do Things with Words* (Oxford: Clarendon Press, 1962),
pp. 94 ff. This distinction can be fitted into the dialectically necessary method I have used to
demonstrate the principle of human rights (1.5).

need for rights as signifying what each person is entitled to because of her necessary agency-needs.[20]

The invocation of rights need not mean that communal attachments or fellow-feeling are not present. If persons' agency-needs are provided for in an institutionally secure way, it may not be necessary to actually invoke rights. Nevertheless, the very security of the protection that is provided would be a sign of the implicit operation of rights, that is, of protections of important interests that ought to be secured to persons for their own sakes. Even if the mandatoriness of this 'ought' is not explicitly invoked against persons charged with fulfilling it, the great importance of the interests in question makes mandatory an at least implicit recognition of the duties and so of the correlative rights.

Just as rights are not only compatible with but necessary for even the most solidaristic kind of community, so from the other side the invocation of rights need not be egoistically adversarial. For one thing, persons may and do act for the rights of others; for example, thousands of whites demonstrated on behalf of the civil and personal rights of blacks in eras ranging from that of the slavery institution in the United States to that of apartheid in South Africa. It is hence a mistake to hold that all rights-talk is exclusively concerned with fulfillment of one's own selfish interests. For another thing, rights can serve to moderate as well as to express adversarial relations among persons. When important rights are threatened or violated, forceful insistence on their fulfillment is quite in order and indeed mandatory. But when mutual rights are effectively recognized, and especially when this recognition is stabilized in effective institutions, the adversarial stance can and often does give way to an atmosphere of the kind of mutual respect and civility which is an important part of the value of community. The reason for this is not only the rights' enforcement as such but also that this brings to emphatic awareness that previously subjugated persons are owed certain important kinds of affirmative consideration and assistance, and are owed these as equal members of the relevant community. An ex-

---

20. This claiming aspect of rights is stressed by Robert E. Goodin to disconnect rights from mutuality and community. See Goodin, *Reasons for Welfare* (Princeton, N.J.: Princeton University Press, 1988), pp. 116–17: "Under mutual-aid arrangements, a beneficiary has no strong rights against his benefactor. . . . He has no right to *demand* assistance, and the neighbor is under no strict duty to render it. . . . From the perspective of communitarians, it is important that this should be so. If the goal is to produce a strong sense of community, with each subordinating his own interests (and perhaps even his own identity) to that of the group, then the individualist's business of demanding one's rights and pressing one's claims seems wholly out of place." If, however, the objects of mutual aid are necessary goods of action, then persons have rights to them even if they do not have to demand them because they are spontaneously given. On this point, see also Allen Buchanan, *Marx and Justice* (Totowa, N.J.: Rowman and Allanheld, 1982), pp. 76–77.

ample of this contrast is provided by the relations between whites and blacks in the American South before and after the passage of civil rights legislation. Thus the desiderated removal of adversarial relationships and the fostering of community may well depend on the implementation rather than the rejection of rights.

3.6. COMMUNITY AND CONCEPTIONS OF THE SELF

The adversarial conception of the relation between rights and community derives much of its support from a contrast between two opposed ontological conceptions of the human self. As against the mutuality emphasized above, some communitarians hold that the invocation of rights assumes a Hobbesian view of persons as essentially competitive individuals who have no specific social ties to one another, who have their identities independent of one another, and who have no positive obligations to one another. The communitarian position, in contrast, is said to uphold a "constitutiveness" doctrine according to which the self's identity is at least partly constituted by its roles in the communities to which it belongs. Far from being "unencumbered" by social ties, these ties are essential to personhood so that humans are inherently social beings.[21]

This constitutiveness doctrine has important merits. It brings out that the sense of belonging, of being part of a larger nurturing whole, is a valuable component of human additive well-being. It serves to emphasize that what exist are not bare, abstract individuals such as figure in many traditional theories of natural rights, but rather persons whose self-identity and self-awareness are partly constituted by their being members of specific cultural groupings demarcated in terms of family, race, class, gender, nationality, ethnicity, religion, ideology, neighborhood, occupation, and other partly interpenetrating variables. The doctrine also brings out the historical locatedness of human selves, for the communities to which they belong and in which they function have definite historical dimensions. This view stands in contrast to the ahistorical abstractions found in many "liberal" theories of the self. Moreover, the doctrine is in accord with the social contribution thesis presented above (3.3), which holds that humans are "social products" in that the society as a community of rights makes indispensable contributions toward fulfilling its members' rights of agency, and that the

21. See Michael J. Sandel, *Liberalism and the Limits of Justice* (Cambridge: Cambridge University Press, 1982), pp. 150 ff., 161, and *Liberalism and Its Critics* (New York: New York University Press, 1984), pp. 5–6; Alasdair MacIntyre, *After Virtue* (Notre Dame, Ind.: University of Notre Dame Press, 1981), pp. 204–9; Charles Taylor, "Atomism," in his *Philosophical Papers* (Cambridge: Cambridge University Press, 1985), vol. 2, pp. 187–210.

members have corresponding obligations both to one another and to their community.

The constitutiveness thesis nevertheless, in the unqualified form in which it is presented, incurs serious difficulties. First, when the communitarian says that the self is partly "constituted" by its roles in the communities to which it belongs, which "communities" are intended? Each of us belongs to many different communities, ranging from the family to church, university, bowling team, and on to various political units, race, gender, ethnicity, and so forth. Is the self equally constituted by all these communities, or by some more than others; and by what criterion is the decision to be made? Presumably the family has priority; but, as many philosophers, psychologists, and sociologists have noted, commitment to one's family is compatible with a wide variety of social stances, including very antisocial ones.[22]

Second, what sort of "constitutiveness" does the self bear to its various communities? Does its membership in these communities so exhaust its selfhood that it has no independent resources for deciding among them or even for rejecting some of them in favor either of further communities or of aspects of its own individuality that, at least in some degree, fall outside its various communities? Is the self's freedom and rational autonomy exhausted by its membership in communities? A negative answer to these questions is suggested by one communitarian's statement that "*certain* of our roles are *partly* constitutive of the persons we are."[23] These restrictions seem, then, to leave an important place for the individual autonomy of thought and action on which the principle of human rights insists.

Third, what are the precise moral bearings of the self's being constituted by the communities to which it belongs? Must the demands or obligations deriving from the communities always be fulfilled, regardless of their impact on one's rationally grounded moral rights? If Nazism, Stalinism, Maoism, and South African apartheid represent kinds of communities, then the duties that stem from them, far from being mandatory, must be rejected because of their violations of human rights. It must not be forgotten that two of the prime kinds of *koinōnia* or "community" in Western thought, those of Plato and Aristotle, sanctioned slavery and other forms of extreme inequality. The particularism stressed by some communitarians, with their dedication to the values of local or partial communities, must here be corrected by the universalism of the principle of human rights.

22. See, e.g., the discussion of "amoral familism" in Edward C. Banfield, *The Moral Basis of a Backward Society* (New York: Free Press, 1958), pp. 83 ff.

23. Sandel, *Liberalism and Its Critics*, p. 5; emphasis added. See also David Miller, *Market, State, and Community* (Oxford: Clarendon Press, 1989), pp. 234–36; Will Kymlicka, *Liberalism, Community, and Culture* (Oxford: Clarendon Press, 1991), pp. 53–61.

In place of such communitarian extremes, the PGC as the principle of human rights upholds a conception that may be called *the reasonable self*.[24] Such a self is aware of its own agency needs and rights, and it has a sense of personal responsibility for their fulfillment, but it also takes due account of the agency needs of other persons, respecting their rights as well as one's own and maintaining a certain equitableness or mutuality of consideration between oneself and others, as required by the universality of human rights. Thus the reasonable self recognizes that it has obligations toward others as well as rights against others, and that these must be embodied not only in individual actions but in social and political institutions, which thereby constitute a community of rights. Individuals have duties to support such communities precisely because of this embodiment. Thus in requiring respect for the human rights of each person, the conception of the reasonable self requires also support of the whole system of mutually sustaining rights and duties. In this way, the emphasis on individual rights is not only compatible with, but requires a conscientious concern for, the common good, where 'common,' from its initial distributive meaning, takes on also the collective meaning of the community that is constituted by and is the protector of human rights. Military service in a just war is one form that this support may take, but there are many others.

As was suggested above, this reasonableness can also take a strongly affective form. Precisely because the corporate community protects its individual members' rights, the individuals have a loyalty and indeed devotion to the community. For the reasonable self, this devotion is not based, at least in the first instance, on ethnic or racial factors, because she recognizes that this could violate the universality of human rights. It is based rather on an awareness of the justice and rightness of the communal protection of rights.[25] On this basis, the community itself also becomes a good for its members; it fosters communal attachments that they prize. But if this basis in the protection of rights is removed, so that persons are held to prize the good of "community" as such, without regard to how it treats its individual members, then this would remove an indispensable moral justification for the community.

In this context it may well seem impertinent to raise the problem of the "free rider," the purely self-interested individual who greedily takes advantage of others' adherence to the community's moral requirements while flouting them himself. But it is important to avoid utopian idealization

24. On the reasonable self, see also Alan Gewirth, *Political Philosophy* (New York: Macmillan, 1965), pp. 14–16, and "The Rationality of Reasonableness," *Synthese* 57 (1983): 225–47.

25. See Per Bauhn, *Nationalism and Morality* (Lund, Sweden: Lund University Press, 1995).

here: not all persons are reasonable, nor are reasonable selves always reasonable. Moreover, one commits the fallacy of composition when one argues from the reasonableness of individuals to the reasonableness of the whole society composed of them. On these grounds it may be contended that what I have called the community of rights cannot be relied on to fulfill the principle of human rights even if all or most of its members accept the principle.

While this problem has various ramifications, including those found in the Prisoner's Dilemma, in the present context it must suffice to note that to the justificatory concepts of reasonableness and mutuality there must be joined a motivational component that takes account of these possible departures from reasonableness. Or, to put it within motivation itself, the motivational pull of narrow self-interest must be recognized as threatening the motivations persons derive from their rational recognition of the reasonableness and mutuality required by the principle of human rights. Hence, the community must have laws that threaten punishment to persons who, out of narrow self-interest, violate the requirements it sets up in accordance with the principle of human rights. This is why it must be the state through its coercive laws, uniformly enforced, that is the primary respondent of the positive rights to welfare and other redistributive policies (2.5). But the state as a community of rights must also have the educational and other institutions that help to provide the guidance and motivation for persons' becoming reasonable selves. These requirements must be maintained within a democratic political order whose laws and sanctions apply to the elected rulers as well as to those who elect them (see 8.1).

This point also bears on the communitarian's assertion that his is "a politics of the common good."[26] In the phrase "common good" the word "common" is ambiguous, in that it can have either a distributive or a collective meaning. In its distributive meaning, "common good" means that some good is equally common to, equally shared by or distributed among, all the members of a community. But in its collective meaning, "common good" means that the good in question pertains to the collectivity as a whole, but not necessarily to its individual members taken separately.

Now if the communitarian intends "common good" in its distributive meaning, then in upholding it he is close to the liberal individualism he officially deplores; and if the goods in question are sufficiently important, then he is committed to upholding human rights to these goods as well as the community of rights, where "community" has not only its main, institutional meaning of the supportive state but also the distributive, adjectival meaning of commonness, whereby the human rights are common to and

26. Sandel, *Liberalism and Its Critics*, pp. 6, 7.

equally had by all the members of the society. If, however, the intended meaning of "common good" is collective, then this may involve a conception of the 'good' that many members of the community do not share; and institutional enforcement of that common good may involve oppressive coercion of at least those members. South African apartheid is an example of such a collective conception of a common good; other examples are the Puritans' enforcement of religious uniformity and other forms of religious, nationalist, and ethnic intolerance.[27] It should not be forgotten that it was Aristotle who first formally classified constitutions as justified or unjustified on the basis of whether or not they aimed at the common good[28]— a classification that was enormously influential on subsequent political thought. But according to Aristotle, the kind of constitution that best exemplified this devotion to the common good was an aristocracy in which a small elite upheld and enforced its ideals of moral and intellectual excellence even though most members of the political community did not share those ideals, and farmers and mechanics were to be slaves.[29]

If the communitarian replies that such modes of association are not genuine communities because they do not embody equal consideration for all their members, then the communitarian is admitting, in effect, that a necessary condition of a genuine community is that it respect and protect human rights. As was noted above, such respect may be found without an adversarial insistence on the rights. Nevertheless, the communitarian who wishes to avoid the inegalitarian and oppressive potentialities of various traditional communities is committed to a conception of the self wherein persons are aware of the necessary goods of their agency and are aware also of their rights to these goods, as entitlements of which they cannot be justifiably deprived simply because their communities demand it of them. As we have also seen, the communitarian's sound emphasis on social solidarity is not only accommodated but made mandatory by the principle of human rights.

These considerations also serve to show that there is no necessary opposition between autonomy and community as here conceived. Such opposition might be thought to arise from the potential divergence between the self-reliance or independence and personal responsibility that figure in au-

27. See Amy Gutmann, "Communitarian Critics of Liberalism," *Philosophy and Public Affairs* 14 (1985): 308–22; Will Kymlicka, *Contemporary Political Philosophy* (Oxford: Clarendon Press, 1990), pp. 224–30. See also the discussion of communitarian relativism in Carlos Santiago Nino, *The Ethics of Human Rights* (Oxford: Clarendon Press, 1991), pp. 102–10.

28. Aristotle, *Politics*, 3.6–7.

29. Aristotle, *Politics*, 7–8; for the slavery of farmers and mechanics, see 7.9, 1328b39, 1329a25; 7.10, 1330a25.

tonomy and the cooperativeness and mutual dependence emphasized in communitarian conceptions of human association (see also 4.2). But justified cooperation with others involves knowledge of the merits of the group in question, and the attainment and evaluation of such knowledge are matters for autonomous scrutiny on the part of agents. To be sure, this evaluation may be based, at least in part, on standards one has learned from one's community. Nevertheless, it is also possible to evaluate those standards by rational criteria that are not relative to a particular community. This does not mean that communal attachments must be constantly reevaluated; habit and tradition may have their own independent value. But the reasonable self can apply its own autonomous standards for the justification of such group activities.

Let us connect these considerations with the communitarian objection about the abstractness of the individuals who figure in traditional theories of natural rights. It must be admitted that there is a sense in which the conception of the self that enters into the principle of human rights is indeed abstract. This abstractness, however, as part of the conclusion that all humans have equal rights, is not based, as with John Rawls's conception of the "original position," on an arbitrary or artificial stripping away of all particularizing properties of human selves (1.7). The argument for the PGC does not involve any denial of the rich communal attachments and diversities of actual human beings. On the contrary, the argument takes humans as they actually are, but with a focus on the generic features that constitute all humans as actual, prospective, or potential agents. Arbitrariness pertains rather to arguments that insist on tying the possession of human rights, or other general moral conclusions, to human characteristics that are not in this way necessarily connected with the context of action. For it is this context that logically must be accepted by every actual or prospective agent, so that its generic features and the moral principle implied thereby cannot be rejected by any agent without self-contradiction. From this it follows that all humans equally have the generic rights as a matter of moral principle, regardless of the different communities to which they may belong.

3.7. ETHICAL INDIVIDUALISM, SOCIALISM, AND THE ECONOMIC CONSTITUTION

The project of conciliating rights and community, as I have envisaged it here, is now complete. As I noted earlier (3.4), I have not tried to include in my use of "community" all the diverse attributes that various communitarian writers have attached to that notion, such as certain particularisms, smallness of scale, and opposition to individualism. My main emphasis in this respect has been on what I regard as the most valuable aspect of the communitarian doctrine, its concern for social solidarity and mutuality of positive consideration among persons. For the reasons indicated above (which will be further spelled out in the following chapters), I believe that this crucial aspect of community has been shown to be conciliated with the principle of human rights.

It can be readily understood in this context how rights and community come together. The rights have as their objects the necessary goods and interests of individuals, to which they are entitled and which they may justifiably claim as their due. But it is the community that protects and fulfills these rights, especially for the persons who do not effectively have them, on the basis of the mutuality that characterizes human rights and the consequent solidarity of the society whose members are brought together by their recognition and fulfillment of common needs. Thus rights require community for their effectuation, and community requires rights as the basis of its justified operations and enactments.

It will help to elucidate some of the complexities of this conciliation if one of its main ideas is put in bold relief. The principle of human rights on which the conciliation is based embodies a certain kind of ethical individualism. This individualism is not to be understood, however, in the perhaps more usual sense that the individual's judgment or conscience is to be the decisive source or criterion for determining what is morally right and wrong.[30] By "ethical individualism" I mean to refer to ends or values rather than to epistemic or decisional sources. Nor is ethical individualism the same as ethical egoism; it is not a reflexive relation whereby each individual should aim only at his own benefit. It is rather a social relation bearing on the ends of social policies and institutions. It is the equal goods and rights of individuals, including their rational autonomy, that constitute the primary objects of human rights as social concerns and hence the primary criterion or end of moral rightness as set forth in the principle of human rights. Thus, as we have seen, the state or society itself is to be viewed as valuationally instrumental, not final; in its primary basis as a community of rights it is a means to protect the equal rights of individuals rather than an end or good in itself.

This ethical individualism receives a strong communitarian specification, however, in at least three ways. First, what the principle of human rights justifies is not the egoistic drives of some individuals as against others but rather a whole system of equal and mutually supportive rights and duties. This system comprises a common good in the distributive sense that goods are common to—equally held by—each of the individual members

---

30. See Steven Lukes, *Individualism* (Oxford: Basil Blackwell, 1973), pp. 101–6.

of the community; but it adds the requirement of mutuality whereby persons not only must refrain from removing from others the necessary goods of action but must also help others to obtain these goods when they cannot obtain them by their own efforts. This mutuality requires a context of institutional rules that are central to community. Second, these rules require systematic contributions by all persons, so far as possible, to maintain the society that supports the human rights of each. Rewards in the way both of monetary income and of social recognition are allocated in accord with such social contributions. In certain extreme situations the contributions may require heavy sacrifices by individuals to preserve their communities. Third, the individuals can develop a loyalty to their community, a shared social sentiment of support and advocacy. This loyalty stems in the first instance from the community's securing their own equal individual rights. But it is also fostered by the group interests, the social bonds that persons maintain through their participation in cooperative activities and that make them communal as well as individual beings. So in these ways ethical individualism is reconciled with communitarianism.

The communitarianism thus developed has some important ties to socialism. Socialism has been defined in many different ways: sometimes as upholding equality above all, sometimes as advocating public ownership of the main means of production, sometimes as central planning of the economy, sometimes as class or party dictatorship. Each of these definitions incurs difficulties of specification, of implementation, and of justification. But many of the persons who called themselves socialists had in mind a more graphic, more distinct, and less technical conception. Above all, they were saddened, indeed revolted, by the spectacle of immense human physical suffering and economic deprivation—hunger, malnutrition, illness, squalor, homelessness, depressive work conditions, unemployment, exploitation— from which the sufferers could not defend themselves because of their poverty and political powerlessness. The socialists wanted above all to do away with this massive deprivation, and they believed it was the duty of the state to protect people from it. They believed the sufferers did not deserve, and had done nothing to deserve, the miserable conditions under which they lived, and they believed that these conditions were the effects of a whole social and economic system in which the strong dominated the weak, or at least were indifferent to their fate. They believed that the suffering masses, whom they identified largely with the working classes, had equal rights which the system violated, and they were animated by strong compassion for these masses.[31]

31.   Apart from the reference to "rights," the above characterization is as true of Marx and Engels as of those they called "utopian" socialists. See Marx and Engels, *The Communist*

Some part of what now passes as communitarianism shares the conception which I have identified with socialism. The general idea of what I here present as the community of rights is largely composed of this fundamental conception, which I have denominated—I think with much historical justification—as both socialist and communitarian.[32] How this conception is related to other parts of the broad tradition, or set of traditions, that have gone under the name of socialism, will be touched on at a few points in what follows. But political dictatorship is rigorously excluded, and so too is central planning, except perhaps where large state corporations may be needed for certain kinds of large-scale industry and public utilities.[33]

As I mentioned at the outset, the human rights with which I shall be especially concerned here are the economic ones that bear on persons' livelihoods. It needs no emphasis here how heavily the human suffering that consists in the infringement of freedom and well-being is caused by poverty, unemployment, lack of productive skills, and other economic deprivations. This is not, of course, to suggest that all human suffering is encompassed solely within economic contexts; the sufferings caused by war, by political oppression, and by psychological and medical problems, among others, can in no way be gainsaid. But these are often intertwined with economic problems. And the economic contexts have their own special urgency in the relief of human suffering. In showing what are the human rights that must be fulfilled in order to relieve this suffering, I shall be tracing a sequence of "economic biography" whereby even the poorest can gradually surmount their economic and related afflictions and move closer to equality by, among other things, developing relevant abilities, but also by appropriate and justified macroeconomic policies and institutions. In

---

Manifesto, pt. 3, in Robert C. Tucker, ed., *The Marx-Engels Reader*, 2d ed. (New York: W. W. Norton, 1978), pp. 491–99; Friedrich Engels, *Socialism: Utopian and Scientific* (New York: International Publishers, 1935). See also Marx, *Capital*, vol. 1 (New York: International Publishers, 1967), esp. chap. 10, "The Working Day." See in general G. D. H. Cole, *A History of Socialist Thought*, 5 vols. (London: Macmillan, 1963–65); Leszak Kolakowski, *Main Currents of Marxism*, vol. 1 (Oxford: Oxford University Press, 1978). See also Gertrude Himmelfarb, *Poverty and Compassion: The Moral Imagination of the Late Victorians* (New York: Vintage Books, 1992), book 5, "We Are All Socialists Now" (pp. 309–13). While emphasizing that "the word 'socialism' was used in the most latitudinarian sense" by those who claimed to be socialists (p. 309), Himmelfarb also says, "The word was not used lightly and its usage was significant. That so many serious, thoughtful people were prepared to identify themselves as socialists testifies to the gravity of their social concerns" (p. 312).

32. See David Miller, "In What Sense Must Socialism Be Communitarian?" *Social Philosophy and Policy* 6, no. 2 (spring 1989): 51–73.

33. See Alec Nove, *The Economics of Feasible Socialism Revisited* (London: Harper Collins, 1991), pp. 213–15.

this way they will attain the main economic dimensions of the freedom and well-being to which they have equal rights. The help toward this development will be presented not as matters of charity or private beneficence but rather as objects of equal rights. As we shall see, the biography will also encompass ethical and other humanistic cultural values and virtues whose attainment the economic development makes possible. This sequence will also develop pari passu an "economic constitution" for the state as the community of rights. This constitution will provide for the progressive fulfillment of the economic rights of persons who need help to overcome their economic deprivations. Thus what from the individual standpoint is a biography, from the social standpoint is a constitution that incorporates, in a stable legal institutional form, the policies that foster the biographical development.[34] It must be emphasized, however, that this constitution, as I shall here present it, does not purport to deal with all the many phases of the economic structure. It will be selective, just as is the economic biography; it will focus on those aspects of the system that are especially relevant to the economic rights to be developed here. But they are, I think, crucial for the community of rights. In chapter 8 I shall discuss some of the political dynamics of this constitution-making for the economic human rights.

As my use of the word "human" indicates, these rights pertain to women as well as to men, as do the economic deprivations that the rights are designed to remedy. In some contexts, such as the welfare system discussed in chapter 4, problems of dependence and child care that have come especially to afflict women will receive prominent attention. In many other contexts, although I shall not be dealing with the theme of suffering in the ways that distinctively characterize women as against men, the analysis to be presented here should accommodate the general economic needs of both genders. The same factors also obtain with regard to the economic needs of different races, and indeed, mutatis mutandis, of the inhabitants of different countries.

The community of rights that will be developed in the following chapters is in the dual position of being both means and end, both process and product. The various institutions and policies through which the commu-

---

34. For the idea of an economic constitution, see Franz Neumann, "On the Preconditions and Legal Concept of an Economic Constitution," in Otto Kirchheimer and Franz Neumann, *Social Democracy and the Rule of Law,* ed. Keith Tribe (London: Allen and Unwin, 1987), pp. 44–65. Neumann's essay, first published in German in 1931, is largely occupied with a critique of the capitalist economy of the Weimar Republic. See also the discussion of the constitution of the Mondragon cooperatives in W. F. Whyte and K. K. Whyte, *Making Mondragon* (Ithaca, N.Y.: ILR Press, 1988), pp. 35–41. See more generally Friedrich A. Hayek, *The Constitution of Liberty* (Chicago: University of Chicago Press, 1960); Stephen L. Elkin and Karol Edward Soltan, eds., *A New Constitutionalism: Designing Political Institutions for a Good Society* (Chicago: University of Chicago Press, 1993).

nity functions constitute ways in which the state undertakes to promote the equal rights of its individual members, especially those who are most deprived, to attain as full a measure as possible of freedom and well-being. The ideal, or at least the envisaged, outcome of these institutions and policies is a society in which this attainment is fully operative. In aiming at this attainment the state is a community of rights that are to be promoted; in having succeeded in this attainment the state is a community of rights that have been fulfilled. There is no anomaly in this dual position. On the contrary, so long as the actual is not confused with the ideal, a society that recognizes the actualities of its pervasive violations of rights can be animated by a relatively clear idea of what must be done to correct the violations and thereby to move from the actual to the ideal.

3.8. The Problems of Rights Inflation and Specification

I have now presented the main general components of the community of rights. In the following chapters I shall apply them to what I take to be the chief lines of economic and social policy that are required for the fulfillment of the community. The applications will involve arguments to the effect that, by virtue of having the generic human rights to freedom and well-being, persons also have certain more specific positive rights, whose objects include welfare, education, property, employment, and other conditions that will be presented as means both for the relief of suffering and for the development and use of productive agency. The society, as a community of rights, is charged with helping to provide these conditions for all persons, and thus with fulfilling their rights to the necessary conditions of action.

In invoking these more specific rights, explicit notice must be taken of two interrelated kinds of problems: rights inflation and specification.

The phrase "rights inflation" is used by critics who decry what they consider to be excessive, unwarranted proliferations of claims of rights.[35] Sometimes the criticisms are primarily directed against the alleged subjects of rights, as when it is held that trees, animals, fetuses, children, or mentally deficient persons have rights.[36] I have tried to deal with this issue through the Principle of Proportionality (2.6). More usually, the criticisms focus on the objects of rights. Here the main areas of discussion have included not

35. See, e.g., Richard E. Morgan, *Disabling America: The 'Rights Industry' in Our Time* (New York: Basic Books, 1984), esp. chap. 10; R. G. Frey, *Rights, Killing, and Suffering* (Oxford: Basil Blackwell, 1983), pp. 168–69.

36. See, e.g., Thomas C. Pocklington, "Against Inflating Human Rights," *Windsor Yearbook of Access to Justice* 2 (1982): 77–86.

only the human rights dealt with in this book but also rights allegedly based on the American Constitution. In each area it has been charged that there has been an unjustified expansion of what persons are held to have rights to. And in each area the main source of the difficulty has been held to be that there is no clear, determinate decision procedure for ascertaining to what objects persons may be justifiably said to have rights. Thus, with regard to asserted new human rights, attention has been called to "the haphazard, almost anarchic manner in which this expansion is being achieved."[37] And with regard to American constitutional rights and to right-claims in general it has been charged that claims of their existence rest on arbitrary, personal or parochial "intuitions."[38]

How do these criticisms bear on the rights I shall here be deriving from the PGC as the principle of human rights? There would seem to be ample room for the procedural vagueness on which the critics have focused. After all, "freedom" and "well-being" are very general words, so how can they be shown to imply or justify specific policy recommendations about rights such as those I shall present below? And with regard to the objections about constitutional rights, an additional basis for suspicion may be derived from the assertion, with which I agree, that "the PGC is the constitutional norm of any legal order."[39]

To deal with this problem, we must first note that the concepts of freedom and well-being have been given extensive elucidations in *Reason and Morality* in connection with their positions in the whole context of agency. My general point can be put as follows: Since the context of agency is inescapable for all humans as actual or prospective agents, and since freedom and well-being, as elucidated, are necessary goods for all agents, the human rights based on these goods have in turn a kind of necessity that exempts them from the critics' charges of arbitrariness.

37.   Philip Alston, "Conjuring up New Human Rights: A Proposal for Quality Control," *American Journal of International Law* 78, no. 3 (July 1984): 607. See also R. G. Mulgan, "The Theory of Human Rights," in K. J. Keith, ed., *Essays on Human Rights* (Wellington, New Zealand, 1968), p. 20; Loren E. Lomasky, *Persons, Rights, and the Moral Community* (New York: Oxford University Press, 1987), pp. 4–7.

38.   See R. M. Hare, *Moral Thinking* (Oxford: Clarendon Press, 1981), pp. 153 ff.; Leonard Levy, *Original Intent and the Framers' Constitution* (New York: Macmillan, 1988).

39.   Deryck Beyleveld and Roger Brownsword, *Law as a Moral Judgment* (London: Sweet and Maxwell, 1986), p. 162; see also pp. 200, 278, and chap. 7. This book provides searching analyses of methods and principles of legal judgment and interpretation, especially in the contrast between legal positivism and natural law theory. Analogues may be found between the difficulties of interpreting the broad phrases of the United States Constitution and the problems of specifying the rights upheld by the PGC. For a convenient collection of readings on diverse methods of interpreting the Constitution, see Susan J. Brison and Walter Sinnott-Armstrong, *Contemporary Perspectives on Constitutional Interpretation* (Boulder, Colo.: Westview Press, 1993).

For the further understanding of this matter it is important to note the distinction between direct and indirect applications of the PGC (*RM*, 200–201, 272–74). In the direct applications, the PGC's requirements are imposed on the interpersonal actions of individual persons. According to these applications, actions are morally right and their agents fulfill their moral obligations if they act in accord with their recipients' generic rights, allowing the recipients to participate in their transactions with freedom and well-being. On this basis, rights and duties bearing on freedom and the three levels of well-being can be deduced in a quite determinate way, ranging from duties not to kill innocent persons and duties to rescue drowning persons if one can, through duties not to lie or break one's promises, to duties to develop one's prudential virtues by education and other means, and duties to refrain from violence, coercion, and deception (*RM*, chap. 4). The derivation of these duties and their correlative rights from the PGC, as well as the adjustments needed to deal with their possible conflicts, can be obtained without the vagueness or arbitrariness emphasized by the critics of "rights-inflation."

In contrast to the PGC's direct applications, in the indirect applications the PGC's requirements are imposed in the first instance on various social rules that govern multiperson activities and institutions, and the requirements of these rules are then in turn imposed on the actions of individuals who participate in the activities and institutions in accordance with their governing rules. Thus, the PGC is here applied to the actions of individual persons only through the mediation of social rules. These rules are morally justified, and the persons who act according to them fulfill their moral obligations, when the rules conform to the PGC's requirements that agents act in accord with the generic rights of their recipients as well as of themselves. I have distinguished four general kinds of social rules and institutions that conform in these ways to the PGC (*RM*, chap. 5). Two kinds are primarily applications of the right to freedom: voluntary associations (including the family) and the democratic state through its use of consensual procedures (although the state is not a voluntary association; see *RM*, 304–7). Two other kinds are primarily applications of the right to well-being: the minimal state, which embodies the criminal law, and the supportive (or "welfare") state, which provides for supplying basic goods, such as food and shelter, to persons who cannot obtain them by their own efforts, as well as education and other additive goods. Most generally, the community of rights embodies all three kinds of state: the minimal, the democratic, and the supportive, although it is the last of these that most specifically promotes equality of freedom and well-being for the deprived groups who are most lacking in these goods.

While all four of these indirect applications involve considerably more

complexities than do the direct applications, their derivation from the PGC
is relatively straightforward. By far the most controversial applications
bear on the supportive state; and since the rights that will be presented and
developed in this book fall within the general lineaments of such a state
(which is, indeed, largely identical with what I am calling "the community
of rights"), it will be especially important to take account of the criticisms
of "rights-inflation."

The main problem in deriving these applications is that of specification. Even if, as I have held, the general justification of the supportive state
as the community of rights is attained by deriving the functions of that state
from the PGC as the principle of human rights, it is a further and more controversial step to derive specific economic and social rights from the supportive state. The general pattern of the derivation is as follows. First, all
humans have rights to freedom and well-being as the necessary conditions
of their action and generally successful action. Second, some good, X, is
required for persons to have freedom or well-being or both. Third, therefore persons have a right to X. So the general pattern of the argument is that
if A has a right to Y, and X is needed for having Y, then A has a right to X.

There are two main difficulties with this line of argument. One difficulty is normative. Even if A must have X if she is to have Y, someone else
may already have a right to that X, and this would preclude A from having
a right to X. This problem arises especially when the X that is needed for
A's having Y is the private property of someone else, B, so that here B's private property right may come in conflict with, for example, A's welfare
right. The criterion of degrees of needfulness for action (2.4) is intended to
deal with this problem. But, as we shall see, there remain many complexities.

The other main difficulty with the above line of argument is factual or
empirical. Assertions of the form "X is needed (or required) for having Y"
usually make strong assumptions about factual or causal connections. In
the biological sphere, it is not controversial that oxygen is required for
breathing and hence for life. But in the socioeconomic sphere there are often many alternative means to given ends, and there is the further factual
question of whether a given X is indeed needed or required for the attainment of some Y—for example, whether or how much education is required
for the development of productive agency, whether or how much or what
kind of employment is needed for well-being, and so forth.[40] The difficulty
may also attach to the concepts of freedom and well-being themselves that

---

40.   Compare the discussion of the need for "specificatory premises" to move from general to specific moral precepts in Alan Donagan, *The Theory of Morality* (Chicago: University
of Chicago Press, 1977), pp. 30–31, 68–74, 134, 143. See also *RM*, 278–82.

represent the generic rights, the ends or values to which ultimate appeal is made to justify the rights to more specific objects. It may be held that these concepts are too general, diffuse, and porous to enable determinate, more specific rights to be derived from them. I have already presented grounds for rejecting this criticism.

These difficulties of specification will require serious attention. In each of the rights-derivations for which I shall argue in the following chapters as contents of the community of rights, careful consideration will have to be given both to the aspects of freedom and well-being that provide the justificatory ends of the argument and to the alleged connection with them of the more specific goods that are held to be required for the attainment of those ends, as well as the various empirical constraints that may limit such attainment.[41] Of particular importance will be the context of agency that supplies the foundation both of the ends and of the means. The general point to be kept in mind throughout is that the central justification of all the human rights, including the more specific ones, is their contribution to the equal fulfillment for all persons of the generic needs of agency, consisting in the proximate necessary conditions of action and generally successful action. The objections about "anarchy" and "intuitionism" raised by the critics of "rights inflation" can be warded off to the extent that this central justification can be shown to provide the warrant for each of the rights that figure in the community of rights. Thus while the dialectically necessary method will continue to uphold the normative necessity of the generic rights (1.5), the more specific rights that will be derived from them may have elements of contingency—only, however, as to their derivation, not as to the requiredness of their enforcement or fulfillment (see also 8.2).

These rights all presuppose as their background the minimal state and the democratic state, whose relevant rules and justifications have been presented in *Reason and Morality* (chap. 5). While I shall return to certain problems of political democracy in the last chapter of this book, the discussions of rights all occur within a context wherein certain rights to basic well-being are secured by the criminal law and rights to civil liberties are secured by the democratic state.

41. See also the warning "against simple applications of moral and political philosophy" in Karol E. Soltan, "What Is the New Constitutionalism?" in Elkin and Soltan, eds., *A New Constitutionalism*, p. 14.

FOUR

THE RIGHT TO
PRODUCTIVE AGENCY

4.1. The Right to Welfare and the Deprivation Focus

In the above three chapters I have tried to fulfill this book's first chief aim: to show that rights and community have a relation of mutual support. We are now ready to take up the second chief aim of this book: to show how the community of rights, through the principle of human rights on which it is based, serves to justify and fulfill the economic and social rights of the most deprived members of society. The central concern of this principle is that each person be equally protected in having the freedom and well-being that are the proximate necessary conditions of action and generally successful action. To trace how economic and social rights are derived from this principle, it will be helpful to compare the procedure followed by a traditional philosophical way of effectuating political and civil rights. In the modern doctrines that begin with Hobbes (which have their ancient parallels) the first step is one of deprivation: a "state of nature" that shows what human life would be like in the absence of law and government. As is well known, for Hobbes this is a life of suffering, a life that is "solitary, poor, nasty, brutish and short." [1] The two following steps are a social contract, and thereby the establishment of government, law, and order, including a bare modicum of effective political and civil rights, with peace and prosperity in the offing.

In the economic sphere, analogously, we may also begin from a condition of deprivation. Unfortunately, to elucidate this condition does not require recourse to an imaginary state of nature; the afflictions of starvation, homelessness, unemployment, insecurity, and other grinding effects of poverty are only too palpably present in the modern world. To be poor is to be in a condition of severe deprivation, suffering, and powerlessness; it is, indeed, to live a life that, even if not solitary, comes very close to being "nasty, brutish, and short." When one is poor one is unable to provide for

1. Thomas Hobbes, *Leviathan,* chap. 13.

oneself the necessities of life, the basic well-being that includes having food, shelter, clothing, medical care, and other essential preconditions of successful action. It may also include a lack of various nonsubtractive and additive goods, such as education.[2] The persons who are thus poor include some of the very old, the physically or mentally handicapped, the very ill, the poorly educated, and mothers who receive little or no support from their children's fathers, so that there has been a "feminization of poverty."[3] Disabilities imposed by race often exacerbate these afflictions. Other persons may suffer deprivations that, while less deep, may also threaten their supply of basic goods because they are unemployed through no fault of their own, or because the prices at which the commodities they produce are bought are not sufficient for their basic needs, or because of other adverse circumstances. There are also distinctions between those who are temporarily unemployed after a period of employment, those who have contributed to the funds, governmental or other, from which they subsequently derive income, and those who have never worked because welfare has become for them a relatively permanent condition. The latter must also be distinguished from persons who are incapable of working because of age or illness.

An obvious beginning point for the kind of economic deprivation that is analogous to the political deprivation of the state of nature is the joint condition of starvation and homelessness: the lack of food and shelter that is a severe threat to basic well-being. I shall not, however, begin with these. I have already briefly discussed starvation above (2.5); and the homelessness that has increasingly disfigured modern cities in the last decades of the twentieth century is itself largely (though not entirely) a product of the poverty which is the central basis of economic affliction.

To see how these and related afflictions should be dealt with, we do not need to appeal to an imaginary social contract, as is done in the modern tradition of political philosophy. For the principle of human rights is already available as the basis for justified evaluation and action, both as a

2. See the discussion of "absolute" versus "relative" poverty with their respective bases in "capabilities" and "commodities," in Amartya Sen, "Poor, Relatively Speaking," in his *Resources, Values, and Development* (Cambridge, Mass.: Harvard University Press, 1984), pp. 325–45. See also Amartya Sen, *Poverty and Famines* (Oxford: Clarendon Press), pp. 17, 22. See the discussion of "the objectivity of need" in Len Doyal and Ian Gough, *A Theory of Human Need* (New York: Guilford Press, 1991), pp. 49–59. For an analysis of poverty in terms of "relative deprivation," see Peter Townsend, *Poverty in the United Kingdom* (Berkeley and Los Angeles: University of California Press, 1979), chap. 1. On the "political changes in the definition of poverty," see Christopher Jencks et al., *Inequality* (New York: Basic Books, 1975), p. 5. See also the discussion of well-being above, 1.4.

3. See Barbara Ehrenreich and Frances Fox Piven, "The Feminization of Poverty," *Dissent* (spring 1984): 162–70.

fundamental moral norm and, in its reference to the state as the community of rights, as providing for its effectuation, although this effectuation raises complex problems both theoretical and practical (8.1, 4). The existence of poverty is an at least prima facie violation of human rights. As we have seen, all persons have rights to the necessary goods of action, and these rights entail correlative duties to provide them for persons who cannot obtain them by their own efforts. For the reasons given above (2.5), the state, as the community of rights, should be the primary respondent of these rights. In this way, then, there is a moral right to welfare, and it must also be a legal right.[4] So here rights and community are brought together, for in fulfilling the right to welfare for persons who need it, the society exhibits the cooperation, mutuality, and compassion that are characteristic of community. Rights are required here because there must be guarantees that the needed welfare help will be forthcoming as something that is owed or due to the recipients for their own sakes, and not as something that is optional for the donors. This nonoptionality derives from the consideration that the objects of welfare provision are necessary goods of action (3.3).

In contrast to the political sequence, then, I shall assume the kind of welfare states that exist in many modern societies. The condition with which I shall begin is the one commonly called "welfare." I shall trace a sequence of economic biography wherein persons obtain the welfare to which they have a right, but then develop the ability and use of productive agency to emerge from welfare, which involves further economic and social rights—all this through the community of rights with its mutual rights and obligations.

In one of its more familiar meanings, "welfare" signifies the support that governments provide for impoverished segments of the population in the form of monetary and other grants for food, rent, clothing, medical care, and other necessities of life. Examples of such measures in the United States are Aid to Families with Dependent Children (AFDC), Medicaid, Supplemental Income Security, and various kinds of general assistance. The definition of "welfare" can, however, be extended to include Social Security, Medicare, and other kinds of entitlements that go to recipients regardless of need. A still further extension has sometimes been used to describe the massive doses of financial aid that the federal government has contributed to bail out huge corporations like Lockheed and the Continen-

4. For the recent development and contents of the right to welfare in the United States, see Edward V. Sparer, "The Right to Welfare," in Norman Dorsen, ed., *The Rights of Americans: What They Are—What They Should be* (New York: Vintage Books, 1971), pp. 65–93; Sar A. Levitan, *Programs in Aid of the Poor,* 5th ed. (Baltimore: Johns Hopkins University Press, 1985); Theodor R. Marmor, Jerry L. Mashaw, and Philip L. Harvey, *America's Misunderstood Welfare State* (New York: Basic Books, 1990).

tal Illinois Bank, to maintain the incomes of wealthy agribusinesses, to help middle-class homeowners by letting them deduct for income tax purposes the interest paid on their mortgages, and so forth. As these examples indicate, the modern welfare state gives financial assistance to many groups besides the poor.[5] But it is primarily to the poor that "being on welfare" is attributed, especially to otherwise unsupported mothers and to men on "general assistance." Although I shall refer below largely to welfare mothers, it must be emphasized that the considerations I shall discuss also apply in important part to men.

Two initial observations must be made. First, regardless of the background causes that have generated the need for welfare assistance, persons who suffer from poverty and related afflictions do not then and there have the power (analogous to what persons in the state of nature may be thought to have) that would justify charging them with the task of surmounting their own deprivations. Circumstances may, of course, vary; but it will be recalled that persons have positive rights to be helped only when they cannot attain relevant well-being by their own efforts (2.3). From the standpoint of human rights it is appropriate to begin from this condition of relative powerlessness and then to examine how it can be remedied.

A second initial observation concerns the areas of deprivation that will receive primary attention in this book. The list of these areas is not, of course, exhaustive; there are many other economically based kinds of affliction besides the ones that will be discussed here. The whole vast area of illness and required health care is a prominent example. My justification for focusing on the areas I discuss here is that they are strategically important for the problem of attaining for all persons the freedom and well-being that are the necessary conditions of human action and generally successful action. The incurring of disease and the availability of health care are themselves strongly influenced by economic factors.

Two objections may be raised against this beginning point of poverty and welfare. First, it may be charged that to begin from poverty seems to assume that poverty will always be with us as part of a just society or a community of rights; but poverty is a violation of rights. The reply is that poverty is a fact of life that sets an important part of the problem that the community of rights is designed to rectify. To overlook this problem is to be utopian, and to proceed without addressing it is to act as if its solution were

5. See Robert E. Goodin and Julian LeGrand et al., *Not Only the Poor: The Middle Classes and the Welfare State* (London: Allen and Unwin, 1987); Brian Barry, "The Welfare State versus the Relief of Poverty," *Ethics* 100, no. 3 (Apr. 1990): 503–29; Christopher Jencks, *Rethinking Social Policy* (Cambridge, Mass.: Harvard University Press, 1992), p. 76. See also Thomas Howard Tarantino and Rev. Dismas Becker, eds., *Welfare Mothers Speak Out* (New York: W. W. Norton, 1972), pp. 17–22.

already effectively at hand and operative. One of the main ends projected by the community of rights is indeed the elimination of poverty; but it is vitally important not to confuse this end either with the beginning or with the steps that must be taken to achieve it.

A second objection concerns universality, in several different respects. It may be contended that the particularistic focus on the poor and, subsequently, on the working class is incompatible with the universality of human rights. The poor and the workers are only a part of humanity, albeit a large part. But if human rights involve the impartial application of universally relevant moral standards, it may be thought inconsistent to emphasize the particularistic perspective of poverty and welfare. This point is exacerbated by the fact that some of my discussion deals largely, though not exclusively, with conditions in the United States.

The most direct reply to this objection is that because human rights impose requirements that equally protect the fundamental agency-related interests of all persons, those deprived persons whose interests are protected inadequately or not at all must become the focus of the rights so far as concerns their effectuation. I shall call this the *deprivation focus*.[6] I use "deprivation" rather than "poverty" in order to include groups, like some of those mentioned above, whose livelihoods are threatened by unemployment, illness, and other adversities, including feelings of hopelessness. Two of the main parts of the deprivation focus are political and economic, having to do respectively with power and with property. There is, then, no contradiction between the empirical recognition of the existence of drastically unequal classes and the moral principle of equal human rights. The emphasis here falls not only on equality as such but also on the material consideration of the needs of agency; leveling down may yield equality as well as leveling up, but since the aim of the human rights is that persons have the abilities of successful agency, the fulfillment of the rights requires increasing rather than decreasing those abilities when they are inadequate to the general aim (see 3.1).[7] The deprivation focus thus bears not only on basic well-being but on the other levels of well-being also, as well as on freedom.

---

6. Compare "the preferential option for the poor" as set forth in Catholic social teaching. See, e.g., U.S. Catholic Bishops, "Economic Justice for All: Catholic Social Teaching and the U.S. Economy," pars. 170, 186 (reprinted, unpaged, in Thomas M. Gannon, S.J., ed., *The Catholic Challenge to the American Economy* [New York: Macmillan, 1987]). The deprivation focus, however, is not, strictly speaking, an "option"; it is a morally necessary requirement as deriving from the principle of human rights, which is itself both rationally and morally necessary. See also the exhaustive discussion of forms of deprivation in Townsend, *Poverty in the United Kingdom*, chaps. 11–14.

7. A distinction must be drawn between the moral and the political aspects of the deprivation focus. The moral aspect was given above. But from a political, tactical point of view the moral objectives of helping the needy may be best achieved through "policies which serve a

A related objection is that the universality of human rights is misrepresented when the concentration falls so heavily on American conditions, as it does here. In reply, this concentration need not detract from the universal applicability of the discussion, for several reasons. Although the problems, histories, and traditions of each country are to some extent unique, the American experience can be taken to be broadly representative of many other Western countries, although the social-democratic policies of some of them are in advance of the American situation (7.1). Moreover, insofar as other countries have been developing economically according to Western patterns, the American problems can be taken at least in part to apply to them as well, either in the present or in the not too indefinite future. More generally, since the whole argument is rooted in the needs of agency that are common to all humans, the concentration on those whose needs are least fulfilled serves to assure its applicability, in principle, to all other humans as well. So concentration does not entail exclusiveness.

A reverse objection about universality is that although, as was noted above, "welfare" applies primarily to poor women with children through AFDC, I shall here be discussing the plight of men as well as women. In reply, it involves no derogation from the overwhelming presence of women among welfare recipients to recognize that males are implicated in the welfare web as well as women. They are implicated as absent, unskilled, poorly educated, usually unemployed fathers; as young boys who struggle with the debilitating effects of poverty in their households; and as adolescents who will grow up in turn to be absent, unskilled, poorly educated, unemployed fathers. The pathology of poverty afflicts both genders, and even though it may strike more vehemently at women, men also suffer greatly from it. This is in no way to overlook the special problems faced by mothers as caretakers of children, although this one-sided responsibility should also be reversed. Hence, the state as the community of rights must be concerned with helping both genders to overcome the deprivations that require welfare, through the mutuality of obligations that serves both as means and as end in this process.

To return to the deprivation focus in general, it is worth noting its relation to the modern tradition of political philosophy. The economic deprivations with which I shall here be concerned are obviously antithetical to at

---

broad slice of the population." See William Julius Wilson, *The Truly Disadvantaged* (Chicago: University of Chicago Press, 1987), pp. 150–57. See also Michael B. Katz, *The Undeserving Poor* (New York: Pantheon Books, 1989), p. 233; Joel F. Handler and Yeheskel Hasenfeld, *The Moral Construction of Poverty* (Newbury Park, Calif.: Sage Publications, 1991), pp. 231–32; Theda Skocpol, "Sustainable Social Policy: Fighting Poverty without Poverty Programs," *The American Prospect*, no. 2 (summer 1990): 58–70. This broader application, however, is a matter of effective means rather than of ends.

least one important kind of equality. The moral equality of persons has been a dominant theme of modern moral and political philosophy. But where political philosophers have dealt in great detail with the political deprivation focus as it affects this equality, few have gone into the sphere of economic deprivation and suffering in sufficient detail to bring out the specific lines of the problems and their proposed solutions. Marx and Mill are two conspicuous nineteenth-century exceptions. But in the twentieth century, despite the overwhelming weight of the economic deprivations, no major political philosopher has dealt with the specifics of the moral problems they raise. Among the partial exceptions, by far the most important is John Rawls. It is greatly to his credit to have made "the least advantaged" the central point of his "difference principle," according to which social and economic inequalities are unjustified unless they serve to maximize the expectations of those persons who are "least advantaged." [8]

There are, however, serious limitations in Rawls's treatment of the least advantaged in relation to the whole vast range of economic problems that specifically affect them. Apart from a brief discussion of a "social minimum" and an even briefer reference to "reasonably full employment in the sense that those who want work can find it," [9] Rawls does not take up the specific economic problems encountered by the "least advantaged," including especially what they themselves can do to increase their advantages. The poor are left in a condition of passive recipience as beneficiaries of the wider society's principles of justice, and without a sense of personal responsibility for helping themselves.

In view of the vast impact of Rawls's magisterial treatise, it is worth noting that there are three main differences between his treatment of the

8. John Rawls, *A Theory of Justice* (Cambridge, Mass.: Harvard University Press, 1971), pp. 98, 302. See also André Gorz, *Strategy for Labor,* trans. M. A. Nicolaus and V. Ortiz (Boston: Beacon Press, 1967); Nicholas Rescher, *Welfare: The Social Issues in Philosophical Perspective* (Pittsburgh: University of Pittsburgh Press, 1972); Peter G. Brown et al., eds., *Income Support: Conceptual and Policy Issues* (Totowa, N.J.: Rowman and Littlefield, 1981); Raymond Plant et al., *Political Philosophy and Social Welfare* (London: Routledge, 1981); Henry Shue, *Basic Rights: Subsistence, Affluence, and U.S. Foreign Policy* (Princeton, N.J.: Princeton University Press, 1980); Carl Wellman, *Welfare Rights* (Totowa, N.J.: Rowman and Littlefield, 1985); Mary Gibson, *Workers' Rights* (Totowa, N.J.: Rowman and Allanheld, 1983); Kenneth Kipnis and Diana T. Meyers, eds., *Economic Justice: Private Rights and Public Responsibilities* (Totowa, N.J.: Rowman and Littlefield, 1985); James W. Nickel, *Making Sense of Human Rights* (Berkeley and Los Angeles: University of California Press, 1987), chap. 9; David Braybrooke, *Meeting Needs* (Princeton, N.J.: Princeton University Press, 1987); Frank Cunningham, *Democratic Theory and Socialism* (Cambridge: Cambridge University Press, 1987); G. A. Cohen, *History, Labour, and Freedom* (Oxford: Clarendon Press, 1988); David Schweickart, *Against Capitalism* (Cambridge: Cambridge University Press, 1993).

9. Rawls, *A Theory of Justice,* pp. 275–77.

least advantaged and the present concern with the deprivation focus (see also 5.4). First, "least advantaged" is relative or comparative. It is true, as we saw in connection with the idea of equality (3.1), that comparative considerations are important in their own right. But the scope of the comparisons, the distance between the items compared, also helps to determine how important are the comparative considerations. Now "least advantaged" does not necessarily mean poor or greatly deprived. In every society that is not completely egalitarian there will be some persons who are economically less advantaged than others, but still they might even be quite affluent or reasonably well off. It is true that Rawls at some points suggests that the least advantaged are to be specified as the class of "the unskilled worker." But this specification is not inherent in the idea of the "least advantaged." The deprivation focus, on the other hand, singles out those groups who lack essentials of basic and other well-being. This specification is not primarily relative or comparative but absolute, in terms of fundamental unfulfilled needs of agency, while at the same time it also calls attention to the vast inequalities that disfigure modern societies (see also note 2 to this chapter).

Second, where the least advantaged are treated, especially in the difference principle, primarily as passive recipients of the agency of other persons,[10] in the deprivation focus there is a double emphasis: both on the society's helping the poor to develop their own abilities of productive agency and, concomitantly, on what the poor can do for themselves to become productive agents on their own behalf through developing and implementing their own sense of personal responsibility and thereby contributing to the society. This difference has an important bearing on human dignity, and it is a result of the human rights principle's central concern that all persons have the proximate necessary conditions of action and generally successful action.

Third, in Rawls's theory the motivation or rationale for maximizing the benefits of the least advantaged is not directly to help economically deprived persons. It is rather a matter of pure self-interest on the part of persons who choose their society's constitution behind a "veil of ignorance" of their personal qualities. These persons, in Rawls's scenario, try to make sure that the pay-off to themselves will be as large as possible regardless of where they land through the natural lottery, and it is only for this reason that they are concerned with what happens to the least advantaged. In important respects, then, the Rawlsian society is not a community in the sense

10.   This emphasis is not counterbalanced by Rawls's brief references to "work" (ibid., pp. 290, 529), as well as to the "Aristotelian Principle" (pp. 424–39). Rawls several times refers to the least advantaged as "the unskilled worker" (pp. 78, 80, 98).

envisaged here. The basis in self-interest may add a refreshing note of realism to Rawls's argument. But at the same time, because of the calculus through which he argues to principles of impartial justice, those principles have a deep element of contingency that is antithetical to the moral necessity of human rights. In the deprivation focus, on the other hand, the direct concern, through the mutuality of the principle of human rights, is to help economically deprived persons to fulfill their needs of agency. This is a concern for persons' freedom and well-being for their own sakes; it is not part of a self-interested probability calculus but reflects rather an awareness of the principled mutuality of needs and rights and the rational and moral necessities that underlie them. The justification of this concern does not require a contrarational ignorance on the part of any of the protagonists. Persons know who they are and are considered as they are; but they also know the principle of human rights and thus the rights and duties that they share with one another (see 1.7). The implications of this principle for the deprivation focus will be examined below.

4.2. THE WELFARE SYSTEM AND AUTONOMY

With a view to tracing the economic biography that begins from a condition of severe economic deprivation, let us now look at certain aspects of the welfare system that aim to relieve this condition. The system is in a paradoxical position. On the one hand, as we have seen, it is morally justified as fulfilling the human right to basic well-being. But, on the other hand, it rests on two morally problematic foundations, one relating more to the past and present, the other more to the future. The system derives its moral justification from a set of conditions, encapsulated as poverty, that is itself morally unjustified. These conditions are humanly caused, unlike much of the physical disease that afflicts many persons in ways beyond their control and that provides the moral justification for the practice of medicine. To rest content with the welfare system because of its moral justification would seem, then, to entail resting content also with the morally unjustified conditions that operate to require the existence of the system.[11]

11. There may be a parallel here to the criminal justice system which, while morally justified, presupposes the existence of crime. But poverty, unlike crime, is not the intentional commission of a morally wrong action. The "paradox of the Good Samaritan" that arises in deontic logic may also be found here. Giving welfare to someone who is in poverty implies that someone is in poverty. Hence, if it ought not to be the case that someone is in poverty, then it ought not to be the case that one gives welfare to someone. This inference may be criticized on the ground that the wrongness of poverty does not necessarily transfer to the attempt to relieve or abolish poverty. On the "good Samaritan paradox," see, e.g., A. N. Prior, "Escapism: the Logical Basis of Ethics," in A. I. Melden, ed., *Essays in Moral Philosophy* (Seattle: University of Washington Press, 1958), pp. 135–46, at p. 144.

Moreover, for those persons who are more than spasmodic recipients of welfare, their condition is morally problematic because, involving as it does dependence on the efforts of other persons, it is antithetical both to certain aspects of the mutuality of human rights and to the autonomy to which, as an aspect of freedom, all humans have rights. I shall here deal mainly with the latter problem, since the former is at least in part entailed by it.

In discussing these morally problematic foundations of the welfare system, it is important both to keep in mind the vital respect in which it is morally justified and to avoid the fallacy of division: the fallacy of attributing the faults of a whole system, together with the conditions that generate it, to its individual members or recipients. This fallacy is especially vicious when the persons to whom the system's faults are attributed are those who are most heavily affected by it while at the same time having the least power to change or influence its functioning or its causes. This does not mean that none of the poor ever bear any responsibility for their poverty. But it does require that, before blaming the victims, one try to become aware of the background causes of the whole system of poverty that generate the need for welfare. In view of the condition of extreme deprivation from which welfare recipients come and in which they live, including its severe blunting of their abilities of agency, it is gratuitous at best to criticize them for being in this condition and for manifesting its effects.[12]

Let us now turn to the morally problematic characteristic of the welfare system as it concerns autonomy. The person who is dependent on welfare for her income lacks a certain important kind of autonomy. As has often been noted, 'autonomy' regarded etymologically means setting one's law for oneself. Obviously there are relevant distinctions about kinds of 'law,' kinds of 'self,' kinds of 'setting,' and so forth. But in any case autonomy belongs to the same family of concepts as does freedom, in the sense in which freedom is one of the necessary conditions of action and generally successful action. This family bears on the procedural features of action:

12. For standard criticisms of the American welfare system as exacerbating rather than ameliorating the problems of poverty, see Edward C. Banfield, *The Unheavenly City* (Boston: Little, Brown, 1968), esp. chaps. 10–11; George Gilder, *Wealth and Poverty* (New York: Basic Books, 1981); Charles Murray, *Losing Ground: American Social Policy, 1950–1980* (New York: Basic Books, 1984); Lawrence Mead, *Beyond Entitlement: The Social Obligations of Citizenship* (New York: Free Press, 1986). For various replies and opposed recommendations, see Wilson, *Truly Disadvantaged;* Robert E. Goodin, *Reasons for Welfare* (Princeton, N.J.: Princeton University Press, 1988); David T. Ellwood, *Poor Support: Poverty in the American Family* (New York: Basic Books, 1988); Lisbeth B. Schorr, *Within Our Reach: Breaking the Cycle of Disadvantage* (New York: Doubleday, 1988); Katz, *Undeserving Poor;* Marmor, Mashaw, and Harvey, *America's Misunderstood Welfare State;* Handler and Hasenfeld, *The Moral Construction of Poverty;* and Jencks, *Rethinking Social Policy.*

features that characterize the initiation and control of one's behavior. In this context, as we have seen (1.4), freedom consists in controlling one's behavior by one's unforced and informed choice while having knowledge of relevant circumstances, so that one's unforced choice is the sufficient condition of one's behavior. Autonomy has the same general reflexive structure of self-control or self-determination as does freedom. It shares with freedom the idea that one's behavior stems from one's own unforced and informed choice, including one's own personal responsibility, so that the choice must not be based upon ignorance of relevant circumstances or be confined to alternatives that are undesirable products of threat or compulsion.

Autonomy differs from freedom, however, because it includes the idea of a 'law' or 'rule.' There are two interrelated aspects here. First, 'rule' implies some degree of generality; thus autonomy requires that one exercise control not only over particular actions or behavioral episodes but also over the general pattern of one's behavior, including the ends of one's actions as well as their means. Second, autonomy requires some degree of awareness of this general rule, including one's ends, as being adopted or maintained by and for oneself. Thus autonomy is not only occurrent but also dispositional; it involves long-range, principled, reflective control over one's behavior, including both what one does and what happens to one. But, as with freedom, this control must derive from one's informed and unforced choice as the sufficient condition of one's behavior.[13]

---

13. Some accounts of autonomy have focused less on persons' control over their external behavior or actions and more on their internal desires, choices, or preferences; they have upheld "desire-autonomy" instead of "behavior-autonomy." On these accounts, autonomy pertains to the "inner citadel" ; it primarily concerns the way in which desires or preferences are formed, "the actual psychological condition of self-government" ; "a property of preference or desire formation" ; it is "a second-order capacity of persons to reflect critically upon their first-order preferences, desires, wishes and so forth and the capacity to accept or attempt to change these in light of higher-order preferences and values." The first two quotations are from John Christman, ed., *The Inner Citadel* (New York: Oxford University Press, 1989), introduction, pp. 6, 13; the third quotation is from Gerald Dworkin, *The Theory and Practice of Autonomy* (Cambridge: Cambridge University Press, 1988), p. 20. While this internalist conception has important merits, it cannot be viewed as the primary conception of autonomy for at least two reasons. First, an autonomy that focuses solely on desires or desire-formation is compatible with nonautonomy of action. One may have formed one's desires in the self-critical way invoked in the internalist conception but may be unable to act on those desires because the general conditions of one's behavior are controlled by other persons. The internalist conception hence leaves obscure or unfulfilled some of the main moral and political grounds on which autonomy has been valued in both personal and institutional settings. Second, in the present context where the necessary goods of action are given primary consideration, it is irrelevant or redundant to ask about the process by which the desires for those goods have been formed or arrived at. If someone wants to have food, shelter, work, protec-

It can be readily seen why autonomy as thus conceived, like freedom and well-being, must be regarded as a necessary good by every actual or prospective agent. This goodness bears both on one's dignity as a self-determining agent who has a sense of personal responsibility and on the instrumental connection of such self-determination with one's attainment of one's purposes. To the extent that one lacks autonomy so that what happens to one is controlled by other persons, one has no assurance that one will succeed in achieving the purposes for which one wants to act.

This necessary goodness of autonomy can withstand the critical views of feminists and communitarians who object to autonomy as being excessively individualistic and impervious to the requirements of caring and cooperation (see 3.5).[14] For autonomy does not exclude the latter qualities. The procedural fact that one sets the rules of one's behavior for oneself does not dictate any particular noncooperative content. It is indeed true that autonomy as here conceived provides no guarantee of moral goodness or rightness. To attain the latter, autonomy must be rational, in that the rules or laws that one sets for oneself have been arrived at by, or are at least compatible with, a correct use of reason so that one recognizes that all other prospective agents have the same rights one necessarily ascribes to oneself: an inference that culminates in the PGC as the principle of human rights (1.5; see *RM*, 138–39). As we have seen, this principle requires a mutualist concern for the positive rights of other persons. Thus rational autonomy, far from being self-centered, incorporates the interconnectedness and concern for others emphasized in communitarian and feminist doctrines. So here rights and community are brought together. At the same time, as I noted above in discussing communitarian conceptions of the self (3.6), autonomy enables each person both to subject to critical scrutiny, through self-aware reflection, the social contexts that bid for one's allegiance or concern, and to make one's decisions based on such scrutiny.

Let us now return to the relation of autonomy to welfare. The welfare recipient lacks certain important aspects of autonomy because, in crucial phases of her life bearing on her very livelihood, she must adhere to rules set by other persons with regard to her receipt of necessities of life. Her receipt of these necessities is not under her control but under the control of others; an important part of her personal responsibility has been removed. She is dependent on others for her continued existence. This relation of de-

---

tion against violence, civil liberties, and so forth, it is inapposite to ask, "How did you come to have these desires?" Similar considerations apply to the discussion of autonomy in Andrew Levine, *Arguing for Socialism* (London: Verso, 1988), p. 35.

14. See Carol Gilligan, *In a Different Voice* (Cambridge, Mass.: Harvard University Press, 1982), pp. 71, 98.

pendence is antithetical to autonomy. We must therefore examine the relation of welfare dependence as it concerns both autonomy and mutuality.

4.3. WELFARE DEPENDENCE, AUTONOMY, AND MUTUALITY

In the context of welfare recipience, "dependence" is a controversial word. The controversies bear especially on whether the dependence with which welfare recipients are regularly charged is unique to them or whether it characterizes many other groups as well. If the latter alternative is correct, then some at least of the criticisms directed against the welfare system should also apply to other social groups or policies.

In general, dependence, as a relation between two or more persons, may be analyzed as follows: For A to be dependent on B for commodity X means that B, or B's activity, is a necessary condition of A's having X. This involves that there is no source other than B from which A can receive X. It also involves, so far, that A and B are different persons, as against the self-dependence that will be referred to below. Thus, if welfare recipients are in this way dependent on others for their sustenance, then without these others they will not have sustenance. This point can also be translated into power terms: if A is dependent on B for commodity X, then B has a certain power over A with regard to X. And from this it can be seen that dependence is in important respects antithetical to autonomy as well as to a certain kind of mutuality.

The above analysis may present a too absolutist notion of the dependence relation. Workers are dependent on their employers for their livelihood, so that the latter have a high degree of power over the former; yet, insofar as a worker who leaves his job can get another, his employer is not a necessary condition of his having work. Nevertheless, a significant part of the general point about necessary condition can be maintained for at least two reasons. First, the worker normally is dependent on *some* employer for work, so that the relation of necessary condition still holds for workers and employers in general. Second, the worker is dependent on the employer in an asymmetrical way, in that the employer can usually survive economically without the worker far more readily than the worker can without the employer (see 5.2; 6.1, 9). At the same time, however, so long as there is the possibility of moving from one employer to another, the dependence relation is weakened. If A has some member of a class of B's as the necessary condition of her receiving X (where a multiplicity of such members is available), this is a less stringent mode of dependence than where a single B holds a monopoly as provider of X.[15]

---

15. On the historical development of the concept of dependence, see the important article by Nancy Fraser and Linda Gordon, "A Genealogy of 'Dependency': A Keyword for the

Let us now connect these considerations about dependence with the discussion in the preceding section of the relation between welfare recipience and autonomy. As we have seen, the autonomous person controls the general rules of her behavior, her general ways of conduct, including what happens to her. But what happens to the welfare-dependent person, on the vitally important matter of her receipt of life-sustaining income, is controlled by the government or by officials acting in its name. For the autonomous person, the rules she herself makes or accepts for herself are the necessary and sufficient conditions of her behavior; but the rules of the welfare dependent's behavior, so far as concerns her receipt of income, have as their necessary conditions the decisions made by other persons; an important part of her personal responsibility has been removed.

The better to understand this opposition, including its moral bearings, we must consider the frequently repeated charge that the giving of welfare assistance both constitutes and encourages a certain unique and undesirable kind of dependence on the part of its recipients, a dependence which does not characterize other adult persons. It may be contended that the regularized characterization of welfare as a condition of "dependence" is simply a rhetorical device by right-wingers who resent the welfare system and who utilize the faintly pejorative connotation of the term when it is applied to adults. I think there is some truth to this. But the device would not even begin to be successful unless "dependence" could indeed be attributed to welfare recipients in a way that is different from the manifold other relations of dependence in which human adults stand to one another.

There are, however, at least two initially plausible arguments against the charge that the receipt of welfare constitutes a unique kind of dependence. One argument is that the charge overlooks the salient fact that in complex modern societies all persons are dependent on one another. As Adam Smith pointed out, "In civilized society, [man] stands at all times in need of the cooperation and assistance of great multitudes." [16] City-dwellers depend on farmers for their food; farmers and others depend on industrial workers for the machines and other products they use; we depend on journalists and broadcasters for information, and on many other persons as well for cultural and spiritual goods. Much, though not all, of this vast web of *inter*dependence is organized through contractual relations in which persons mutually pay for the goods and services they receive. But

U.S. Welfare State," *Signs: A Journal of Women in Society* 19, no. 2 (winter 1994). On less stringent modes of dependence, see Robert E. Goodin, *Protecting the Vulnerable* (Chicago: University of Chicago Press, 1985), pp. 195, 200, and *Reasons for Welfare*, p. 176.

16.   Adam Smith, *Wealth of Nations*, bk. 1, chap. 2 (New York: Modern Library, 1937), p. 14.

these contractual relations are themselves structured through a system of political and economic order in which all persons in a society mutually depend on one another to obey the rules that enable the various parts of the order to function. Hence, this argument concludes that it is a mistake to single out welfare recipients as being somehow uniquely dependent; we are all one another's necessary conditions for living and living well; we are all mutually dependent on one another for the necessities and emoluments of civilized society.

A second argument is that welfare policy, far from constituting or encouraging dependence, rather does the opposite; it fosters *in*dependence on the part of the recipients. For insofar as welfare consists in legally enforced entitlements, its recipients do not have to rely on the vicissitudes of private charity or the often invidious discretionary power of public officials or bureaucrats. On the contrary, the recipients can have the kind of stability and security of income that enables them to take care of themselves and plan their own lives. Because of the laws, officials are no longer necessary conditions of their receipt of income. Thus, welfare entitlements are an indispensable basis of independence on the part of their recipients.[17]

There is much plausibility in these two arguments; but they leave untouched an important basis of the charge that welfare involves a unique kind of dependence. This basis consists in the fact that the various interdependences adduced in the first argument comprise a relation of mutuality which has important moral implications. To put it schematically, person A depends on person B for some commodity X; but person B in turn depends on person A for commodity Y. In modern societies, where money, not barter, is the characteristic mode of exchange, persons are one another's monetary recipients in the various areas of interdependence. Each gives to the other something he or she values, and receives something valued in return, or its monetary equivalent.

In contrast to this mutuality of interdependence, in the welfare situation the recipient obtains money or equivalent goods but does not give anything in return. Here again it must be emphasized that this is not a criticism of the welfare recipients per se but rather of the institution and the socioeconomic conditions that make it necessary. The welfare recipients are dependent in a nonsymmetrical way; they take but do not give, that is, they are not taken from. This is a unilateral relation of dependence because the recipient depends on other persons who do not in turn depend on her; they are necessary conditions of her having sustenance, but she is not in any similar way their necessary condition. These other persons depend on their own productive efforts to obtain needed commodities from others who in

17. See Goodin, *Reasons for Welfare*, chap. 6.

turn depend on their own productive efforts to obtain needed commodities. In such mutual relations each participant's productive agency is his or
her own necessary condition for receiving commodities from others. Because of this self-dependence, the persons in question are in an important
respect independent—that is, not uniquely dependent on other persons.
This point also applies to unemployed persons who have previously done
income-generating work and have made contributions in the form of unemployment insurance or social security. The welfare recipient does not
have this self-dependence, so that he is dependent in a far more conclusive
way. This point about unilateralness is not removed by the fact of legally
enforced entitlements to welfare, because it concerns relations of mutuality
that are antecedent to such entitlements.

The contrast between mutual and unilateral relations bears directly on
the concept of dependence as comprising necessary conditions. It must be
emphasized, however, that this contrast is subject to important qualifications. Like the example of workers and employers mentioned above, the
persons involved in relations of interdependence can have, at least to some
extent, alternative sources of income or goods because, partly through
their mutuality, they may not have only one person or group as the necessary condition of their receipt of the relevant goods. The power contained
in their mutual dependence is diffused both for this reason and because
they may be able both to give and to withhold the goods they have to offer.
The relation of necessary conditions is hence also diffused. But none of
these mitigating circumstances are found in the relation of welfare dependence. The welfare recipient has no goods or services to withhold and has
no alternative potential source of supply. It must also be recognized that
many kinds of workers themselves become dependent on welfare when
economic circumstances force them out of the relation of mutuality of interdependence, that is, when they lose their jobs and they lack, or run out
of, unemployment insurance.

This point about the nonmutuality of the welfare relation does not remove the more general point about the mutuality of human rights: that all
persons have rights against one another and duties to one another. That
welfare recipients are unable to fulfill positive rights of other persons does
not invalidate the principled mutuality of human rights, including the positive duties of other persons to welfare recipients, as required by the community of rights. It is an important objective of social policy that welfare
recipients, through developing their abilities of productive agency, be enabled to make their own effective contributions to this mutuality and
thereby to be the agents or respondents as well as the recipients or subjects
of human rights.

It might be argued that welfare recipients do indeed participate actively in relations of mutuality by giving something of value to other persons or to the society at large, so that they are not as exclusively dependent as has just been alleged. For, by not rebelling against or attacking the affluent persons or the environing public institutions, welfare recipients help to maintain the social order. Amid their poverty and miserable living conditions, they hold their peace and thereby enable the other members of society to go their various ways.[18] So the rest of society depends on the poor to maintain civil peace, while the poor depend on the rest of society for their sustenance—so that welfare recipience does involve a mutual, symmetrical relation of interdependence after all. This point may also be put in terms of Pareto optimality. When persons are taxed to provide welfare, they are not made worse off because they are compensated through the social peace they acquire thereby. So, while the welfare recipients are made better off, no one is made worse off.

This argument depicts humans as being in sharply adversarial relations to one another, with force or the threat of force and intense rivalry over resources as dominant features of human relations. Welfare policy, according to this argument, is for its recipients a kind of adaptive mechanism whereby their implicit militant strengths are brought to bear on the rest of society to assure their survival.

Nevertheless, the argument is not satisfactory. It amounts to saying that welfare recipients hold the rest of the society hostage for their good behavior. While there may indeed be situations in which rebellion, violence, or at least civil disobedience is justified, the abstention from violence cannot legitimately be adduced as a regular, normal "commodity" or "emolument" which one class in society provides for others. On the contrary, peacefulness, law-observance, and civility are goods which all persons owe to one another except in societies (like Nazi Germany) that are so pathological in their hateful oppression of some of their members and their rejection of democratic methods that only defiance and revolt are justified. So this argument to prove the nondependence of welfare recipients is unacceptable. Nevertheless, it calls attention to the need for alleviating the conditions that make for welfare recipience.

The argument from nonrebellion is also unsatisfactory for the further reason that, taken in its own terms as threatening richer persons' self-interest, it can be countered by hiring more police, building more prisons, and geographically isolating the welfare recipients in hermetically sealed

18. See Patricia Roberts Harris, "Comment on the Rightful Limits of Freedom," in Eugene V. Rostow, *Is Law Dead?* (New York: Simon and Schuster, 1971), pp. 103–9; Robert M. Fogelson, *Violence as Protest* (Garden City, N.Y.: Doubleday, 1971); Frances Fox Piven and Richard A. Cloward, *Regulating the Poor* (New York: Pantheon Books, 1971).

ghettoes. That these expedients already exist to some extent shows, at least, the incongruence of arguments based solely on richer persons' self-interest and the moral appeal to mutuality.

There is another, sounder reply to the charge that welfare recipience is asymmetrical or unilateral. Welfare recipients do give something good in return; for by using welfare to sustain themselves and their children, they enable the whole society to have more healthy and happy persons than would otherwise be the case. Indeed, the point can be put more directly, without envisaging the health or happiness of welfare recipients as mere means toward the good of society. For on the Kantian view that each human being has value or worth in her own right and should be treated as an end, not merely as a means, the giving of welfare helps to sustain this intrinsic value, and by this very fact the welfare recipient, by being sustained and thus sustaining herself, gives something good in return.

It may still be replied that when welfare enables its recipients to take care of themselves, and mothers to give care to their children, this does not meet the moral requirement of mutuality. For this requirement is an interpersonal relation. But when welfare recipients benefit themselves, they do not thereby benefit others. The same consideration also applies, *mutatis mutandis,* to the care that mothers give their children; for there is too close an identification between them for this to be regarded as benefiting persons *other than* the recipients.

There is, nonetheless, an important ground for holding that the caretaking function does benefit other persons and indeed the society at large. To understand this thesis in proper perspective, we may counterpose to it an antithesis that focuses not on beneficial consequences but on antecedent causes.

Thesis. Mothers perform a vitally important service not only for their children but also for the whole society as a community of rights. Maternal nurturing is necessary for children's proper development in both physical and mental health. And the rest of society benefits from having a mature, well-developed cohort. So welfare mothers' relation to society is not one of asymmetrical dependence or nonmutuality; on the contrary, they give something of great value to society, and society depends on these mothers as contributing to a healthy, effective population. Consequently, mothers have a right to public compensation in a way similar to the soldier: "To call such a person a 'dependent' is . . . as monstrous as to call the Librarian of Congress a 'dependent.' He is paid for his work, she for hers." [19] To ignore

19. Susan Tiffin, *In Whose Best Interest? Child Welfare Reform in the Progressive Era* (Westport, Conn.: Greenwood Press, 1982), p. 125. See also Wendy Sarvasy, "Reagan and Low-Income Mothers," in Michael K. Brown, ed., *Remaking the Welfare State* (Philadelphia:

this maternal contribution and to regard welfare mothers' dependence as unilateral is to uphold both "the injustice of mothers whose needs for income are defined as dependency, while payments to the unemployed, veterans, or retirees defy such labeling . . . [and] the injustice of a dual antipoverty system in which people who tend machines are more protected than people who tend other people." [20]

Antithesis. It is irresponsible to bring children into the world if one cannot support them. The responsibility for proper support rests with both parents, since it is they who perform the act that generates the need for support. So when mothers go on welfare they are asking society—other persons—to shoulder a burden that is properly theirs and the fathers'. Society does indeed need healthy children, but if the parents cannot promote this health without asking for support from other persons, whatever contribution the parents make to other persons is given at a cost that those others are required to pay without antecedently agreeing to do so, and without making their own judgments about the values or benefits they receive at that cost.[21]

There is merit in both these arguments. The thesis has a strong case for three reasons, all based on the principle of human rights. It emphasizes the mutuality whereby maternal nurturing gives to as well as receives from society. It brings out the crucially important consideration that maternal nurturing helps to develop children's abilities of agency. And it reinforces the general point that persons have a positive human right to be helped when they cannot attain basic well-being by their own efforts—a right that is not contingent on the optional agreements of other persons.

But the antithesis also has an important point. In view of the squalor and crime amid which so many welfare recipients have to live because of inadequate governmental provision (including inadequate public schools and hence low levels of education), it is not surprising that in so many cases the children of welfare mothers exhibit pathological conditions of delinquency, such as crime, drug dependence, teenage pregnancy, or failure in

---

Temple University Press, 1988), pp. 254, 269–71; "With the issue of dependence, we see that the state and some men are actually dependent on women to provide essential services for them" (p. 271).

20. Deanna Bonner, "Women, Work, and Poverty: Exit from an Ancient Trap by the Redefinition of Work," in David A. Gil and Emma A. Gil, eds., *The Future of Work* (Cambridge, Mass.: Schenkman, 1987), p. 83. See also Marilyn Power, "From Home Production to Wage Labor: Women as a Reserve Army of Labor," *Review of Radical Political Economics* 15 (1983): 71–91.

21. See Mead, *Beyond Entitlement*, p. 244. See also Alan Donagan, *The Theory of Morality* (Chicago: University of Chicago Press, 1977), p. 101; and Jencks, *Rethinking Social Policy*, pp. 21, 189–90, 229.

school, instead of development of abilities of agency. Moreover, the thesis does not apply to males, whether fathers or not, who receive certain forms of nonwork related welfare. The antithesis calls attention to the need for changing the conditions that give rise to the need for welfare.[22]

4.4. ORGANICIST RELATIONS AND WELFARE RECIPIENCE

The issue of the contributions made by welfare recipients raises ontological questions about the broader nature and context of human relationships and society. It will be helpful to go into these issues here, albeit briefly, because, although they go beyond the specific problems of welfare, they call attention to the underlying assumptions, metaphysical as well as moral, that must be taken account of if the morally justified policies concerning welfare are to be clearly understood (see also 2.5).

On a certain extreme organicist position, we are all parts of one another in the way that my heart or my liver is a part of the whole organism which is myself or my body, so that the good of any one part is constitutive of the good of the whole.[23] Hence, welfare recipients, in sustaining the intrinsic value that they directly embody in themselves, would also be doing good for the whole social organism and thus for all the other persons who constitute that organism.

It is important to distinguish between such an extreme organicist position whereby each person has value only as a part of the whole and the more moderate position of ethical individualism whereby each person, as a prospective purposive agent, has worth and dignity in her own right and not merely as a part of some greater whole, while at the same time there are institutional provisions for mutual support where needed. The former position, which can perhaps be assimilated to some of the extreme versions of the "constitutiveness" thesis upheld by communitarians (3.6), not only has obvious totalitarian dangers; it is also much more difficult to sustain on the basis of objective ethical argument.

The organicist doctrine is much more plausible when it is confined to more restricted human relations, such as marriage and the family. Here the members do indeed view themselves as parts of one another; this derives from the deep intimacy and mutual support that constitute the purposes

22. See Jencks, *Rethinking Social Policy,* pp. 181–203. For some qualifications about the subsequent careers of teenage mothers, see Katz, *Undeserving Poor,* pp. 221–23.

23. This position (which can be traced back at least to Plato and forward in important respects to Hegel) was developed by medieval political thinkers as the idea of mankind as a "mystical body." See Otto von Gierke, *Political Theories of the Middle Age,* trans. F. W. Maitland (Cambridge: Cambridge University Press, 1900), pp. 22–30. This was usually given a strongly hierarchical, inegalitarian interpretation.

for which they enter into marriage: and, as we have seen, it provides the paradigm for a certain conception of community (3.4). Even in the family, however, there remains the need for each member's personal integrity and indeed rights. This is indicated by the consideration that even in an ideal marriage concepts like "not being taken advantage of," "being respected for oneself," and "being treated fairly" have a place, at least dispositionally and implicitly even if not occurrently and explicitly. In such familial relationships, to benefit one member is also to benefit the others. A related pattern of beneficence can be found in what Titmuss called "spontaneously altruistic" transactions, "acts of 'voluntaryism' which carry with them no wish for return acts or return gifts." [24] Examples are not only Titmuss's own discussion of the "gift relationship" involved in the free unpaid giving of blood but also the heroic Christian Poles, Germans, and others who risked their lives to protect Jews from the Nazis during World War II. Such relationships are unilateral, but the focus of this unilateralness is on the giving side, not the receiving side, unlike the case of welfare dependence. Even in such cases, however, a principled relation of mutuality can be discerned insofar as the recipients recognize that they should have acted similarly had they been in the position of the agents.

A society organized around such spontaneous generosity and altruism corresponds closely to one of the chief kinds of "community" upheld by critics of individualism. It would be a very different society from one dominated by the limited generosity that Hume called one of the two leading circumstances of justice.[25] There are at least two reasons, however, for not using such an altruistic conception to exempt welfare dependence from the criticism that it departs from mutuality (see also 2.6). First, we must distinguish between crisis situations where human life is directly at stake and the more protracted kinds of situations that bear primarily on alternative institutional arrangements. The former situations call for immediate actions with no regard for mutuality or reciprocity except in the general background sense that recipients of rescue actions must be prepared to act likewise if reverse conditions obtain. The welfare situation is usually not of this kind; hence there is a legitimate basis for contrasting it with certain aspects of mutuality.

A second reason concerns empirical applicability. There is no need to invoke the untenable position that all human motivation is exclusively self-interested or to ignore the ways in which social policies can influence atti-

24. Richard Titmuss, *The Gift Relationship* (New York: Vintage Books, 1972), p. 215.
25. David Hume, *Treatise of Human Nature*, 3.2.2, ed. L. A. Selby-Bigge (Oxford: Clarendon Press, 1928), pp. 486–88, and *Enquiry Concerning the Principles of Morals*, sec. 3, pt. 1, ed. L. A. Selby-Bigge, 2d ed. (Oxford: Clarendon Press, 1962), pp. 184–88.

tudes and motivations. But since welfare dependence occurs in a world not characterized by spontaneous and universal generosity, to interpret such dependence by the standards of a very different world would remove the interpretation from the context that is directly and descriptively relevant to it. These standards also depart from the mutuality upheld by the reasonable self (3.6). None of this is meant to ignore that individual human motivations can have important social causes. Societies constructed around spontaneous gift-giving or heroic acts of self-sacrifice generate quite different motivations from those that are more self-centered. But by taking the more limited kinds of motivations as our starting point, we can make our conclusions relevant to a wider range of social contexts and have them carry conviction with those persons and groups who are not initially wedded to the social character of the conclusions (see also 1.2).

4.5. WORKFARE AND ITS PROBLEMS

We have now filled in the elements noted above of the morally paradoxical character of the welfare system: that the system is morally justified as fulfilling human rights, while it both rests on and maintains morally unjustified conditions of dependence and nonmutuality. The principle of human rights requires that welfare dependents be supported, but it requires also that strenuous efforts be made to remove the morally unjustified conditions that generate the need for such dependence. In keeping with these efforts, the community of rights follows two interrelated lines of policy. One line concentrates largely on individuals: their lack of autonomy and mutuality is to be rectified by developing their capacities for productive agency, including their ability to effectively implement their sense of personal responsibility. Through such development they can participate actively in the production process, paying their own way and thereby controlling their own destinies (chaps. 4 and 5). The other line concentrates on the larger economic structure with its related political institutions: a system of full employment is to be established so that all persons can work with adequate pay at jobs appropriate to their abilities of productive agency, and a system of economic democracy is to be maintained both within and between firms (chaps. 6 and 7).

Each of these lines of policy reflects the mutuality required by the principle of human rights, whereby persons have duties to help fulfill one another's needs of agency insofar as they cannot fulfill them by their own efforts. Each line of policy requires some interference with the free market system: poor persons, with their lack of effective demand, are not left to bid for their productive development on the open market; and the guarantee of full employment is not made contingent on the job offers of employers who seek to maximize their profits. Nevertheless, within the parameters set by these lines of policy, market relations are maintained. Each line of policy is organized and subsidized by the state as a community of rights. For the state, in seeking to fulfill for each person the rights to productive agency and employment, thereby protects for each person his or her fundamental interests in freedom and well-being. So here again rights and community support one another.

Let us first deal with the line of policy that concentrates on individuals. Here a salient initial point is that they often lack the work skills that would enable them to fill jobs whereby they could earn sufficient income to support themselves. It is indeed true that some welfare recipients work to supplement their welfare allotments. The percentages at various times range from one-third to one-sixth.[26] The work, however, is unstable and, even with welfare, usually insufficient to cover basic needs.

I now wish to examine the proposals for what has come to be called "workfare." The avowed aim of these proposals is to remove the dependence relation of welfare recipience, so that to this extent they would institute the autonomy conditions of agency and the mutuality upheld by the principle of human rights. Most directly, according to workfare, welfare recipients would be required to work in return for their allotments. There has also been proposed a "new style" for workfare whereby it would include, in addition to the work requirement, "a variety of employment and training services and activities: job search, job training, education programs, and also community work experience." [27]

These proposals point in the right direction. But they also incur serious problems, both factual and moral, which show that they require supplementation in at least four ways. The first concerns the psychological conditions needed for participating in such programs. Many welfare recipients come from a background in which the debilitating effects of poverty have already left a heavy mark. It is hence naive to expect that these persons will directly have the emotional and intellectual abilities, including relevant

---

26.   See Mildred Rein, *Work or Welfare?* (New York: Praeger, 1974), pp. 26–30; Jencks, *Rethinking Social Policy*, p. 167.

27.   Katz, *Undeserving Poor*, p. 226. See also Family Support Act of 1988, U.S. Congress, Public Law 100-485; Richard Nathan, "Will the Underclass Always Be with Us?" *Society* 24 (Mar.–Apr. 1987): 57–62. On workfare more generally, see Katz, *Undeserving Poor*, pp. 223–35; Wilson, *Truly Disadvantaged*, pp. 159–63; Mead, *Beyond Entitlement*, pp. 104 ff. There has been considerable change since the Special Task Force to the Secretary of Health, Education, and Welfare wrote in 1971: "It is not even clear that anyone other than the mother has the legal or moral right to make that decision [i.e., whether or not to "take a job"], or that anyone other than the mother can make the decision that is best for her and her children" (*Work in America: Report of a Special Task Force to the Secretary of Health, Education, and Welfare* [Cambridge, Mass.: MIT Press, 1973], p. 177).

skills and an effective sense of personal responsibility, needed to take adequate advantage of the opportunities they may be offered. In this regard, it is vitally important to seek out their children at a very early age and to put them into educational programs in which these debilitating effects can be strongly countered. The Head Start program is a valuable example of such early intervention (4.10).

Second, the need for child care raises an especially pressing problem. If adequate child care is not available except at a prohibitive price, this removes much of the incentive and justification for a work requirement for welfare mothers. It has been contended, in opposition to this, that since many nonwelfare mothers work, this weakens the argument for welfare mothers' not working: "As more and more non-welfare mothers entered the labor force, it became clear that allowing women on welfare to stay at home would violate the principle of equity." [28] This "violation" could be mitigated by the idea that for some nonwelfare mothers working is a matter of their individual choice; hence such choice should also be open to welfare mothers. But the situation is altered where work is necessitated by economic need. In any case, there is far greater justification for an arrangement whereby welfare mothers would "combine part-time employment with care for children, as many more privileged American mothers still do." [29] This would again require extensive support by the state as a community of rights.

A third problem concerns the spirit in which work is offered. As workfare has actually been designed and developed, it has been charged, with considerable justification, with exhibiting an unfortunate kind of "moral ambiguity." For it seeks to combine two mutually incompatible objectives. One objective is deterrent and indeed punitive: by making receipt of welfare conditional on welfare recipients' working at jobs that are onerous, stigmatized, and unpaid or very low-paid, they "will be deterred from choosing welfare over work." The other objective is educative: to teach work skills and proper work attitudes and to inculcate self-esteem. These objectives are incompatible because the former functions, and is intended to function, so as to grind down the workers, to make them detest work, to regard it as punishment, not as reward.[30]

28. Mildred Rein, *Dilemmas of Welfare Policy: Why Work Strategies Haven't Worked* (New York: Praeger, 1982), p. 7. See also Murray, *Losing Ground*, p. 231; Mead, *Beyond Entitlement*, p. 74; Jencks, *Rethinking Social Policy*, p. 229.

29. Theda Skocpol and William Julius Wilson, "Welfare As We Need It," *New York Times*, Feb. 9, 1994, national edition, p. A15.

30. See Handler and Hasenfeld, *The Moral Construction of Poverty*, pp. 38, 197–200. See also Mary E. Hawkesworth, "Workfare and the Imposition of Discipline," *Social Theory and Practice* 11, no. 2 (summer 1985): 163–81.

To deal with this conflict of objectives it is important to recur to the principle of human rights. This principle requires, especially in its components of nonsubtractive and additive well-being, that the self-esteem of persons, as well as their development of a sense of personal responsibility, not be attacked by subjecting them to insults or to a general atmosphere of disparagement. Whatever be the handicaps with which they enter the work situation, workfare to be justified requires, on the part of those who offer and control it, an attitude of support, cooperation, and respect, such as is required by the positive human rights in general.

A fourth problem, which is directly continuous with the third, concerns the nature of the work that is offered. When it is held that welfare recipients should work in return for their benefits, there is often assumed a certain idealized conception of work. Indeed, it must be acknowledged that work often generates an important kind of self-esteem and indeed self-respect because of the mutuality it embodies. But it must also be recognized that, amid the vast variety of kinds of work, there are two broad modes of work that are at extreme opposites to one another. One mode may be called "depressive," the other "creative." The work offered to welfare recipients is almost always of the former sort. I shall here characterize them in words largely taken from Marx; for the passage of over a century has not altered their defining features.

Depressive work is toil, drudgery, stressful, and deadening. Marx called this mode of work a "curse, a negation of tranquillity," whereby one sacrifices one's freedom and leisure in order to obtain commodities.[31] Such work is "done out of necessity." "Its alien character emerges clearly in the fact that as soon as no physical or other compulsion exists it is avoided like the plague." [32] And as to the process of work, the worker has "little choice about how and when the work is done." [33] His work procedures are dictated to him by others: managers, supervisors, efficiency experts, so that his work situation is characterized by powerlessness and loss of initiative and autonomy.[34]

At the opposite extreme from this depressive mode of work is what may be called a creative mode. One reason for this terminology is that in

31. Karl Marx, *Grundrisse,* trans. M. Nicolaus (Harmondsworth, England: Penguin, 1973), pp. 610–16.

32. Karl Marx, *Economic and Philosophic Manuscripts of 1844,* in Robert C. Tucker, ed., *The Marx-Engels Reader,* 2d ed. (New York: W. W. Norton, 1978), p. 74.

33. Gregory Pence, "Towards a Theory of Work," *Philosophical Forum* 10, nos. 2–4 (1978–79): 307.

34. See Robert Blauner, *Alienation and Freedom: The Factory Worker and His Industry* (Chicago: University of Chicago Press, 1964); Harry Braverman, *Labor and Monopoly Capital* (New York: Monthly Review Press, 1974).

this mode of work the emphasis often falls on its valuable product, as in "work of art" or "master work," rather than on the arduous process. But the process of work itself is also very different from the depressive mode. In the creative mode work is not only instrumental to the fulfillment of needs but is itself a need, for in its overcoming of obstacles it is "a liberating activity," a "positive, creative activity," so that it is intrinsically satisfying to the worker. Such work makes use of persons' higher mental faculties; it is taken on freely and gladly and the worker has a justified sense of personal responsibility and achievement, for it is a form of "self-realization." Important aspects of this mode are emphasized by Marx's graphic statement that "Milton produced *Paradise Lost* as a silkworm produces silk, as the activation of his own nature." [35]

While work as actually undergone by most persons exhibits a wide diversity between these two extremes, there is abundant evidence that for most workers in America it is far closer to the depressive extreme than to the creative one.[36] The principle of human rights requires that welfare recipients as well as all other persons be given realistic hope that they can develop their abilities of productive agency so that they are not forced to work at the lowest levels of their competence, but are instead enabled to come as close as their latent abilities permit to the creative mode of work. This provides a way to move from the deterrent and punitive objectives of workfare to the educative objective. In the transitional stages, however, the self-esteem that comes from mutuality of participation in income-generating work can also provide a valuable incentive. More generally, as we shall see in chapter 7, various aspects of economic democracy can help to ameliorate the deficiencies of depressive work and thereby help to support the workers' dignity.

4.6. PRODUCTIVE AGENCY AND PRODUCTIVIST WELFARISM

The point we have now reached is that the state as the community of rights is to relieve the morally wrong condition of poverty, with its related welfare

---

35. Karl Marx, *Results of the Immediate Process of Production*, in Marx, *Capital*, vol. 1, trans. Ben Fowkes (New York: Vintage Books, 1977), p. 1044. Cf. Frank H. Knight, *The Ethics of Competition* (London: Allen and Unwin, 1935), p. 59: "participation in economic activity as a sphere of self-expression and individual achievement."

36. See, e.g., *Work in America*, pp. 30 ff.; chaps. 2–3. See also Studs Terkel, *Working* (New York: Pantheon Books, 1972); Blauner, *Alienation and Freedom*. For a recent version of the distinction between depressive and creative work, see Robert B. Reich's classification of "three broad categories of work" : "routine production services, in-person services, and symbolic-analytic services" (*The Work of Nations* [New York: Alfred A. Knopf, 1991], pp. 174–80).

dependence, by enabling persons to develop their abilities of productive agency. Viewed from within the specific context of our discussion so far, productive agency consists in having the abilities needed for earning income so that one becomes relatively autonomous or self-sufficient with regard to well-being. Thereby one does not have to depend on welfare recipience with its nonmutuality and lack of autonomy. Insofar as all persons have rights to autonomy and to relations of mutuality, they also have a positive right to the development of their productive agency, especially when they cannot develop it by their own efforts. The state as the community of rights, through its provisions for education and training, contributes importantly to this development, so that here again rights and community support one another.

For a better understanding of the complex concept of the "productive," we must view it from a somewhat broader analytical and historical perspective. Let us begin with the relation between action and production.[37] Action has been defined here as voluntary and purposive behavior, that is, as behavior that the agent controls by her unforced choice while having knowledge of relevant circumstances with a view to achieving some outcome she desires or intends. This outcome may consist either in emitting the behavior itself or in something that results from the behavior. Agency is the proximate capacity to engage in action as thus defined.

What, then, is productive agency? At a minimum, it is the agent's ability to achieve the outcome he desires or intends, and a productive agent is one who does thus achieve. So we may say of a weight lifter, for example, that his actions or efforts were productive if he succeeded in lifting the weight he was trying to lift. In this respect "productive" is synonymous with the additiveness referred to earlier in the phrases "additive goods" and "additive well-being" (1.4). For additive goods as viewed by an agent consist in his achieving the purposes for which he acts, and additive well-being consists in one's having the general abilities and conditions needed for such achievement. By additive well-being, then, one increases one's capabilities for purposive action and one's general level of purpose-fulfillment. To be a productive agent is to maintain such additive well-being in one's actions, that is, to achieve one's purposes. Productive agency is the continuing proximate capacity or disposition for being a productive agent.

---

37. Aristotle distinguished between action (*praxis*) and production (*poiēsis*) on the ground that production has an end other than itself while action (or at least good action, *eupraxia*) is its own end (*Nicomachean Ethics* 6.4.1140b4–5). This distinction is not apposite for present purposes because "action" is used here in a broader sense as encompassing all voluntary and purposive behaviors, including "productive" ones, that are the objects of both moral and other practical precepts, including technical and artistic precepts. See *RM*, 25–30, 346–47.

Thus, just as for every agent her purposes seem to her to be good (according to whatever criterion enters into her actions), so for every agent productive agency, in the general sense just defined, is itself a necessary good. And all persons have positive rights to the development of such general productive agency as part of their generic rights to both freedom and well-being.

For most persons this development requires, as a necessary if not sufficient condition, that they have, or be able to acquire, wealth or income sufficient at least for protecting their freedom and well-being. And again for most persons, as a matter of empirical fact they have to acquire wealth or income through their own work. Thus in the economically relevant sense, it is in the ability for such acquisition that productive agency consists. So, for a reason continuous with that just given, all persons have positive rights to the development of their productive agency in this further, economic sense.

In this economic sense (as against the general achievemental sense just discussed), the concept of productive agency has three additional components which also serve to define a general concept of work or labor. (a) What is produced must not consist simply in one's own purpose-fulfillment; in addition, these purposes must be embodied in products, services, or objects of some kind that are external to the agent, at least in some form that is observed or experienced by other persons. (b) The products must be valued by other persons; they must be use-values for other persons. (c) The use-values must also be exchange-values, in that they are effectively demanded by other persons who are willing and able to pay for them. In this way, by working to produce exchange-values, productive agents obtain income, so that they acquire the means to be productive agents in the first, general purpose-fulfilling sense distinguished above. But since additive well-being presupposes basic well-being, income also serves the more elemental purposes of having food, clothing, shelter, and of fulfilling other basic needs. And by earning such income persons escape the need to receive welfare and achieve a measure of autonomy, including an effective sense of personal responsibility. Although there is also a general concept of work or productive agency that consists solely in the first of the three components just distinguished (including purpose-fulfillments that may be solely personal), the relation of work to the earning of income is crucial to the problem of welfare dependence. It is this additional factor that converts work into employment, whether one is self-employed or employed by others. But the third component of work listed above, exchange value, also serves to emphasize in another way the vital contribution made by the social context. If there is no demand for one's products, then the work one does is ineffective from the standpoint of economic productive agency, and effective mutuality is not achieved. This fact sets an important limit to what can be accomplished by the right to productive agency, including the extent to which what one earns by one's work can be attributed solely to oneself. As we shall see, there is a right to employment that serves to counter this factor (chap. 6).

Like action in general, work is the expenditure of effort for some end or purpose preconceived and aimed at by the worker. Indeed, so close is the connection between action and work that some thinkers have tended nearly to equate them. Thus Veblen tried to derive the "instinct of workmanship" directly from the very nature of human agency:

> As a matter of selective necessity, man is an agent. He is, in his own apprehension, a center of unfolding impulsive activity—"teleological" activity. He is an agent seeking in every act the accomplishment of some concrete, objective, impersonal end. By force of his being such an agent he is possessed of a taste for effective work, and a distaste for futile effort. He has a sense of the merit of serviceability or efficiency and of the demerit of futility, waste, or incapacity. This aptitude or proximity may be called the instinct of workmanship.[38]

Despite Veblen's glowing testimonial, there are at least two potential differences between action and work. Unlike action in the strict sense, the worker may not control his behavior by his unforced choice; his choice to do the work may in various ways be forced. And action may not result in an externally observed product; for example, an agent may run in some secluded woods for pleasure. Intellectual work may come close to this internalist description, although it may also eventuate in some written product.

For the development of productive agency in the economic sense, however, work requires abilities and opportunities for earning income. The right of all persons to be assisted in such development has an important consequence for the welfare system. It entails a normative thesis which I shall call *productivist welfarism*.[39] This thesis is a direct consequence of the

38. Thorstein Veblen, *The Theory of the Leisure Class* (New York: New American Library, 1953), p. 29. See the comments on this passage in Ernest Gellner, *Plough, Sword, and Book* (London: Collins Harvill, 1988), pp. 29–31. See the complementary thesis of Ludwig von Mises that the entrepreneurial function "is inherent in every action. . . . The term entrepreneur as used by catallactic theory means: acting man exclusively seen from the aspect of the uncertainty inherent in every action" (*Human Action: A Treatise on Economics*, 3d rev. ed. (Chicago: Henry Regnery, 1967), p. 256. This thesis is repeated in Israel Kirzner, *Competition and Entrepreneurship* (Chicago: University of Chicago Press, 1973), pp. 86–87.

39. I here use "welfarism" in a sense directly related to the welfare system discussed above. This is different from the sense used by Amartya Sen, "Utilitarianism and Welfarism," *Journal of Philosophy* 76 (1979): 463–89, where "welfarism" is the thesis that the goodness of a state of affairs is determined by the sum of the individual utilities in that state. See also the discussion of "political welfarism" in Joseph Raz, *The Morality of Freedom* (Oxford: Clarendon Press, 1986), pp. 137–45.

right to well-being as specified by the PGC as the principle of human rights. Most normative theories of distributive justice involve dependence and passive welfarism. Their primary concern is with persons as dependent recipients of money or economic goods that are produced by other persons. In contrast, productivist welfarism focuses directly not on distributing products but rather on distributing or fostering personal productive abilities or resources. It involves helping persons to develop their own capacities for producing goods or commodities, including their own effective sense of personal responsibility, so that they can then dispense with help from others to secure their basic well-being. Such productivist welfarism is directly connected with the PGC's central orientation in the needs of agency. The ultimate purpose of the generic rights, whose equal distribution the PGC requires, is to secure for each person a certain fundamental moral status: that each person have rational autonomy in the sense of being a self-controlling, self-developing agent who can relate to other persons on a basis of mutual respect and cooperation, in contrast to being a passive, dependent recipient of the agency of others. Even when the rights require positive assistance from other persons, their morally justified point is not to reinforce or increase dependence but rather to give support that enables persons to be agents, that is, to control their own lives and effectively pursue and sustain their own purposes and their own sense of personal responsibility without being subjected to domination and harms from others. In this way, agency is both the metaphysical and the moral basis of human dignity. Now, so far as possible, such agency involves, both as end and as means, participation in the productive process, that is, work that produces valued commodities, although, of course, the nature of this value can vary enormously. But it is because of the connection between work and agency, including autonomy, that an emphasis on participation in the productive process is required for economic justice as the rights to freedom and well-being. This applies to economic justice on the international as well as the national level (see above, 2.5).

It is important, then, to reject a purview that assumes a permanent class of welfare dependents (whether domestic or international), with a permanent division between affluent agents and poor, dependent recipients. Instead, the PGC's emphasis on the rights of agency requires that all persons have the necessary conditions of action, including property, and that welfare programs (whether domestic or international) aim at fostering for all persons their acquisition of the conditions and abilities needed for successful agency and hence a cessation of exclusive dependence on others for basic goods. Thus the "welfare state" must aim at abolishing some of the most basic aspects that give it the appellation of "welfare."

Productive agency, in both the general and the economic senses, entails certain personal prudential virtues. Persons who have productive agency as an enduring disposition or capacity have corresponding traits of character, which may be summed up as three of the four traditional cardinal virtues (see *RM*, 242–43). They have courage, which includes fortitude, perseverance, and a sense of personal responsibility in the face of obstacles; they have temperance, controlling their appetites and inclinations judiciously; they have prudence, whereby they can calculate the most efficient means to achieving their ends and can ascertain which of their possible ends are most worth pursuing in light of their overall capacities and deepest aspirations. When, moreover, productive agency is put into the context of the mutuality required by the principle of human rights, it also entails the moral virtue of justice. For the productive agent then acts in accord with the generic rights of his recipients as well as of himself. Their general purposes then become his own both negatively, in that he must refrain from interfering with their freedom and well-being, and positively, in that he must help them to attain these necessary goods when they cannot do so by their own efforts. In this latter regard the productive agent, as a reasonable self (3.6), supports governmental measures that aim to help deprived persons to attain their own abilities and conditions of productive agency through the policy of productivist welfarism.

4.7. HUMAN CAPITAL AS A FORM OF PRODUCTIVE AGENCY

It will be helpful to connect the productive agency just discussed with the idea of human capital. There are long-standing disputes about the nature of capital,[40] but capital may be regarded as a kind of second-order wealth, that is, wealth that can be used to produce more wealth; hence, if land is excluded, capital is "produced means of production." [41] Human capital then consists in skills and abilities that have economic value because of their use in income-yielding activities. Such skills and abilities are means of production, and they are "produced" in that they have resulted from investments in education, health, and other conditions of successful agency.[42]

In an important respect, then, human capital is identical with what I

---

40. See Mark Blaug, *Economic Theory in Retrospect*, 3d ed. (Cambridge: Cambridge University Press, 1978), chap. 12.

41. This is E. Böhm-Bawerk's definition; see Joseph Schumpeter, *History of Economic Analysis* (New York: Oxford University Press, 1954), p. 630.

42. See Theodore W. Schultz, "Investment in Human Capital," *American Economic Review* 51 (Mar. 1961): 3; Schultz, *The Economic Value of Education* (New York: Columbia University Press, 1963), pp. 10, 64; Schultz, *Transforming Traditional Agriculture* (Chicago: University of Chicago Press, 1983), p. 175.

have called productive agency. Nevertheless, they can be distinguished in several ways. As we saw above (4.6), productive agency in the general sense need not be confined to narrowly economic abilities; it can also be applied to a broader range of skills and aptitudes that help persons to attain other values, moral, intellectual, aesthetic, and prudential, that reflect the wide range of purposes pursued by actual and prospective agents. In this respect, productive agency is more inclusive within what I have called additive well-being. On the other side, the fact that human capital, as capital, is itself produced serves to call attention to the various means or instrumentalities, including especially education, that can be used to develop human productive abilities. I shall return to this in a following section.

Although the concept of human capital has now come to be widely recognized by economists, this very fact can help to bring out certain distinctive features of the concept as used here, features that derive from its place within a moral theory grounded in the principle of human rights. First, despite its orientation to increased productivity, human capital as viewed here is primarily the possession of the individual agent and is oriented to her benefit. It consists in her having skills and knowledge that enable her to improve her purposive actions on the economic side; it thus enables her to be a more effective and autonomous agent. This is in accord with the ethical individualism of the principle of human rights (3.7). Second, because human capital is oriented toward increasing one's levels of purpose-fulfillment and one's economic capabilities, it is a dynamic notion as part of a person's economic biography. It involves the idea of the agent's self-improvement, his development of certain personal virtues and sense of personal responsibility with a view to being able to participate more effectively in the productive process. But as before, the primary focus is on helping the agent to develop his capabilities for purpose-fulfilling action. Third, through the development of one's human capital one is enabled to contribute to fulfilling other persons' needs and wants and thereby to maintain moral relations of mutuality. In this way one can participate actively in the community of rights.

Since every agent has rights to freedom and well-being, she has rights to the development of her human capital. In the first instance, these rights are negative, in that their correlative duties require that this development not be interfered with through restrictions or discriminatory policies, including obscurantist repression of educational achievement. The rights are also positive, however, although in varying ways. Children have a right to education in the positive sense that they must be helped to develop basic intellectual skills as well as related physical and emotional dispositions (4.9, 10). Other persons have rights to be helped to develop their human capital insofar as they cannot do so by their own efforts, although certain distinctions must be observed here. Persons who are poorly educated or mentally or physically handicapped have positive rights to be helped to overcome these deficiencies through the development of their human capital. But parallel help for developing human capital is owed to such workers as physicians, farmers, teachers, architects, carpenters, and others whose skills are needed to protect persons' basic and additive rights to health, food, shelter, and other basic goods. But this help must be fitted into a context where the workers in question also take personal responsibility for developing their own abilities. In these cases, the positive rights belong to the workers not only for their own sakes but also because they are mutually instrumental to protecting or promoting the rights of other persons within the community of rights. But more generally when the welfare state helps persons to develop their human capital, this helps both to promote autonomy and to reduce economic inequality.[43]

The idea of human capital has been criticized on both empirical and moral grounds. The moral criticisms, however, are largely based on a utilitarian interpretation of human capital in terms of economic growth rather than an interpretation in terms of individual rights.[44] Thus one objection has been that it is demeaning to human dignity to regard persons as mere means of production; this is to put them on a par with machines and other inanimate instruments, and it overlooks that humans are the ends for which society, including the productive process, exists. The objection continues that to use and evaluate human labor from the standpoint of its efficiency in the productive sphere is to encourage all the dehumanizing excesses of Frederick Taylor's atomization and depersonalization of the labor process.[45] The objection culminates in the observation that the human capital concept has also been applied to slaves in the American South.[46] In a related way, Marx held that because the "material elements of the labor

43.   See Julian LeGrand, "Markets, Equality, and Welfare," in LeGrand and Saul Estrin, eds., *Market Socialism* (Oxford: Clarendon Press, 1989), pp. 207–8.

44.   The utilitarian emphasis as it applies in the United States is prominent in David W. Hornbeck and Lester M. Salamon, eds., *Human Capital and America's Future* (Baltimore: Johns Hopkins University Press, 1991). See also Theodore W. Schultz, "Reflections on Investment in Man," *Journal of Political Economy* 70, no. 5, pt. 2, suppl. (1962): 3: "In these reflections I shall restrict myself mainly to the role that investments in man play in economic growth."

45.   See Neil W. Chamberlain, "Some Second Thoughts on the Concept of Human Capital," in Ronald W. Wykstra, ed., *Human Capital Formation and Manpower Development* (New York: Free Press, 1971), pp. 205–15. See, however, Schultz, "Investment in Human Capital," p. 2.

46.   R. W. Fogel and Stanley Engerman, *Time on the Cross: The Economics of Negro Slavery* (Boston: Little, Brown, 1974), pp. 147, 232–34. See also Gary S. Becker, *Human Capital*, 2d ed. (Chicago: University of Chicago Press, 1980), pp. 7–8.

process have been purchased by the capitalist, they represent his capital" ;[47] thus human capital consists in labor that is owned by the capitalist and used for maximizing his profits. On this ground Marxists have also held that, by making labor part of capital, "'labor' disappears as a fundamental explanatory category and is absorbed into a concept of capital in no way enriched to handle labor's special character." [48] A related objection is that investment in human capital, especially in the sphere of education, is made with a view to efficiency by obtaining the maximum rate of return, and this may result in extending and reinforcing existing social and economic inequities. For example, it may lead to reducing or eliminating money investments in education for blacks as against whites, or for women as against men, or for the handicapped as against the physically whole, and so forth.[49]

An underlying assumption of these moral objections is that the human capital concept involves a cost-benefit calculus whereby all values are estimated in pecuniary terms. Since the aim of investing in human capital is to increase productivity, it follows that education itself is evaluated only for its monetary output, and this tends to downgrade forms of education that are "merely" cultural or that are for the sake of "consumption" rather than "investment." [50]

For the most part, these objections result from viewing the human capital concept in a utilitarian framework. For that framework is primarily aggregative, not distributive; it focuses on maximizing productivity or economic growth for a whole society, not on the rights and interests of each individual severally. But when human capital is interpreted primarily in terms of individual rights and ethical individualism, the picture is different. For on this interpretation, each individual is the owner of his own human capital, and he uses it in the first instance for his own sake, not merely as a means of producing a maximum which does not belong to him, let alone producing it solely for the expansion of capital. Hence he also controls his use of human capital, so that he is not a Taylorian machine, let alone a slave. For this reason, also, he is not subject to an efficiency calculus whereby investment in his education or his health, for example, is determined by comparing its rate of return with alternative uses of available

47. Marx, *Results of the Immediate Process of Production*, p. 996.

48. Samuel Bowles and Herbert Gintis, "The Problem with Human Capital—A Marxian Critique," *American Economic Review* 65, no. 2 (May 1975): 74.

49. See Henry W. Shaffer, "Investment in Human Capital: A Comment," *American Economic Review* 51 (Nov. 1961): 1031.

50. See Chamberlain, "Second Thoughts," p. 210; Thomas Balogh and Paul P. Streeten, "The Coefficient of Ignorance," in Wykstra, *Human Capital Formation*, pp. 197–201; Michael W. Apple, *Official Knowledge* (New York: Routledge, 1993), p. 101.

funds. To be sure, the application of human capital in the productive process involves the mutuality whereby persons provide exchange values for
one another and fulfill their obligations to society (3.4). This double emphasis reflects the PGC's requirement that each agent act in accord with his
recipient's generic rights as well as his own (1.5). These interpersonal aspects will be taken up in the next section. But in the context of human rights
with its ethical individualism, the initial emphasis falls on each person's
possession, development, and use of her own abilities of productive agency.
In this respect, it is an important form of self-ownership (5.4).

Although pecuniary criteria are indeed prominent and perhaps even
central in the idea of human capital, as it is in the economic concept of productive agency, this is mitigated not only by the fact that the money in question belongs in the first instance to the individual worker but also that,
because she has autonomy as controlling her own human capital, she can
help to determine the extent to which her education, especially at higher
levels, will comprise noneconomic as well as economic factors. More generally, the subsumption of human capital under additive well-being entails
that pecuniary criteria are to be limited by, and ancillary to, the broader
values comprised within the whole range of purpose-fulfilling capabilities.

In opposition to this individual-distributive interpretation of human
capital, it may be contended that the aggregative interpretation cannot be
evaded. For even if human capital belongs to the individual worker, unless
he is self-employed his participation in the productive processes will depend on his being hired by an employer, who in turn is concerned to maximize his profits. For this maximization to occur, the worker's marginal
product must be equal to his price, that is, the wage or salary he gets for his
work. But since the worker's human capital is reflected in his marginal
product and hence in what he earns, it follows that human capital as it operates in the productive process will usually not be able to escape the aggregative, maximizing criterion.

The answer to this objection is that we must avoid confusing two possible meanings of "human capital": (a) human skills and labor that operate as capital, and (b) human skills and labor that belong to and are used in
the interest of the capitalist.[51] Thus a distinction must be drawn between
the criteria of the employer or entrepreneur and the criteria of the worker
with his human capital. Even if the entrepreneur views his workers' human
capital only in terms of maximizing his profits, and even if, in the macroeconomic sphere, human capital is viewed only as a means of fostering economic growth, it does not follow that the individual worker must also view

---

51. Cf. Karl Marx, *Capital*, vol. 1, chap. 14, sec. 5 (New York: International Publishers,
1967), p. 360.

his human capital in the same way. Instead, he may view it as a means to, or as a component of, his overall freedom and well-being. He may indeed be concerned to maximize his well-being; but since this has many components besides narrowly economic or pecuniary ones, the role of his human capital is correspondingly diversified.

None of this is meant to deny that government should be concerned to invest in human capital for the sake of economic growth. But such growth is valuable, in final analysis, because of the contribution it can make to the well-being of individuals and especially, through the deprivation focus, of those individuals who cannot maintain their basic well-being by their own efforts. In this way the state functions as a community of rights, helping persons to attain autonomy and abilities of productive agency. An indispensable value of the human capital concept is that it provides for many such individuals the capabilities for this self-help, including developing an effective sense of personal responsibility. Economic growth can also assist in moving social structures in more egalitarian directions, but it will do so for the most part only if strenuous efforts are made by governments and organized groups, including especially the workers and those who suffer from economic deprivation. Like other phases of human rights, the interpretation of human capital in terms of individual rights requires for its effectuation a supportive context of appropriate institutions in the community of rights. This is an important field for the social contribution thesis (3.4).

4.8. PRODUCTIVE AND UNPRODUCTIVE LABOR

As we have just seen, human capital is to be interpreted primarily as promoting each individual's development of his own abilities of productive agency. But from the moral standpoint of the principle of human rights, the application of these abilities is rewarded in important part because of the mutual relations whereby producers contribute to the fulfillment of one another's needs and wants—relations epitomized as exchange values. Thus, as we saw above (4.6), in the economic sense of productive agency one not only earns an income by making an input; in so doing one interacts with other purposive agents as buyers of one's output and as pursuers of their own purposes. To be productive is, in some relevant sense, to benefit other persons as well as oneself; it involves mutuality of benefits. So we must consider such further questions about the productive as the following: What is produced? Who produces it—that is, who makes a productive contribution? For whom or for what end is it produced? What is, or should be, the relation between such production and both the producer's income and the recipient's or consumer's benefit? These questions are important for the fuller understanding of the productive agency whose development, as fostered by the community of rights, is an essential part of the economic biography that is being traced here.

Going back at least to the classical economists, these questions have been discussed in terms of a distinction between "productive" and "unproductive" labor.[52] Paradoxically, while the distinction has often been disparaged by economists, and the classicals explicitly separated it from moral concerns, there have been many disputes, continuing down to the present, over who or what is "productive," and these disputes have often had sharply moral overtones. The reason for this is that the distinction between productive and unproductive labor is "a powerful tool of social critique."[53] And the reason for this, in turn, is that, amid the seeming verbal disputes over what is to be called "productive," the debates have revolved around normative assumptions concerning (a) what is genuinely valuable, at least within some given economic system; (b) what contributes to the making or providing of what is thus valuable; and (c) what alone is therefore deserving of income as reward. The labor that is "productive" has been implicitly defined in terms of these three assumptions. So to categorize certain work or activity as "unproductive" is to hold that it is undeserving of rewards and thereby to suggest an important criticism from within a relevant economic context; and at the extreme it has been used to cast doubt on the rightness of a whole economic system. Important questions about mutuality, at least in the economic sphere, thus revolve around the distinction between productive and unproductive labor.

Even on a purely verbal level it is clear that "productive" is often an evaluative term, if not a morally evaluative one. To say that something is "productive" is, if not necessarily to approve of it, at least to indicate that it makes an affirmative contribution to some end or purpose—which returns it to the generic sense of productive purposive action referred to above (4.6). By the same token, to call something "unproductive" is, in some degree, to disparage it. In this distinction the emphasis falls not on how work is experienced by the worker but rather on its outcome, including its relation to the persons who presumably receive or benefit from that outcome. Thus (to use the terminology of chap. 5), although the "productive" is directly an antecedentalist concept, in various of its uses it also has important specific consequentialist implications. In each case, questions of mutuality of contributions are at least implicitly involved.

52. See references in Blaug, *Economic Theory in Retrospect,* index, s.v. "labor," p. 747. See also Sidney H. Koontz, *Productive Labour and Effective Demand* (London: Routledge and Kegan Paul, 1965).

53. Paul Baran, *The Political Economy of Growth* (New York: Monthly Review Press, 1957), p. 31.

For a clearer understanding of these issues, it will be helpful if we look briefly at the discussions by some of the classical economists about the distinction between "productive" and "unproductive" labor. Two aspects of that discussion are especially relevant. One is that they specified what labor is "productive" from within the context of profit-seeking capitalism. Thus Adam Smith gave two different answers to the question of what productive labor produces. On the one hand, he said that labor is productive which "adds to the value of" the object worked on, so that the "master" or employer realizes a profit in this "improved value." Here it is the capitalist recipient of profit generated by labor that is emphasized as the criterion of labor's being productive. On the other hand, Smith said that labor is productive which brings about an enduring material object having exchange value: such labor "fixes and realizes itself in some particular subject or vendible commodity, which lasts for some time at least after that labor is past," so that the commodity "can afterwards, if necessary, put into motion a quantity of labor equal to that which had originally produced it." [54] Thus, what productive labor produces, according to these two respective criteria, is added value for capitalists and material "vendible" objects. These criteria have been called, respectively, the "value version" and the "storage version" of productive labor.[55] In both versions the primary recipient of the product is the employer or capitalist entrepreneur (although in a secondary sense Smith is also thinking of a whole nation's increase in wealth); and those workers are productive who produce these products. Here mutuality figures only in a very attenuated way, since the emphasis falls not on what the capitalist does for the worker or for other persons but on what the worker does for the capitalist.

Marx, while rejecting Smith's second criterion, gave the first an interpretation which emphasized its direct historical connection with the capitalist mode of production: "That laborer alone is productive, who produces a surplus-value for the capitalist, and thus works for the self-expansion of capital. . . . Hence the notion of a productive laborer implies . . . a specific, social relation of production, a relation that has sprung up historically and stamps the laborer as a direct means of creating surplus-value." [56] Here what is produced is surplus value, and the primary recipient is the capitalist. John Stuart Mill, on the other hand, took over Smith's second, "storage" criterion; he understands "by productive labor only those kinds of exertion which produce utilities embodied in material ob-

---

54. Smith, *Wealth of Nations*, bk. 2, chap. 3; p. 314.
55. Hla Myint, *Theories of Welfare Economics* (New York: Augustus M. Kelley, 1965), p. 73.
56. Marx, *Capital*, vol. 1, chap. 16 (International Publishers), p. 509.

jects," although this "embodiment" may also be indirect, when the labor is such that "an increase of material products is its ultimate consequence." [57] Thus these economists confined the productiveness of labor to its being profit-generating for employers or its issuing in "vendible" or "marketable" material objects. The former criterion, in particular, allies the "productive" with efficiency in the sense that the benefits it generates outweigh its costs, although benefits and costs are assayed solely (or at least primarily) from the standpoint of the profit-seeking capitalist. So mutuality remains only in a very attenuated form.

A second aspect of the economists' definitions is that they explicitly abstracted from broader consequentialist moral considerations of need or usefulness. Thus Adam Smith, adducing his two criteria, classified as "unproductive" the "labor of some of the most respectable orders of society," including not only all governmental officials but "churchmen, lawyers, physicians, men of letters of all kinds," on the ground that "[t]heir service, how honorable, how useful, or how necessary soever, produces nothing for which an equal quantity of service can afterwards be procured." [58] Although Smith seemed to hold that all productive labor is useful, even if not conversely, Marx went further and said that "[t]he use-value of the commodity in which the labor of a productive worker may be embodied may be of the most futile kind" ;[59] "the designation of labor as productive labor has nothing to do with the determinate content of the labor, its special utility, or the particular use-value in which it manifests itself." [60] Thus, "An actor, for example, or even a clown, according to this definition, is a productive laborer if he works in the service of a capitalist (an entrepreneur) to whom he returns more labor than he receives from him in the form of wages" ;[61] similarly, the labor of "actors, musicians, prostitutes, etc." is productive insofar as it provides the "entrepreneurs of theatres, concerts, brothels, etc. . . . with wages and profit." [62] On the other hand, without this relation to the generation of profit, the labor of writers, singers, physicians, tailors, cooks, waiters, and so forth is "unproductive." [63] In a similar

57. J. S. Mill, *Principles of Political Economy*, 1.3.3, ed. W. J. Ashley (London: Longmans Green, 1950), p. 48.

58. Smith, *Wealth of Nations*, bk. 2, chap. 3; p. 315.

59. Karl Marx, *Theories of Surplus Value*, pt. 1 (Moscow: Progress, 1968), p. 158.

60. Ibid., p. 401.

61. Ibid., p. 157.

62. Ibid., p. 166.

63. Ibid., p. 158; Marx, *Results of the Immediate Process of Production*, p. 1044. In some passages, however, Marx seems to give a moral cast to the distinction. See Marx, *Theories of Surplus Value*, pt. 1, pp. 175–76, 289. Cf. E. K. Hunt, "The Categories of Productive and Unproductive Labor in Marxist Economic Theory,"*Science and Society* 43 (1979–80): 305–25.

vein, Mill wrote that "all labor, according to our present definition, must be classed as unproductive, which terminates in a permanent benefit, however important, provided that an increase of material products forms no part of that benefit. The labor of saving a friend's life is not productive." [64] Thus the concept of the productive was rigorously confined to the criterion of economic efficiency for the capitalist. And considerations of mutuality are rigorously restricted to exchange values that bring profits to capitalists.

What emerges from this brief historical survey is that the classical economists defined productive labor by criteria that had a relatively narrow focus in both antecedentalist and consequentialist terms. The consequences that make labor productive consist in profits for capitalists, not in broader effects or benefits for other persons. Those workers alone are productive who are the efficient causes, in whole or in part, of those profits.

Although a considerable measure of agreement can be found in these three economists, subsequent writers, including but not limited to Marxists, have disagreed sharply with their central focus on profit-generation for capitalists.[65] These critics have decried the general equation of "productive" activity with the "ability to fetch a price in the market," with "all activities in capitalist society that earn a monetary reward." [66] For this equation serves to make the criteria of market capitalism the sole evaluative bases of the productive and of mutuality. The equation leaves out many activities, such as housework or artistic creation, which, though unpaid, are productive in the sense of mutually providing valuable services or outputs; and it includes as productive many useless and even harmful activities, such as prostitution and drug dealing. These criticisms, however, may also bear on my own characterization of productive agency in the economic sense as involving income-generating work (4.6). I shall deal with them below.

The criticisms about the "productive" have centered sometimes on consequentialist considerations about the outputs of activities and sometimes on antecedentalist considerations about the activities themselves.

64. Mill, *Principles of Political Economy,* 1.3.4, p. 49.

65. There have also been many debates over the proper interpretation of Marx's distinction. Besides Hunt, "Categories," see Ian Gough, "Marx's Theory of Productive and Unproductive Labour," *New Left Review* 76 (Nov.–Dec. 1972): 47–72; James C. O'Connor, "Productive and Unproductive Labor," *Politics and Society* 5 (1975): 297–332; Scott M. Lash, "Productive Labor, Class Determination and Class Position," *Science and Society* 42 (1978–79): 62–81; Peter Meiksins, "Productive and Unproductive Labor and Marx's Theory of Class," *Review of Radical Political Economics* 20 (1988); Braverman, *Labor and Monopoly Capital,* chap. 19.

66. Baran, *Political Economy of Growth,* p. 31 and n. See *Work in America,* pp. 2–3: The definition of work "as 'paid employment' . . . utterly ignores its profound personal and social aspects and often leads to a distorted view of society."

With regard to the former, it has been urged that the "productive" should be confined to outputs that are "socially useful," [67] "the satisfaction of needs," that which "contributes to increasing well-being," [68] the demand for whose products derives "from a rationally ordered society." [69] It has also been held that unproductive labor is that which results "in the output of goods and services the demand for which is attributable to the specific conditions and relationships of the capitalist system." Examples are "armaments, luxury articles of all kinds, objects of conspicuous display and marks of social distinction." [70]

With regard to activities, unproductiveness has been ascribed to "government officials, members of the military establishment, clergymen, lawyers, tax evasion specialists, public relations experts . . . advertising agents, brokers, merchants, speculators, and the like." [71] The epithet "unproductive" has also been applied to administrators as being mere "parasites" on productive labor.[72] Capitalists and landlords have also been classed as unproductive: "I find it hard to accept that merely allowing others to use my money, or my land, is a 'productive' activity, on a par with actually working." [73] It has also been held that only "direct producers" are "productive" while "indirect producers" are not, the former being sometimes confined to manual workers (factory workers and farmers) while at other times they also include providers of social services, such as physicians and teachers.[74] In all these contexts the mutuality of contributions that enters into the moral principle of human rights is given different interpretations based on divergent interpretations of economic and social value.

In the light of these conflicting criteria of what is "productive" and "unproductive," it has sometimes been contended that the distinction is a barren one and should be given up.[75] With certain qualifications, however,

67. Ellen Turkish Comisso, *Workers' Control under Plan and Market* (New Haven, Conn.: Yale University Press, 1979), citing Antonio Gramsci.

68. Ibid., pp. 13–14, citing Branco Horvat.

69. Baran, *Political Economy of Growth*, p. 32.

70. Ibid.

71. Ibid. See Braverman, *Labor and Monopoly Capital*, p. 301 n.: "Banking corporations produce nothing but merely profit from the mass of capital in money form at their disposal. . . . they have mastered the art of expanding capital without the necessity of passing it through any production process whatsoever. (The magical appearance of the feat merely conceals the fact that such corporations are appropriating a share in the values produced elsewhere.)"

72. Comisso, *Workers' Control*, pp. 161, 171.

73. Alec Nove, *The Economics of Feasible Socialism Revisited* (London: HarperCollins, 1991), p. 4.

74. Comisso, *Workers' Control*, pp. 161, 171.

75. See Alfred Marshall, *Principles of Economics*, 8th ed. (London: Macmillan, 1930), pp. 66–67, incl. notes; Irving Fisher, *The Nature of Income and Capital* (New York:

I think it is important to retain the distinction. The qualifications bear on the point, which is suggested by the variety of opinion just canvassed, that what is to be regarded as "productive" and what "unproductive" is relative to context. We saw in the case of the classical economists that the context they chose for defining the distinction was the capitalist and his profits. This led to the various moral and other anomalies against which the critics protested. Now since all modes of the productive are kinds of action, the primary, and indeed inescapable, context for distinguishing between productive and unproductive labor is the freedom and well-being that are the necessary goods of action and the objects of human rights. In this way the productive-unproductive distinction can be tied to, and derived from, the principle of human rights with its requirement of the equal and mutual protection of all persons' needs of agency.

What is productive in this primary context is work that contributes to the protection and development of these necessary goods. This sense of "productive" fits directly into the broader consequentialist justification of property rights (5.2), and it is morally more fundamental than either of the two senses of productive agency—general and economic—that were previously distinguished (4.6). But it must be kept in mind that the well-being which is an object of the productive labor just defined includes not only basic well-being but also nonsubtractive and additive well-being. Hence, productive labor as here construed comprises a wide range of work activities; they include making available food, clothing, shelter, medical care, and other goods that serve to protect life, health, and safety; they include also fostering of education, including humanistic and scientific culture, and opportunities for earning an income that is adequate for all the levels of well-being, and thus for being a productive agent in the economic sense previously distinguished. Sufficient training and remuneration must be provided to assure that relevant workers, from farmers to medical doctors, can provide these necessary goods. The society, as a community of rights, must see to it that these needs of the necessary goods of action and generally successful action are fulfilled, with due recognition both of the availability of resources and of the personal preferences and sense of personal responsibility on the part of the workers in question. In these ways the community of rights promotes the essential values on which it is grounded, including the mutuality and equality of the human rights of agency, and thereby it also contributes to its own flourishing. Here again rights and community support one another.

On this criterion, then, what emerges as unproductive is work or activ-

Macmillan, 1906), p. 58; Joseph Schumpeter, *History of Economic Analysis* (New York: Oxford University Press, 1954), p. 631.

ity that does not contribute to the fulfillment of these fundamental needs of agency. This is, indeed, the burden of many of the criticisms mentioned above: that much of what is produced and paid for in a capitalist economy does not fulfill any real needs, but is either a response to demands artificially stimulated by advertisers or a result of financial manipulations that enrich speculators without adding any goods to the economy.

Once the requirements of the primary context of the necessary goods of action and generally successful action are fulfilled, however, it is possible to shift to a broader market context wherein the "productive" is defined by reference to the multitude of desires and preferences whose satisfaction is effectively demanded in a market economy. Thus, whereas in the primary context one can accept Galbraith's contention about "the dependence of wants on advertising," [76] with its implied corollary that work that caters to such wants is unproductive, one can also agree with Hayek, against Galbraith, that most of the amenities of civilized life are also the effects of culturally induced wants.[77] Hence, completely to remove such amenities from the sphere of the "productive" would be to overlook much of what makes human life not merely possible but worthwhile and enjoyable. Thus in this alternative market context the productive includes "the musical performer, the actor," as well as the servants, the government officials, and so forth, that Mill and Smith had classed as "unproductive."

This duality of contexts is confronted by the apparent anomalies of persons who do productive work according to the first context but not according to the second. The unpaid housewife is a prime example; so too perhaps are struggling artists and novelists. And on the other side stand the paid and hence "productive" prostitute and pornographer. To deal with these anomalies, the context of the principle of human rights must again be invoked, in three ways. First, the actions and institutions that are sanctioned as productive must satisfy the moral standards set by that principle. Hence the services of gunmen, drug dealers, and others who are paid for their criminal activities are not productive on the present account, and this also applies to prostitutes, pornographers, and other paid agents whose operations are harmful to the human dignity upheld by the principle of human rights.[78] Second, even if the housewife is not paid by external cus-

76. John K. Galbraith, *The Affluent Society* (Boston: Houghton Mifflin, 1958), pp. 156–57.

77. F. A. Hayek, "The *Non Sequitur* of the 'Dependence Effect,'" in Edmund S. Phelps, ed., *Private Wants and Public Needs* (New York: W. W. Norton, 1965), pp. 37–42. See also Nove, *The Economics of Feasible Socialism Revisited*, pp. 227–28.

78. For a contrary view regarding prostitution, see Janet Radcliffe Richards, *The Sceptical Feminist* (Boston: Routledge and Kegan Paul, 1980), pp. 199–202; Igor Primorack, "What's Wrong with Prostitution," *Philosophy* 68 (April 1993): 159–82.

tomers, she ought to be paid by her husband, at least in the sense that she ought to share with complete equality in his earned income. It must be understood that she makes an essential mutualist contribution to his productivity by giving him the love and support he needs in order to carry on his own paid work, so that in this way she too is a productive agent. It is morally outrageous to exclude her, even in part, from the financial proceeds that are made possible by their functioning as a family unit. This point applies whether or not she also takes care of their children.[79] The same thing applies, of course, if it is the husband who stays home with the children, as well as where both spouses work. Third, as for the unpaid novelist, as well as the mother who rears children without a husband, such cases fall in large part under the positive welfare right to basic well-being presented above. But as we have seen, where persons are not productive agents in the sense presented here, they have a positive right to be helped to develop and use their capacities for productive agency. In addition, recognition must be given to the wide varieties of cultural work that contribute to additive well-being, so that such workers stand in mutual productive relations. In these complex ways, then, the productive agency to whose development all persons have rights figures in the economic biography that is being traced here. The community of rights that fosters this development contributes thereby to the mutual protection and promotion of the freedom and well-being of all persons both as productive agents and as recipients of other persons' productive agency.

4.9. EDUCATION FOR PRODUCTIVE AGENCY

Education is a prime means for the development of productive agency. It can help persons to acquire the abilities and skills both for raising their general levels of purpose-fulfillment and, more specifically, for performing income-generating work. Thus while education has economic value for persons in the form of increasing their human capital, it can also promote cultural, intellectual, aesthetic, and other values that contribute to additive

79. On women's unpaid housework, see Carol Lopate, "Pay for Housework?" *Social Policy* 5, no. 3 (Sept.-Oct. 1974): 27–31; W. Seccombe, "The Housewife and Her Labor under Capitalism," *New Left Review* 83 (1974): 3–24. See also Veronica Beechey, *Unequal Work* (London: Verso, 1987); Harriet Bradley, *Men's Work, Women's Work* (Minneapolis: University of Minnesota Press, 1989). It has also been held that "procreation and nurturing are production in the broadest Marxist sense of being necessary to human life and they are increasingly productive in the capitalist sense of falling within the market" (Alison M. Jaggar and William L. McBride, "Reproduction as Male Ideology," *Hypatia* 8, no. 3 [1985]: 194–95; quoted in Virginia Held, *Feminist Morality* [Chicago: University of Chicago Press, 1993], p. 131). Held comments: "Giving birth and bringing up children may be closer to artistic expression than it is to the production of material objects" (p. 131).

well-being, including an effective sense of personal responsibility. It enables persons to make informed choices about the values that guide their lives, to have knowledge of their and other persons' human rights, to take on the rights and obligations of democratic citizenship, and to develop the personal virtues conducive to well-being. Since, as we have seen, persons have rights to productive agency, they also have rights to education. In this regard the society, operating through public governmental institutions, functions as a community of rights: it helps to fulfill persons' positive rights to the proximate necessary conditions of action and generally successful action.[80] By this means, persons are also enabled to avoid welfare dependence. So here again rights and community have a relation of mutual support. And by improving their skills, education can enable persons to

80. According to the "voucher" system advocated by Milton Friedman, "governments could require a minimum level of schooling financed by giving parents vouchers redeemable for a specified maximum sum per child per year if spent on 'approved' educational services. Parents would then be free to spend this sum and any additional sum they themselves provided on purchasing educational services from an 'approved' institution of their own choice" (*Capitalism and Freedom* [Chicago: University of Chicago Press, 1962], p. 89). While this proposal has many merits it incurs at least three difficulties: (*a*) Since more affluent parents would be allowed to supplement the voucher sum, this would reintroduce all the inequalities of the market system. The richer, paying more, would have better schools, and the poorer would be left with schools of minimum standards. (*b*) The proposal could derogate, as Friedman recognizes, from an important communitarian ideal: the schools' ability to "provide the common core of values deemed requisite for social stability" (ibid., p. 90). More specifically, the proposal may obscure the social and even communitarian concern for the shared values that enter into the community of rights both as the source and as the partial end of education (for a related but not identical criticism, see Amy Gutmann, *Democratic Education* [Princeton, N.J.: Princeton University Press, 1987], pp. 64–70). (*c*) The proposal may also be open to the objection that parents whose children are most in need of educational help may be least capable of making the relevant informed choices. A result could be schools of markedly unequal degrees of adequacy. On this point, however, I think the parental involvement required by Head Start and other early intervention programs (see below, 4.10) provides a sound medium between such situations and those where parental choice is almost entirely absent. For a spirited defense of the voucher proposal, see Anthony Flew, "Libertarians versus Egalitarians," in Tibor Machan, ed., *The Libertarian Reader* (Totowa, N.J.: Rowman and Littlefield, 1982), pp. 257–58.

Besides the early intervention programs, improvement of inner-city education can also be achieved by the oft-proposed and oft-defeated policy of mingling urban and suburban property taxes used for schools. For qualified support of a voucher system from a socialist standpoint, see Raymond Plant, "Socialism, Markets, and End States," in LeGrand and Estrin, *Market Socialism*, pp. 72–74, and LeGrand, "Markets, Welfare, and Equality," pp. 198–204. In any case it must be recognized that apart from the issue of community, the voucher dispute is a circumstantial one over means. But supporters and opponents of vouchers agree that children have a positive right to education and that government must be the primary respondent of this right, regardless of whether it directly employs persons to run the schools or pays private groups to run them. See also below (8.4) on the distinction between legislative and executive meanings of "privatization."

acquire jobs in which the depressive aspects of work are sharply reduced even if not completely eliminated. Although I shall here concentrate on education as a process that leads children to productive agency, much of my discussion will also apply to "manpower programs" whereby the government sponsors "skill training programs" for adults.[81]

It must be admitted that the relation between education and the removal of the depressive mode of work requires changes other than those contributed by education itself. The changes in question bear on the whole area of the social organization and control of work. I take this up in chapter 7. In the present context I focus mainly on education as a necessary, not a sufficient condition of the removal of welfare dependence and depressive work.

The education that is here in question is not narrowly vocational. Entirely apart from the contributions of education to the expansion of persons' cultural horizons—which is itself an important part of additive well-being—even in its specifically economic effects education can foster the acquisition of broad skills of analysis, understanding, resourcefulness, and problem-solving, as well as of diligence, dependability, and self-reliance that constitute personal virtues or excellences.

The cultural aspects of education also have communitarian effects. They contribute to a shared understanding of the heritage and traditions of one's own social milieu, of other cultures, and of humanity as a whole, and can foster an appreciation of the value of human rights and achievements. In this way students can come to see themselves as part of a larger whole to which they are bound by a mutuality of rights and duties as well as by other important social, political, and cultural values, and they can also appreciate and be motivated by their obligations to their nurturing society (3.4).

Despite these communitarian effects, it is a mistake to hold that the primary end of education is to enable children "to participate effectively in the democratic process." [82] Such participation is indeed a part of productive agency in the general sense; but to make it primary incurs the danger that persons may be regarded and treated as means toward democratic polity, rather than the other way around. From the standpoint of the principle

---

81. See Charles R. Perry et al., eds., *The Impact of Government Manpower Programs* (Philadelphia: Wharton School, Industrial Research Unit, 1975).

82. Gutmann, *Democratic Education*, p. 136. See also John Rawls, *Political Liberalism* (New York: Columbia University Press, 1993), p. 200: "Society's concern with their education lies in their role as future citizens." For a parallel view that the primary purpose of the First Amendment freedom is not to protect "personal autonomy" but to foster "an improved public capable of self-government," see Stephen Holmes, "Liberal Constraints on Private Power," in Judith Lichtenberg, ed., *Democracy and the Mass Media* (Cambridge: Cambridge University Press, 1990), pp. 32–33.

of human rights, with its ethical individualism, states and governments exist to secure the human rights of persons. Toward such securing, democratic polity and citizenship, within a rights-protecting constitution, are indeed necessary means; but to make them the sole ends may lead to an at least comparative neglect of persons' needs for autonomy and productive agency for their own sakes. These needs include far more than democratic citizenship, important though that is. It is indeed the case that persons cannot be effective citizens unless they are "economically independent and self-supporting" ;[83] but this economic empowerment must be a concern for children's well-being for their own sakes, not solely or mainly for the sake of the polity. As some communitarians have insisted, participation in the polity is, indeed, a part of persons' well-being; but it is only a part, not the whole. Similarly, persons have obligations to their society; but this is in return for its contributions toward fulfilling their rights (3.4), in ways that involve both reciprocity and mutuality.[84]

From the standpoint of the principle of human rights with its deprivation focus, our main concern must be with the impact of education on the life chances of the poor, especially regarding their development of productive agency and an effective sense of personal responsibility. Conditions of inveterate poverty condemn millions of persons to welfare dependence. These conditions, while continuing through all phases of the life cycle, have their biographical origins in infancy. The children of poor, uneducated parents often become, in turn, poor and uneducated adults. Thereby their rights to freedom and well-being go unfulfilled. They lack autonomy; they are not in control of important phases of their lives; instead, they are victimized by their adverse conditions of life, including their very limited abilities of purpose-fulfillment. Lacking self-esteem and a feeling of hope for the future, they turn to crime, drugs, and teenage pregnancy, thereby helping to continue their abysmal conditions.

All such persons have rights to a kind of education that will prevent the perpetuation of these conditions and will enable them to develop their abilities of productive agency. These rights are continuous with the rights previously discussed, all of which derive from the human rights to freedom and well-being. The state as the community of rights must be the primary respondent of these rights, based on the mutuality of rights and duties (2.5).

83. Rawls, *Political Liberalism*, p. 200.

84. It is an interesting confluence of ideas that the libertarian Milton Friedman comes close to Rawls and Gutmann in his thesis that government support of education is justified by its "promoting a stable and democratic society," but not by its providing "purely vocational training, which increases the economic productivity of the student but does not train him for either citizenship or leadership" (*Capitalism and Freedom* [Chicago: University of Chicago Press, 1962], pp. 86, 88).

That education can help toward the development of productive agency has been denied both on the hereditarian ground that the genetic makeup of disadvantaged persons precludes any substantial improvement[85] and on various environmental grounds. Among the latter, three are especially prominent. According to one, the promotion of equality of educational opportunity can come only at the price either of lowering standards of merit or of impugning the autonomy of the family.[86] According to a second, Marxist criticism, because of the pervasive influence of capitalism, attempts to equalize the education of disadvantaged children and thereby to promote equality in society must fail because they serve to reproduce the inequalities of the social relations of capitalist production.[87]

A third ground has appealed to somewhat more specific social-scientific findings. Here, however, there seems to be a conflict between two schools which emphasize, respectively, human capital and equal opportunity. Human capital thinkers have adduced several kinds of evidence for the proposition that education is an investment in human capital that helps to increase both national and personal income. One kind is that the growth in national income has been much greater (three times as great in mid-century) than the growth in the quantity of labor and physical capital that has been used to produce that income. This divergence has been explained by the increase in schooling beyond the eighth grade: such schooling improves the quality of workers' productivity and thus yields a higher output.[88] Another kind of evidence is that persons' earnings tend to increase with their years of schooling: "More highly educated and skilled persons almost always tend to earn more than others . . . inequality in the distribution of earnings and income is generally positively related to inequality in education and other training." [89] It has not escaped the notice of human capital theorists that the correlations they adduce may be explained more

85. See A. R. Jensen, "How Much Can We Boost IQ and Scholastic Achievement?" *Harvard Educational Review* 39 (1969): 1–123; Richard J. Herrnstein and Charles Murray, *The Bell Curve* (New York: Free Press, 1994). These hereditarian theses, which have received well-grounded criticisms, do not militate against the roles assigned to education in this and the next section.

86. James S. Fishkin, *Justice, Equal Opportunity, and the Family* (New Haven, Conn.: Yale University Press, 1983).

87. Samuel Bowles and Herbert Gintis, *Schooling in Capitalist America* (New York: Basic Books, 1976).

88. See Schultz, "Investment in Human Capital," pp. 5–6; Theodore W. Schultz "Investment in Man: An Economist's View," *Social Service Review* 33 (1959): 115; Schultz, *Economic Value of Education*, pp. 42–48; and Schultz, *Investment in Human Capital* (New York: Free Press, 1971), pp. 64–77.

89. Becker, *Human Capital*, p. 10. For some important qualifications, see pp. 105–17. See also Schultz, *Economic Value of Education*, pp. 53, 64–65, and *Investment in Human Capital*, p. 63.

fully by such factors as family background than by schooling per se.[90] But this has not invalidated a significant causal role for the latter.

That schooling has such differential effects on personal income has, however, been denied by other social scientists, whose main emphasis has been on equality of educational opportunity.[91] They have pursued intensive empirical research over a wide range of testing of children's intellectual skills in various schools and on the relation of such skills to personal income. On the first point they have concluded that "differences between schools account for only a fraction of difference in pupil achievement," [92] so that the degree of development of intellectual skills cannot be explained by any concomitant variations in kinds of educational facilities. On the relation between intellectual development and personal incomes it has been concluded that "Neither family background, cognitive skill, educational attainment, nor occupational status explains much of the variation in men's incomes." [93]

This divergence between the theorists of human capital and of equal opportunity can perhaps be explained by differences in areas of concentration, such as whether one concentrates on individuals or on groups,[94] on elementary schooling or on higher education, and so forth. But it is also important to note that theorists of equal opportunity, amid their comparative concerns, have pointed out correlations both between the economic status of children and their scores on tests of intellectual skills, and between that status and children's ability to profit from improvements in educational facilities. In the famous Coleman report of 1966 it was shown that, on various tests of intellectual skills, African-American children at every grade level scored much lower than white children, and their schooling did not help to close this gap: "For most minority groups, then, and most particularly the Negro, schools provide little opportunity for them to overcome this initial deficiency; in fact they fall farther behind the white majority in the development of several skills which are critical to making a living and participating fully in modern society. Whatever may be the combination of nonschool factors—poverty, community attitudes, low educational level of parents—which put minority children at a disadvantage

90. See Becker, *Human Capital*, pp. 117–20.

91. James S. Coleman, *Equality of Educational Opportunity* (Washington, D.C.: U.S. Government Printing Office, 1966); Christopher Jencks et al., *Inequality: A Reassessment of the Effect of Family and Schooling in America* (New York: Harper and Row, 1973).

92. Coleman, *Equality*, p. 22.

93. Jencks et al., *Inequality*, p. 226.

94. See Donald M. Levine and Mary Jo Bane, eds., *The Inequality Controversy* (New York: Basic Books, 1975), pp. 7–8; Nathan Keyfitz, "Can Inequality Be Cured?" *Public Interest*, no. 31 (spring 1973): 94–95.

when they enter the first grade, the fact is the schools have not overcome it." At the same time, however, it was also shown, on the basis of these tests, that African-American children were more affected by the quality of their elementary schools than were white children: "The achievement of minority pupils depends more on the schools they attend than does the achievement of majority pupils" ; hence, "Improving the school of a minority pupil may increase his achievement more than would improving the school of a white child increase his." [95]

These findings suggest that, in contrast to a purely negative and undifferentiated view of the relation between elementary education and the development of skills of productive agency, a far more concentrated attempt to improve the education of initially deprived children can achieve valuable results, not only intellectual but also emotional and cultural, as they bear on the rights to freedom and well-being.

4.10. EARLY EDUCATION AND EQUALITY OF SELF-ACTUALIZATION

A prime example of such an ameliorative attempt is Project Head Start, which was initiated in 1964 as part of the Economic Opportunity Act. Under this program children between the ages of two and four are given intensive services to prepare them for school by advancing their intellectual and emotional development. They are put into small classes; their teachers have assistants and undergo continual training; their parents are closely involved in their learning processes. In these ways the community of rights makes vital contributions to the fulfillment of basic and additive rights. Although estimating the effects of these programs involves many difficulties, there is evidence that the programs have had considerable success, as measured by such criteria as promotion in regular school grade levels, reading and arithmetic achievement, IQ, health, and the significant area of social and emotional development, including "an adequate aspiration level, a healthy self-image, expectancy of success, mastering motivation, curiosity, and independence." [96]

The longer-range effects of Head Start programs have been less positive.[97] But this indicates that further intensive educational programs are

95. Coleman, *Equality,* p. 21.

96. Edward Zigler, "Project Head Start: Success or Failure?" p. 498, and see also Francis H. Palmer and Lucille W. Anderson, "Long-Term Gains from Early Intervention: Findings from Longitudinal Studies," pp. 433–66, both in Zigler and Jeanette Valentine, eds., *Project Head Start: A Legacy of the War on Poverty* (New York: Free Press, 1979).

97. The "Westinghouse Report," focused on narrowly interpreted intellectual criteria, reported that Head Start's favorable effects did not carry through to children in the first and

needed to avert the continuing effects of poverty and a disabling environment. It is a serious mistake to think that the severely debilitating effects of poverty can be permanently overcome by giving preschool children a few years of intensive intellectual and emotional nurturing and then throwing them back into their original deprivational maelstrom, including schools that are seriously deficient both absolutely and relatively.[98] What is needed is a continuation of the nurturing begun by Head Start into the middle teen years. There has been some recognition of this in the Follow Through program begun in 1967, which extended early intervention services into the beginning years of elementary school; but this has been spasmodic and poorly funded.[99] This is especially anomalous because such programs, despite the large financial outlays they require, save far more money than they cost.[100]

It must be emphasized that the contribution of early educational programs is not only intellectual but also emotional and motivational. To recognize that persons care for them and want to help them can be a strong encouraging and motivating factor, especially for children in dysfunctional families. Without such early and continuing care, children may lack the motivation to take advantage of opportunities that come to them later; they may fail to develop a sense of personal responsibility.[101]

---

second grades. See Westinghouse Learning Corporation, *The Impact of Head Start: An Evaluation of the Effects of Head Start on Children's Cognitive and Affective Development*. Ohio University. Report to the Office of Economic Opportunity (Washington, D.C., 1969). For critiques of the Westinghouse Report, see Marian S. Stearns, *Report on Preschool Programs: The Effects of Preschool Programs on Disadvantaged Children and Their Families* (Washington, D.C.: U.S. Department of Health, Education, and Welfare, Office of Child Development, 1971), pp. 117–34, and Lois-Ellin Datta, "Another Spring and Other Hopes: Some Findings from National Evaluations of Project Head Start," in Zigler and Valentine, *Project Head Start*, pp. 417–24.

98. See Alex Kotlowitz, *There Are No Children Here* (New York: Doubleday, 1991); Jonathan Kozol, *Savage Inequalities: Children in America's Schools* (New York: Crown, 1991).

99. See Levitan, *Programs in Aid of the Poor*, p. 103; Datta, "Another Spring," pp. 419–21.

100. "Longitudinal studies of Head Start indicate that by reducing the likelihood of later handicaps and repeated grades, the program actually leads to a net reduction of public expenditures. . . . Head Start children were also less apt to be arrested (31 percent compared with 51 percent) or to seek welfare payments (18 percent compared with 32 percent). Based on these findings, the investigators estimated that taxpayers save nearly $5 in reduced crime, welfare, public education costs, and increased tax revenues for every $1 invested in preschool compensatory education programs (or $3,100 for each child in the program)." Levitan, *Programs in Aid of the Poor*, p. 102.

101. The following is a not untypical example of this phenomenon: "Harrison Steans and Burt Kaplan, wealthy businessmen from posh suburbs, thought that poor kids from Chicago would jump at the chance to earn a college scholarship. So in 1987, Steans and Kap-

An important factor contributing to the valuable results of Head Start programs is the provision for parental involvement. In its most salient form, this consists in parents' learning simultaneously with their children: "Parents had to learn *with* their children, particularly how to *be* parents. . . . Parents were encouraged to assist in the classroom, accompany children on field trips, and participate in adult education." [102] By such active involvement welfare mothers and other deprived parents can participate together with their children in overcoming the debilitating effects of their environments. They can acquire realistic feelings of hope that they can control their own destinies in ways that improve their abilities of productive agency and thereby take on the mutual rights and duties of the community of rights. [103]

There have been disputes over the proper function of parental involvement. In contrast to emphases on parental learning, an awareness of the central institutional deficiencies that impose the need for welfare has led to demands that parents actively control their local Head Start programs. By such means parental self-determination would be more direct and effective. [104]

There is no necessary conflict, however, between these two conceptions, especially when it is kept in mind that the former parental-learning model itself requires not mere passive receipt of external instruction but rather, as in all genuine learning, an active inquiring, exploratory frame of mind. The support and encouragement of such an outlook on the part of parents can contribute strongly to both their and their children's development of autonomy and their abilities of productive agency. Moreover, such parental involvement can help to resolve the frequently invoked conflict between equal opportunity and family autonomy, because the parents would

---

lan promised to pay a chunk of college tuition for each of the students in two North Side elementary school classes—if they graduated from high school. Six years later, commencement is here and the donors have learned that any problems involving education and poverty are frustratingly complex—and that money is just one impediment, perhaps not even the most important one, to higher education. Specifically, Steans and Kaplan realized that the immediate lure of drugs, gangs, sex and other temptations in the inner city can be more powerful than the remote idea of a college degree and that many kids are too overwhelmed by the daily pressures of poverty, violence and family troubles to even concentrate on the future." *Chicago Tribune*, July 7, 1993, p. 1. Subsequent correspondence in the *Tribune* modified the strictures of the last sentence.

102. Jeanette Valentine and Evan Stark, "The Social Context of Parental Involvement in Head Start," in Zigler and Valentine, *Project Head Start*, p. 297.

103. See Clara M. D. Riley and Frances M. J. Epps, *Head Start in Action* (West Nyack, N.Y.: Parker, 1967), chap. 10, "Parent Education."

104. For a historical account of these disputes, see Valentine and Stark, "Social Context," pp. 291–311.

themselves participate in the process whereby their children's educational opportunities were rendered more equal to those of children from affluent homes.[105]

The early education fostered by Head Start and similar programs can provide an important kind of equality that is intermediate between the familiar opposites of equality of opportunity and equality of outcomes (see 3.1). All three kinds of equality can be visualized by the metaphor of a journey. Equality of opportunity emphasizes the beginning of the journey, defined in both negative and positive terms: persons who undertake the journey are not to be handicapped by decisions about their race, religion, gender, and other irrelevant factors, and they are to be given equal external assistance of inputs with regard to educational facilities and other assisting goods.[106] Equality of outcomes emphasizes the end of the journey: persons are to arrive at the same place, defined in terms of relevant values such as intellectual achievement or wealth.

Neither of these views takes account of the journey itself, the varying routes whereby one may get from the beginning to the end. Persons may make varying uses of their initial abilities and facilities. Equality of self-actualization, while upholding the negative and positive phases of equality of opportunity at the beginning of the journey, emphasizes that the journey itself is also to be equalized, in that each person is to be enabled to actualize her own productive potentialities.[107] Thus equality of self-actualization, while partaking of phases of each of the other kinds of equality, is identical with neither but is intermediate between them.

To see what this involves, we must first note two negative points. First, the aim is not mere actualization of potentialities. Human potentialities are a very varied lot: humans can be cruel, bestial, and slothful as well as kind, compassionate, and industrious.[108] Moreover, some potentialities are not

105.   On this conflict, see Fishkin, *Justice, Equal Opportunity, and the Family*. Fishkin recognizes that the conflict may be resolved in this way: "there are many government interventions, compatible with both family autonomy and merit in assignment, that may lead to far greater equality of life chances than has been achieved thus far" (p. 148).

106.   See Mary Jo Bane, "Economic Justice: Controversies and Policies," in Levine and Bane, *Inequality Controversy*, pp. 280–91; James S. Coleman, "The Concept of Equal Educational Opportunity," in ibid., pp. 207 ff.

107.   For a somewhat related notion of self-actualization, see A. H. Maslow, *Motivation and Personality* (New York: Harper and Brothers, 1954), chaps. 12–13.

108.   Thus one cannot accept the formula attributed to "the Marxist tradition" according to which "self-realization is the full and free actualization and externalization of the powers and the attributes of the individual" (Jon Elster, "Self-Realization in Work and Politics," *Social Philosophy and Policy* 3, no. 2 [spring 1986]: 101). See, in a similar vein, Milton Fisk's characterization of "ideal justice," as "the realization of the capacities of all" (*The State and Justice* [Cambridge: Cambridge University Press, 1989], p. 90). For reasons why the "actualization of potentialities" formula cannot be attributed to Aristotle, see my essay, "The

controllable by their possessors (such as blinking of the eyes), and some are lacking in depth or moral significance (such as flexing and unflexing one's fingers). What are to be actualized are potentialities for productive agency, as this has been specified above, including the moral restrictions imposed by the mutuality of the principle of human rights. Second, equality of self-actualization may not lead to equality of outcomes. Since persons' productive potentialities vary, their actualizations will also vary. Not everyone can be a Beethoven or an Einstein.

By equality of self-actualization each person is enabled to fulfill herself through the development of her own inherent productive powers. This development occurs through time, in the journey from infancy to later childhood. The productive powers that are actualized need not be thought of as fixed and unalterable; they are more diffuse than that and can be developed in different directions. According to the principle of human rights, these directions must be productive ones in that each person is enabled to attain both the general abilities and conditions needed for successful agency and the abilities for earning income sufficient to be self-supporting. The general abilities include the competences needed by all humans, including the basic tools of learning, in mathematics, literacy, and so forth. The economic abilities that are actualized in a given case will take account of particular aptitudes and interests. The actualized abilities need not be centered on a specific occupation; they may involve various kinds of adaptability and "trainability." [109] This may require more public expenditures in some cases than in others; but in each case the aim is to enable the child to develop her productive capacities at least sufficiently to be self-supporting. Beyond that, aptitudes and interests will differ, and having been given basic tools, each individual must gradually use his own efforts in the directions he favors.

The equality of self-actualization thus comprises a triple equality. First, all children's educations equally enable them to achieve competence, consistent with their inherent abilities, in the basic tools of learning. Second, each child is equally enabled to actualize her particular productive abilities. The equality here is in the first instance proportional: as A's potentialities are to her productive outcome, so are B's potentialities to his. The outcomes themselves may not be arithmetically equal; but they are equal in that they equally develop the respective potentialities, which may

Ontological Basis of Natural Law: A Critique and an Alternative," *American Journal of Jurisprudence* 29 (1984): 95–121.

109. See Burton A. Weisbrod, "Education and Investment in Human Capital," *Journal of Political Economy* 70, no. 5, pt. 2 (Oct. 1962): 113; Lester C. Thurow, "Education and Economic Equality," in Levine and Bane, *Inequality Controversy*, pp. 172, 176.

themselves not be equal. Thus if A becomes an electrical engineer and B a carpenter, they are equal in that they have equally developed their specific potentialities in ways that reflect their aptitudes and interests. Each will have equally actualized his or her particular productive potentialities. There may be difficulties of ascertainment here, just as, at a later stage of the economic biography, there are difficulties in making the distribution of economic rewards proportional to productive contributions (see 5.7). But the difficulties in the educational case are not insurmountable. It is especially important to stress the need for sympathetic and informed guidance counseling, especially in the case of initially deprived children. The educational process will then be a free development because it will have been guided by each person's own interests and aptitudes.[110] Third, each person is equally enabled to earn enough to be self-supporting without having to turn to welfare. Obviously this will also depend on general economic conditions (to be discussed in chaps. 6 and 7); but at least on the side of the individuals themselves their rights to productive agency and their corresponding obligations of mutuality will have been fulfilled.

The economic relation here emphasized between work and the earning of income does not militate against work's also being desired for its own sake or being intrinsically rewarding. The education here envisaged, with its emphasis on aptitudes and interests, should help to move work from the depressive mode to the creative mode. To be a productive agent in the economic sense does not remove one from being a productive agent in the more general purposive sense.

It may be objected that since persons do not deserve their inherent potentialities or the social conditioning that enables them to exert efforts on their own behalf, they also do not deserve the different actualizations they achieve. This objection, however, involves a denial of each person's selfhood and thus his autonomy and sense of personal responsibility. To try to override the effects of persons' inherent potentialities is to cancel what they are and what makes them what they are. The result would be not fulfillment but rather destruction of the person. Persons do not deserve to be

---

110. In *Democratic Education*, p. 124, n. 4, Amy Gutmann presents several criticisms of "proportionality" as an aim of education. These criticisms may not, however, apply to my above formulation; e.g., the criticism that proportionality "offers no standard for setting the proportion" is obviated by my above emphasis on specific aptitudes and interests. Also relevant here are Gutmann's cogent criticisms of "maximization," "equalization," and "meritocracy" (pp. 128–36). The idea of justice as consisting in proportional equality goes back to Plato (*Laws* 6.757) and Aristotle (*Nicomachean Ethics* 5.3). For good recent discussions, see Douglas Rae, *Equalities* (Cambridge, Mass.: Harvard University Press, 1981), pp. 59–63; Peter Westen, *Speaking of Equality* (Princeton, N.J.: Princeton University Press, 1990), pp. 52–57.

born; but this does not entail that they do not deserve anything they may achieve after they are born (see also 5.4).

This actualizing journey is a development from passive to active powers. The initial potentialities are passive in that, in part, they receive instruction and guidance from without. They become active powers in that the individual has achieved productive abilities that enable him to act for his own purposes.[111] By the same token, the actualizing process involves a departure from what one previously was and did; it is a sequence of self-improvement whereby one's earlier inadequacies are supplanted by gradually developed personal excellences or virtues. In this regard, self-actualization is epitomized in such other familiar reflexive phrases as "making the best of oneself" and "doing right by oneself." Self-actualization in this sense is distinct from what Nietzsche probably had in mind when he discussed "how one becomes what one is" [112] and urged "Become who you are!" [113] if this involves a complete identification of one's present with one's past.[114]

In the light of these considerations, let us recur to the important Marxist criticism to which I briefly alluded in the preceding section: that attempts to equalize education and thereby to promote equality in society are bound to fail, because the educational system is part of the superstructure based on the capitalist system of production and hence serves to "reproduce" the inequalities of capitalism.[115] To this it has been added that the "counterculture" of young people who rebel against the values of the wider society is simply a reaction against the educational policies that operate to reinforce the economic disabilities that capitalism imposes on its victims.[116]

In the next chapter I shall discuss the great inequalities of economic power as they are related to the equality of human rights. Here it must suffice to note that in a democratic society that embodies the community of

111.   For the general distinction between active and passive powers, see John Locke, *Essay Concerning Human Understanding*, 2.21.2. The distinction goes back to Aristotle, *Metaphysics*, 5.12; 9.1.

112.   This is the subtitle of *Ecce Homo*.

113.   Friedrich Nietzsche, *Thus Spake Zarathustra*, pt. 4, in Walter Kaufmann, ed. and trans., *The Portable Nietzsche* [New York: Viking Press, 1954], p. 351.

114.   See the important essay by Alexander Nehamas, "How One Becomes What One Is," *Philosophical Review* 92 (July 1983): 385–418. He summarizes Nietzsche's thought as follows: "To become what one is, therefore, is not to reach a specific new state. . . . It is to identify oneself with all of one's actions, to see that everything one does (becomes) is what one is" (p. 411).

115.   Bowles and Gintis, *Schooling*.

116.   See Paul Willis, *Learning to Labor: How Working Class Kids Get Working Class Jobs* (New York: Columbia University Press, 1977).

rights as a process of equalizing effective rights to freedom and well-being, education can and does function in important degree not only independently of the capitalist economic system in which it is embedded but also as a corrective of that system, insofar as education serves to equalize abilities and opportunities. This need not involve a total rejection of the Marxist criticism, but it calls attention to a "paradox" whereby schools, while preparing students to take their unequal places in the system of production, are themselves "more equal and participatory than offices or factories." [117] Beginning with Head Start and continuing its equalizing impact through later school years, public education can serve to develop abilities of productive agency in ways that are not necessarily tied to a drastically unequal economic system. The community of rights helps to fulfill the right to such education, so that it here exemplifies the solidarity and promotes the mutuality whereby rights and community are brought together.

4.11. THE NONNEUTRALITY OF THE COMMUNITY OF RIGHTS

From the above discussion of the relation of government to education, it is clear that the state as a community of rights is not neutral with regard to all values or conceptions of the good. [118] Since human rights are based on the necessary goods of action and generally successful action, the state must respect these goods for all persons and help to provide them when persons' own efforts cannot do so. Accordingly, with regard to education in particular, the state must try to foster for each person the abilities of productive agency. Hence, it must oppose the values that enter into criminal activities, strong drug use, teenage pregnancy, early dropping out of school, the use of violence to resolve personal disputes, and other such destructive modes of action. In contrast, the state must foster and encourage the development of the personal virtues or excellences that characterize productive agency both in general and in the economic sphere, including the mutuality of productive contribution and other exercises of human rights.

The state's promotion of these goods of character and action should, so far as possible, not be coercive but rather a process of encouraging and fostering by way of precept and example. Criminal penalties should be used to punish and deter violations of basic rights; and elementary and secondary

117. Martin Carnoy and Henry M. Levin, *Schooling and Work in the Democratic State* (Stanford, Calif.: Stanford University Press, 1985), p. 2. See also ibid., chap. 6.

118. For doctrines of liberal neutrality regarding personal morality and conceptions of the good, see Ronald Dworkin, "Liberalism," in Stuart Hampshire, ed., *Public and Private Morality* (Cambridge: Cambridge University Press, 1978), pp. 113–43, and Bruce Ackerman, *Social Justice in the Liberal State* (New Haven, Conn.: Yale University Press, 1980), pp. 43–45.

education should be made legally obligatory.[119] But the state, while respecting the right to freedom of choice in ways of life, should make clear that the dysfunctional modes of conduct that are antithetical to productive agency are reprehensible and should pursue policies that enable persons to develop their abilities of productive agency.

In taking sides on such disputed issues of personal conduct, the state does not violate anyone's rational autonomy. We noted above (4.2) a distinction between autonomy in general and rational autonomy. In the latter, the rules or laws by which a person guides her life are rationally justifiable in that they conform to or derive from the principle of human rights. Since this principle obviously takes sides on how persons should live and act, rational autonomy also takes such sides; and states that follow the principle's guidelines do not, therefore, violate persons' rational autonomy. As we have seen, the principle of human rights, including its obligatoriness, can be known by all normal persons. The goods that enter into or derive from the principle are values of human action that can be shared by all the members of the society, so that in this way a prime emphasis of communitarianism is fulfilled.

With regard to conceptions of the good that do not enter into or derive from the principle of human rights, the state must be neutral. These conceptions bear on such areas of concern as religion, sexual orientation, choice of occupation, political activity or ideology, and many other spheres of thought and action.

It may be difficult in some cases to distinguish between these two kinds of values or conceptions of the good.[120] Examples are where, in some religions, physical harms to self or others may be required, or educational opportunities may be restricted or foreclosed. In such cases, however, further careful analysis can elicit on which side the disputed value falls. For example, a life-threatening rejection of a blood transfusion can be temporarily countered while assurance is sought that the endangered person fully understands the consequences of his rejection (see *RM*, 262–64). Children's educations must be fostered in the general ways indicated above regardless of their parents' religiously based objections; in accordance with the ethical individualism of the principle of human rights, the children's

119. This involves that education is a mandatory, not a discretionary right. On this distinction see below, 6.4.

120. The distinction I have drawn in the text between kinds of goods in relation to state neutrality is partly the same as John Rawls's distinction between the goods that enter into a "political conception of justice" and those that enter into some "particular comprehensive religious, political, or moral doctrine" (*Political Liberalism*, pp. 174–75). But the principle of human rights is more than a "political conception;" it bears on personal morality as well. See also Raz, *Morality of Freedom*, p. 136.

rights to the development of their general abilities of productive agency override the parents' rights, based on their religion, to prevent that development.

While the principle of human rights thus authorizes the state to enforce certain conceptions of the good and to prohibit the effectuation of other conceptions, it may be held that the principle is not "perfectionist" because it permits the free exercise of a large variety of conceptions of the good, and corresponding ways of life, so long as they are not antithetical to human rights. Much depends, however, on the scope of the respective kinds of goods—in particular, on how far the principle of human rights sanctions some conceptions of goods and ways of life as against others. Especially relevant here is the right to additive well-being. As we have seen, this right entails the right to productive agency both in general and in the economic sphere; and this includes the development of various personal virtues. Do such virtues include not only the intellectual virtues but also what may be called cultural virtues? Especially for children, is watching television for hours on end as good a use of their time and attention as reading literature that broadens their horizons by enabling them to better understand other people and cultures? Is hanging out on street corners or in taverns through much of the day as conducive to productive agency as the self-discipline required for mastering scientific subjects or learning to play well a musical instrument? One kind of answer to such questions would hearken back to the education discussed above as means of avoiding welfare dependence. But a further answer would emphasize that it is far more in keeping with human dignity and self-actualization to promote some kinds of goods that enter into additive well-being as against others. But again, this should not be by coercion but rather by encouragement and education.[121]

It may be objected that such preferential policies on the part of governments are paternalistic, that they derogate from human dignity because they substitute the government's choices of the right way to live for those of the individual who is to live that life, and that they are dangerous because they open the door to cultural dictatorship. The rejection of coercion as means of implementing the policies, however, removes much of the force of the objections. Moreover, value choices about what ought to be learned enter into the construction of school curricula. And if, as argued above, the contents of human rights are not arbitrary but are objects of rational argument, then so too, although perhaps in more disputable ways, are the contents of the various goods that persons may pursue in their purposive actions.

121. See the valuable discussions of these and related issues in Raz, *Morality of Freedom,* chaps. 5–6, and William A. Galston, *Liberal Purposes* (Cambridge: Cambridge University Press, 1991), pts. 2 and 3.

It should be noted that the sequence of my argument has moved from a universalism of human rights and a corresponding impartiality to an apparently more particularistic thesis that some goods and ways of life are better than others. There is no inconsistency here. The crucial intermediate step has been the emphasis on productive agency and on the education and virtues it requires. This emphasis applies to all persons; it embodies a concern to help them to make the best of themselves through their rational autonomy and self-actualization. Education itself requires choices between competing values; the universalism of human rights is maintained so long as those choices are made available to and are in the rationally justified interests of all persons. The deprivation focus itself aims to fulfill the right to productive agency for those persons whose conditions of life, including their vulnerability to physical suffering, make that fulfillment most difficult. In these ways, the state as the community of rights serves to bring together the rights that enter into productive agency and the community that effectuates these rights through the mutual support that persons owe to one another, as shown by the principle of human rights.

FIVE

THE RIGHT TO PRIVATE PROPERTY

5.1. PRODUCTIVE AGENCY AND TWO JUSTIFICATIONS OF PROPERTY RIGHTS

One of the main purposes of the right to productive agency is to enable persons to earn income for themselves and their dependents through their own work. Such income is a species of private property. Hence, insofar as there is a right to productive agency as I have argued above, there is also a right to private property, at least as represented by one's earned income and accruing wealth. This latter right is primarily a moral claim-right; but it should also comprise legally enforceable powers or controls over external things and other objects of wealth: exclusive powers to possess, use, transmit, exchange, or alienate objects. In this regard property consists not only in things and other objects but also in relations between persons and things whereby persons have rights over things, with correlative duties and other disadvantages placed on other persons. The rights are in the first instance negative: other persons have correlative duties to refrain from interfering with the owner's possessing, using, and otherwise handling the owned things without the owner's consent. But since the property right, as so far envisaged, derives from the right to productive agency, which as we have seen is a positive right, the right to private property is, at least in this indirect way, also a positive right.[1]

---

1. See the analysis of the "incidents" of the "liberal concept" of ownership in A. M. Honoré, "Ownership," in A. G. Guest, ed., *Oxford Essays in Jurisprudence* (Oxford: Clarendon Press, 1961), pp. 107–47. In listing the rights "to use" and "to manage" under ownership (pp. 116–17) Honoré does not distinguish between ownership and control—a distinction made famous by Adolf A. Berle and Gardiner Means in *The Modern Corporation and Private Property* (New York: Harcourt, Brace and World, 1932). But ownership may be construed as including control de jure even if not de facto. For qualifications about the extent to which property rights are claim-rights (as against the other three kinds of Hohfeldian rights), see Lawrence C. Becker, *Property Rights: Philosophic Foundations* (London: Routledge and Kegan Paul, 1977), pp. 21–22; Stephen R. Munzer, *A Theory of Property* (Cambridge: Cambridge University Press, 1990), pp. 24–25.

This brief analysis incurs many ambiguities and leaves many questions unanswered. But the connection so far suggested between private property and productive agency indicates that the line of inquiry to be followed here is guided by the principle of human rights, including its ethical individualism. I am here concerned directly with the relation of property rights to the work and the needs, the freedom and well-being, of individuals, especially those who are most deprived and hence most in need of protection. My direct concern, then, is not a utilitarian one; it does not include such questions as which arrangement of property rights is most efficient for the operations of a market economy.[2] Such questions are by no means negligible; they may well have an important bearing on how much property entrepreneurs and others may accumulate through production and exchange. But at the level of the primary producers whose economic biography I am tracing here, the more direct concern must be with the relation of property rights to their own work and needs.

As we have seen, the state as the community of rights has as one of its positive duties helping persons, especially those who are most deprived, to develop their abilities of productive agency. But although the acquisition of property rights is the envisaged outcome of this development, this does not necessarily mean that the state is also itself to provide property rights for persons. On the contrary, it would seem that persons must use their own productive abilities to attain such acquisition. But this then raises questions about how tight must be the connection between productive agency and private property in wealth and income. In the one direction, even if productive agency in the economic sense distinguished above (4.6) is geared to the earning of income, it may not always succeed in this, because the products may not have any, or sufficient, exchange value. Hence there remains the question of just how, or whether, the state's fulfillment of the right to productive agency bears on the fulfillment of property rights as rights of actual possession. The problem of unemployment will be taken up in the next chapter. In the other direction, there are such questions as the following: Do income and wealth always derive from productive agency? Can the vast inequalities of the former be explained solely or even largely by corresponding inequalities of the latter? Moreover, *should* income derive solely from the exercise of productive agency? In view of the imperative

2. For a focus on this question, see Eirik G. Furubotn and Svetozar Pejovich, eds., *The Economics of Property Rights* (Cambridge, Mass.: Ballinger, 1974), including the editors' "Introduction: The New Property Rights Literature" (pp. 1–9). See also Harold Demsetz, "Toward a Theory of Property Rights," *American Economic Review* 57 (May 1967): 347–59. For discussions of utilitarian justifications of property rights within broader justificatory frameworks, see Becker, *Property Rights*, chap. 5 and Stephen R. Munzer, *A Theory of Property*, chap. 8.

economic needs of human life, needs typically fulfilled by income and property, must it be only through the work or contribution of productive agency that income and property should be derived? Many aspects of these questions have already been considered in our discussion of welfare dependence (4.3). But there remains also the question of mutuality: how is the privacy of property rights related, if at all, to the mutuality of rights and duties required by the principle of human rights?

The right to private property serves valuable purposes for persons regardless of whether or not they have earned it through their own productive agency. Indeed, many justifications of the right to private property have concentrated mainly or even exclusively on the palpable beneficial consequences for persons of their having this right, quite independent of any consideration of work done by the persons who have and enjoy the right.[3] Hence, in view of my above emphasis on the right to productive agency, we must examine whether or to what extent the right to private property can be justified solely in this consequentialist way. Among the issues involved here are questions about the ethical status of persons as agents who are enjoyers of life and consumers of goods, as against their status as productive agents. If personal fulfillment or happiness is an intrinsic good for human beings, then why isn't it a sufficient justification of the right to private property that it subserves this good? And why shouldn't persons have this right in whatever abundance is available for their personal fulfillment?

Marxists sometimes distinguish between "personal property" and "private property," the former consisting in consumer goods directly used by the owner, while the latter is private ownership of the major means of production.[4] While this distinction is useful for some purposes, it may have only a peripheral bearing on the great inequalities of property that figure in questions of justification. For even when persons do not own means of production they may nonetheless have vast amounts of personal property in estates, yachts, expensive condominiums, precious works of art, and so forth. Such persons may have inherited their wealth from past capitalist entrepreneurs, but, whatever its antecedentalist source, the inequalities it embodies and its impact on the freedom and well-being of other persons raise consequentialist questions that require independent scrutiny, regard-

3. See Jeremy Waldron, *The Right to Private Property* (Oxford: Clarendon Press, 1988).

4. This distinction, in one form, can be traced back at least to Marx and Engels, *Manifesto of the Communist Party,* as the distinction between "the right of personally acquiring property as the fruit of a man's own labor" and "bourgeois private property" (in Robert C. Tucker, ed., *The Marx-Engels Reader,* 2d ed. [New York: W. W. Norton, 1978], pp. 484–85). See also David Schweickart, *Against Capitalism* (Cambridge: Cambridge University Press, 1993), p. 4 n. For a closely related distinction, see Anthony Downs, *An Economic Theory of Democracy* (New York: Harper and Row, 1957), p. 12, n. 9.

less of or in addition to the question of private property in major means of production. The understanding of the institutions upheld by the community of rights requires that we attempt to answer these questions.

In making this attempt I shall proceed in four stages. First, I shall separately present two independent justifications of private property rights based first on need and then on contribution. For reasons to be indicated below, I shall use the more general terms "consequentialist" and "antecedentalist" in working out the respective justifications. Second, I shall take up certain "primordialist" questions bearing on the antecedentalist justification. Third, I shall examine the relations between the two justifications. Fourth, I shall consider how the justifications bear on the great inequalities of private property rights, especially as they concern the ownership of nonhuman capital in the major means of production.

Let us proceed to the first task. When it is said that a main purpose of the right to productive agency is to enable persons to earn income through their own work, the component of purpose and the component of work give rise to two different justifications of the right to private property. Each justification is derivable from the principle of human rights; but they emphasize different parts of the principle and have different implications concerning who has property rights to what and the respective roles of the community of rights. One kind of PGC-based justification of property rights is *consequentialist*; it bears on the consequences, for persons as prospective purposive agents, of their having such legal rights; or, in Aristotelian terms, it concerns the final cause, the end or purpose served by persons' having property rights. A second kind of justification is *antecedentalist*; it bears on the antecedents, the prior conditions and work activities that determine who has property rights to what; or, in Aristotelian terms, it concerns the efficient cause, the generating process of work that leads to the acquisition of property rights.

Although the two justifications have complex contents and backgrounds, they can be correlated in a general way with the two kinds of necessary goods that are the objects of the human rights. The consequentialist justification derives from the well-being that is the substantive generic feature of action and generally successful action, and that focuses on the purposiveness, the purportedly good consequences or results aimed at by action. The antecedentalist justification derives from the freedom that is the procedural generic feature of action and that focuses on the voluntariness of action, the agent's initiation and control of her behavior. Both freedom and well-being, however, enter into the contents or objects of each kind of justification. And each kind serves both to raise questions for the other and to limit the other, so that neither justification taken by itself establishes conclusive rights to private property. Since the primary concern of the community of rights is to protect the freedom and well-being of all persons, we shall especially have to consider how this protection figures in the justification of property rights. It will be helpful to begin by discussing the antecedentalist and consequentialist justifications separately, and to do so initially in the context of the biographical development traced in the preceding chapter of the right to productive agency as it emerges from the deprivation focus.[5]

5.2. CONSEQUENTIALIST JUSTIFICATION OF PROPERTY RIGHTS

Let us now take up the consequentialist justification of property rights. In accordance with the ethical individualism of the principle of human rights, it must be stressed that "consequentialist" is here used primarily in a distributive, personalist sense, not in an aggregative, collective, or utilitarian sense. At least in the first instance, the consequences referred to in this justification consist in benefits to individual persons as actual or prospective agents, not in benefits maximized for society at large without regard to how they are distributed. As we shall see, social considerations must be taken into account, and this is one of the reasons why I use the more general term "consequentialist" rather than "need" in analyzing this justification. But its concern is aggregative or maximizing only as ancillary to fulfillment of distributive concerns at the highest level, as was indicated above in my discussion of equality (3.1). As we shall also see, although the consequen-

---

5.   I have previously discussed the distinction between consequentialist and antecedentalist justification in "Economic Justice: Concepts and Criteria," in Kenneth Kipnis and Diana T. Meyers, eds., *Economic Justice: Private Rights and Public Responsibilities* (Totowa, N.J.: Rowman and Allanheld, 1985), pp. 7–32, at pp. 13–17. Although the distinction bears some similarities to Robert Nozick's distinction between "end-state" and "historical" principles of justice (*Anarchy, State, and Utopia* [New York: Basic Books, 1974], pp. 150–64), there are important differences. What he calls "end-state" principles involve some overarching "patterns," such as equality, whose maintenance will require "continuous interference with people's lives" (p. 163). Consequentialist criteria need not, however, require such totalistic patterns; they are concerned in the first instance with the impact of property rights on individuals; and insofar as they bear also on comparative holdings, they may provide for fulfillment of each person's basic needs while leaving taxpayers free to use their remaining money as they wish, so that there is ample room for change and variety. As for "historical" principles, for Nozick these are quite general, bearing on how a distribution "came about" (p. 153). My concern is the more specific one of who produced the goods whose distribution then "came about" so that my antecedentalist justification is not primarily "historical" but rather productivist. Nozick is notoriously vague about the content of "the principle of justice in acquisition" (pp. 150–51); he explicitly rejects Locke's labor theory of acquisition (pp. 174–78). The antecedentalist criterion presented here, on the other hand, puts major, though not exclusive, emphasis on work or labor as a justification of property rights.

tialist justification is universalist in its concern for the human rights of all persons, it also provides an important place for the deprivation focus.

The consequentialist justification of property rights may be stated succinctly as follows: having such rights serves to protect both the well-being and the freedom that are needed for purposive action and generally successful action. Property rights, as represented by one's having a steady, assured, adequate income and savings, provide the economic security that is essential for basic well-being and for at least some degree of additive well-being. And property rights in external things entail that one has both the positive freedom and autonomy whereby one's behavior with regard to those and other purchasable things (or their monetary equivalents) is under one's own control, and also the negative freedom whereby other persons are excluded from taking or using one's things without one's consent. An important function of the state as the community of rights is to protect this freedom. In these consequentialist ways property rights serve the final cause of providing the conditions for generally successful action and indeed, to an important degree, for purposive action as such. To this extent it would seem that property rights should be included as the next step in the economic biography that is being unfolded here. But, as we shall see, this thesis requires serious qualification.

I noted above a distinction about the subjects of the consequentialist justification, the entities for whose sake the consequences are valued (individuals and society). A further distinction must also be noted about the objects in which the consequences consist. The consequentialist justification just presented views these consequences broadly, as comprising the freedom and well-being that are the objects of human rights. Although this broader object-meaning will receive primary emphasis, we shall see subsequently that "consequentialist" can also have a narrower object-meaning as referring to more particular effects of economic activities.[6]

The brief consequentialist argument just given can be interpreted in two different ways. One way is as a conditional statement: if one has private property rights, then one's freedom and well-being are protected. This is at least in part an empirical causal statement (causal in that private property rights are not viewed as being constitutive of freedom and well-being but only as means of securing them). It leaves open the question of whether freedom and well-being can be protected without private property rights. The other interpretation is unconditional: it is morally required that persons have private property rights in order to protect their freedom and

---

6. Although all final-cause *considerations* are consequentialist, not all consequentialist considerations are of final causes, because, among other reasons, not all consequences are desirable ends or purposes. But all consequentialist *justifications* are final causes.

well-being. Here there is a double mandatoriness: because it is morally required that each person's freedom and well-being be protected, it is also
morally required that each have private property rights. It is this latter, unconditional statement of the consequentialist justification that would seem
to be sanctioned by the principle of human rights. But it leaves open at least
three questions. One is whether, or to what extent, the protection of freedom and well-being for each person provides a conclusive justification for
each person's having property rights. In view of the nonmutuality and dependence for which the welfare system was criticized (4.2, 3), the answer to
this question would seem to be negative. A second question concerns the
alleged necessity that property rights be private in order to protect freedom
and well-being. The third question concerns the consequences of private
property rights for persons other than the particular property owner. Both
of the last two questions bear on the social import of private property and
thus on its fuller relation to the community of rights where the community
serves to protect the rights of all persons. I shall postpone dealing with the
first question to the next section.

The question about privacy is this: May not the final cause of protecting persons' freedom and well-being be attained through a system of communal as against private ownership? An important affirmative answer,
which has strong communitarian overtones, is found in the ancient doctrines that friends have all things in common and that the use of property
should be common even if its ownership is private.[7] A somewhat different
kind of affirmative answer is suggested by the apparent empirical facts of
the existence of complex systems of property rights that combine private
and communal elements in various ways.[8] These empirical data are given
moral support by communitarian ideas that stress the need for cooperation
and mutuality. Examples of such ideas are theses about the rightness of
"surplus sharing," "the claims of the community," [9] and the thought of
"societies of mature, healthy, and virtuous humans in which the appropriation involved in personality development does not ground the justification
of private property. Think of a culture in which self-esteem standardly
comes from producing or achieving things that are admirable; . . . where

7. See Aristotle, Nicomachean Ethics, 8. 9. 1159b30; Politics, 2.5. See Terence Irwin,
"Aristotle's Defense of Private Property," in David Keyt and Fred D. Miller, eds., A Compan-
ion to Aristotle's Politics (Cambridge, Mass.: Blackwell, 1991), pp. 200–225.

8. See, for example, Melville J. Herskovits, Economic Anthropology (New York: Alfred
A. Knopf, 1952), esp. pt. 4. See also Lawrence C. Becker, "The Moral Basis of Property
Rights," in J. Roland Pennock and John W. Chapman, eds., Nomos XXII: Property (New
York: New York University Press, 1980), pp. 197–220; A. M. Honoré, "Property, Title and
Redistribution," in Virginia Held, ed., Property, Profits, and Economic Justice (Belmont,
Calif.: Wadsworth, 1980), pp. 84–92.

9. Honoré, "Property, Title and Redistribution," pp. 91, 87.

possessiveness is regarded as a vice." [10] On such grounds it may seem that persons' freedom and well-being can be protected without their having private property rights. Indeed, it may also seem that the very idea of the community of rights requires communal rather than private ownership.

These considerations provide important grounds for modifying but not completely surrendering the privacy of property rights. Amid the valuable communitarian emphases that are incorporated, as we have seen, in the positive rights upheld by the principle of human rights, there are strong reasons for maintaining some privacy for property rights. It must be kept in mind that the community of rights involves the important distributive aspect whereby each person's freedom and well-being are protected by the state. The community as a corporate entity is ancillary to the ethical individualism of this distributive aspect of community. If property rights were common, held by the corporate community on behalf of its members, these rights might well be used to fulfill each member's economic rights to well-being. But such common property rights would, as such, lack the freedom element of individual control over external things, whereby one can exclude others from taking or using one's things without one's personal consent. Thereby, also, the security that comes from being one's own property holder might be jeopardized, and so too with the person's incentive to provide for herself. In this regard, the community's control over roads, police protection, and other public goods is on a different footing from the property rights whose private ownership contributes to individual freedom and autonomy. For the latter are not public goods but are the necessary several goods of each individual as a prospective purposive agent. Thus it is one thing to hold that the community of rights, through the right to productive agency, enables individuals to obtain their own private property, and through its police power protects them therein. It is another thing to hold that the community itself owns the property. And it is still a third thing, for which I have argued above in the social contribution thesis (3.4), to hold that individuals have obligations to the community to share some of their property because they are in part "social products" to whose productive agency the community has contributed. In this regard the mutuality of human rights involves that persons both contribute to one another's acquisition of abilities of productive agency and share some of the resulting property with the wider society. So property rights, while serving to protect each person's freedom and well-being, are not absolute. As we shall see, the doctrine of world ownership also serves to modify the privacy of property rights (5.5).

---

10. Lawrence C. Becker, "Too Much Property," *Philosophy and Public Affairs* 21, no. 2 (spring 1992): 206.

The point about freedom raises a further question about the consequentialist justification of property rights. While such rights protect and promote the freedom of the subject, the property owner, they also at the same time restrict the freedom of all other persons, who are legally excluded from taking or otherwise handling the property object without the owner's consent. In this regard, property relations are asymmetrical relations of power.[11] This asymmetry is a reflection of two familiar general correlativities: the correlativity of rights and duties, where A's negative right to X entails other persons' duty to refrain from interfering with X; and the correlativity of freedom and unfreedom, where A's freedom to do X entails the unfreedom of other persons to interfere with A's doing X.[12] This latter correlativity derives from what is sometimes called the "paradox of freedom." The general point of the paradox may be put as follows: freedom involves unfreedom; or the more freedom there is, the less freedom there is. Two main versions of this paradox may be distinguished: (a) The empirical version points out that total or unlimited freedom would lead to great unfreedom, since it would leave the strong free to tyrannize over the weak.[13] More generally, the more freedom there is for the strong, the more unfreedom there is likely to be for the weak, regardless of whether the "strong" and the "weak" are measured in physical, political, or economic terms. (b) The logical version of the paradox of freedom deals with what is logically implied by anyone's being free: it holds that a freedom for one person entails correlative unfreedom for all other persons, that from the very concept of freedom, 'A is free to do X,' entails 'All other persons are unfree to prevent A from doing X or to determine whether A will do X.'[14] Some examples of the logical version base their point mainly on the relation of freedom to law: any law which gives to A the freedom to do X must make all other persons unfree to interfere with or prevent A's doing X. This point is parallel to the logical correlativity of rights and duties: if A has a

11. See Morris Cohen, "Property and Sovereignty," in C. B. Macpherson, ed., *Property: Mainstream and Critical Positions* (Toronto: University of Toronto Press, 1978), p. 159; G. A. Cohen, *History, Labour, and Freedom* (Oxford: Clarendon Press, 1988), p. 293.

12. See John Gray, "Against Cohen on Proletarian Unfreedom," *Social Philosophy and Policy* 6, no. 1 (autumn 1988): 77–112.

13. See Isaiah Berlin, *Four Essays on Liberty* (London: Oxford University Press, 1969), p. 123; Karl R. Popper, *The Open Society and Its Enemies*, 2d ed. (London: Routledge and Kegan Paul, 1952), vol. 2, pp. 44, 124; S. I. Benn and R. S. Peters, *Social Principles and the Democratic State* (London: George Allen and Unwin, 1959), p. 213.

14. See Jeremy Bentham, *Theory of Legislation*, ed. C. K. Ogden (London: Routledge and Kegan Paul, 1950), p. 94; Sidney Hook, *The Paradoxes of Freedom* (Berkeley, Calif.: University of California Press, 1962), pp. 10 ff.; J. R. Lucas, *The Principles of Politics* (Oxford: Clarendon Press, 1966), pp. 157–58, 167–68, 171; Jan Narveson, *The Libertarian Idea* (Philadelphia: Temple University Press, 1988), p. 50.

right to do X (so that he should be free to do X), then it logically follows that all other persons have the duty to refrain from interfering with A's doing X (so that they should be unfree to interfere).

Apart from these general empirical and logical considerations, by the fact that property rights, while enhancing the owner's freedom, restrict the freedom of other persons, a more specific and serious question is raised: Must the freedom of the property owner always take precedence over the freedom of other persons? This question can also be extended to include well-being: Must the degree of well-being that property owners derive from their property always be maintained regardless of its impact on the well-being of other persons? I shall call these questions about the priority of property rights, but they also bear more generally on economic equality. They arise naturally in the context of the consequentialist justification. For if consequences for property owners are directly relevant to the justification of property rights, then, in view of the universality of the principle of human rights, why shouldn't their consequences for other persons also be relevant to their justification? This latter question is seen to be especially apposite when it is kept in mind that all justifications of property rights derive ultimately from the principle of universal human rights.

These questions are to be answered in part by the consideration that, as we have just seen from the social contribution thesis, property rights are not absolute. This point also emerges from the criterion of degrees of needfulness for action (which is a consequentialist criterion): property may be taxed or otherwise removed if the basic well-being of other persons requires it (2.4). But a further, more general answer is given by the egalitarian structure of the principle of human rights. The consequentialist justification involves that all persons have equal rights to property, although not necessarily rights to equal amounts of property. The protections of freedom and well-being provided by private property through the community of rights must to this extent pertain to all persons. A famous example of this general comparative, egalitarian emphasis is Locke's stipulation that the acquisition of property rights in the state of nature requires that "there is enough, and as good left in common for others." [15] The possibly harmful consequences of property rights when they differentially affect some persons as against others are also invoked in the thesis that one of the "incidents" of property ownership is "the prohibition of harmful use . . . the condition that uses harmful to other members of society are forbidden." [16] Here, the consequentialist consideration likewise refers not only to the

15. John Locke, *Two Treatises of Government*, 2.27. This "proviso" is discussed below, 5.5.

16. Honoré, "Ownership," p. 123. Cf. Becker, *Property Rights*, pp. 111–12; Waldron, *Right to Private Property*, pp. 32–33.

property owner herself but also to the freedom and well-being of other persons; but it is still distributive, focusing on the rights of each person severally.

Overlooking for the present the possible ambiguities concerning what is "harmful," [17] we must note that the "prohibition of harmful use" may have a narrower and a broader import. Construed narrowly, it refers only to use, while leaving untouched the ownership. Standard examples of such "harmful use" include negative externalities like air pollution, unsafe work conditions, and dangerous auto driving; there is a consequentialist disjustification of such uses of one's property. But "harmful" may also be construed more broadly as applying to the property right itself. If it is harmful for A to make certain uses of her property right, this may cast consequentialist doubt on the justifiability of her having this right. In particular, the consequentialist justification of property rights calls attention to their impact on the human rights of other persons, including their own property rights. In this regard, the "harmful use" that the consequentialist justification prohibits includes such wide inequalities in property holdings that some persons can dominate the lives and thus the freedom and well-being of others. I shall refer to this as the *inegalitarian harm thesis*.[18]

A graphic illustration of this strong disjustification was presented in Rousseau's assertion about "civil liberty" : "in respect of riches, no citizen shall ever be wealthy enough to buy another, and none poor enough to be forced to sell himself." [19] To "buy another" who is "forced to sell himself" implies that the person bought becomes the property of the buyer, and hence akin to a slave. That capitalism in the nineteenth century reduced its workers to a condition akin to slavery was maintained not only by Marx[20] but also by J. S. Mill: "The generality of labourers in this and most other countries have as little choice of occupation or freedom of locomotion, are practically as dependent on fixed rules and on the will of others, as they

17.   As Harold Demsetz points out, "property rights convey the right to benefit or harm oneself or others. Harming a competitor by producing superior products may be permitted, while shooting him may not. . . . It is clear, then, that property rights specify how persons may be benefited and harmed" ("Toward a Theory of Property Rights," *American Economic Review* 57 [May 1967], p. 347).

18.   With regard to kinds of harm, see Joel Feinberg's discussion of the "harm principle" in *Harm to Others* (New York: Oxford University Press, 1984). Although his discussion is mainly concerned with the criminal law, he also helpfully examines the nature and kinds of harm in many other contexts throughout the volume.

19.   J. J. Rousseau, *The Social Contract*, 2.11, trans. G. D. H. Cole (New York: E. P. Dutton, 1950), p. 50.

20.   See Karl Marx, *Capital* (New York: International Publishers, 1967), vol. 1, pp. 302, 692.

could be on any system short of actual slavery." [21] The reference to modern workers' enslavement can also be found in a sequence at least from John Locke in the seventeenth century[22] to Frank H. Knight, a founder of the Chicago School of economics, in the twentieth.[23]

The drastic inequalities of power, and thus of freedom, referred to by Rousseau and Mill have to some extent been mitigated by the development of the social-democratic welfare state. Nevertheless, in important respects the inequalities persist, and with them the harmful consequences for the freedom and well-being of those who have inferior power. So far as concerns the power wielded by capitalist employers of labor, especially large corporations, four dimensions of their power may be distinguished. First, especially when work opportunities are scarce, the employers can determine who obtains work and who does not, and hence who can obtain the property rights conferred by work.[24] Second, employers can control the conditions of work, and hence of life, so that the freedom of workers is severely restricted. Third, since the employers try to maximize their profits, which includes minimizing their labor costs, this leads to great inequalities of income. Fourth, because of these inequalities the rich can monopolize the use of resources for their own purposes, as against the needs of the poor, even when their objects are far less needed for action. A salient example in the last decade of the twentieth century in America is the amount of money devoted to the production of luxury housing and governmental subsidies for middle-class housing when millions of homeless persons have little or no means of shelter.[25] Other examples are the well-equipped offices of major industrial corporations in contrast to the abysmal working conditions

21.   J. S. Mill, *Principles of Political Economy*, 2.1.3, ed. W. J. Ashley (London: Longmans, Green, 1915), p. 210.

22.   John Locke, *Essay Concerning Human Understanding*, 4.20.2: "And in this state are the greatest part of Mankind, who are given over to Labour, and enslaved to the necessity of their mean condition; whose Lives are worn out, only in the Provisions for Living."

23.   Frank H. Knight, *Risk, Uncertainty, and Profit* (Boston: Houghton Mifflin, 1921), p. 126: "It is characteristic of the enterprise organization that labor is directed by its employer, not its owner, in a way analogous to material equipment. Certainly there is in this respect no sharp difference between a free laborer and a horse, not to mention a slave, who would, of course, be property."

24.   See Charles E. Lindblom, *Politics and Markets* (New York: Basic Books, 1977), pp. 47–50.

25.   "The homelessness plan raises a politically sensitive issue in noting that prosperous homeowners receive far more in housing subsidies than poor people do. The vehicle for the middle-class subsidy is the deduction of interest on home mortgages, which the plan said cost the Treasury $41 billion last year. Of that amount, the report said, 85 percent went to the most affluent quarter of American taxpayers, who earn more than $50,000 a year" (*New York Times*, Feb. 17, 1994, national edition, p. A10).

that are menaces to the health and safety of industrial and agricultural workers, the lack of adequate medical care and health insurance for millions of persons, and the markedly inferior facilities provided for inner-city public schools. These and other conditions are in major part consequences of the distribution of property in wealth whereby the rich can command resources and services far beyond the abilities of the poor. The word "command" is used advisedly, because it calls attention to the ways in which, as was noted above, property relations are relations of power. Insofar as property rights are justified by their consequences in protecting freedom and well-being, this justification fails, and human rights are violated, in the face of such inequalities.[26]

The analysis I have just presented may be criticized in at least two ways. First, it may be held that the inequalities of property rights can be justified on consequentialist grounds. For they serve as incentives to energetic entrepreneurs to make productive innovations that increase the total amount of goods and make them available at lower prices, so that the poor as well as the rich are thereby benefited. In reply, it must be said that while there is indeed merit in this argument, it does not justify the extreme inequalities whereby masses of human beings are left in conditions of abject poverty and economic insecurity. So the consequentialist objection to the current distribution of property rights can still be maintained.

Second, it may be held that capitalist employers of labor do not by themselves control the availability of employment because, among other things, the rigors of international competition force them to cut costs by laying off workers.[27] While this is an important contributing factor, the vastly greater property rights held by employers give them much greater power to determine both which jobs to maintain and how to respond to global pressures.

There is strong consequentialist moral justification, then, for moving, through the state as a community of rights, toward a greater equalization of property rights. One of the ways in which this can be accomplished is by establishing a system of economic democracy in which the means of production are owned and controlled by the persons who work in them. This will be discussed in chapter 7. A less drastic way, proceeding from the exis-

26. Munzer (*A Theory of Property,* p. 247) sets forth the "gap thesis," which "constrains inequalities of wealth so that they do not undermine a fully human life in society." Unlike my above analysis, which emphasizes the severe consequences for material well-being, Munzer's discussion focuses more on the impact of inequalities on persons' "healthy self-esteem." Although this is a not unimportant consideration, I think it is less serious for human rights, in part because self-esteem can have widely variant bases (see 6.2).

27. See, e.g., Louis Uchitelle, "The Rise of the Losing Class," *New York Times,* Nov. 20, 1994, national edition, sec. 4, pp. 1, 5.

tence of large economic inequalities, would reduce them by a system of economic redistribution; it would subject to extensive taxation the wealthier segments of the population and would use the proceeds to provide more opportunities for productive advancement for those who need them most, especially in the sphere of education (4.9, 10).

There are many different possible modes of economic redistribution, ranging from lump-sum payments in money or in kind through progressive taxation to means-tested benefits.[28] The state, as the community of rights, imposes taxes in order to secure the economic rights of those who are more deprived and thereby to narrow the inequalities that subject them to unwarranted superiorities of power. In this way rights and community reinforce one another, because these economic rights are fulfilled through the mutualist provisions of the community.

It has been held that, so far as concerns "the existence of super-rich people . . . their excess incomes, if redistributed, would make no decisive difference to the welfare of the masses," so that "serious measures of redistribution cannot be confined to taking from 'the rich,' as the amount so obtained would make no significant difference to the poorer segments of the community." [29] Such a view, however, unduly narrows the range of redistribution with regard both to sources and to recipients. The sources need not be confined to static total holdings of the very rich; they can include also increased taxes on various of their differential incomes and other emoluments on a continuing basis. Thus, for example, a memorandum by Robert B. Reich, secretary of labor in the Clinton administration, "suggested that tens of billions of dollars could be raised by changing provisions it called 'tax breaks' for the prosperous. Mr. Reich, for instance, suggested reducing interest deductions for expensive homes or raising taxes on inherited stock." [30] The recipients of such redistribution need not be the poor viewed as having doled out to them, in a single transfer on an individual basis, a certain very large sum of money. Instead, the "billions of dollars" that could be raised would be used to fund programs for developing the abilities of productive agency of the persons who are most in need of such help. The whole economic biography traced in this book, from welfare through education to employment and beyond, is a multiple means of re-

28. See David Collard, Richard Lecomber, and Martin Slater, eds., *Income Distribution: The Limits to Redistribution* (New York: John Wiley and Sons, 1980). See also Lucien Foldes, "Income Redistribution in Money and in Kind," *Economica* 34 (1967): 30–41; Edgar K. Browning, *Redistribution and the Welfare System* (Washington, D.C.: American Enterprise System, 1975); Hillel Steiner, *An Essay on Rights* (Oxford: Blackwell, 1994), chap. 8.

29. Alec Nove, *The Economics of Feasible Socialism Revisited* (London: Harper Collins, 1991), pp. 166, 168.

30. *New York Times*, Feb. 22, 1994, national edition, p. A10.

ducing economic inequalities in a dynamic way, through the mutuality whereby the rich contribute to the development of the poor who thereby contribute through their own work to the well-being of others.

It is sometimes held that increases in well-being for "the average man come not from economic redistribution but from increases in output." [31] While this utilitarian point may well apply to many middle-class persons, it applies far less surely to members of the lower classes, with whom the deprivation focus is especially concerned. It has also been contended that such movement toward greater equality involves adherence to a presumed rigid "pattern" of the distribution of wealth, and that setting up such a pattern must violate individual freedom. For if the pattern is to be maintained, this will require that individual agents be prevented from engaging in free transactions that would upset the pattern. Nozick's Wilt Chamberlain example is the most familiar argument of this kind; its conclusion is "that no end-state principle or distributional patterned principle of justice can be continuously realized without continuous interference with people's lives." [32] The cogency of this argument depends on how one interprets "continuous interference" and "patterned principle." Surely the income tax system involves, in some way, "continuous interference with people's lives," in that a certain percentage of one's earnings is regularly deducted from one's income. But this still leaves persons free to carry on their lives in all other respects without any "interference"; the unqualified phrase "people's lives" unwarrantedly suggests a much more frequent, pervasive, and sinister kind of "interference."

As for the "distributional patterned principle," there are at least two ways in which governmental policy may try to realize this without involving "continuous interference." First, the pattern in question may not be global; instead, it may concern only a certain part of the distribution, especially that whereby certain minima of income are prescribed. Such a partial pattern, apart from the taxation it would specifically require, would still leave persons free to accumulate their further wealth without interference.

31. See John K. Galbraith, *The Affluent Society* (Boston: Houghton Mifflin, 1958), pp. 96–97. Galbraith also notes that "Increasing aggregate output leaves a self-perpetuating margin of poverty at the very base of the economic pyramid" (p. 97).

32. Nozick, *Anarchy, State, and Utopia*, p. 163. See P. T. Bauer, *Equality, the Third World, and Economic Delusion* (Cambridge, Mass.: Harvard University Press, 1981), p. 8: "In an open and free society, political action which deliberately aimed to minimize, or even remove, economic differences (i.e. differences in income and wealth) would entail such extensive coercion that the society would cease to be open and free." See also F. A. Hayek, *The Road to Serfdom* (Chicago: University of Chicago Press, 1944). That redistribution involves a great redistribution in state power is stressed by Bertrand de Jouvenel, *The Ethics of Redistribution* (Indianapolis, Ind.: Liberty Press, 1990), p. 43, 71–72.

Second, even if a more global distributional pattern is envisaged, this may be realized in at least two ways that do not involve "continuous interference." The pattern may be a more egalitarian one that is dynamic rather than static, whereby the leveling aimed at is a leveling up rather than down, so that persons at the lower end of the scale are provided with educational and other opportunities that enable them to improve their productive abilities. Moreover, wealthier groups may be taxed more heavily in ways that still do not remove their incentives to be more productive in their income-generating activities.[33]

5.3. ANTECEDENTALIST JUSTIFICATION OF PROPERTY RIGHTS

We have just seen that the consequentialist justification of property rights yields serious criticisms of the wide economic inequalities found in the United States and other capitalist countries. But the criticisms themselves must now be confronted in turn through the antecedentalist justification of property rights. For a vital question left open by the consequentialist justification is the issue of justified differential rights, including their sources. If property rights are justified by their consequences for freedom and well-being, then, since all persons as actual or prospective agents have needs for these necessary goods of action, this does not, as such, distinguish between the amounts of property that different persons ought to have; nor does it tell us whether work in producing objects of property should give any privileged position to the producers as against other persons. This latter question bears on the issue of the priority of property rights that was briefly considered above. But it also invokes very strongly the centrality of productive agency, the right to which was discussed in detail in chapter 4. After all, a chief point of this right is that persons are to support themselves through their own income-generating work and thereby fulfill their mutual rights and duties in the economic sphere and elsewhere. How is this emphasis related to the consequentialist justification's exclusive focus on the fulfillment of needs and the prevention of harmful uses of property?

The antecedentalist justification of property rights is in large part an

33. The rich may, of course, seek to avoid higher taxes "in a variety of legal ways—everything from borrowing against their houses to increasing gifts to charity to socking away more cash in pension accounts . . . they can also work less" (Peter Passell, "Higher Taxes: Will the Well-Off Pay or Play?" *New York Times*, Sept. 1, 1993, national edition, p. C5). Such maneuvers, however, do not uniquely reflect attempts to change distributional "patterns"; they are found generally when higher taxes are imposed on the wealthy. The very fact that such alternative lines of action are available to the wealthy reinforces the contrast to the poor with regard to the power conveyed by property rights.

attempt to answer these questions. Although there may be diverse antecedentalist justifications,[34] the primary one is based on work or labor: property rights belong to persons who have produced the goods—things or services—that are the objects of the rights. This justification reflects, in the transition from productive agency to property, the consideration that persons earn income through their own work. Thus, just as productive agency required development of certain abilities, so too is it with private property as generated by the use of those abilities.[35]

The need for this antecedentalist justification can be further seen by asking the following interrelated questions: From where come the various goods or external things that are the objects of property rights and that are adduced by the consequentialist justification as protecting their owners' freedom and well-being? Or, to put it otherwise, how are these goods provided to fulfill the ends or purposes for which property rights exist? From what source does A derive his income and the various things he can buy with it? Does this source have any bearing on who should have the objects of property rights? These questions ask, in Aristotelian terms, about the efficient cause of property rights, the generating process that leads to the acquisition of such rights.[36] The questions also echo the traditional doctrine that the distribution of economic goods presupposes their prior production.[37]

It may be contended that these antecedentalist questions can be dispensed with, that the consequentialist justification of property rights is sufficient. If A's having X serves to benefit A as purposive agent without harming anyone else, then why must we also ask how A comes (or should come) to have X? Two interrelated answers, which go back at least to Hume, are that there may be many claimants to X and that X may be in short supply. One may here still proceed in consequentialist terms bearing on degrees of needfulness: among the various claimants to X, that person

34.   See my "Economic Justice: Concepts and Criteria," pp. 13–15.

35.   It has been said that "the right to property . . . does not seem to presuppose a capacity needing development" (Charles Taylor, "Atomism," in Taylor, *Philosophical Papers* vol. 2 [Cambridge: Cambridge University Press, 1985], p. 202). This statement overlooks the background of property as generated by one's work and productive agency.

36.   The phrase "efficient cause" as used in the Aristotelian tradition is not to be confused with the economist's use of "efficient" as meaning the maximizing of output with minimal input. "Efficient cause" means that which effects or generates a result; it is equivalent to what, in modern philosophy following Hume, is called simply "cause" (the other three kinds of Aristotelian "cause" being either eliminated altogether or reduced to efficient causes). For Aristotle's four causes, see *Physics*, 2.3.

37.   See Mill, *Principles of Political Economy*, 2.1.1, p. 200; Karl Marx, *Critique of the Gotha Program*, in Tucker, *Marx-Engels Reader*, pp. 531–32; Karl Marx, *Grundrisse*, trans. Martin Nicolaus (Harmondsworth, England: Penguin, 1973), pp. 88–98.

has an overriding right to X who needs it most for her purposive activity or will benefit from it most. But there remain both the fact that X must in some way have been antecedently produced or made available, and the normative question of whether this antecedent relation to X may also have an important bearing on who has a property right to X. Directly relevant here are the considerations about mutuality and dependence adduced in chapters 3 and 4.

The answer given by the antecedentalist justification is that it is persons' labor, their productive action, that justifies their having property rights in the things they produce or in equivalent goods. This justification, however, has two sides, one tied closely to the consequentialist justification in relation to other persons, the other tied directly to the worker herself. The first side, beginning from the thesis that the having of property promotes persons' freedom and well-being, goes on to point out that persons whose labor produces the objects of property make a special contribution to the final cause or good end that justifies the having of property. The worker's having the property income that promotes this final cause for herself is justified as a reward for the contribution she makes in producing the objects of property for others. This justification reflects the relation of mutuality: A does good for others by producing objects of property, and others do good for A by giving her income that constitutes her own claims to property.

A second side of the antecedentalist justification looks at labor not as being instrumental to the fulfillment of human rights and being rewarded for that fulfillment, but rather as itself an application or exercise of human rights, including the agency whose protection is the ground of the rights. In this relation, productive labor is an application of persons' rights to both freedom and well-being: each person has a right to use his freedom and personal responsibility, to control his behavior, for the end or purpose of producing external goods for himself, so that he should have the abilities and conditions needed for such production. Because, by one's labor, one exercises one's generic rights of action, one should also have rights in what one produces by one's labor.

The labor justification of property rights through the generic rights of agency has its deeper basis in the nature of purposive action itself. The reference to purpose serves to connect, at an elemental level, the efficient-cause justification of property rights with the final-cause justification. Since it is by A's own efforts that X is produced or made available in ways that do not harm any other persons, and since A's direct purpose in so producing is to have X as her own thing either as a use value or an exchange value, to say that A does not have a property right in X would be to say that A's purpose in so acting may rightly be frustrated. But this, when generalized, would be an attack on the whole purposiveness of human action and hence on human agency itself. For all human action is performed with a view to achieving the respective agents' purposes; and such action is morally permissible insofar as it does not violate the generic rights of other persons. It follows that persons have property rights in things they have produced for the purpose of having such rights. This may be called *the purposive-labor thesis* of property.[38]

This point can be extended in a more directly interpersonal direction. If A does not have property rights in his product X, then no restriction is placed on B's or other persons' use or appropriation of X even without A's consent. This would mean that A subserves the freedom or well-being of other persons without receiving any payment from them, so that the requirement of mutuality is violated. It would also mean that the result X that A aims to achieve by his purposive action can be appropriated by other persons, thereby again frustrating the purposes for which he acts. That this would also remove A's incentive to produce is a point stressed by utilitarians; but the more direct underlying wrong would be the attack on purposive agency itself. As we have seen, however, property rights are not thereby left absolute; property can be taxed on grounds justified by the PGC.

It may be objected that to deny property rights in what one produces does not entail a general rejection of all purposive action. For persons may still act to achieve their other purposes without fulfilling any specific purpose of acquiring property rights in external things they work to produce. When A produces a book manuscript, a banana split, or a baseball bat, he may fulfill his purpose without any thought of having property rights in such products. The products are indeed his in the sense that he produced them, but they need not also have been produced by him for the purpose of his having exclusive use or power of disposal over them.[39]

This distinction is sound, but it does not invalidate the purposive-labor thesis's generalization from denial of property rights to denial of purposive agency. For in each of the cases of presumed nonproprietary purposes, the fact remains that *if* A produces what he does for the purpose of having property rights in his products, then he should have those rights. The alternative would be that purposes one acts to achieve without harming other persons may rightly be frustrated, so that in such cases purposive actions would be performed in vain. There would thus still be an attack on purposive agency without any justification of preventing harm. In this regard,

38. This requirement is similar to the version of the labor theory of property acquisition presented by Becker, *Property Rights,* pp. 49–56. Becker explicitly emphasizes that "labor . . . is undertaken for some purpose" (p. 52). The argument I present here is perhaps more general and does not explicitly adduce a principle of desert.

39. Cf. ibid., p. 55.

without going the whole route to "self-ownership" as the basis of property rights (see below), it can be argued that implicit claims to proprietorship are at least potentially present in all purposive action with regard to the proximate effects or results of such action. This is not, as such, an assertion of ubiquitous "possessive individualism" ; a producer may want to give away his products, but this implies the prior recognition that they are his to give away, as having been produced or effected by him for purposes that he has and values.

It must also be noted that this derivation of property rights from purposive action is restricted to *effective* purposive action, that is, to labor activity which produces some use or exchange value that the worker intends to produce. The argument thus does not sanction a move from vague, ineffectual intentions or desires to property rights in their wished-for objects. It is when A produces X with the intention of its belonging to A, at least in the first instance, that A has a property right in X.

It may be objected that the purposive-labor thesis would not enable us to distinguish which property belongs to whom; for two persons may have the same purpose in producing something. The reply is that the thesis does not rely on purposes alone to justify property rights; there must be concomitant acts of production. It will be recalled that for there to be productive agency in the economic sense, one's purposes must be embodied in external objects (4.6). Although in complex acts of production it may be difficult to disentangle who has produced what (see 5.7), this difficulty does not derive from the purposiveness itself. Although the purposive-labor thesis directly provides an antecedentalist justification of property rights, since it deals with the question of who has produced the objects of property, it also has a consequentialist component. For to say that A by his work has produced X is to say that X is a consequence of A's work. Here, however, "consequence" is closely tied to the work activity itself, whereas in the consequentialist justification considered above "consequence" refers rather to the broader impact of property rights on the human rights of persons. It is in this broader sense that "consequentialist" is mainly used here.

Up to this point the purposive-labor thesis has dealt primarily with the relation of the producer to his product. But we must now take preliminary note of the consequentialist consideration adduced in the preceding section in connection with harmful use. The general point is that, as we have seen, property rights have consequences for the freedom and well-being of persons other than the owners. For now I shall use this point only to call attention to the specifically economic fact that the purposive-labor thesis, as such, does not determine that the workers' product will have any exchange value. It is possible that no one else may want or be willing to pay for what the worker produces. In such a case the worker will still have a property

right in her product, but this will not be a right that effectively fulfills the
final cause or purpose of property rights in the way indicated above. Effective demand is a factor in the consideration of property rights that go beyond use values for the individual producer herself. So here the purposes or
desires of other persons are also highly relevant. This consideration involves, more generally, the mutuality of the PGC as the principle of human
rights: If A, having produced X, is to receive from B the income she wants
for having produced X, then X must be something that B wants and is willing to pay for. If he is not willing to pay A's price, then either A may lower
her price, or she may find C, D, or someone else who is willing to pay for X,
or she may decide to produce Y or Z instead. These alternatives raise
broader questions of social policy which will be taken up in chapter 6; and
they also show again that the development of productive agency must be
stressed. This emphasis on the mutuality of the exchange relation in the
antecedentalist justification of property rights is continuous with the criticism presented above of the nonmutuality of welfare dependence (4.3).

A traditional argument for the labor theory of property-acquisition,
going back at least to Locke, relies on the idea of "self-ownership." [40] It is
contended that because persons own, or have property in, themselves, they
should also have property in what they produce by their own labor.

There are several preliminary difficulties with this argument. First,
what one produces results from using not only one's own labor but also
external things and resources, and these, at least initially, are not parts of
oneself. Two points follow from this: Even if one owns one's products, one
does not own them in the same way as one owns oneself, for they are not
literally parts of oneself. And this invalidates the sequence from self-
ownership to ownership of one's products, because the latter result not
only from oneself but also from other things. The thesis of self-ownership is
itself brought into question because one's self is also the product of genetic
and environmental causes to which one has not contributed. (This will be
discussed below, 5.4.) Locke himself accompanied his assertion that "every
man has a property in his own person" with the thesis that men are the
"property" of God because they are his "workmanship." [41] But even if one
rejects this theological doctrine, it can still be plausibly argued, as in the
social contribution thesis (3.4), that humans are the "workmanship" or
products both of their parents and of external social causes. Nevertheless,
self-ownership, in the sense of the right of autonomous self-determination,
can still be saved even on a productivist or labor doctrine if it is recognized

---

40. See Locke, *Two Treatises of Government*, 2.27: "every man has a property in his
own person." See also Knight, *Risk, Uncertainty, and Profit*, pp. 56, 77, 354; Nozick, *Anarchy, State, and Utopia*, p. 172.

41. Locke, *Two Treatises of Government*, 2.6.

that humans, while using external factors, can control their own choices and actions. The normative thesis of self-ownership would hold in addition that persons have the right of such control, so that it is in this way equivalent to the human right to freedom.

But even with acceptance of the thesis of self-ownership, there is a major difficulty in the attempt to derive from it property rights in external things, especially in the version which holds that removal of any of those rights by taxation is equivalent to loss of self-ownership. The difficulty may be put as a *modus tollens* argument. If self-ownership entails ownership of what one has produced, then ceasing to own the latter, or part of it, entails ceasing to own oneself, or part of oneself. Hence, if it is permissible to remove, by taxation, part of what one has produced, so that one's ownership of this part ceases (even without one's explicit consent), then it would also be permissible to remove part of one's self, such as, for example, one's eyes or kidneys, without one's consent, if these can be used to help persons who lack these organs. There need not be an exact fit between what one has produced and the parts of one's self, or of one's body, by which one has produced it; it is sufficient that the "self" which one diffusely "owns" has worked to make its product. Hence, if removal of part of the product is justified, then so too is removal of part of the self, since ownership of one's self is held to carry through to, or to entail, ownership of what one's self has produced. The possibility of such an argument for self-mutilation or self-destruction is sometimes adduced by libertarians to reject taxation of one's "holdings," on the ground that taxation is tantamount to removing part of oneself.[42]

It is perhaps laboring the obvious, however, to point out that this contention about taxation ignores the vital difference between one's self with its bodily parts and one's holdings in external things. If some of the former are removed this may drastically decrease or even endanger one's overall well-being. But this need not be the case if some of one's external goods are removed by taxation, especially where one retains sizable amounts of such goods.[43] More generally, one's bodily parts are literally parts of oneself and parts of one's personhood as an actual or prospective agent, in a way that is

42. See Nozick, *Anarchy, State, and Utopia,* pp. 171–72. For critical discussion, see Becker, *Property Rights,* pp. 39–41; Waldron, *Right to Private Property,* pp. 178–81, 398–401.

43. Munzer attempts to deal with this problem by qualifying the idea of self-ownership such that, while "persons do not own their bodies . . . they have limited property rights in their bodies" (*A Theory of Property,* p. 43). He goes on to criticize this distinction on the ground, among others, that "the concept of ownership is compatible with significant restrictions" (p. 44). Cf. Ronald Dworkin, "In Defense of Equality," *Social Philosophy and Policy* 1, no. 1 (autumn 1983): 38–39.

far more intimate and direct than is the case with any external things. Hence, the argument for property rights in external things cannot be securely based on the idea of self-ownership, at least in the sense in which it has been considered here. The criterion of degrees of needfulness for action (2.4) is again directly relevant here. These considerations do not, however, invalidate the purposive-labor thesis as stated above.

5.4. PRIMORDIALIST OBJECTIONS TO THE PURPOSIVE-LABOR THESIS: SELF-OWNERSHIP

The purposive-labor thesis of property rights is confronted by two further questions of a kind I shall call *primordialist*. They concern persons' primordial rights of ownership both over themselves and over the external things on which they work. One question returns us to the thesis of self-ownership just considered. If persons' use of their free purposive agency to produce commodities is to justify their exclusive ownership of these commodities, it would seem to be because the producers are the owners of their respective abilities, their skills and talents, by the use of which they achieve such production. But do they have exclusive rights to these abilities? If, as Rawls has famously claimed,[44] the initial distribution of abilities is morally arbitrary, in that no person deserves the skills and talents that derive from his genetic endowments and from the ways these are molded by the various environmental influences he undergoes, then how can any person have an exclusive moral right to what results from his use of his abilities, including what he contributes to the productive process? The other question bears on persons' rights to exert their purposive agency on external things and resources in such a way as to produce from them things they claim as their private property. If, as many medievals and moderns have contended, the earth was originally owned by all its inhabitants jointly,[45] then how can any of their descendants have a right to make any parts of it their private property without the consent of all the other original owners?[46] Following G. A. Cohen, I shall refer to these two questions as dealing respectively with "self-ownership" and "world ownership." [47]

44. John Rawls, *A Theory of Justice* (Cambridge, Mass.: Harvard University Press, 1971), pp. 60 ff., 104, 302.

45. See Locke, *Two Treatises of Government,* 2.26: "God . . . hath given the world to men in common." On the medieval doctrines, see R. W. Carlyle and A. J. Carlyle, *A History of Mediaeval Political Theory in the West,* vol. 1 (Edinburgh: W. Blackwood & Sons, 1940), chap. 12.

46. See John Exdel, "Distributive Justice: Nozickian Property Rights," *Ethics* 87, no. 2 (Jan. 1977): 142–49.

47. G. A. Cohen, "Self-Ownership, World Ownership, and Equality," in Frank S. Lucash, ed., *Justice and Equality Here and Now* (Ithaca, N.Y.: Cornell University Press,

Let us first discuss self-ownership in connection with Rawls's challenging criticism of it. Although he does not explicitly reject self-ownership, his "difference principle" sets up as the primary determinant of property rights not the antecedentalist consideration of the purposive-labor thesis, with which the doctrine of self-ownership may be associated, but rather a certain consequentialist consideration. According to the difference principle, any departures from economic equality are justified only if they are "to the greatest benefit of the least advantaged" [48] (the maximin effect). This is a distributive consequentialist principle in that it bases economic rewards not primarily on antecedent contributions or productive agency but solely on the comparative consequences of distributing those rewards in one way rather than in another. Economic differentials are justified only insofar as they generate incentives for productive agents that have the maximin effect. The principle is thus compatible with arrangements whereby the "least advantaged" contribute nothing to the productive process but are left in a condition of complete passivity and dependence (see also above, 4.1). For the principle's central emphasis is on maximally benefiting the "least advantaged" regardless of any productive contributions they may themselves make.[49] This emphasis is thus quite different from the focus on productive agency and purposive labor that has been developed here.

Rawls bases his difference principle in part on certain primordialist theses about the ultimate causation of human abilities, achievements, and efforts. According to these theses, the economic rewards or income that persons receive from their productive activity are not to be attributed to

---

1986), pp. 108–135; "Self-Ownership, World Ownership and Equality: Part II," *Social Philosophy and Policy* 3, no. 2 (spring 1986): 77–96.

48. Rawls, *A Theory of Justice*, p. 302.

49. This charge may be contested on various exegetical grounds, including (*a*) Rawls's stipulation that "offices and positions" are to be "open to all under conditions of fair equality of opportunity" (ibid., p. 302); (*b*) his provision for a "stabilization branch" which "strives to bring about full employment in the sense that those who want work can find it" (p. 276); (*c*) his view of the "distributive function of prices" as "determining the income to be received by individuals in return for what they contribute" (p. 273); (*d*) his assertion that "[w]hat men want is meaningful work" (p. 290); (*e*) his definition of "the least advantaged" in terms of "the unskilled worker" (p. 98; cf. pp. 78, 80); (*f*) his invocation of the "Aristotelian principle" according to which "human beings enjoy the exercise of their realized capacities (their innate or trained abilities)" (p. 426). None of these items, however, remove the possibility indicated in my text. Rawls does not develop his fleeting reference to "full employment," nor does he indicate why the "least advantaged" should be represented by the "unskilled worker" and not by impoverished welfare recipients who remain in semipermanent conditions of dependence from which they are to be maximally benefited by the work of others. For a valuable attempt to develop Rawls's vague suggestions on some of these matters in ways that avoid the idea criticized here, see Rex Martin, *Rawls on Rights* (Lawrence: University Press of Kansas, 1985), chaps. 8, 9.

their own desert, because persons do not deserve either their natural or their socially derived abilities. For these abilities stem from genetic or environmental sources beyond the agent himself, "for which he can claim no credit" ; hence, their economic "outcome is arbitrary from a moral perspective." [50] "Even the willingness to make an effort, to try, and so to be deserving in the ordinary sense is itself dependent upon happy family and social circumstances." [51] From this it follows that persons also do not deserve whatever income and wealth they may acquire through these externally generated abilities, so that, to this extent at least, the antecedentalist purposive-labor justification of property rights is to be rejected.

As has been frequently pointed out, Rawls's argument rests on a kind of transitivity assumption: If A does not deserve X (the abilities he derives from the natural and social conditions of his starting point in life), and if X is a necessary condition of Y (the income and wealth he acquires through using these abilities), then A does not deserve Y. This assumption, however, overlooks the possibility that A may make an independent contribution to his getting Y, since X is only a necessary, not a sufficient condition of his getting Y. There is a difference between *having* externally derived abilities and *using* them; one may deserve what one gets by the latter.[52]

This distinction, however, may not capture the full force of Rawls's thesis. It is to be noted that the causal relations asserted in his thesis are conveyed by rather vague expressions: a person's ability, character, or effort, together with the wealth and income that he may attain thereby, is "determined," "decided," "settled," "affected," "strongly influenced by," "is itself dependent upon," "is the cumulative effect of," "depends in large part upon," [53] his natural and social conditions, "for which he can claim no credit" and which he therefore does not deserve. This raises the question of the extent of such "dependence" or "influence" or being "affected." What Rawls seems to suggest, without saying so explicitly, is a determinism so complete that the person himself contributes nothing either to his own actions or to the development of his own character and abilities.[54] A realistic sense of personal responsibility is thereby rejected. The picture given is suggestive of Descartes's view of the motion of material objects: each motion is the result of the impact on it of external objects moving according to natural laws; no object has any independent causal influence on its own

50. Rawls, *A Theory of Justice*, pp. 74, 104.
51. Ibid., p. 74; see also p. 312.
52. See Martin, *Rawls on Rights*, pp. 164–65. See also Derek L. Phillips, *Toward a Just Social Order* (Princeton, N.J.: Princeton University Press, 1986), pp. 359–60.
53. Rawls, *A Theory of Justice*, pp. 72, 74, 104, 312.
54. See Nozick, *Anarchy, State, and Utopia*, p. 214.

motions.[55] Applied to Rawls's conception, this raises the question: How can it be that each person's actions, character, and outcome are so completely "determined," "settled," "affected," "influenced by" and "dependent upon" only factors *other* than the agent himself? Is each of these factors in turn similarly "determined" only by still other factors? If not, then why should independent causal efficacy be attributed to (some of) these other factors and not to the individual agent himself? If, on the other hand, none of these factors has independent causal efficacy, then how does the whole process get started? Is there some Initiating Cause that sets these natural and social forces in motion, imparting to them from without a seemingly exclusive and exhaustive causal efficacy that is not to be attributed to their own powers or behaviors?

Despite such problems, there is indeed plausibility in Rawls's claim that persons' actions and characters are influenced by external natural and social conditions. This point precludes unqualified acceptance of the opposed view that blames the plight of poor people on their "laziness" or "stupidity" with no recognition of their debilitating social circumstances, and that attributes the achievements of the more successful solely to their own intelligence and efforts. Such frequently expressed pejorative and laudatory judgments fail to take account of the diverse causal backgrounds to which Rawls's thesis directs emphatic attention, and which also enter into the social contribution thesis discussed above (3.4).

What is needed is an intermediate position that views persons' actions and characters neither as completely determined by external natural and social forces nor as completely independent of those forces. A tenable position of this sort may be suggested in two steps. The first develops the comparative perspective just suggested. It must be kept in mind that Rawls's discussion of desert occurs in the context of various interpretations of equality of opportunity, so that it is on considerations of comparative rights or entitlements that his thesis is focused. Now certain comparative judgments of economic desert are plausible and well founded. For example, if A is born poor and otherwise disadvantaged, then he deserves more credit for his productive work than if he had been born rich and otherwise advantaged; and so, concomitantly, he deserves more credit than does well-born B. Such comparative judgments have two interrelated grounds. One is antecedentalist; it calls attention to the much greater obstacles A had to overcome in order to become a productive worker, and to the much greater degree of effort he had to exert in this overcoming. The other ground is in a certain sense consequentialist; it focuses on the goods

---

55. See Descartes, *Principles of Philosophy*, pt. 2, sec. 37.

A produces by his efforts. Even if these goods are modest by comparison with what B produces, A may still deserve more credit for producing them than does B, at least so far as concerns the agent-oriented considerations of obstacles and effort. The case is clearer still if A's and B's products are roughly similar as embodying beneficial effects.

The sense in which A is said to "deserve" credit is that it is fitting or appropriate that A receive appreciation or commendation not only for the good he has personally done but also for the personal qualities of effort and control he has had to exert in overcoming the obstacles to his being capable of such productivity.[56] A is an economically productive agent and the thesis of nondesert does not apply to him (even if it does to B). This thesis hence does not preclude that the purposive-labor justification of property rights applies to A's work.

Such a comparative perspective is more cogent than the blanket assertion that "[e]ven the willingness to make an effort . . . is itself dependent upon happy family and social circumstances."[57] When A exerts his efforts, is none of this "dependent upon" himself, especially in view of his lack of "happy family and social circumstances"? This brings me to the second step toward the intermediate position mentioned above. Even if happy family and social circumstances may facilitate development of the willingness to make an effort, they are not sufficient conditions of such development. On the contrary, once an at least minimally facilitative upbringing has done its part, what kind of character one develops, including one's willingness to make appropriate efforts, is then up to the individual herself, through her own actions that are under her own control and her own sense of personal responsibility. As we have seen, the deprivation focus requires that special assistance be provided for those persons whose initial circumstances are most adverse to the development of productive agency. But for all persons education and other conditioning can operate not as exclusively determining actions and character but as laying foundations for autonomous action, so that once these foundations are laid it is then within the person's power to choose to act in one way rather than in another. The foundations in question include training whereby persons learn to control their direct emotions in the light of knowledge about available alternatives and also to develop their capacities for productive agency. It is in this context that the comparative considerations referred to above become especially apposite. Thus, for example, if a person born poor is given education, the use he makes of it—whether to neglect the opportunities it offers

56. See Joel Feinberg, *Doing and Deserving* (Princeton, N.J.: Princeton University Press, 1970), pp. 56–58, 82; George Sher, *Desert* (Princeton, N.J.: Princeton University Press, 1987), chaps. 4, 6.

57. Rawls, *A Theory of Justice*, p. 74.

or to pursue them—will depend on his or her own choices or decisions. In this way he can be held to be responsible for what he does and to deserve punishment or reward. But without such upbringing, the extent of his responsibility and desert will be correspondingly much more limited.[58]

This position is a modification of the agent-cause theory of human action, according to which actions are caused by persons themselves through their own free choices, as against being caused by beliefs and desires over which they have no control.[59] If persons themselves are identified with their autonomous choices, then such a view of action is true of persons once they have undergone appropriate habituation. The need for habituation, education, and training is not thereby denied; on the contrary, as was emphasized in chapter 4 above, it is indispensable for the development of productive agency and human capital. This theory can directly accommodate the freedom which is one of the generic objects of human rights, consisting in control of one's behavior by one's unforced choice while having knowledge of relevant circumstances.

I conclude that the primordialist objection against self-ownership does not refute the antecedentalist justification of property rights as represented by the purposive-labor thesis and the sequence from productive agency to property rights.

Although desert did not figure explicitly in the purposive-labor thesis as it was presented in the preceding section, it can now be fitted directly into the thesis. Just as one deserves credit for one's efforts in producing

---

58. The double aspect of education and autonomous action can be traced back to Aristotle, who says on the one hand that persons who are to benefit from instruction in ethics "must have been brought up in good habits" (*Nicomachean Ethics*, 1.4.1095b4), and on the other hand that persons are responsible for the development of their own characters through the actions they voluntarily perform (ibid., 3.5.1113b3 ff.). The implication of these two sets of passages is that a suitable early upbringing is a necessary condition of autonomous action, but that given this upbringing, what persons do, including the characters they form by their actions, are up to them. On the other hand, without such upbringing persons lack the necessary condition of moral understanding and responsibility. A similar double emphasis can be found in John Dewey, *Human Nature and Conduct* (New York: Henry Holt, 1922), pt. 1, secs. 1, 2; see also Dewey, *Democracy and Education* (New York: Macmillan, 1916), chap. 4. For an application of this double consideration in the sphere of social work, see Helen Harris Perlman, "Self-Determination: Reality or Illusion?" in F. E. McDermott, ed., *Self-Determination in Social Work* (London: Routledge and Kegan Paul, 1975), pp. 65–80.

59. See Roderick Chisholm, "Freedom and Action," in Keith Lehrer, ed., *Freedom and Determinism* (New York: Random House, 1966), pp. 11–44; Richard Taylor, *Action and Purpose* (Englewood Cliffs, N.J.: Prentice Hall, 1966); Alan Donagan, *Choice: The Essential Element in Human Action* (London: Routledge and Kegan Paul, 1987), chaps. 9, 10. For a representative sample of difficulties, see Irving Thalberg, "How Does Agent Causality Work?" in Myles Brand and Douglas Walton, eds., *Action Theory* (Dordrecht, Holland: D. Reidel, 1976), pp. 213–34.

goods, one also deserves income or wages as a reward for such production.
The two desert bases here indicated—effort and production—are not identical. Effort may not be productive of anything good, and one may still deserve credit for one's efforts alone. There may also be institutional rules or
agreements that entitle persons to rewards if they try to produce some designated outcome, even if they fail. But, quite apart from such antecedentalist grounds, persons deserve income for the goods they produce. The
income is a way of recognizing and responding favorably to the benefits one
receives from persons who do not have a distinct obligation to provide
those benefits.[60] This point is an application of the mutuality upheld by the
principle of human rights. The connection between desert based on effort
and desert based on productive contribution is that there is normally a
causal sequence between effort and contribution. After all, the point of trying is to succeed; and in the work situation as such, success consists in producing what one was trying to produce. This is an important part of the
general sense of productive agency (4.6). Effortless contributions (in one
sense of "effort") are unusual, although they may occur.

5.5. PRIMORDIALIST OBJECTIONS TO THE PURPOSIVE-LABOR THESIS: WORLD OWNERSHIP

Let us now turn to the other primordialist objection to the purposive-labor
thesis about property rights. This bears on world ownership: the doctrine
that because the world was originally owned in common, no one can claim
exclusive ownership of any part of it through one's own work or in any
other way. On this doctrine one may be tempted to say, with Hume, that
since the original ownership of external things is unknown and since "the
rule concerning the stability of possession [is] not only useful but even absolutely necessary to human society," [61] we should not try to probe into the
primordialist question of original ownership but should instead accept
things—the distribution of external objects—as they are. But this would be
to overlook both the known antecedent historical circumstances of the violence and treachery that have been the means of so much acquisition of land
and resources,[62] and also the continuing harmful consequences of those

---

60. Cf. Becker, *Property Rights*, pp. 49–56; Munzer, *A Theory of Property*, chap. 10.
61. David Hume, *Treatise of Human Nature*, 3.2.3., ed. L. A. Selby-Bigge, p. 501.
62. See Mill, *Principles of Political Economy*, 2.2.3, pp. 208–9; Marx, *Capital*, vol. 1,
pt. 8, "The So-Called Primitive Accumulation," pp. 713–74. For parallel accounts of American capitalist accumulation, see Gustavus Myers, *History of the Great American Fortunes*
(New York: Modern Library, 1936); Matthew Josephson, *The Robber Barons: The Great
American Capitalists, 1861–1901* (New York: Harcourt Brace, 1934). For an opposed view,
see F. A. Hayek, ed., *Capitalism and the Historians* (Chicago: University of Chicago Press,

immoralities for the freedom and well-being of so many of their victims. These points indicate at least that current ownership may rest on immoral foundations in that rightful past owners have been wrongly dispossessed. Hence, current ownership may not provide a morally sound justification of property rights in external things. In addition, there is also the problem of how private property rights can be generated on the basis of original common ownership.

The implication of the primordialist consideration of world ownership would seem to be the following: if A produces X with the help of resources Y, which he does not personally own but which is owned by H (where H comprises all humans or at least all the members of A's own society), then A is not the sole owner of X; instead, X is at least partly owned also by H. I shall call this the "world ownership thesis."

Now this thesis can be interpreted in at least two different ways. In one, H's ownership of Y is so complete that no special right of ownership of X can belong to A. In the other, A has a privileged position with regard to ownership of X, but he must share some of this ownership with H. The former interpretation should be rejected, for it fails to recognize the special contribution A has made to the production of X. Even if the original or primordial acquisition of resources Y has been immoral, still insofar as A, working subsequently to that acquisition, has produced some X which uses but is not identical with Y, to this extent his ownership of X is at least partially justified. Moreover, the results of A's work then become also available to other persons through various forms of gift or exchange. If A is put on a par with all the other members of H regarding the ownership of X, then the moral requirement of mutuality is violated; for A would then be in the position of producing something for the others without their in turn producing anything for him. As we shall see, this last statement needs qualification.

The reference to "H" as comprising all humans or all members of one's society is, of course, very vague, as is also the reference to H's original "ownership" of the world. Modern theories of corporate ownership may cast some light on the matter; but H is not an explicit corporation in which a group of persons explicitly band together for some common purpose. The difficulties of such a conception continue to mar contractualist theories of state or society. Nevertheless, the world ownership thesis can be de-

---

1954); for a critique of Myers by L. M. Hacker, see Hayek, *Capitalism and the Historians*, p. 79. See also Alfred D. Chandler, *The Visible Hand: The Managerial Revolution in American Business* (Cambridge, Mass.: Harvard University Press, 1977), and Richard B. Du Boff and Edward S. Herman, "Alfred Chandler's New Business History: A Review," *Politics and Society* 10, no. 1 (1980): 87–110.

fended on the basis of the principle of human rights. All humans, as prospective purposive agents, have certain interests in common, in the distributive sense that each needs the necessary goods of freedom and well-being both for the very possibility of action and for generally successful action. As such, they all collectively comprise H, and they have a distributively common interest in being able to use the world and its resources for their various purposes. This interest, as we have seen, comprises the consequentialist justification of private property. But it is also, in an important respect, antecedentalist, not in the sense that each person has put labor into her pursuit of her interest, but in that each has a claim to the world's resources that is temporally prior to that of any particular producer precisely because the world, with each person's interest in its use, exists prior to any particular labor that is expended on it.

What follows from this is that in one respect there should be common or public ownership of the means of production, but in another respect not. There should be public ownership insofar as those means are in the position of Y in my initial statement, but not insofar as they are in the position of X. It will be recalled that Y is the elemental resources that are used to produce X; they consist in the land and other raw materials that exist prior to and independently of human productive actions. Because they are thus indispensable means of production and not owned by the individual producer(s) A but rather by H, they should be publicly owned by the state as the community of rights. On the other hand, insofar as the means of production consist in the objects X—machines and other artificial instruments —that have been produced on the basis of Y through human work, those means should be the private property of the persons who have worked to produce them. The analysis of who these workers are, and in what proportion they should own the means of production, will be taken up below in connection with the contribution principle (5.7). What this divided ownership should come to in practice is that the private owners cannot claim their X's, their products, exclusively for themselves; it is justified that they pay rent or taxes to the other members of H through national and international fiscal agencies.[63] The proceeds should be used to help fulfill basic rights

---

63. For similar suggestions of such combinations of ownership, see Cohen, "Self-Ownership, World Ownership, and Equality: Part II," pp. 77–96; John E. Roemer, *Free to Lose* (Cambridge, Mass.: Harvard University Press, 1988), chap. 10; James O. Grunebaum, *Private Ownership* (London: Routledge and Kegan Paul, 1987), chap. 7. One of the proximate ancestors of this position is John Stuart Mill; see Mill, *Autobiography* ([1873]; Indianapolis, Ind.: Bobbs Merrill, 1957), chap. 7: "The social problem of the future we considered to be, how to unite the greatest individual liberty of action, with a common ownership of the raw material of the globe, and an equal participation of all in the benefits of combined labour" (p. 149).

and rights of productive agency, as well as for public goods. When persons see that in these ways they are common beneficiaries of the arrangements made on the basis of world ownership, this serves to strengthen their sense of community and of the rights they share as members of the community. Important implications of this thesis for economic democracy will be discussed in chapter 7.

This conclusion points in the same direction as the social contribution thesis discussed above (3.4). Just as that thesis held that persons have obligations to support their society because of its contribution to fulfilling their human rights, so the divided ownership thesis holds that private owners have obligations to the other members of their society because the former have made use of primordial natural resources that are not their private property but are in some sense collectively owned. In these ways the community of rights helps to protect the generic rights of all persons while also recognizing the specific property rights of persons who have worked to produce valued commodities. Here too rights and community are mutually supportive.

An important implication of the above argument needs explicit attention. As was noted above (5.2), Locke held that the acquisition of property rights in the state of nature requires that "there is enough, and as good left in common for others." [64] This "Lockean proviso" seems to presuppose the world ownership thesis, and to many philosophers it has seemed clear that the proviso cannot be satisfied because if one "removes" any object "out of the state that Nature hath provided, and left it in," [65] then it cannot be the case that "there is . . . as good left in common for others." This negative view, however, gives an exclusively static interpretation of the labor that "removes" something from the natural state. But if one views labor in accordance with the productive agency stressed above, the labor is dynamic instead of static; it uses the preexisting natural materials to generate new products, so that what is now "left in common for others" is "as good" as, and indeed perhaps even better than, what existed before.[66] This point does not, of course, apply to all "primitive accumulation"; it must be sharply qualified by the brigandage and other immoralities that have char-

---

64. Locke, *Two Treatises of Government*, 2.27.
65. Ibid.
66. See ibid., 2.36: "the Inhabitants think themselves beholden to him, who, by his Industry on neglected, and consequently waste Land, has increased the stock of Corn, which they wanted." On this point, see also David Schmidtz, *The Limits of Government* (Boulder, Colo.: Westview Press, 1991), chap. 2, and "The Institution of Property," *Social Philosophy and Policy* 11, no. 2 (summer 1994): 42–61. I am indebted to Schmidtz's discussion, in which he also gives references to philosophers who have said that the Lockean proviso cannot be fulfilled. Schmidtz does not, however, adduce the qualifications I indicate in the text.

acterized past acquisitions of property. The point also does not, as such, indicate how the products are to be distributed; nor does it change the divided ownership thesis that imposes, on the part of private property owners, obligations to the other members of society. But, within these limits, the fulfillment of the Lockean proviso shows that the world ownership thesis is compatible with the existence of private property rights on both consequentialist and antecedentalist grounds.

This section and the preceding one have two main upshots. One is that although the purposive-labor justification of property rights requires some modification because of the primordialist objections about world ownership, social contribution, and nondesert for one's productive work, these objections do not refute the justification: an important place is left for property rights through one's productive work. The other upshot is that the nonabsoluteness of private property rights, which was previously upheld on the consequentialist grounds of degrees of needfulness for action and prevention of harmful use, has been reinforced on antecedentalist grounds. The arguments for the world ownership and social contribution theses indicate that part of what one produces by one's labor is owed to others or to society at large, not for the utilitarian consequentialist reason that this will serve to maximize utility, but because of the indispensable contribution that worldly resources and social conditions make to one's own productive abilities and activity. And the modified self-ownership thesis has shown that although part of what one produces can be attributed to one's own causal efficacy as a purposive agent, background social circumstances also have an important place in facilitating such efficacy. These upshots in the limitation of property rights have served to buttress the communitarian (and to some extent socialist) emphases that figure in the community of rights and that exemplify the mutual support between rights and community.

5.6. RELATIONS BETWEEN THE TWO JUSTIFICATIONS

The consequentialist and antecedentalist justifications of property rights, as they have been considered so far, have provided arguments both for private property and for limiting it in the interest of greater equality. The consequentialist justification culminated in the statement of the grave harms done by vast economic inequalities through their deleterious effects on the freedom and well-being both of deprived persons and of many others. What was called for was a drastic reduction of such inequalities. The antecedentalist justification, while sustaining the purposive-labor thesis, also presented arguments from world ownership and social contribution that upheld policies requiring owners of huge accumulations of wealth to share them with others, especially those who are most deprived. Through both these justifications, then, the need for much greater economic equality has been defended, and thereby the justice of greater sharing of wealth as provided for by the community of rights. In these ways the ethical individualism of the principle of human rights has been turned in a communitarian direction.

Although the two justifications have in this way had similar upshots, there remain serious questions about their compatibility with one another in their respective relations to property rights. I shall deal with these questions in two main steps. First, I shall point out the oppositions between the consequentialist and antecedentalist justifications and shall indicate how I think they are to be resolved. Second, I shall consider further the issue of unequal property rights as they emerge from the antecedentalist justification, and I shall examine how a principle of contribution sets the stage for dealing with these inequalities (5.7).

To begin with, the two justifications pull in contrary directions, in at least two ways. First, the consequentialist justification is universalist and appeals to a "general right" of property, while the antecedentalist justification is particularist and appeals to a "special right" of property.[67] The consequentialist argument aims to secure property rights for all persons as fulfilling their respective needs of agency; it is not contingent on any special actions or transactions on anyone's part. The main thrust of the argument is thus egalitarian. The antecedentalist argument, on the other hand, justifies property rights for each person only insofar as she has contributed to the production of goods or services through her own labor. Since persons' productive abilities are unequal, even after the equality of self-actualization provided for in early education (4.10), this argument may eventuate in a markedly unequal distribution of property and, at the extreme, in some persons' having no property at all and thus having quite minimal abilities for effective purposive action. Although, as we have seen, the world ownership and social contribution theses serve to limit these inequalities, the antecedentalist justification, with its exclusive emphasis on productive agency, may exert strong pressure for economic inequality. It may seem, then, that by virtue of upholding each of these justifications the principle of human rights is at war with itself.

A second conflict between the two justifications takes the form of an apparent contradiction between their respective assumptions. For the con-

---

67. The distinction between "general" and "special" rights was set forth by H. L. A. Hart, "Are There Any Natural Rights?" *Philosophical Review* 64 (1955): 183 ff., and is extensively developed with regard to property rights by Waldron, *Right to Private Property*, chap. 4. Waldron, however, argues primarily for a general right to private property; see his chap. 8.

sequentialist justification holds that property rights are required for fulfilling the needs of productive agency, while the antecedentalist justification holds that productive agency is required to generate property rights. Thus, the first justification assumes that productive agency is not available to persons until they have property rights, while the second justification assumes that productive agency is already available to persons as means of their getting property rights. So the two justifications together seem to imply that productive agency both can and cannot exist without the having of property rights.[68]

The solution to the latter problem involves a temporal consideration. To be a productive agent requires that one have at least minimal property in what one uses to engage in action, and this is justified through an initial consequentialist argument. But once one thus has abilities of productive agency, the use of those abilities justifies, through the antecedentalist argument, the acquisition of more property, and this furthers one's additive well-being by increasing one's abilities of purpose-fulfillment, so that the final cause is more extensively served.

The solution to the first conflict of justifications is more complex. It requires, to begin with, that, in accordance with the consequentialist justification, the agency needs of all persons must be met if they cannot fulfill the antecedentalist justification's requirement that they provide for themselves through their own work. In brief summary: persons have rights to private property because, as the consequentialist justification has shown, these rights enable them to fulfill their needs of agency. The rights are positive in two respects: first, persons are to be helped to develop the productive agency that enables them to earn income sufficient for their needs of well-being; second, they are to be given welfare payments insofar as they cannot earn sufficient income. These positive rights entail correlative positive duties, enforced by the state as the community of rights, whereby property holders are taxed from their surplus to help fulfill these needs. This involves that the PGC's mutuality requirement is limited by the principle that 'ought' implies 'can.' If A has a positive right to be relieved from starvation or destitution through B's taxes, then B does not have a parallel effective positive right against A if A is unable to provide such relief. Nevertheless, as we have seen, the mutuality and universality of the positive rights obtain as a matter of principle: everyone has the right to be treated in the appropriate way when she has the need, and when others have the relevant ability (2.5).

---

68. This problem and its solution are parallel to the objection I raised against myself in *RM*, 68, that it is "pointless" for an agent to claim rights to freedom and well-being because, as an agent, he already has these generic features of his actions.

Taxation of property is also justified if, through the democratic political process, it can be shown in other ways to be required with a view to fulfilling persons' needs of agency. These requirements include safe drinking water, roads, national defense, and other public goods and collective rights that redound directly or indirectly to the support of human agency. The requirements also include, more generally, prevention of the harms generated by great inequalities of property rights. Only after these requirements have been fulfilled do property rights become negative, in that persons' property is not to be removed or interfered with.

Once this consequentialist justification of property rights has been made effective, the antecedentalist justification takes over: persons are to acquire property through their own productive work. It is this work that justifies their having the general property rights to whose beneficial effects for freedom and well-being the consequentialist justification was addressed. Thus the general need for property to protect one's freedom and well-being does not, of itself, justify persons' actually having any specific property, except in the two ways connected with positive rights. Apart from this, the property income must be earned by one's work (see also 6.4).

This consideration serves to bring out further why the antecedentalist or efficient-cause justification for property rights is needed as well as the consequentialist or final-cause justification. The latter justification, taken alone, is compatible with complete passivity on the part of persons whose needs are fulfilled. But the antecedentalist justification calls direct attention to how these needs get fulfilled and who should fulfill them. To be one's own productive agent, so far as possible, rather than being the passive recipient of the agency of other persons, is required by the PGC as the principle that aims to secure the effective rights of purposive agency and autonomy for all persons, and with them the ethical goods of dignity and self-respect. In these ways rights and community are brought together, because the community helps persons to secure and exercise those rights. In addition, as we have seen, the antecedentalist justification, involving as it does the labor or productive agency of all prospective agents, serves to uphold the mutuality of contribution that is opposed to the asymmetrical relation whereby only some persons are providers or productive agents while other persons are only passive recipients of the agency of others.

The two justifications are also brought closer together by the consideration of economic growth. The consequentialist justification, as we have seen, argues for economic equality while the antecedentalist justification involving productive contributions to total output upholds economic development and growth. It has long been held that rapid economic growth requires economic inequality rather than equality because, among other reasons, only if some persons are very rich will they have the resources and the desire to save and invest.[69] More recent experience in East Asia and elsewhere, however, has shown that rapid economic growth is fostered by policies that promote universal education and other means of equalizing abilities of productive agency.[70] As education becomes more widespread, it expands the productive abilities of hitherto submerged groups, with corresponding increases of human capital. Although growth as an economic concept is primarily utilitarian or aggregative rather than individualist, it is significant that the economic growth that helps to fulfill the right to well-being for all is promoted by fulfillment of the equal right to productive agency. In this way the consequentialist justification of equal property rights moves in the same direction as the antecedentalist justification through productive work. To this extent such societies function as communities of rights, although they may violate political rights in the course of fulfilling economic rights. This conflict will be further discussed in chapter 8.

On the basis of these considerations, we can combine the consequentialist and antecedentalist justifications of property rights by setting up a simplified model of what I shall call a "minimally ideal property situation," as follows: each person is both the efficient cause and the final cause of his property rights. Each person is the productive agent of the goods that fulfill his agency-needs, so that each person is self-reliant and economically autonomous. No one needs assistance from others except to help maintain a stable, legally ordered system. We have here an instantiation of an essential part of the PGC's requirements: Each person, both as efficient cause and as final cause, acts in accord with his own rights to freedom and well-being without violating any other persons' rights. This minimally ideal property situation does not, of course, preclude persons' producing for one another. But such production is provided for through mutual voluntary exchange of produced goods, so that each person thereby fulfills her own agency-needs while being in a mutualist relation with others.

The initial basis for calling such a reflexive situation "ideal" is moral. For the alternative arrangement would seem to be that if A gets property, income, or external goods at all, he gets them from other persons without giving anything in return. But this would violate an important part of

69.   See Nicholas Kaldor, "Capital Accumulation and Economic Growth," in Kaldor, ed., *Further Essays in Economic Theory* (New York: Holmes and Meier, 1978). See also Simon Kuznets, "Economic Growth and Income Inequality," *American Economic Review* 45 (Mar. 1955): 1–28.

70.   For documentation, see Nancy Birdsall, David Ross, and Richard Sabot, "Inequality and Growth Reconsidered." Paper presented at St. Antony's College, Oxford, February 1994. I am greatly indebted to this paper, which fits in with the work on human capital by Theodore W. Schultz cited above (4.7).

the PGC's requirement of mutuality. Nevertheless, the minimally ideal property situation is not feasible for persons who cannot, through self-employment, offer exchange values simply on their own. As has often been pointed out, its simple barter system gets complicated by the introduction of money and the vast transactions that money makes possible. In the complex conditions of modern society, for most persons a necessary condition of their earning income is that they sell their labor power to other persons, who thus become their employers.[71] These latter, especially when they are large corporations, own the extensive means of production that must be used by the former. While this ownership raises questions of both antecedentalist and consequentialist justification, I want to merge it into the question of economic inequality.

5.7. THE CONTRIBUTION PRINCIPLE AND ECONOMIC INEQUALITY

Let us now turn to the second issue distinguished above: how the antecedentalist justification bears on unequal property rights. We have seen that the theses of world ownership and social contribution set limits to the rights. But, as so far considered, it is not entirely clear how much of a differential impact the theses may have, because they apply to all persons who derive income for their productive work. All workers may be required to pay taxes on a proportional basis in return for the use they have made of the world-owned resources and their social context in earning their incomes; these taxes may be used to support the indigent, to help develop productive agency, and to provide for various public goods. But this would still leave it open for the antecedentalist justification to issue in markedly unequal amounts of income, contrary to the egalitarianism of the consequentialist justification. What is needed is a further look at the antecedentalist justification, with special reference to two questions. First, just what does productive work consist in? What kind of work justifies the earning of income? This question has been answered in part by my discussion of the two contexts of the distinction between productive and unproductive labor (4.8), but more must be said on the subject. In particular, the question bears on the role played by capitalists in the productive process. I shall re-

71. There has, of course, been enormous change since Marx wrote (1865) of the United States that "Capital . . . cannot prevent the labour market from being continuously emptied by the continuous conversion of wages labourers into independent, self-sustaining peasants. The position of wages labourers is for a very large part of the American people but a problematical state, which they are sure to leave within a longer or shorter term" (*Wages, Price, and Profit*, sec. 14, in *Marx Engels Selected Works* [Moscow: Foreign Language Publishing House, 1958], vol. 1, p. 444).

cur to this question, but only after discussing a second question: How much property or income should persons derive from their work? As we shall see, much depends on how work is interpreted. But if work is correlated with wages, the normative question becomes: How should the level of wages be determined?

On the factual question of how wages are in fact determined, historians have traced a sequence from a "subsistence" theory to the classical "wages fund" theory to the theory of marginal productivity, and from this to more recent conceptions based partly on labor union pressures and other manifestations of power.[72] To these may be added further emphases on technological developments and the international movement of capital, including competition from low-wage foreign workers. Since, however, property as money income enables its owners to acquire property in other goods, from which they can exclude other persons who may also want the goods, the normative question should also be put in comparative terms: How much work-derived income should workers get in relation to one another? Still ignoring the question of kinds of "workers," this is in large part a question of how rich, or how poor, persons should be relative to one another, how much relative command they should have over the resources needed for living and living well, including the services of other persons. Thus the question has an important bearing on the class structure of a society, in one of the main meanings of "class." Who are able to get other persons to work for them; who are able to outbid other persons for the necessities and amenities of life? In broadest terms, this is the question of the criterion of distributive justice.

The traditional antecedentalist answer to this question has seemed plausible to a long line of thinkers from Aristotle[73] through Marx[74] to the present. This answer is the *contribution principle*: distribution should be determined by contribution; or, in comparative terms, how much goods or rewards persons get relative to one another should be determined by, and be proportional to, how much, by their prior work, they have contributed

---

72. See John T. Dunlop, ed., *The Theory of Wage Determination* (London: Macmillan, 1964), including essays by Dunlop, "The Task of Contemporary Wage Theory," pp. 3–30, and Clark Kerr, "Wage Relationships—The Comparative Impact of Market and Power Forces," pp. 173–93. See also Maurice Dobb, *Wages* (Cambridge: Cambridge University Press, 1927), chap. 4; and Richard Perlman, ed., *Wage Determination: Market or Power Forces?* (Boston: D. C. Heath, 1964). The influence of racism and sexism does not figure in these historical accounts.

73. Aristotle, *Politics*, 3.9.1281a3.

74. Marx, *Critique of the Gotha Program*, p. 530: "The individual producer receives back from society—after the deductions have been made—exactly what he gives to it." Marx is here referring to the transitional "communist society . . . as it emerges from capitalist society," not to the "higher phase of communist society" (pp. 529, 531).

to the total product. This principle has the same justificatory ground as the two sides of the antecedentalist justification presented above (5.3): one's work is rewarded for producing goods for others, and it is itself an application of one's human rights of agency. In the reward doctrine, in particular, how much one is rewarded should be determined by how much one produces. The comparative version of the contribution principle enables it to avoid the rejoinder, made by Marx and others, that persons should not receive the full value of what they have contributed because part of the product must be allocated for future investment and other purposes. The comparative version is also the basis of the justified feminist demand that women workers should be paid according to the "comparable worth" of their work.[75] The mutuality requirement of human rights also enters here, for persons are to contribute to one another not only according to their respective needs but also according to their productive efforts.

The concept of exploitation as an unfair transaction between persons can be defined in terms of the contribution principle: if A in working for B produces X units of value but (apart from necessary deductions) B pays A the equivalent of less than X units, then B exploits A. This relation obtains regardless of whether the X units are held to consist in A's marginal product[76] or in the value of the hours he works.[77] Similarly, in comparative terms, B exploits A if B, while distributing to himself an amount greater than what he has contributed, distributes to A an amount less than what A has contributed. This comparative conception of exploitation has the advantage that it can acknowledge different kinds of contribution to the final product, as against attributing value solely to labor. In each case exploitation violates the contribution principle, and hence the antecedentalist justification, for what it distributes to the exploited person is not equal or proportional to what the person has produced or contributed. In this regard, the requirement of mutuality is also not fulfilled.[78]

75. See Henry J. Aaron and Cameron M. Lougy, *The Comparable Worth Controversy* (Washington, D.C.: Brookings Institution, 1986). See also Donald Treiman and Heidi Hartmann, eds., *Women, Work, and Wages: Equal Pay for Jobs of Equal Value* (Washington, D.C.: National Academy Press, 1981); Dobb, *Wages,* pp. 170–72. Cf. Universal Declaration of Human Rights, art. 23: "Everyone, without any discrimination, has the right to equal pay for equal work" (in Ian Brownlie, ed., *Basic Documents on Human Rights,* 2d ed. [Oxford: Clarendon Press, 1981], p. 25).

76. A. C. Pigou, *The Economics of Welfare,* 4th ed. (London: Macmillan, 1952), pp. 549–51, 556–60.

77. See Marx, *Capital,* vol. 1, chaps. 9, 10, 11, 15, 25 (pp. 218, 298, 303, 395, 618). For contentions that Marx also had more general conceptions of exploitation, see Allen Buchanan, *Marx and Justice* (Totowa, N.J.: Rowman and Allanheld, 1982), chap. 3.

78. A different comparative conception of exploitation is presented by John E. Roemer, *A General Theory of Exploitation and Class* (Cambridge, Mass.: Harvard University Press,

The contribution principle incurs familiar conceptual, empirical, and moral difficulties. Just how is the value of any contribution in general to be ascertained or measured? "Effective market demand" as an answer raises the problems about the "productive" considered above (4.8). Moreover, how are the particular contributions of particular individuals to be disentangled from one another? Both questions raise severe problems for the theory that persons should be paid according to their marginal product.[79] But they also recur to the primordialist issues considered earlier (5.4, 5) as well as to the social context that helps both to shape one's productive abilities and to determine the demand for one's products (3.4; 4.6).

These difficulties show that the contribution principle, even if it is supplemented by the consequentialist justification, cannot be accepted in an unqualified way as determining the justified extent of persons' property rights through the purposive-labor thesis. In his acute discussion of the contribution principle, Rawls holds that it is "but one among many secondary norms, and what really counts is the workings of the whole system," that is, the system based on his two principles of justice.[80] While recognizing the strong merits of Rawls's approach, the one I follow here does not proceed entirely or mainly on an ideal level in which principles of justice are regarded as being already effective and thus as shaping economic policy. Instead, having begun from the existing imperfections of a society whose large violations of human rights are reflected in the deprivation focus and elsewhere, I have tried to show, in sequential fashion, how these violations should be removed. In keeping with this approach, I shall use the contribution principle while recognizing its limitations. To give it up completely would require, at the least, a major reorientation of the antecedentalist justification of property rights. For that justification, especially through the purposive-labor thesis, holds that persons earn property in-

---

1982): "An individual or coalition is considered to be exploited if he (or they) has (have) some alternative which is superior to the present allocation" (p. 20; see also chap. 7). Here the comparison is not between groups who receive more or less from the production process, but rather between general alternative states of affairs. For criticism of Roemer's model, see Jon Elster, "Roemer versus Roemer: A Comment on 'New Direction in the Marxist Theory of Exploitation and Class,'" *Politics and Society* 11, no. 3 (1982): 363–73. For a collection of essays that offer varying analyses of exploitation, see Andrew Reeve, ed., *Modern Theories of Exploitation* (London: Sage Publications, 1987). For an analysis of exploitation as "a breakdown or failure of reciprocity," see N. Scott Arnold, *The Philosophy and Economics of Market Socialism* (Oxford: Oxford University Press, 1994), pp. 57–59, 65–70.

79. See Arthur M. Okun, *Equality and Efficiency: The Big Tradeoff* (Washington, D.C.: The Brookings Institution, 1975), pp. 40–50; Lester C. Thurow, *Generating Inequality* (New York: Basic Books, 1975), pp. 211–30; David Miller, *Social Justice* (Oxford: Clarendon Press, 1976), pp. 103–9; Derek L. Phillips, *Toward a Just Social Order*, pp. 365–72.

80. Rawls, *Theory of Justice*, p. 309.

come through their work. The justification thus requires that some means be available for correlating work with income. The attempted correlation has all the difficulties noted above. But it can still be invoked in connection with large issues of economic inequality as it is reflected in the capitalist system of production. This brings us to the first question distinguished above.

It will be recalled that that question concerns the nature of productive work, especially as it justifies the earning of income. Here a vital addition must be made to the concept of purposive labor in its relation to property rights. As we have already noted (5.1), there is an important distinction between persons whose property rights include the major means of production and other workers. I have thus far used "work" and "labor" without regard to this distinction. The deprivation focus has assumed that the workers referred to are those who must sell their labor power in order to live, and whose property rights thus derived do not extend from ownership of their labor to other means of production. To be sure, just as capital is produced means of production, so "means of production" may be interpreted literally to include workers' own hammers, word processors, or sewing machines whereby they produce other commodities. But when workers are distinguished from capitalists in terms of ownership of the means of production, what are referred to are the far more impersonal and extensive mechanical, electronic, and other instruments that are used in large-scale industrial and postindustrial production.

Three additional restrictions must be noted in the customary definition of capitalism as a system of private ownership of the means of production. First, where "factors of production" were traditionally divided into three groups—labor, land, and capital[81] (with entrepreneurship or "management" sometimes added as a fourth group)—since labor is not legally owned by anyone other than the laborers themselves, it is excluded from the "means of production" that are owned by capitalists. Second, since modern capitalist organizations are characterized by a separation of ownership from control, so that the dominant form is not "family capitalism," "entrepreneurial capitalism," or "financial capitalism" but rather "managerial capitalism," the result is that both short-term operations and long-term policies are determined by salaried managers whose main concern is not to maximize current profits but rather to foster "the long-term stability

---

81. See Alfred Marshall, *Principles of Economics,* 8th ed. (London: Macmillan, 1930), bk. 4, chap. 1, pp. 138–43. See Marx's critique of "the trinity formula" in *Capital,* vol. 3, pt. 7, chap. 48, pp. 814–31; Marx, *Theories of Surplus Value,* pt. 3 (Moscow: Progress, 1971), pp. 453–540. See also David Harvey, *The Limits to Capital* (Chicago: University of Chicago Press, 1989), pp. 40–41.

and growth of their enterprises." [82] Third, although "private" ownership is contrasted with "public" ownership, where the latter means ownership by the state, in many corporations ownership does not belong to a narrow group of entrepreneurs or capitalists but is instead widely diffused over a large number of stockholders, so that in important degree the ownership is "public" though not by the state.

These three restrictions leave capitalism to be defined as a system where the large-scale means of production are owned by stockholders but are controlled by managers acting in their behalf as well as for entrepreneurs and providers of extensive capital. How is the system as thus defined related to the right of private property? I have already considered certain aspects of this question so far as it bears on the consequentialist justification's concern about the harms done by vastly unequal property rights (5.2). We must now ask about the antecedentalist justification, especially as it bears on the vast property rights that corporate employers of labor amass in capitalist societies. Do the purposive-labor and contribution justifications apply to them?

I shall first deal with this question by outlining the beginning of a negative answer. Its point is suggested in the following critique by J. S. Mill of "the present [1852] state of society with all its sufferings and injustices . . . the institution of private property necessarily carried with it as a consequence, that the produce of labour should be apportioned as we now see it, almost in an inverse ratio to the labour—the largest portions to those who have never worked at all, the next largest to those whose work is almost nominal, and so in a descending scale, the remuneration dwindling as the work grows harder and more disagreeable, until the most fatiguing and exhausting bodily labour cannot count with certainty on being able to earn even the necessaries of life." [83] As this passage suggests, Mill holds that the "equitable principle" of private property consists in "proportion between remuneration and exertion." [84]

It is easy to sympathize with Mill's condemnation of the "inverse ratio" between labor and reward, the flagrant violation of the contribution principle exhibited in the nonmutualist contrast between the idle rich and the suffering toilers. Although he puts his criticism in terms of "exertion,"

82. See Chandler, *Visible Hand*, pp. 9–10. See also the classic discussion of the separation of ownership from control in Berle and Means, *The Modern Corporation and Private Property*.

83. Mill, *Principles of Political Economy*, 2.1.3, p. 208.

84. Ibid., p. 209. In his later work, *Utilitarianism* (1861), Mill holds that there are "conflicting principles" of "superior remuneration," including effort and contribution, and that the conflicts can be resolved only by an appeal to utility (chap. 5 in *Utilitarianism, Liberty, and Representative Government* [London: J. M. Dent, 1910], pp. 53–54).

its basic point reflects the contribution principle: under capitalism, distribution, far from being proportional to contribution, is the reverse of proportional, so that the workers are exploited, in the specific comparative sense of "exploitation" noted above. While Mill was presumably referring especially to idle landowners when he said that the largest remuneration goes to "those who have never worked at all," his criticism can be applied to the contemporary question of antecedentalist justification with regard to those groups who provide "means of production" other than labor: entrepreneurs, managers, and capitalists. Do they, through their distinctive activity or work, make a contribution to the total product? And are the rewards they obtain proportional to that contribution? These questions invoke the mutuality requirement of human rights, for they ask whether the various groups obtain income in a way that is proportional to what they contribute to one another in the productive process. Although these three groups may coincide in the same persons, their roles may also be filled by different persons. In any case, the question of antecedentalist justification applies directly to the roles: are contributions to the total product made by entrepreneurs, managers, and capitalists as such, in their distinctive roles, through their distinctive activities? It will be noted that this question assumes that, at least to some extent, the contribution principle can be meaningfully applied.

Although a satisfactory answer to this question involves many complexities, the answer seems relatively clear with regard to the first two of these groups. Entrepreneurs play an important role in conceiving new, more efficient methods of production and new products, and in accumulating the risk capital to support their ventures.[85] Managers also play an important role in coordinating production, supervising various stages of the production process, and ironing out difficulties that threaten to impede the process.[86] In this perspective, both entrepreneurs and managers may be classed as productive workers who fulfill the requirements of the purposive-labor justification of property rights. Hence there is a basis for applying the contribution principle to each of them: as each contributes to the process of

---

85. See Israel M. Kirzner, *Competition and Entrepreneurship* (Chicago: University of Chicago Press, 1973). Joseph Schumpeter, while extolling the "supernormal intelligence and energy" of past entrepreneurs (*Capitalism, Socialism, and Democracy* [London: George, Allen and Unwin, 1950], p. 16), held that the entrepreneurial function "is already losing importance and is bound to lose it at an accelerating rate in the future" (p. 132). For opposed views, see A. Heertje, ed., *Schumpeter's Vision: Capitalism, Socialism, and Democracy after Forty Years* (New York: Praeger, 1981), and Janos Kornai, "Market Socialism Revisited," in P. A. Bardhan and J. E. Roemer, eds., *Market Socialism: The Current Debate* (New York: Oxford University Press, 1993), pp. 58–61.

86. See Chandler, *Visible Hand,* chaps. 12, 13; Marx, *Capital,* vol. 3, chap. 23, pp. 383–90.

production, so each should have a share in the resulting proceeds. Of course, the size of the share is still left indeterminate.

This brings us to the capitalists, the persons or groups who, as owners of great wealth, supply capital for the productive process. Do they, as such, contribute to the process or outcomes of production? It might seem obvious that if capital, as produced means of production, is necessary for production, and so contributes to production, then the providing of capital to be so used also contributes to production. Nevertheless, that the provision of capital is a "productive activity" has been disputed. Thus it has been said that "ownership of means of production literally creates nothing," "ownership of capital, considered as such, cannot be said to . . . produce what has value." But since such ownership reaps vast financial rewards, it follows that "capitalist property in means of production is theft" and is hence "morally illegitimate." [87]

Part of the dispute on this issue arises because "productive" is used in a confused way. We may here distinguish between two different senses, both of which fall within the economic kind of productive agency discussed above (4.6). In the consequentialist, "objective" sense, X is productive if it eventuates in the production of commodities. In this sense, it seems clear that providing capital is a productive activity. In the antecedentalist, "subjective" sense, on the other hand, X is productive if it consists in persons' activities or expenditures of effort or energy from which produced outcomes or consequences can be traced. These two senses are distinct because, for example, a capitalist's provision of capital may yield positive consequences for production but he may make this provision without any effort, exertion, or sacrifice on his part. He may simply let his capital (inherited or otherwise acquired) be used by others. In this case what he does is productive in a consequentialist sense but not in an antecedentalist sense: *he* has not done any productive work to obtain his capital or to put it to this use.

Let us look somewhat more closely at how this distinction underlies some of the main polemics over the question of whether capitalists qua capitalists contribute to production and so are "productive." A traditional argument may be divided into three parts. The first part focuses on the "ab-

---

87. Cohen, *History, Labour and Freedom*, pp. 223, 227, 234, 235. See Nove, *The Economics of Feasible Socialism Revisited*, p. 4: "I find it hard to believe that merely allowing others to use my money, or my land, is a 'productive' activity, on a par with actually working. . . . Why should vast riches go to those who have had the luck to own some oil-bearing land, or to have forebears who were given land in exchange for services rendered (sometimes in bed) to some long-dead monarch? This has nothing to do with any contribution to production or welfare in any sense." See also Schweickart, *Against Capitalism*, chap. 1.

stinence" of the capitalist:[88] by investing his wealth and so forgoing immediate consumption, he allows it to be used by others to produce goods. Such abstinence, however, has two sides. On its objective-consequentialist side, the question concerns what abstinence does for production; and there can be no doubt that it helps to make production possible by putting some wealth aside to be used for production. But on this side, abstinence need not be a characteristic of a person who is a capitalist; it could pertain just as well to the state as making capital available for production instead of using it for direct consumption by individuals and groups. At this point the argument's second part returns the focus to the capitalist by dwelling on the subjective-antecedentalist side of abstinence: the capitalist is held to deserve profits or income because, by abstaining from immediate consumption, he has gone against the normal "time preference" of persons.[89] Normally, persons prefer present to future consumption, both because of the desire for immediate gratification and because present realities are more certain than future ones. By going against this normal time preference, the capitalist has made a "sacrifice," has undergone a "privation," and so deserves a reward.[90]

There are at least two replies to this second part. First, as before, such time preference need not be a feature of individual capitalists; it may also characterize the state acting through its officials. They may also feel an urge to dispense publicly owned capital for immediate consumption instead of investing it in productive resources. Immediate gratification may here take the form of popularity with various constituents. Hence, the appeal to time preference does not, as such, justify the conclusion that rewards for abstinence must go to the individual capitalist or that he makes a productive contribution. Second, to portray the individual capitalist's going against his time preference as his incurring a "subjective cost" and a "sacrifice" opens the thesis "to ridicule on the grounds that abstaining from the present enjoyment of income is hardly painful to the average saver in the upper income brackets."[91] "Now sacrifice arguments have always appeared ludicrous to critics of capitalism. (Does the owner of a mine really sacrifice

88. See Mill, *Principles of Political Economy* 1.2.2, p. 22; 2.15.1, p. 405; Marshall, *Principles of Economics*, 4.7.8, pp. 232–34. See also Mark Blaug, *Economic Theory in Retrospect*, 3d ed. (Cambridge: Cambridge University Press, 1978), pp. 201–4.

89. See N. Scott Arnold, "Capitalists and the Ethics of Contribution," *Canadian Journal of Philosophy* 15 (Mar. 1985): 87–102.

90. See Ludwig von Mises, *Human Action*, 3d rev. ed. (Chicago: Henry Regnery, 1963), p. 846 n.: "Saving is privation (*Entbehrung*) in so far as it deprives the saver of an instantaneous enjoyment."

91. Blaug, *Economic Theory*, pp. 201–2.

more than a miner? A major stockholder in General Motors more than an autoworker?)" [92] The obvious weakness of the appeal to abstinence on its subjective-antecedentalist side does not, however, remove the soundness of the argument on its objective-consequentialist side.

The third part of the argument is therefore the crucial one. If the consequentialist investment functions of the capitalist can be performed by the state, then is his ownership of capital justified in the first place? To say that he deserves to own capital because he has abstained from immediately consuming his wealth is, of course, question-begging, for the question concerns whether the wealth is "his" as his property right in the first place. This is a question of justification and, as before, it can be divided into two subquestions, one about efficient causes or antecedents, the other about final causes or consequences.

Suppose we give the most favorable answer to the efficient cause question. Ignoring the historical evidence of brigandage, as well as the possibility of state provision of capital, let us concede that the capitalist has accumulated his capital through his own work, savings, and investments, and that, by investing his capital in productive enterprises, he makes a contribution to the productive process. Let us also take emphatic note of the vast outpouring of consumer goods that characterizes this process under capitalism. There remain two important questions. One is the antecedentalist question of whether the capitalist's contribution determines how much he should get in the way of reward. Surely the vast inequalities of rewards between capitalists and workers cannot be justified by any comparative contribution principle. What is operative here is that the capitalist uses his preexisting economic power to extract a reward that is grossly disproportional to the value of his contribution.[93] In this regard it is unjustified for the capitalist to be the "residual claimant" who, just as he owns the firm, also owns the net proceeds of the firm's production process.[94] The comparative contributions made by workers and capitalists justify a far more equal distribution of the proceeds. This subject will be resumed in chapter 7.

92. David Schweickart, *Capitalism or Worker Control?* (New York: Praeger, 1980), p. 22. See Marx, *Capital*, vol. 1, chap. 24, sec. 3, pp. 597–98).

93. See Frank H. Knight, *Freedom and Reform* (New York: Harper and Brothers, 1947), pp. 222–23, also pp. 9, 67; Charles E. Lindblom, *Politics and Markets* (New York: Basic Books, 1977), pp. 46–47; Elliott Jacques, *Equitable Payment* (New York: John Wiley and Sons, 1961), pp. 26–27; Warren J. Samuels, "On the Nature and Existence of Economic Coercion," *Journal of Economic Issues* 18 (Dec. 1984): 1027–48.

94. On the "residual claimant," see Armen A. Alchian and Harold Demsetz, "Production, Information Costs, and Economic Organization," *American Economic Review* 62, no. 5 (Dec. 1972): 782–83, 791; David Ellerman, *The Democratic Worker-Owned Firm* (Boston: Unwin Hyman, 1990), chap. 1.

The other question is the consequentialist one. If the consequence of the capitalist's contribution, what he plays an important role in contributing to, is a society marked by vast inequalities of wealth and resultant severe suffering and violation of rights for millions of persons, then this strongly limits the extent to which the antecedentalist justification through the capitalist's contribution can residually justify the distribution of property rights.[95] That contribution accommodates too little in terms of the equal rights to freedom and well-being. Hence, even if full credit is given to the provision of capital for the productive process, the distributive consequences in question warrant a search for a different antecedentalist ground, a different way of providing and controlling capital, that does not have such deleterious consequences for the human rights to freedom and well-being.

This point does not remove the importance of the antecedentalist consideration of productive agency in its bearing on the millions of workers who are not capitalists. There is still a need to produce goods and to participate in the productive process. The superseding of the antecedentalist question by the consequentialist one in the case of the capitalist is largely motivated by the aim of enabling the productive agency of the masses of workers to obtain, so far as possible, the full fruits of their labor and to avoid the crippling effects of vast unjustified economic inequalities.

The upshot of these considerations about the right to private property is at least twofold. First, the state as the community of rights must provide for effectuating the right to productive agency for all persons through, among other things, a system of universal education. Persons must be free to use their abilities and talents in productive work. Second, the theses about harmful use, social contribution, and world ownership set requirements of redistribution on both consequentialist and antecedentalist grounds. By these requirements the effects of great economic inequalities are warded off. The state as the community of rights acts thereby to help fulfill the equal rights of all persons to freedom and well-being. So rights, far from being antithetical to community, supply the contents that the community uses to enable all persons to mutually help one another to meet their respective needs of agency and thereby to live lives of dignity as purposive autonomous agents.

95. See Blaug, *Economic Theory*, p. 253: "One may believe that capital is productive, and even that capitalists are productive—another proposition altogether—and yet believe that the price we pay for free enterprise in the form of recurrent slumps and gross inequalities in the distribution of income is too great to warrant its perpetuation."

Six

The Right to
Employment

6.1. The Argument from Productive Agency
and Basic Well-Being

We have now reached the point of economic biography where persons, through developing their abilities of economic productive agency, can earn income sufficient for their well-being and can thereby acquire property rights. This development has required not only the efforts of the individuals directly concerned but also positive assistance through socio-political institutions that comprise a community of rights. The institutions have mandated such policies as free public education, welfare payments for transitional learners as well as for persons unable to work, protection of private property combined with redistributive taxation to prevent abuses of the power conveyed by great wealth, and other systemic provisions to secure the equal rights to freedom and well-being. These provisions are embodied in the economic constitution of the state as a community of rights.

These communal policies are now confronted by a further challenge: unemployment. During many of its phases modern capitalism has been afflicted by greater or lesser amounts of unemployment, sometimes reaching crisis proportions such as during the Great Depression of the 1930s when 25 percent of the labor force was unemployed. In 1994 in western Europe roughly nineteen million people, about 11 percent of the workforce, were unemployed.[1] It must be stressed that unemployment with its attendant insecurities also afflicts many members of the middle class.

The community of rights must be deeply concerned about unemployment for several familiar reasons, all bearing on the negative impact of unemployment on the human rights whose securing is the prime function of the state. Since for most persons paid work is the source of their livelihoods, unemployment threatens their basic well-being. It can bring about severe undernourishment, homelessness, lack of needed medical care, and

---

1. *New York Times,* Mar. 14, 1994, national edition, p. C4.

inability to obtain other necessities of life.[2] Moreover, unemployment can undermine one's self-esteem. For unemployed persons are in effect told that they are "of no use."[3] In extreme cases, unemployment, coupled with the threat to livelihood, can lead not only to deep depression but to suicide.[4] On these and other grounds, including the considerations about productive agency and private property presented in chapters 4 and 5, all prospective purposive agents have a right to employment, a right to be effectively able to earn their livelihoods through their own productive work and thereby to ward off such negative impacts. As we shall see, the state as the community of rights is in certain crucial respects the respondent of this right.

In opposition to this thesis, it may be contended on free-market grounds that the state should not be concerned about unemployment, let alone provide work for unemployed persons. If would-be workers are unable to sell their products or services by free exchange, this shows that those products or services are not sufficiently valued by other persons. What justification is there, then, for government's rewarding such workers by directly or indirectly paying them for their products? (I shall call this the "exchange-value objection.") Moreover, workers are like all other participants in a market economy, including entrepreneurs, in that they contract to sell commodities that they make, own, or are entrusted with: in their case, their labor.[5] Now if other entrepreneurs are unable to sell their offerings, we do not think they are entitled to help from the government, such that the government buys their goods and pays for them. (But the government has bailed out Lockheed and other corporations.) After all, in a market economy each entrepreneur knowingly incurs risks, including the risk that the commodities he offers for sale will not be bought, either at all or at a market-clearing price. There is always the possibility of bankruptcy—a risk that accompanies the decision to do business on the market. Why, then, should it be any different with workers who offer their labor on the market? (I shall call this the "entrepreneurial objection.")

These and other free-market objections will be answered in some detail in what follows. But, in addition to the impacts on well-being noted

2. See Peter Townsend, *Poverty in the United Kingdom* (Berkeley, Calif.: University of California Press, 1979), chap. 17.

3. See William Beveridge, *Full Employment in a Free Society* (New York: W. W. Norton, 1945), pp. 18–20. See also Richard T. DeGeorge, "The Right to Work: Law and Ideology," *Valparaiso University Law Review* 19, no. 1 (fall 1984): 15–35, at p. 18.

4. See Stephen Platt, "Unemployment and Suicidal Behaviour: A Review of the Literature," *Social Science and Medicine* 19 (1984): 93–115; P. Warr, *Work, Unemployment and Mental Health* (Oxford: Clarendon Press, 1987).

5. See Armen A. Alchian and Harold Demsetz, "Production, Information Costs, and Economic Organization," *American Economic Review* 62, no. 5 (Dec. 1972): 777, 783.

above, unemployment poses an important challenge to the phases of the
community of rights that are concerned with equal freedom and power.
Apart from "frictional" unemployment, where workers leave their jobs in
order to find something better or for other reasons, it may be held, as in the
exchange-value objection, that the direct underlying cause of a person's being unemployed, both in structural and in cyclical unemployment, is that
there is no, or insufficient, effective demand for his work, or, in other
words, his work lacks exchange value: "Other people no longer can or
want to keep on paying for what he is able to offer."[6] But although this
simple statement (which may overlook other causal factors)[7] applies both
to self-employed persons and to persons who work for others, the statement's "can or want" reflects three inequalities of power that operate to the
marked disadvantage of workers. First, even when work is performed well,
large corporations eliminate thousands of jobs in order to maintain or increase profits, so that the interests of stockholders are given precedence
over the interests of workers, regardless of considerations of productivity
or further investment.[8] Second, the workers cannot of themselves control
whether their work will have sufficient exchange value, that is, will be effectively demanded, in contrast to the ability of large corporations, through
advertising and other means, to help to determine (though without complete assurance) that their products are effectively demanded.[9] Third, with
minor exceptions the workers cannot control the decisions of their em-

6. Charles E. Lindblom, *Politics and Markets* (New York: Basic Books, 1977), p. 83.
7. For alternative theories that stress structural or cyclical factors rather than (or in ad-
tion to) demand, see Edmond Malinvaud, *Mass Unemployment* (Oxford: Basil Blackwell,
1984), pp. 11–13; Lawrence M. Summers, *Understanding Unemployment* (Cambridge,
Mass.: MIT Press, 1990), pts. 2 and 3; and, for a more general discussion, Assar Linbbeck and
Dennis J. Snower, "Explanations of Unemployment," *Oxford Review of Economic Policy* 1,
no. 2 (summer 1985): 34–59. The thesis that "the major cause of high unemployment, both
cyclical and secular, is government itself" is upheld by Richard K. Vedder and Lowell E. Gallo-
way, *Out of Work: Unemployment and Government in Twentieth-Century America* (New
York: Holmes and Meier, 1993), back cover; see also chap. 15.
8. See Louis Uchitelle, "Strong Companies Are Joining Trend to Eliminate Jobs," *New
York Times,* July 26, 1993, national edition, p. 1. See the multiple reports in the *New York
Times* (within a few weeks of one another) of many thousands of jobs cut by leading industrial
companies with a view to maintaining profits: 60,000 jobs, IBM (July 28, 1993); 10,000 jobs,
Kodak (Aug. 19, 1993); 9,000 jobs, U.S. West (Sept. 18, 1993); 40,000 jobs, Daimler-Benz
(Sept. 18, 1993). For broader overviews on massive unemployment, see Morley Gunderson,
Noah M. Meltz, and Sylvia Ostry, eds., *Unemployment: International Perspectives* (Toronto:
University of Toronto Press, 1987); Bob Rowthorn and Andrew Glyn, "The Diversity of Em-
ployment Experience Since 1973," in Stephen A. Marglin and Juliet B. Schor, eds., *The
Golden Age of Capitalism* (Oxford: Clarendon Press, 1990), pp. 218–66.
9. See Edward L. Bernays, ed., *The Engineering of Consent* (Norman: University of
Oklahoma Press, 1955), esp. pp. 54–93; John K. Galbraith, *The Affluent Society* (Boston:
Houghton Mifflin, 1958), chaps. 10, 11.

ployers with regard to their having continued employment (see also above, 5.2).[10]

These inequalities of power reflect in turn the imperatives of market operations in which every corporate board uses "the single criterion of profit maximization upon which to base its decisions."[11] But they are also inequalities of legal property rights, which are legally protected interests of these and other corporations. In view of the sharp contrasts of these inequalities to the equalities mandated by moral rights, the question arises of whether they are morally justified. While many aspects of this question have been discussed above (5.7), further consideration of it is needed with regard to unemployment.

The inequalities of power that underlie the phenomenon of unemployment mean, among other things, that even when persons' economic biography has reached the point where their abilities of productive agency have been adequately developed, they may still not obtain the income that should be the reward of their using those abilities according to the purposive-labor thesis and the contribution principle (5.2, 7). Such a situation is a violation of the principle of human rights according to both the antecedentalist and the consequentialist justifications of the right to private property.

The right to employment provides an important step toward correcting this violation and thereby counteracting the inequalities of power. This right is continuous with the right to productive agency. For the latter is a right not only to acquire but also to exercise the abilities of productive agency, including its economic components. In this regard, the right to employment inherits all the arguments that buttressed the right to productive agency as a means of securing the rights to freedom and well-being without unilateral dependence on other persons, and also the right to private property with its consequentialist and antecedentalist justifications. I shall first deal with it as a moral right; but, as we shall see, it is a right that the government provide certain legal rights to persons who are unemployed.

The right to employment is both a negative and a positive right. It is a negative right in that all other persons and groups have the correlative duty, consistent with the moral requirements of the principle of human rights, to refrain from interfering with an agent's obtaining, performing, or retaining productive and remunerative work. This duty to refrain includes the duty not to impose obstacles that prevent persons from working because of considerations of race, religion, gender, or other criteria that are irrelevant to the ability to perform the kind of work that is in question. It also includes

10. See the discussion of employment at will, below (6.9).

11. Neil H. Jacoby, *Corporate Power and Social Responsibility* (New York: Macmillan, 1973), p. 265.

the duty not to exclude persons from jobs, or fire them from jobs they already have, because they have objected to their work conditions on grounds of health or safety.[12]

Even more stringently, this negative right entails the duty of corporate employers to refrain from policies that throw people out of work, in pursuit of profits that disregard the adverse impact on workers' continued employment. A relevant proposal, which invokes the inequalities of power referred to above, emphasizes the causal role of corporate policies in generating unemployment and the responsibility of government to help to control those policies:

> A government committed to the same full employment objective might first establish and enforce standards of behavior and decision-making on private capital—and particularly the large, concentrated, globally-oriented corporate and financial firms—focused on their job-creating, job-destroying decisions and choices. Public policy would apply incentives and rewards, penalties and obligations, analogous to those used in enforcing standards of environmental protection, consumer health and safety, and protection of investors' savings. Like the environmental impact statement now required before investment or land-use decisions may be implemented, employers would be required to develop 'employment impact' statements wherever a decision about location or relocation, change of methods, scale, and process involved significant effects on jobs, skills, and earnings.[13]

This proposal is continuous with the consequentialist restriction on the "harmful use" of private property considered above (5.2). The state, as a community of rights, should seek to secure the negative right to employment by enforcing on private corporate employers the duty not to infringe this right through policies that disregard their severe impact on the employment security of workers. Some of the issues raised by this proposal will be further considered in chapter 7.

The negative right to work receives a further interpretation wherein its correlative respondents or duty-bearers are labor unions. This interpretation is used by employers who object to having union membership made a condition of employment. The inequalities of power referred to above, however, make this interpretation of the right morally unacceptable. Labor unions have traditionally been the chief means by which workers have been able to counteract the enormous powers of corporate employers on matters

12. See Mary Gibson, *Workers' Rights* (Totowa, N.J.: Rowman and Allanheld, 1983), chap. 3.

13. Sumner M. Rosen, "The Right to Employment," *Monthly Review* 45 (Nov. 1993): 5–6.

including wages and working conditions. They are therefore important protections of the equality of rights that is essential to the PGC as the principle of human rights.[14] And the state, as a community of rights, must protect the ability of unions to provide such protection. The right to employment, insofar as it is a morally justified negative right, hence does not include this interpretation of it.

The right to employment is also a positive right because of the crucial impact of unemployment on both freedom and well-being. Insofar as the market, as represented by private employers, fails to provide work, its primary respondent must be the state as the community of rights. It is the state, acting through the government, that has the correlative duty to take the steps required to provide work for unemployed persons who are able and willing to work. In this way the government, acting for the community of rights, becomes the guarantor of full employment. In so acting the state carries out the mutuality of human rights. For since each person has rights to freedom and well-being against all other persons who in turn have these rights against him or her, the state, as the persons' representative, sees to it that these mutual rights are fulfilled. Employment, as an important segment of well-being and of autonomy as reflected in productive agency, is one of the economic objects of these rights. So the state, in helping unemployed persons to obtain employment, enables its other members to fulfill positive duties that, in principle, are incumbent on all persons who can provide the needed help. The state as a community of rights thereby effectuates the solidarity which is an essential part of community. The claims for

14. That right-to-work laws have "real and significant effects" in reducing union organizing and membership is shown by David T. Ellwood and Glen Fine, "The Impact of Right-to-Work Laws on Union Organizing," *Journal of Political Economy* 95, no. 2 (Apr. 1987): 250–73. See also Raymond L. Hilgert and Jerry D. Young, "Right-to-Work Legislation," *Personnel Journal* 42, no. 11 (Dec. 1963): 549–59; Sidney C. Sufrin and Robert C. Sedgwick, *Labor Economics and Problems at Mid-Century* (New York: Alfred A. Knopf, 1956), chaps. 4-9; Paul Sultan, *Right-to-Work Laws: A Study in Conflict* (Los Angeles: Institute of Industrial Relations, UCLA, 1956). On the role of labor unions, see Sumner H. Slichter, James J. Healy, and E. Robert Livernash, *The Impact of Collective Bargaining on Management* (Washington, D.C.: Brookings Institution, 1960); Richard Freeman and James Medoff, *What Do Unions Do?* (New York: Basic Books, 1985); Henry S. Farber and Daniel H. Saks, "Why Workers Want Unions: The Role of Relative Wages and Job Characteristics," *Journal of Political Economy* 88 (Apr. 1980): 349–69; Thomas A. Kochan, "How American Workers View Labor Unions," *Monthly Labor Review* 102 (Apr. 1979): 23–39; H. Gregg Lewis, *Unionism and Relative Wages in the United States: An Empirical Inquiry* (Chicago: University of Chicago Press, 1963); H. Gregg Lewis, *Union Relative Wage Effects: A Survey* (Chicago: University of Chicago Press, 1986); Thomas Geoghegan, *Which Side Are You On? Trying to Be for Labor When It's Flat on Its Back* (New York: Farrar, Straus and Giroux, 1991). For a more negative view, see Sylvester Petro, *The Labor Policy of the Free Society* (New York: Ronald Press, 1957).

such a positive right and duty regarding employment can be traced back at least to Thomas Paine,[15] and in the twentieth century it has been forcefully upheld in President Franklin D. Roosevelt's "economic bill of rights,"[16] in the Universal Declaration of Human Rights promulgated by the United Nations in 1948,[17] and elsewhere.[18]

The governmental assistance toward such full employment may take several different forms which are not mutually exclusive. One form, continuous with the education for productive agency discussed above (4.9), provides for retraining workers whose skills have been made obsolete by technological advances or shifts of markets. The government may also establish or expand information services that enable unemployed workers to learn what jobs are available both in their own areas and elsewhere. Another proposal, which may require governmental enforcement if it is to be maximally effective, shortens the length of the work week so as to make more jobs available.[19] In addition, the government may pursue such macroeconomic policies as giving tax credits to employers who hire previously jobless workers and greatly enlarging governmental spending for education, housing, and other projects. These policies would focus on private-sector employment.[20]

Distinct from all such policies is governmentally provided public-

15. Thomas Paine: "Employment at all times for the casual poor in the cities of London and Westminster" (*The Rights of Man,* chap. 5 [Harmondsworth, England: Penguin, 1969], p. 280).

16. "The right to a useful and remunerative job in the industries or shops or farms or mines of the nation" (Franklin D. Roosevelt, Message to the Congress on the State of the Union, January 11, 1944; quoted in Philip Harvey, *Securing the Right to Employment* [Princeton, N.J.: Princeton University Press, 1989], p. 127).

17. "Everyone has the right to work, to free choice of employment, to just and favourable conditions of work and to protection against unemployment. . . . Everyone who works has the right to just and favorable remuneration ensuring for himself and his family an existence worthy of human dignity" (art. 23, Universal Declaration of Human Rights, in Ian Brownlie, ed., *Basic Documents on Human Rights,* 2d ed. [Oxford: Clarendon Press, 1981], p. 25).

18. "Swedes are not particularly religious, but one thing we do hold almost sacred is everybody's right to work" (Berit Rollén, quoted in Helen Ginsburg, *Full Employment and Public Policy: The United States and Sweden* [Lexington, Mass.: D. C. Heath, 1983], p. 122).

19. See Bob Kuttner, "Jobs," in Irving Howe, ed., *Alternatives: Proposals for America from the Democratic Left* (New York: Pantheon Books, 1984), pp. 31–33; Roger Cohen, "Europeans Consider Shortening Workweek to Relieve Joblessness," *New York Times,* Nov. 22, 1993, national edition, pp. A1, A6.

20. See Robert Eisner, "A Direct Attack on Unemployment and Inflation," *Challenge* (July–Aug., 1978): 49–51; Leon Keyserling, "The Humphrey-Hawkins Act Since Its 1978 Enactment," in David C. Colander, ed., *Solutions to Unemployment* (New York: Harcourt, Brace Jovanovich, 1981), pp. 225–29; Harvey, *Securing the Right to Employment,* pp. 11, 14, 107, 112.

sector employment. Here the government itself becomes the employer, guaranteeing to all persons who are able and willing to work jobs on various publicly funded projects. The jobs offered would be aimed, so far as possible, to match existing abilities of the applicants, but there would be an especially strong emphasis on fulfillment of important needs for which there has not been an effective demand.

This last form of governmental assistance is in important respects preferable to the other forms. While the tax credit policy has an appearance of voluntarism because of its reliance on fiscal inducements to employers, it cannot take care of the involuntary employment that arises when employers refuse to hire workers at the previously prevailing wage because of "efficiency wage" considerations (see 6.5). In other ways, also, the tax credit solution may not lead enough employers to hire sufficient numbers of unemployed.[21] For the government itself to guarantee work in the public sector for all unemployed persons would be the most direct recognition and fulfillment of the right to employment as a human right.[22]

This right has two different grounds in the principle of human rights. First, the positive right to employment, when made effective, serves to counter the threat that unemployment poses to basic well-being, as was noted above. The positive right provides the economic security that enables persons not only to survive but also to have confidence that they will have stable and assured livelihoods.[23]

Since the right to employment involves governmental intervention in the operations of a free market, it incurs objections based directly on market considerations. It will be recalled that the entrepreneurial objection holds that workers, like entrepreneurs, must take their chances in the mar-

21. For discussion of some of these factors, see Keyserling, "Humphrey-Hawkins Act," pp. 225–29; Harvey, *Securing the Right to Employment*, chap. 1; Michael Rustin, "A Statutory Right to Work," *New Left Review*, no. 137 (Jan.–Feb. 1983): 48–67. For an opposed view, see James Tobin, "Unemployment in the 1980's: Macroeconomic Diagnosis and Prescription," in his collection, *Policies for Prosperity: Essays in a Keynesian Mode* (Cambridge, Mass.: MIT Press, 1987), pp. 386–414.

22. See Richard Lewis Siegel, *Employment and Human Rights: The International Dimension* (Philadelphia: University of Pennsylvania Press, 1994). It has been objected that the right to employment cannot be a human right because both its subjects and its objects are less than universal: as set forth in the U.N. Universal Declaration of Human Rights (art. 23; see above, n. 17), it is compatible with some persons' being unemployed and it is restricted to socially useful work. See Rex Martin, *A System of Rights* (Oxford: Clarendon Press, 1993), pp. 288–90, and Bernard Cullen, "The Right to Work," in J. D. G. Evans, ed., *Moral Philosophy and Contemporary Problems* (Cambridge: Cambridge University Press, 1987), p. 169. See also James W. Nickel, "Is There a Human Right to Employment?" *Philosophical Forum* 10, nos. 2–4 (winter–summer 1978–79): 165–67. See my discussion of the universality of positive rights, above, 2.6.

23. See Nickel, "Is There a Human Right to Employment?" pp. 158–62.

ket. The objection does indeed have some point. Workers, as purposive agents, should be encouraged to fend for themselves so far as possible; this is an important aspect of personal responsibility. They should try to sell their skills in the market, including applying them to develop new or better products, and to acquire new marketable skills—all these as ways of developing and utilizing their productive agency.

It must also be recognized, however, that these expedients are usually subject to severe limits. Workers often lack effective entrepreneurial skills, so that there remain sharp divisions between them and the entrepreneurs for whom they work. In this regard the entrepreneurial objection requires recognition of the inequalities of power between workers and other market participants, in addition to the inequalities mentioned above. First, entrepreneurs normally have had alternatives between which they could choose, including alternative means of support. They could have chosen to obtain income by means other than the business ventures they undertook. Workers, on the other hand, normally have no other means of support than their labor. They are therefore far more dependent on their jobs for their livelihoods; so if they are thrown out of work and cannot get other jobs, they face severe hardship (see 4.3). Second, even if entrepreneurs voluntarily incur risks, why should ordinary workers have to shoulder those risks? If they are averse to risks, as most of them are because of their slender financial margins, it is unfair to subject them to entrepreneurial risks that they would rather not undergo. Third, if business firms fail and go into bankruptcy, they are not totally deprived of government support; the government may help them to avoid total liquidation of their assets by laws providing for rehabilitation of their estates, whereby payments are deferred or their indebtedness is reduced. Such entrepreneurs are thus enabled to try again.[24] While the cases are not entirely analogous, the worker who is rescued from unemployment by a governmentally guaranteed job is not treated in a completely different way than other "entrepreneurs." Fourth, an assumption of the doubt concerning government support is that mar-

24. "Despite the stigma of bankruptcy and the evidence it gives of financial failure, debtors find it no harder to get credit after bankruptcy than they did before. Creditors take the risk of losses on bad debts in order to do business" (Daniel T. Stanley and Marjorie Girth, *Bankruptcy: Problem, Process, Reform* [Washington, D.C.: Brookings Institution, 1971], p. 3; see also chaps. 6, 7). See also Ted Nicholas, *How to Get out of Debt* (Wilmington, Del.: Enterprise, 1980); Harlan D. Platt, *Why Companies Fail: Strategies for Detecting, Avoiding, and Profiting from Bankruptcy* (Lexington, Mass.: D. C. Heath, 1985), chaps. 9–11. There are, however, dire possibilities in the opposite direction. See, e.g., the report of a "perpetually optimistic entrepreneur" who committed suicide when his lingerie business failed (Michelle Quinn, "Success, Bankruptcy, Suicide," *New York Times*, Sept. 26, 1993, national edition, sec. 3, p. 4).

kets should be the sole sources for the allocation of work. Strictly applied, this would mean that needs, no matter how basic or pressing, should not be fulfilled unless there is a specific effective demand for their fulfillment through money held by private buyers or investors. But the arguments presented in chapter 4 have shown that every mentally and physically competent person has a right to be a productive agent who can engage in mutual relations of need-fulfillment. This right should not be completely subjected to the vagaries of market demand.

6.2. THE ARGUMENT FROM SELF-RESPECT AND SELF-ESTEEM

Let us now turn to a second argument that the principle of human rights provides for a governmentally guaranteed right to employment. It may be objected that the protection of basic well-being adduced in the first argument can be achieved just as well by giving persons an adequate money income without their having to work. This would reinstate the dependence and passivity of the welfare system, for whose surmounting the right to productive agency was seen to be essential. In contrast to this, the second ground for the right to employment invokes the interrelated values of self-respect, mutuality, and self-esteem. To get something for nothing, that is, without having contributed to the production of what one receives, or of its equivalent, is a violation of the PGC's requirement of mutuality, according to which each person has duties to others as well as rights against others. To fulfill this requirement is an important basis of self-respect as a moral quality. For a person to respect herself, she must be realistically aware that she has fulfilled the essential moral requirement of acting in accord with the rights of others as well as of herself (1.5). In the economic sphere this involves that, parallel to deriving use-values for oneself from other persons' work, one makes a contribution to their well-being by producing commodities that have use-value for them. Self-respect here derives from one's awareness that one effectively acknowledges in other persons the same right to purpose-fulfillment as one claims for oneself. Such self-respect is thus an essential moral condition for fulfilling the principle of human rights and thereby promoting and participating in the community of rights.

Distinct from the moral virtue of self-respect is the prudential virtue of self-esteem. Although each of these virtues figures importantly in justifying the positive right to employment, they differ in their objects, that is, in what aspect of the self is valued. In self-respect what one values is one's moral qualities. One respects oneself insofar as one treats other persons fairly or justly, with the mutuality discussed above. In self-esteem what one values is various of one's own nonmoral qualities, including one's effectiveness in attaining one's desired goals.[25] To have self-esteem is to have a secure sense of one's own worth, and this includes having the conviction that one's plans and purposes are worthwhile and that one has the ability to carry them out.[26] Such self-esteem is a significant component of additive well-being, for it enables one to increase one's capabilities of purpose-fulfillment and hence to achieve more of one's goals (see *RM*, 240–42).

Now to be paid for one's work provides an important basis of self-esteem, for it gives the assurance both that one can support oneself, including at least some of one's goals, and that other persons value the contributions one makes to the common stock of goods. Self-esteem is thus closely tied to productive agency in both the general and the economic senses (4.6). This relation may not be appreciably altered even if one's work is more on the depressive side than on the creative (4.5), unless, perhaps, one feels that the work is so far beneath one's abilities that one feels belittled thereby. But even then the fact of self-support may bolster one's feeling of self-worth.

There is, then, a close connection between self-esteem and the government's providing employment for persons who are mentally and physically capable of working but who cannot find or perform paid work. In this context work performs the liberating function of assuring persons that they have abilities whose worth is recognized by others. The positive right to employment is thus justified on the ground of self-esteem as well as self-respect.[27]

25. For related ways of distinguishing self-respect from self-esteem, see Alan Donagan, *The Theory of Morality* (Chicago: University of Chicago Press, 1977), pp. 239–42; Stephen R. Munzer, *A Theory of Property* (Cambridge: Cambridge University Press, 1990), pp. 116–17. For a discussion of some ordinary uses of these expressions (but without the specific interpretation presented in my text above), see David Sachs, "How to Distinguish Self-Respect from Self-Esteem," *Philosophy and Public Affairs* 10 (fall 1981): 346–60.

26. See John Rawls, *A Theory of Justice* (Cambridge, Mass.: Harvard University Press, 1971), pp. 178–79, 440–46; Robin Attfield, "Work and the Human Essence," *Journal of Applied Philosophy* 1, no. 1 (1984): 144–50.

27. Employment also has further important features that serve to reinforce this justification. "Employment, like every other institution, has latent consequences that enforce on all who participate in it certain inescapable categories of experience. . . . There are at least five major such categories stemming from the organization of employment: it enforces a time-structure on the working day; it enlarges the social horizon by requiring regular contact with people beyond family and self-chosen friends; it enforces participation in a collective effort; it defines a person's place in society; and, last but not least, it demands regular activity" (Marie Jahoda, "Unemployment—Curse or Liberation?" in Pauline Marstrand, ed., *New Technology and the Future of Work and Skills* [London: Frances Pinter, 1984], pp. 21–22). See also B. Södersten, "New Attitudes to Work," in Edmond Malinvaud and Jean-Paul Fitoussi, eds., *Unemployment in Western Countries* (New York: St. Martin's Press, 1980), pp. 443–59; Jon Elster, "Is There (or Should There Be) a Right to Work?" in Amy Gutmann, ed., *Democracy*

There are at least two serious objections against this way of tying self-esteem to the positive right to employment. The first bears on the individual's own scale of values. Self-esteem is so variable in its causal factors that work is neither a necessary nor a sufficient condition of a person's having it. For self-esteem, like esteem in general, depends on what one values, what one regards as worth doing or emulating, and this may vary greatly from one person or group to another.[28] Thus someone who does no paid (or other) work at all may nonetheless derive self-esteem from his prowess in other fields, such as the idler roué who seduces many women or the saint who spends all his days in prayer; hence, paid work is not a necessary condition of self-esteem. And someone who works hard and gets paid well for it may nonetheless be strongly lacking in self-esteem because his work does not measure up to his own or others' standards; examples are a professional ballplayer who regards his batting average as too low or a professor whose laboriously worked-out articles are rejected by prestigious journals. So paid work is not a sufficient condition of self-esteem.

One way of dealing with this objection is to recur to the moral virtue of self-respect and thereby to restrict the relevant self-esteem to what is morally justified. But, with due recognition of the variability of the specific objects of self-esteem, the justification given above for the positive right to employment, in terms of basic well-being, also provides an important ground for answering the objection. For to secure one's own livelihood plays such a strategic role in relation to one's other purposes and projects that it serves to buttress one's ability to carry them out. Even if one's paid work is not completely indispensable for such achievement, it is normally highly conducive to it. So the objects of self-esteem do not comprise a completely unordered set.

A second objection, which invokes the "exchange-value objection" presented above (6.1), emphasizes the social basis of self-esteem. If would-be workers are unable to sell their products or services by free exchange, this shows that those products or services are not sufficiently valued by other persons; hence, to have the government pay them for their work will not contribute to their self-esteem.

> It would be . . . self-defeating to create a right to work for the purpose of promoting self-esteem, because self-esteem depends essentially on the freely accorded esteem of others. Work that has no purpose other than assuring

---

and the Welfare State (Princeton, N.J.: Princeton University Press, 1988), pp. 53–78, at pp. 62–69.

28. See, for example, the essays in Andrew W. Mecca, Neil J. Smelser, and John Vasconcellos, eds., *The Social Importance of Self-Esteem* (Berkeley and Los Angeles: University of California Press, 1989), incl. pp. 10–21, 178–87, 221–25.

self-esteem would also fail in this regard. To engender self-esteem, work must first of all result in production of a good or services that is valued by consumers or taxpayers. . . . It follows that if the purpose of work is to promote self-esteem, a right to work that was visibly realized by heavy subsidies would be self-defeating. . . . If the work one does is esteemed enough to provide one with self-esteem, there will be a demand for it and no need to provide it as of right. If there is no demand for it, so that it has to be provided by a separate right, it cannot promote self-esteem.[29]

This objection fails because it trades on ambiguities in words like "value," "demand," and "productive." These words can refer either to what is effectively demanded as backed up by money or to what would be effectively demanded if persons had the money, because it meets important needs. The words are also ambiguous as between what is wanted by large numbers of persons but not attained because of ineffective coordination of means to satisfy the wants, and what government can do to effectively coordinate these wants. Now when the state, as a community of rights, provides for employment on various public service projects, its objective is to supply what is wanted and productive in the second of each of these senses. Such governmental action, while not proceeding according to market wants as measured by effective demand, can nevertheless be justified as meeting real needs for productive work. So here again rights and community are brought together, because the state, in providing employment, operates as a solidaristic community that represents its members in fulfilling important needs that are objects of rights.

The trouble with the above objection, then, is that it assumes that the only criterion of value is effective market demand. But persons may value and indeed need various goods and services for which they are unable to pay; hence, there is not effective demand for them.

> It is in the public sector . . . that unsatisfied social needs are extremely urgent, and sometimes alarmingly so—in medical attention, crime prevention, mass transportation, environmental control, education, public facilities for recreation and the arts, care of the aged and infirm, and others. If resources otherwise idle—that is, the unemployed—were given the opportunity to work in the public sector, the social contribution could easily be materially greater than the estimate of private output lost.[30]

29. Jon Elster, "Is There (or Should There Be) a Right to Work?" pp. 74–76. See to the same effect J. Donald Moon, "The Moral Basis of the Democratic Welfare State," in Gutmann, *Democracy and the Welfare State*, p. 48; Harold Cox, *Economic Liberty* (London: Longmans, Green, 1920), p. 70.

30. Melville J. Ulmer, "The Economic Consequences of Public Employment," in Alan Gartner, Russell A. Nixon, and Frank Riessman, eds., *Public Service Employment* (New

The services here indicated coincide to a large extent with the first kind of "productive labor" distinguished above, which contributes to fulfilling fundamental needs of agency (4.8). The provision of such services could be an important source of self-esteem for the respective workers because they both would themselves recognize and would receive social recognition for the value of these contributions, for which they would be fully deserving of the pay they receive. There must, then, be a realistic awareness of the gap between genuine needs and the inability of the needy to pay for them. Just as fulfilling the right to employment would effectuate an important human right, so the satisfaction of those other pressing needs would also contribute to the fulfillment of other basic and additive human rights.[31] Thus, to the traditional criticisms of capitalist economies that they manifest "poverty amid plenty," there can be added the further criticism that governmental failure to subsidize employment manifests the phenomenon of vast important unfulfilled needs amid plenteous means of fulfilling them.

This point serves to refute the objection that a full employment program would be so obsessed with the aim of funding jobs that their content—the products of the work—would be of secondary concern, and would be as trivial as leaf-raking and hole-filling. The persons thus employed would be "a second-rate work force,"[32] "a second-class employment ghetto."[33] Such a pejorative view is obviated by the important needs that a full employment program would aim to meet. Because its primary focus would be on the needs for whose fulfillment all persons have rights, this focus would apply as much to the work to be done as to the workers themselves operating within the community of rights.

Questions may be raised about the precise relation between the social-needs consideration and the consideration about employing the unemployed. Which is for the sake of which? Is the employment consideration primarily a means to fulfilling the vast unmet social needs, or is the fulfillment of these needs primarily a means (and a justification) of providing full

---

York: Praeger, 1973), p. 103. See also Clive Jenkins and Barrie Sherman, *The Collapse of Work* (London: Eyre Methuen, 1979), p. 169; Cullen, "Right to Work," pp. 179–80; Peter Sinclair, *Unemployment: Economic Theory and Evidence* (Oxford: Basil Blackwell, 1987), pp. 281–83; Stanley Aronowitz, "Why Work?" in David G. Gil and Eva A. Gil, eds., *The Future of Work* (Rochester, Vt.: Schenkman, 1987), pp. 27–28.

31.   Besides the other essays in Gartner, Nixon, and Riessman, *Public Service Employment* (above, n. 30), see also Robert F. Cook et al., eds., *Public Service Employment: The Experience of a Decade* (Kalamazoo, Mich.: W. E. Upjohn Institute for Employment Research, 1985).

32.   Elster, "Is There (or Should There Be) a Right to Work?" p. 74.

33.   Harvey, *Securing the Right to Employment*, p. 62. See also Robert Lekachman, "Toward Equality through Employment," *Social Policy* 5, no. 3 (Sept.–Oct. 1974): 6.

employment? If the former is upheld, then there is no necessary connection between fulfilling unmet social needs and employing the unemployed. It is indeed the case that the private market sector will not provide for these needs: "A market economy is simply incapable of producing and distributing the quantity of public goods and services which citizens really want."[34] But even if it is granted that governmental intervention through public service employment is required for this purpose, why must the government wait for people to become unemployed before it gives them the relevant jobs in the public sector? Why should the government operate as an "employer of *last* resort" when it hires people to fulfill these pressing needs?[35]

If, on the other hand, providing employment is primary, and fulfilling unmet social needs is mainly justified as providing a useful outlet for such employment, then there might be less concern with the social value of the work to be done, and a greater concern with getting workers into the private sector. In this case, paying less than market wages may be upheld as a means of pushing workers off the public payroll.

The conflicting tendencies of each of these alternatives, however, are to be rejected. The pressing social needs are objects of positive rights to well-being, and so too is employment. But employment which is to provide not only a living wage but also self-respect and self-esteem for the worker is best achieved when it is meaningful in terms of valued social functions. Fulfillment of such functions is not, then, a mere means of providing work; it is itself intrinsically connected with the value of such work both for the workers themselves and for the community at large. Nor is public service employment a mere means of fulfilling vital social needs; on the contrary, it has its own justification as fulfilling an important right to well-being. On the other hand, the private sector cannot be counted on to fulfill both sets of rights. So public service employment has this double, intrinsically interconnected justification, and a society that provides such employment is in a double way a community of rights.

In addition to such needs, governmentally provided employment could also fulfill wants for legal services, music, art, museums, lifelong education, and many other amenities that help to improve people's well-being even while economic disabilities or priorities leave them without effective demand. "An explosion in employment is possible in all of these people-oriented service industries."[36] Here too the fulfillment of such values would help to bolster the workers' self-esteem.

34. Bennett Harrison, "Comment of a Radical Economist," in Gartner, Nixon, and Riessman, *Public Service Employment*, p. 118.
35. See Michael Harrington, "Government Should Be the Employer of *First* Resort," in Colander, *Solutions to Unemployment*, pp. 209–17; emphasis in original.
36. Jenkins and Sherman, *The Collapse of Work*, p. 169.

6.3. Is There No Need for Work?

Despite the above arguments, it has been objected on at least two grounds that the right to employment is pointless. One objection bears on the object of the right, the other on its subject. While the right's direct object is, of course, employment, the argument from basic well-being has held that the primary justification of the right is that it enables persons to fulfill their needs for the necessities of life. To this it has been objected that work for this purpose is no longer required since modern technology has developed to the point where all persons' basic needs can be readily fulfilled without working. A second objection contends that because all unemployment is voluntary, this removes an underlying assumption of the right to employment so far as it bears on the alleged right-holder. Let us consider each of these objections in turn.

According to the first objection, technological developments have made, and will continue to make, human work progressively less needed. The "microprocessor revolution"—the new technology of microelectronics—has resulted in vast displacements of workers both in manufacturing and in service employment. Small electronic machines are enormously more productive than traditional manual or mental workers; as a result, the latter are thrown out of work at rapidly increasing rates. Hence, in contrast to the claimed right to employment with its mandate to provide work for all persons who want it, work in the traditional sense is becoming more and more obsolete, and the claimed right is simply a reflection of outmoded ways of thinking. The main inference that has been drawn from this development is what I shall call the *no-work solution:* income should be separated from work; persons, including those capable of working, should be enabled to live at leisure while drawing an "unconditional basic income" set "at the highest sustainable level."[37]

This solution is undeniably attractive, echoing as it does the utopian themes found in Marx and many others: an economy of such abundance that the inveterate human conflicts over scarce resources, which Hume declared to be one of the main circumstances of justice, would give way to an era of maximal harmony and self-development.

37. See Jenkins and Sherman, *The Collapse of Work;* Colin Gill, *Work, Unemployment, and the New Technology* (Cambridge: Polity Press, 1985); Fred Block, "The Myth of Reindustrialization," *Socialist Review* 14, no. 1 (Jan.–Feb. 1984): 59–79; Clive Jenkins and Barrie Sherman, *The Leisure Shock* (London: Eyre Methuen, 1981); André Gorz, *Paths to Paradise: On the Liberation from Work* (Boston: South End Press, 1985); Philippe van Parijs, "Why Surfers Should Be Fed: The Liberal Case for an Unconditional Basic Income," *Philosophy and Public Affairs* 20 (spring 1991): 105; Claus Offe, "Full Employment: Asking the Wrong Question?" *Dissent* (winter 1995): 77–81; Jeremy Rifkin, *The End of Work* (New York: G. P. Putnam's Sons, 1995).

There are two kinds of difficulty with this no-work solution, one empirical, the other moral. Even if its predictions are confirmed by further technological developments, it glosses over all the kinds of work that will still be needed even amid its envisaged abundance. Machines will still have to be produced, food harvested, houses built, clothes made, and so forth. Even if these processes will require far less human labor than previously, they still require some. But, in addition, the technological revolution of material things will not remove the vast needs for many kinds of services, including the personal relations that make them fully helpful and, in many cases, even possible. Medical care, education, and many other contributions to well-being, which figured prominently in the reply to the objection about self-esteem (6.2), will still furnish extensive areas for the right to employment. Hence, instead of the no-work solution, a more realistic and feasible response to the technological revolution would be to reduce the hours of work and raise wages.

If the no-work solution is taken literally, it also incurs serious moral difficulties. Let us call "loafing" the opposite of working. If everyone loafs, who will supply the subsistence and other goods needed or wanted by the loafers? The no-work solution ignores the arguments given above to show that the right to private property requires an antecedentalist justification as well as a consequentialist one (5.3). It may be replied that not everyone will loaf, either because some enjoy working or because they prefer the greater income they receive by working to the smaller income they receive while loafing. But the loafers would still violate the moral requirement of mutuality, for they would live, as parasites, off the work of others without contributing anything in return. This is unfair; it would violate the antecedentalist contribution principle that distribution should be determined by contribution (5.7). The loafers would make exceptions in their own favor, for by choosing not to work while having at least their basic needs fulfilled by others, they would take advantage of the latter's practice of work while refusing to engage in the practice themselves. This would generate a morally justified sense of resentment toward the loafers who, as free riders, would be exploiting the workers.

It may be replied that the no-work solution helps to maximize freedom because it leaves the choice between work and no-work to personal preferences. But this still raises the question of why those who prefer to work should have to support those who do not.

A related argument against the no-work solution is the following. The loafers' receipt of subsistence is not proposed merely as an act of charity or benevolence. For if it were, there would be nothing mandatory about it, so that the loafers could not count on getting it; it would be a purely optional or contingent arrangement. On the contrary, the "basic income" policy is proposed as a mandatory arrangement such that loafers have a legal right to receive at least subsistence. But if some loafer A has a positive right to receive subsistence, then some other person or persons—call them B— have a positive duty to provide the subsistence. Fulfillment of this duty would require that B work. But if B has a duty to work because she is able, or is in a position, to fulfill the subsistence needs of other persons (where this "because" is that of sufficient condition), then all persons who are able, or are in a position, to fulfill the subsistence needs of other persons also have a duty to work. Hence A and any other would-be loafers have a duty to work insofar as they are able, or are in a position, to fulfill the subsistence needs of other persons. Hence, the exemption from working that the no-work solution proposes cannot be justified, for it claims to exempt the loafers from a generalization to which they are logically committed when they set forth the duty to fulfill their claimed right to receive subsistence.

This objection to the no-work solution is not removed by the theses of social contribution and world ownership (3.4; 5.5). For those theses, while emphasizing that persons' productive activities are aided by the natural re- sources they use and the social nurturing they receive, still leave an impor- tant place for the contributions made by those activities themselves. That the distribution of income must recognize the helps provided by these ex- traindividual factors does not militate against the mutualist requirement that persons make their own contributions on the partial basis of these fac- tors.

6.4. Is There a Duty to Work? When Do Right-Holders Have Corresponding Duties?

As the above considerations indicate, there is a duty to work as well as a right to work; and the right and the duty pertain to the same persons. The subsistence and other goods of well-being, whose attainment constitutes an important part of the justification of the right to work or employment, must, so far as possible, be provided by the persons who benefit from this attainment. So the right to work is a mandatory, not a discretionary right, in that whether one exercises one's right to work is not to be left to one's optional choices or preferences.[38]

The basis of this duty is the moral requirement of the mutuality of hu- man rights: just as A has generic rights against other persons, they have

38. On this distinction, see Martin P. Golding, "Towards a Theory of Human Rights," *The Monist* 52, no. 4 (Oct. 1968): 521–49, at pp. 541–48; Joel Feinberg, "Voluntary Eutha- nasia and the Inalienable Right to Life," in his collection *Rights, Justice, and the Bounds of Liberty* (Princeton, N.J.: Princeton University Press, 1980), pp. 221–51, at pp. 232–38. I use Feinberg's terminology.

generic rights against A. In the present context the rights in question consist in required protections or promotions of interests comprised in the various levels of well-being. The protections are provided through the acquisition of commodities, including services, ranging from the subsistence goods of basic well-being to other varieties of goods. This provision occurs within a network of transactions in which other persons fulfill A's rights to the various levels of well-being. But these other persons have concomitant rights against A, who therefore has correlative duties to them. This is another way of saying that, just as A has rights to receive the products of other persons' work, so they have rights to receive the products of his work. Normally this mutuality of receipt occurs through market transactions of mutual payment, either in money or in kind. Only if persons are unable to participate in this mutual productive process are they exempt from its duties. The community of rights is partially constituted by this mutual universality of rights and duties in the sphere of work and commodities (see also 1.2).

The duty to work, as so far discussed, is a moral duty. Should it also be a legally prescribed duty? The latter course would arouse justified fears about state compulsion. The former Soviet "parasite laws" provide a graphic example of this sort of tyranny.[39] Such laws violated the right to freedom, the right of persons to be let alone, to pursue their life plans as they see fit as long as they do not violate the rights of others. In addition, by giving a tendentious, partisan interpretation of "socially valuable commodities," the Soviet police were authorized to prosecute liberal thinkers, writers, artists, and others who did not toe the party line. The legal duty to work thus came to mean the duty to work at pursuits that did not displease the authorities.

Despite these cautionary considerations, the duty to work can be fitted into a legal context without incurring such tyrannical compulsions. For, as is seen in many developed countries, the duty can be effectively instituted apart from laws that explicitly and directly require persons to work. It is sufficient that, in addition to policies guaranteeing employment, there be laws that protect property rights by prohibiting theft and related operations. The result procured by such laws is that persons, while maintaining

---

39. On this whole topic, see the important essay by Lawrence C. Becker, "The Obligation to Work," *Ethics* 91 (Oct. 1980): 35–49. See also Tom Campbell, *The Left and Rights* (London: Routledge and Kegan Paul, 1983), pp. 185–92, where it is held that for socialism the moral basis of the duty to work is not reciprocity but utilitarianism. For a Marxist source, see Marx and Engels, *The Communist Manifesto* 2, where one of the measures "of entirely revolutionizing the mode of production" is "Equal liability of all to labour. Establishment of industrial armies, especially for agriculture" (in Robert C. Tucker, ed., *The Marx-Engels Reader,* 2d ed. [New York: W. W. Norton, 1978], p. 490).

freedom to choose their modes of work, are effectively required to work in order to fulfill their needs and wants unless other persons voluntarily provide for them. Inheritance taxes, especially of large fortunes, are also justified here. If one cannot earn income by one's own efforts, then, as we have seen, one has a positive right to welfare, that is, to receive income from other persons through the state (4.1). But here, as we have also seen, one has rights of productive agency whereby the state enables one to acquire skills and other abilities whereby one can make productive contributions and thereby support oneself. If suitable employment is not obtainable, then the state has the correlative duty to provide it.

The duty to work, then, need not involve the draconian methods of "parasite laws" or any other direct legal prescriptions. The duty is rather to avoid becoming a burden on others and to make contributions to others that are mutual with the contributions one receives from others. It is also a duty that is conditional upon the fulfillment of two kinds of important rights: the right to develop one's abilities of productive agency and the right to have employment.

Although the right to work is a mandatory right that entails the duty to work, not all rights are in this way mandatory. Indeed, more generally, it is not the case that every right to some X entails a correlative duty *of the rightholder* with regard to that X. For example, if I have a right to receive ten dollars from you because of a promise you have made to me, nothing follows from this alone about my having any duty to you or anyone else with regard to the ten dollars. I do indeed have some duties in this regard—for example, I may not threaten to shoot you if you do not give me the ten dollars, and I may not use the ten dollars to bribe someone or to buy lethal drugs—but these duties are not correlative with or logical consequences of the right to receive the ten dollars from you; rather, they derive from more general moral rights which set correlative duties of persons *other than* the right-holders themselves.

The logical relation that holds between all rights and duties, then—as against the relation that holds specifically in the case of mandatory rights—involves what I shall call *diversity relations,* in that the subjects or holders of rights are diverse from the respondents or bearers of the correlative duties. The duties regularly entailed by rights are not duties of the right-holder but rather duties of other persons to respect those rights.

We are left, then, with two questions. First, why is the right to work a mandatory right that entails the right-holder's duty to work, while other rights are not thus mandatory? Second, is there some other way in which rights, while not being directly mandatory, may nonetheless entail duties of the right-holder that are directly related to the objects of the rights?

On the first question, it will be recalled that the right to work entails the duty to work because of the mutuality of human rights. Every person has human rights against all other persons, who in turn have human rights against him, so that he has duties to them as well as rights against them (1.2). In this way community and rights are brought together, because the community helps to fulfill and coordinate these rights and duties. To see how this relation helps to account for the mandatoriness of the right to work, we must note that the reason for this mandatoriness is that a person's exercising the right is beneficial not only to himself but also to other persons.[40] By virtue of its being beneficial to himself, he has a right to work; by virtue of its being beneficial to others, he has a duty to work. A similar relation obtains for other human rights; for example, the right to eat entails the duty to eat, insofar as one's not eating will remove one's company from other persons who want it and will impose on them the burden of feeding one. Relations of a similar reflexive sort may be found between the right to be educated and the duty to be educated, the right to vote and the duty to vote, the right to have self-esteem and the duty to have self-esteem, the right to maintain one's dignity and the duty to maintain one's dignity, and similarly for many other conditions including maintaining one's justified freedoms, acquiring the knowledge needed for citizenship, and so forth. In a closely parallel way, the rights not to be harmed or deceived or discriminated against entail the duties to see to it, so far as one can, that one is not harmed or deceived or discriminated against. While all these duties are moral ones, they are not all legal duties. In all such cases the grounds of the duties are not directly paternalistic; for although performance of the duties is beneficial to the duty-bearers, what directly makes them duties is that they are beneficial to other persons. Hence, mutuality is here preserved.

These manifold reflexive relations indicate the large area within which there is a harmony of interests between oneself and other persons insofar as the interests are the objects of moral rights. This harmony is an important basis for the community of rights, in the adjectival sense where rights are distributively common to persons. Because they are thus common, a person's right to a kind of interest X among the necessary goods of action entails his duty to maintain or fulfill that interest for himself because his maintaining or fulfilling it also protects that kind of interest X for other persons. Thus whereas A's special right to receive a promised ten dollars from B does not entail any duty of A with regard to those ten dollars, A's general right that promises to himself be kept does entail A's duty to see to it that promises to himself are kept, because he thereby helps to reinforce the institution of promise-keeping which is an important good for all per-

---

40. For a related point, see Campbell, *The Left and Rights*, pp. 177, 189–90; Feinberg, "Voluntary Euthanasia," p. 247.

sons as actual or prospective agents (see *RM,* 232–39). Mandatory rights, then, obtain at the generic level where kinds of rights are beneficial to many persons other than the right-holders, so that maintenance or fulfillment of the rights is also a duty of the right-holder to other persons. This mutuality is an important basis of the concept of the "reasonable self" that is characteristic of the community of rights (3.6).

Let us now turn to the second question raised above: Is there any other way, besides rights' being mandatory, whereby rights may entail duties of the right-holder that are directly related to the objects of the rights? The answer I shall give does not entirely depart from the basis of mandatoriness just indicated, but it is more specific. Its direct principle is what I shall call *criterion-based obligations.*[41] If some person A has or claims a right to X by virtue of her fulfilling certain criteria Y, then, insofar as A claims the right, she has a duty to fulfill those criteria. For example, if A claims the right to inspect the naked body of B by virtue of A's having relevant medical expertise (as evidenced by her having appropriate medical training and related qualifications), then, insofar as A claims the right, she has a duty to have and use that expertise. For otherwise her right-claim would be unfounded and hence unjustified because based on intentional falsehood and dishonesty. Such criterion-based obligations are also found in many other work contexts where the right to perform a specific kind of work entails the right-holder's duty to have the relevant ability for that work.

The criterion-based obligation can also be construed as the justifying ground for the duty to work, but perhaps in a less direct way. If one claims the right to work on the consequentialist ground that one's work will be beneficial to others as well as to oneself, then one has the duty to see to it that one has work abilities that are thus beneficial to others. Here the mutuality of rights is again invoked. Although its main specific reference may be to market conditions wherein effective demand is the criterion of one's work's being beneficial to others, in nonmarket relations of the community of rights it is the fulfillment of agency-needs that provides the criterion. In either case the claim that one has a right to work, as based on such a criterion, entails the duty both to be ready to work using the abilities referred to in the criterion and to actually work using those abilities. This is, so far, only a prima facie duty, because other requirements bearing on pay and work conditions must also be met, as well as the right to strike.[42]

---

41. I have previously presented this argument in my chapter "Human Rights and Academic Freedom," in Steven M. Cahn, ed., *Morality, Responsibility, and the University: Studies in Academic Ethics* (Philadelphia: Temple University Press, 1990), pp. 8–31, at pp. 21–23.

42. See L. J. Macfarlane, *The Right to Strike* (Harmondsworth, England: Penguin, 1981).

6.5. IS ALL UNEMPLOYMENT VOLUNTARY?

Besides the objection that technological developments render work unnecessary, a second argument for the pointlessness of the right to employment is that all unemployment is voluntary. This voluntariness may be held to contradict an underlying assumption of the right to employment. For this right, like most positive rights, can be analyzed as a set of individual claims, such as a claim on the part of some person A that he be given some object X (see also 3.5). The underlying assumption of the claim is that X is not already under A's control, so that he needs to be helped or protected by other persons if he is to have (or continue to have) X. If, however, all unemployment is voluntary, then it is under A's control whether he has employment. But this contradicts the underlying assumption of the claim that A, or any other person, has a positive right to employment. Hence, the alleged right is pointless.

This objection obviously depends in important part on the meaning assigned to "voluntary." In the statement of the objection just given, I have interpreted "voluntary" in the sense used from the beginning of this book to characterize the procedural necessary condition of action: in voluntary behavior the agent controls her behavior by her unforced choice while having knowledge of relevant circumstances (1.4; see *RM*, 31–35). On this definition, the allegation that all unemployment is voluntary may well be contradicted by the phenomena of the anguish, despair, and feverish searches for work that have long characterized the unemployed (see 6.1). But let us here assume that such phenomena could, at least prima facie, be consistent with the control-and-choice conception of voluntariness. It is this conception that enters into typical statements of the classical economic thesis that unemployment is voluntary, such as the following:

> Unemployment in the unhampered market is always voluntary. In the eyes of the unemployed man, unemployment is the minor of two evils between which he has to choose. The structure of the market may sometimes cause wage rates to drop. But, on the unhampered market, there is always for each type of labor a rate at which all those eager to work can get a job.[43]

On this view, then, to say that all unemployment is voluntary is to say that every unemployed person has an effective choice between being employed and being unemployed, such that it is under his control whether he has a job (he "always . . . can get a job").

This thesis rests on several interrelated grounds. It can be viewed as reflecting the "economic approach to human behavior" according to

---

43. Ludwig von Mises, *Human Action: A Treatise on Economics*, 3d rev. ed. (Chicago: Henry Regnery, 1966), p. 599.

which all human conduct and choices are analyzed as attempts to maximize utility on the basis of stable preferences within market equilibrium.[44] Another, more specific ground is partly derived from Say's Law, according to which supply creates its own demand.[45] From this it is inferred that, in a competitive market system, the alternatives between which persons choose include work at an equilibrium wage where the demand for labor equals the supply. If the worker cannot sell his labor at the price he wants, he can, eventually, by reducing his price, find a buyer.[46]

There are at least two difficulties with this thesis, one bearing on the voluntariness of the choice to be unemployed, the other on the availability of employment when wage demands are lowered. First, when it is said that unemployment under market conditions "is always voluntary," or that "there is also a voluntary element in all unemployment,"[47] the precise meaning assigned to "voluntary" requires scrutiny. It may be contended that "the issue here [of voluntariness] is just a matter of semantics."[48] But it also involves a serious moral point about social and economic policy.[49] If all unemployment is voluntary, in some specific and plausible sense of "voluntary" like the one given above, this suggests that unemployed workers have only themselves (or their union leaders) to blame for their lack of paid work. For if, in voluntary behavior, the agent controls his behavior *by his own unforced choice,* then it is under his own control whether he is employed or not; no further directly causal factors or remedial measures need to be considered.

A crucial question, then, is whether the worker's choice between employment and unemployment is voluntary in the sense that he controls his behavior by his *unforced* choice. A choice is forced when one is compelled

44. See Gary S. Becker, *The Economic Approach to Human Behavior* (Chicago: University of Chicago Press, 1976).

45. See Mark Blaug, *Economic Theory in Retrospect,* 3d ed. (Cambridge: Cambridge University Press, 1978), chap. 5.

46. See the explication of this view in John Maynard Keynes, *The General Theory of Employment, Interest, and Money* (London: Macmillan, 1936), p. 26. See also James J. Hughes and Richard Perlman, *The Economics of Unemployment* (New York: Cambridge University Press, 1984), pp. 53–55; Vedder and Gallaway, *Out of Work,* p. 99.

47. Robert E. Lucas, Jr., *Studies in Business Cycle Theory* (Cambridge, Mass.: MIT Press, 1981), p. 242.

48. Carl Shapiro and Joseph E. Stiglitz, "Can Unemployment Be Involuntary? Reply," *American Economic Review* 75, no. 5 (Dec. 1985): 1215. See also Richard Layard, Stephen Mickell, and Richard Jackman, *Unemployment: Macroeconomic Performance and the Labour Market* (Oxford: Oxford University Press, 1991), p. 41: "The question is fruitless."

49. "Quarreling about words, usually a rather sterile activity, here becomes of some importance because of the powerful influence that a suggestive, colorful phrase may have upon the shaping of views with regard to economic policy" (Trygve Haavelmo, "The Notion of Involuntary Economic Decisions," *Econometrica* 18, no. 1 [Jan. 1950]: 1–2).

to choose between two severely undesirable alternatives set by someone else. There are thus three elements in forced choice: (*a*) it is between alternatives both of which are severely undesirable to the chooser; (*b*) the alternatives are set by someone else, who has superior bargaining power; (*c*) the chooser is compelled to make the choice, whether he wants to or not (see *RM*, 32–35).

Consider, for example, a case where Ms. Smith must choose between sleeping with her boss and losing her job. Although she is desperate for work at a wage sufficient to support herself and her children, she nonetheless rejects the boss's demand. It may be held that she has become unemployed voluntarily, because she has chosen this alternative. But because she had to choose between two severely undesirable alternatives set by her boss, her choice was forced; hence, her being unemployed is not voluntary.

It may be objected that this example, involving coercion by the boss, does not fit the stipulation of an "unhampered market" within which choices are to be made. But "unhampered" cannot mean that there are no adverse constraints or "evils" between which a choice must be made. In this and other cases the choice must be made within a context of alternatives that is not itself chosen but is rather resented, and the alternatives are set by someone else who has superior bargaining power.[50]

These considerations about forced choice also apply to the situation of many other unemployed workers. If they choose unemployment over working for starvation wages at life-threatening occupations that would require their moving very far from their homes, they have not chosen to be in the situation where they are confronted by such undesirable yet compulsory alternatives. Hence there is an important respect in which their choice of unemployment is forced, involuntary.[51]

It may still be objected that the worker does indeed choose the context in which his unemployment occurs. For in taking any job he knows that there may be risks: of lowered profits, of severe competition, and other possibly adverse conditions. To enter a market economy is to subject oneself to the risk of losing one's job or undergoing other economic adversities (6.1). Moreover, it is unrealistic to ask that one should always be able to choose the alternatives or contexts in which one makes choices. After all, one does not choose one's initial context of being brought into the world; and when

---

50. On this point, see Joel Feinberg, *Harm to Self* (New York: Oxford University Press, 1986), pp. 249–53.

51. See Lucas, *Studies in Business Cycle Theory*, p. 242: "Thus there is an involuntary element in *all* unemployment, in the sense that no one chooses bad luck over good" (emphasis in original). See also Peter Sinclair, *Unemployment: Economic Theory and Evidence* (Oxford: Basil Blackwell, 1987), p. 116; David Schweickart, *Against Capitalism* (Cambridge: Cambridge University Press, 1993), p. 108.

one is lucky enough to be born in a constitutional democracy, the fact that many of one's choices occur within this unchosen context does not render them involuntary or forced.

To answer these objections, we must recur to the three elements involved in forced choice. Since being alive is presumably desirable and the newborn make no choice, the elements of undesirableness and compulsory choice do not characterize someone's being born. And a constitutional democracy is also marked by the absence of these two elements, while the third element, the external setting or control of the alternatives, is strongly negated or at least mitigated by the civil liberties and electoral systems of democratic institutions (see 8.1).

As for the worker's choice of the market context with its risks of unemployment, it is precisely here that the factor of forced choice becomes prominent when unemployment looms. This forcedness arises from the undesirableness of the unemployment he may undergo, the compulsoriness of the choice he may have to make, and the fact that the conditions under which he becomes unemployed are beyond his control. He does not normally have any alternative to entering the market economy with its risks.

It is this kind of market imperfection, as it affects the unemployed worker, that emphasizes the need for a governmentally sanctioned full employment policy. If such a policy can be made available, then the worker can avoid a context of forced choice in which his loss of employment is a genuine possibility. The community of rights here operates to fulfill a vitally important human right on the basis of a solidaristic commitment of the society to mutual assistance.

It is important to see further that the involuntariness and forcedness that are here attributed to the choice of unemployment do not apply to all conduct in which choices are made. Lionel Robbins has written: "Everywhere we turn, if we choose one thing we must relinquish others which, in different circumstances, we would wish not to have relinquished. . . . Economics brings into full view that conflict of choice which is one of the permanent characteristics of human existence. Your economist is a true tragedian."[52] This overblown statement ignores the characteristics of forced choice as against other choices. It is not a feature of all conduct and choice that they occur in contexts where both the available alternatives for choice are set by factors outside the chooser's control and are repugnant or emphatically undesirable to the chooser, as against simply being less inclusive of overall desire-fulfillment because of the infinity of human desires. To

52. Lionel Robbins, *An Essay on the Nature and Significance of Economic Science* (London: Macmillan, 1952), pp. 15, 30.

disregard this difference is like assimilating the cancer patient's terrified choice between two risky, painful therapies and the tycoon's reluctant choice to spend his precious vacation time on the Riviera, thereby forgoing the pleasures of a safari in Kenya.

Let us now turn to a second difficulty of the thesis that all unemployment is voluntary. This bears on the empirical claim that "the unemployed worker at any time can always find *some* job at once."[53] If other employment is "always" readily available, then his remaining unemployed is the result of his own choice, hence voluntary; hence, no governmental measures to provide employment are needed. The basis of this claim is that there will always be an equilibrium point where the supply of and the demand for workers are equalized; if the employment market does not clear, this is because wage demands are too high. So all the worker need do is lower his wage demands sufficiently to meet the wage offers of potential employers.[54]

We may consider this empirical-theoretical claim in abstraction from the considerations about forced choice just presented. The question now is: Even if the worker is willing to reduce his reservation wage quite substantially, does this guarantee that he can always find some work? A negative answer was given by Keynes in his definition of involuntary unemployment:

> My definition is, therefore, as follows: *Men are involuntarily unemployed if, in the event of a small rise in the price of wage-goods relatively to the money-wage, both the aggregate supply of labour willing to work for the current money-wage and the aggregate demand for it at that wage would be greater than the existing amount of employment.*[55]

53. Lucas, *Studies in Business Cycle Theory,* p. 242; emphasis in original.
54. "If commodities cannot be sold and workers cannot find jobs, the reason can only be that the prices and wages asked are too high. He who wants to sell his inventories or his capacity to work must reduce his demand until he finds a buyer. Such is the law of the market" (Von Mises, *Human Action,* p. 577). See also Patrick Minford, *Unemployment: Cause and Cure* (Oxford: Martin Robertson, 1983), pp. 2–8; Layard, Mickell, and Jackman, *Unemployment,* pp. 19–31.
55. Keynes, *General Theory,* p. 15; emphasis in original. See John N. Smithin, "The Definition of Involuntary Unemployment in Keynes' General Theory: A Note," *History of Political Economy* 17, no. 2 (1985): 219–22. See also A. G. Hines, "Involuntary Unemployment," in Malinvaud and Fitoussi, *Unemployment in Western Countries,* pp. 141–64, and the following essays in Robert Lekachman, ed., *Keynes' General Theory: Reports of Three Decades* (New York: St. Martin's Press, 1964): D. G. Champernowne, "Unemployment, Basic and Monetary: The Classical Analysis and the Keynesian" (pp. 153–73); Abba P. Lerner, "The General Theory" (pp. 203–22); Jacob Viner, "Mr. Keynes on the Causes of Unemployment" (pp. 235–53).

In other words, there is involuntary unemployment when persons cannot find work even when they are willing to work for real wages that are lower than the prevailing wage.

One reason for this inability derives from the theory of the "efficiency wage." An employer may not want to hire workers at lower wages than the hitherto prevailing wage because this may result in lower productivity and eventually higher labor costs. The employer may fear that persons who offer to work for lower wages will be less capable than higher-paid workers; that his current workforce will resent the new workers and refuse to train them; that his current workforce will have reduced incentives and consequently develop shirking behavior; or that the lower wages will encourage undesirable labor turnover.[56]

These empirical considerations thus point to a different aspect of involuntary employment than the thesis about forced choice in the first objection presented above. The objection now focuses directly not on the "supply" factor of the behavior of the worker but rather on the "demand" factor of the behavior of the employer and the specific market conditions that influence his behavior. Since the employer's behavior with regard to "efficiency wages" is not under the worker's control, there is nothing he can do, in the way of reducing his reservation wage, to obtain employment, so that his being unemployed is involuntary on his part.

The theory of the efficiency wage is a species of the more general doctrine presented by Keynes that unemployment results from deficient effective demand for labor and other goods. Keynes's doctrine proceeds in macroeconomic terms: unemployment is explained by the functioning of the whole economic system. Prices may rise without a corresponding rise in wages; since workers' households can therefore buy less, there is "overproduction" and workers are fired. This unemployment is not under the workers' control; even if they offer to work for lower wages, the offers may not be accepted, not only for "efficiency wage" reasons but also because effective demand, given the workers' lower real wages, will not be sufficient to buy the resulting products, so that profits will not increase.[57]

On these grounds, then, the arguments for the pointlessness of the

56. See Janet L. Yellen, "Efficiency Wage Models of Unemployment," *American Economic Review* 74, no. 2 (1984): 200–205; Shapiro and Stiglitz, "Can Unemployment Be Involuntary? Reply," pp. 1215–17; George A. Akerlof and Janet L. Yellen, eds., *Efficiency Wage Models of the Labor Market* (Cambridge: Cambridge University Press, 1986). See also Layard, Mickell, and Jackman, *Unemployment*, chap. 3; Andrew Weiss, *Efficiency Wages* (Princeton, N.J.: Princeton University Press, 1990); Sinclair, *Unemployment: Economic Theory and Evidence*, pp. 54–55.

57. See Keynes, *General Theory*, chap. 3. See also Sinclair, *Unemployment: Economic Theory and Evidence*, pp. 67–71.

positive right to employment are to be rejected. This right, and with it the correlative obligation of government to provide employment for persons able and willing to work, remain unaffected by the thesis that all unemployment is voluntary.

6.6. FULL EMPLOYMENT AND INFLATION

The envisaged outcome of the right to employment is full employment:[58] Everyone who is able and willing to work has a job. It has long been objected that full employment leads to inflation, that is, to a continuing increase in the general level of prices, so that the value of money falls, with corresponding negative effects on economic well-being. These effects are serious enough; but they can be further characterized as attacks on property rights in one's income and savings and thus on one's nonsubtractive rights (1.4). Thus just as a necessary consequentialist condition of morally justified property rights is that they must not be put to "harmful use" or have harmful effects (5.2), so it can be argued in reverse that for an economic policy to be morally justified it must not have harmful effects on property rights, especially as these belong to persons at the lower end of the economic scale. It may be held that such effects are antithetical to the community of rights in that an inflationary social policy violates important property rights. The criterion of degrees of needfulness for action (2.4), however, must also be operative here.

The most direct way of explicating the causal route from full employment to inflation is through the traditional theory of supply and demand. With full employment the supply of available workers for jobs is scarce, so that the demand for workers is greater than the supply; hence the price of labor, the wage rate, rises, and this in turn leads to a rise in the prices of the goods produced by labor. This thesis is buttressed by the "Phillips curve," which purports to show, on the basis of extensive empirical data, that there is an inverse relation between the percentage rate of change of money wages and the rate of unemployment.[59] Hence economic policy is confronted with a dilemma: if unemployment is decreased (with full employment at the limit), inflation will increase, while if inflation is decreased, unemployment will increase.

58.   On some of the variations in the interpretation of this concept, see Richard B. Du Boff, "Full Employment: The History of a Receding Target," *Politics and Society* 7, no. 2 (1977): 1–25.

59.   See A. W. Phillips, "The Relation between Unemployment and the Rate of Change of Money Wage Rates in the United Kingdom, 1861–1957," *Economica* 25 (Nov. 1958): 283–99. See also Karl Brunner and Allan H. Meltzer, eds., *The Phillips Curve and Labor Markets* (Amsterdam: North Holland, 1976).

Partly in reaction to this dilemma and partly on the basis of further empirical data, it has been argued that there is a "natural rate of unemployment": a level of unemployment at which inflation indeed exists but is not accelerated, so that unemployment below that level does accelerate inflation, and unemployment above that level accelerates deflation.[60] The apparent implication for policy is that one should be satisfied to hold unemployment at this "natural rate," which, in the United States, may range from 4 percent to 7 percent of the labor force, where each percent would comprise approximately one million workers. This recommendation smacks of the utilitarian contention that the well-being of some persons may be sacrificed through their being unemployed if this leads to greater good on the whole. But it is difficult to accept as morally justified a policy that subjects millions of persons to the trauma of unemployment for the purpose of maintaining a general level of well-being in which they do not share.

The Phillips curve has generated an immense amount of critical discussion, which cannot be gone into here.[61] The discussion has focused not only on the curve's alleged policy implications but also on the empirical data from which it is constructed. Those data (with their variations for subsequent decades) have been interpreted not only as correlations but also—and this is where the policy implications are especially emphasized—as indicating causal connections. The curve argument holds that there are two main causal connections (comprising both necessary and sufficient conditions): (a) As the available supply of workers decreases (so that unemployment declines) while demand persists or increases, this causes the price of labor—the level of wages—to increase. (b) The increase in the level of wages causes an increase in the level of prices. Cogent reasons have been provided, however, for rejecting each of these causal connections and with them the inflation argument against full employment.[62] I shall briefly sum-

---

60. Milton Friedman, "The Role of Monetary Policy," *American Economic Review* 58 (Mar. 1968): 1–17, at pp. 7–11.

61. For developments to 1978, see Anthony M. Santomero and John J. Seater, "The Inflation-Unemployment Tradeoff: A Critique of the Literature," *Journal of Economic Literature* 16 (June 1978): 499–544. See also Milton Friedman, "Nobel Lecture: Inflation and Unemployment," *Journal of Political Economy* 85 (June 1977): 451–72; David Wheeler, "Is There a Phillips Curve?" in Michael J. Piore, ed., *Unemployment and Inflation: Institutionalist and Structuralist Views* (White Plains, N.Y.: M. E. Sharpe, 1979), pp. 46–57.

62. For an objection of a different kind, which holds that changes in the rate of inflation cause changes in the level of unemployment, rather than conversely, see Milton Friedman, *Unemployment versus Inflation? An Evaluation of the Phillips Curve* (London: Institute of Economic Affairs, Occasional Paper no. 44, 1957). For a critique, see John W. Nevile, "How Voluntary Is Unemployment? Two Views of the Phillips Curve," *Journal of Post-Keynesian Economics* 2, no. 1 (fall 1979): 110–19.

marize two kinds of arguments that have been presented against each connection.

(a) There is a standard contention, both polemical and realistic, that capitalists, in opposition to the community of rights, want to have a large "reserve army of the unemployed" in order to keep wages down.[63] This contention conforms directly to the Phillips curve's causal connection between a fall in unemployment and a rise in wages. Nevertheless, although in extreme cases of great labor scarcity or abundance, supply and demand will affect the rise or fall of wages, the Phillips curve hypothesis must be rejected insofar as it assumes that wages move in a flexible, functional relation with the supply of and demand for workers. On the contrary, there are relatively fixed and self-contained "wage contours" that define relationships between various groups of workers falling into different job groups or "clusters." "Internal standards of job comparison, formal or informal in character, are a much more adequate explanation of many wage differentials than are market forces." Thus, apart from extreme conditions, it is these contours, rather than supply and demand, that directly determine the level of wages. The contours, in turn, are determined by job-content comparisons, especially as to required skills, and more generally by various historical factors of custom and of economic development, including industrialization.[64]

On this view, inflation occurs when external "shocks" operate to "distort" the relationships of wage contours by increasing the wages of one group in relation to other relevant groups within the contour, and the latter groups "then react to restore the original differentials." The control of such inflation must hence aim at preventing the initial distortion-producing shocks through various private and governmental interventions that focus on considerations of equity. Once the distortions have occurred, the attempts to restore the original wage relationships should be evaluated and guided through direct participation by the labor and management groups directly concerned.[65] In this way a certain relevant autonomy can be maintained.

According to this conception, then, wage increases (as well as increases

---

63. Marx, *Capital*, vol. 1, chap. 25, sec. 3 (New York: International Publishers, 1967), pp. 628–40; see also pp. 478, 487.

64. E. Robert Livernash, "Job Clusters," in Piore, ed., *Unemployment and Inflation*, pp. 75–93, at p. 76; see also Michael J. Piore, "Unemployment and Inflation: An Alternative View," and John T. Dunlop, "Wage Contours," in ibid., pp. 5–16, 63–74.

65. Piore, "Unemployment and Inflation: An Alternative View," p. 7. See also James Tobin, "The Cruel Dilemma," in Arthur M. Okun, ed., *The Battle against Unemployment*, rev. ed. (New York: W. W. Norton, 1972), pp. 50–51.

in inflation) are not caused by increased employment, so that the Phillips curve objection against full employment is inapplicable. The government can increase levels of employment by Keynesian monetary and fiscal policies to increase demand, and this without increasing inflation.

Another response to the Phillips curve partly accepts its thesis that the level of wages is determined by the supply of labor, but nonetheless rejects its further thesis that the labor shortages reflected in reduced levels of unemployment must lead to higher wages. For since these labor shortages occur for the most part in jobs requiring high levels of skill, a greater supply of skilled workers (through increases in human capital) would reduce or remove the inflationary pressures increasing wages. Accordingly, "manpower policies" can be used to recruit and train workers from less crowded fields to fill the skilled-labor vacancies, and to train unemployed workers to take the jobs thus vacated. In this way unemployment can be reduced without leading to wage increases.[66] This would be continuous with other policies of education for productive agency (4.9, 10).

(b) The Phillips curve assumes that there is a direct causal sequence from wages to prices: prices rise because wage rates rise, with the latter rise in turn being caused by decreased unemployment. But, entirely apart from profit markups, what determines prices is not wages alone but rather unit labor costs, that is, the amount of wages paid for each unit produced. Hence, if an increase in wages is accompanied by a corresponding increase in productivity (partly through increases in human capital), unit labor costs will remain unchanged, so that there is no need for prices to change. Thus, even with full employment there need not be an increase in inflation if the productivity of labor is increased.[67] The general idea is that the increased wages pay for themselves in the increased goods they produce, so that there is no need to raise prices to pay for the increased wages.

This counterargument to the Phillips curve hypothesis raises the question of what determines productivity growth and decline. Here it is to be noted that psychosocial factors of worker motivation and commitment have contributed strongly to the productivity declines experienced in the United States since the mid-1960s. But such declines are not inevitable if steps are taken to improve worker motivation as well as management competence. Such motivation would reflect the solidaristic emphasis of the

66. See R. A. Gordon, *The Goal of Full Employment* (New York: John Wiley and Sons, 1967), pp. 180–81; Charles C. Holt *et al.*, *The Unemployment–Inflation Dilemma* (Washington, D.C.: Urban Institute, 1971), pp. 67–69, 80–81.

67. See David M. Gordon, "Six-Percent Unemployment Ain't Natural: Demystifying the Idea of a Rising 'Natural Rate of Unemployment,'" *Social Research* 54, no. 2 (summer 1987): 223–46.

community of rights. Hence, full employment, and with it fulfillment of the right to employment, does not necessarily lead to an increase in inflation.[68]

Another argument against the Phillips curve thesis that wage increases must lead to price increases is that price increases can be avoided if the wage increases are absorbed by corporations as reductions of profits and dividends.[69] In this way the cost of wage increases would not be imposed on all buyers indiscriminately, with the most deprived carrying a disproportionate share of the burden in relation to income. Instead, the persons who stand to benefit most directly from workers' increased productivity would bear most of the costs. This would be an application of the criterion of degrees of needfulness for action insofar as that criterion requires giving preferential status to those whose needs are greatest.

It will have been noted that the above replies to the Phillips curve hypothesis are not all mutually consistent. According to one reply, the supply of labor—the level of employment and unemployment—is not causally related to the level of wages, while according to another reply it is; and one reply denies that wage increases alone lead to price increases, while another holds that wage increases will lead to price increases unless profit and dividends are concomitantly reduced. I cannot go here into all the considerations that could remove or mitigate these inconsistencies. But the policies leading to full employment need not involve similar inconsistencies: they converge in important part on increasing human capital and thus productivity as well as on norms of mutuality and equity both between different groups of workers and other segments of the economy. My main concern here has been to show that the argument for full employment, based on the principle of human rights, contains sufficient resources to withstand the objections about inflation.

6.7. WAGE COSTS OF FULL EMPLOYMENT

An important problem for a full employment policy providing public service employment concerns costs: How would the extra employment be paid for? Milton Friedman has presented a set of arguments to the effect that, if the program is not to be inflationary, it would fail in its aim of increasing total employment because, whatever the source of the funds to pay the newly employed workers, these workers "would simply replace" other, already employed workers:

68. See Samuel Bowles, David M. Gordon, and Thomas E. Weisskopf, *Beyond the Waste Land* (Garden City, N.Y.: Anchor Press//Doubleday, 1984), chap. 6.

69. See R. A. Gordon, *Goal of Full Employment,* p. 75; Lekachman, "Toward Equality through Employment," p. 11.

If the funds came from reducing other government expenditures, new government employees would simply replace other government employees with no gain in total employment and very likely a loss in efficiency.

If the funds came from imposing higher taxes, the taxpayers would have less to spend, which would reduce the number of workers they employ directly or indirectly. New government employees would simply replace persons employed in the private sector. "Make work" would replace employment that met the private demands of taxpayers.

If the funds came from borrowing from the public, less credit would be available to lend to others. New government employees would simply replace persons employed in building houses or factories or machines that would have been financed by savings now absorbed by the public service program. Make-work would replace employment devoted to adding to our productive wealth.[70]

I shall here focus on the second, fiscal argument, since the taxation approach is most in keeping with the PGC's criterion of degrees of needfulness for action and the mutuality required by the community of rights. There are many difficulties with Friedman's argument. For one thing, it would apply to the increase of taxes for any reason, not just to pay for public service workers. It would apply to increased health care expenditures, military expenditures, antipollution expenditures, and indeed to the "negative income tax" that Friedman himself advocates.[71] Increased taxes for these and any other purposes would also mean that "the taxpayers would have less to spend," with a corresponding reduction in private sector workers. But if at least some of these interferences with the market are in any degree desirable, as Friedman concedes, then the fact that the public service employment program could be financed through higher taxes does not of itself affect the program's desirability any more than it affects the desirability of these other public expenditures.

Second, if the program is targeted to meet the important public goods and services indicated above (6.2), as against "the private demands of taxpayers" for various goods, the need for which is far less pressing, then it is false to apply to public sector employment the pejorative label of "make work."

70. Milton Friedman, *There's No Such Thing as a Free Lunch* (LaSalle, Ill.: Open Court Publishing Co., 1975), pp. 118–19. For Friedman's more technical argument focused on economic stability, see "The Effects of a Full-Employment Policy on Economic Stability: A Formal Analysis," in Friedman, *Essays in Positive Economics* (Chicago: University of Chicago Press, 1953), pp. 117–32. For an older version of Friedman's second and third arguments, see Harold Cox, *Economic Liberty* (London: Longmans, Green, 1920), p. 72.

71. Friedman, *There's No Such Thing*, pp. 198–201. See also Friedman, *Capitalism and Freedom* (Chicago: University of Chicago Press, 1962), pp. 190–95.

Third, the increased taxes for the public service employment program should be levied mainly against large corporations and the persons with the highest incomes, such as those in the top fifth of the income distribution, and also against industries that contribute excessively to environmental depletion.[72] The justification for this is provided by the criterion of degrees of needfulness for action. And since the funds so derived would be used to pay for work done, not merely as transfer payments, they would encourage self-reliance rather than dependence.

Fourth, the argument seems to assume a kind of "spending fund" doctrine whereby actual spending is not only limited by but is also determined by the availability of funds to taxpayers. But the fact that "taxpayers *would have* less to spend" does not entail that taxpayers would actually spend less. Especially for the upper-income taxpayers who would pay the largest amount of new taxes, they could readily maintain their spending levels while saving somewhat less. So the availability of less funds for private sector spending need not mean that "new government employees would simply replace persons employed in the private sector."

The lesser savings of some upper-income taxpayers would be considerably offset by the increased spending of the newly employed public sector workers, which would give employment to private sector workers. So again no "replacement" need occur: there would be an absolute increase in employed workers. In addition, paying the costs of the program would be helped by the increased tax revenues derived from the wages of the newly employed workers, as well as by reduced expenditures for welfare payments and unemployment compensation.[73]

Besides the costs incurred by the government to pay for the public service program, there are other potential costs that may also raise serious problems. Among the groups affected are employers of low-wage labor whose increased labor costs could result in reduced demands for their products or in loss of markets to foreign competitors who have much lower labor costs. Rising affluence in such countries could eventually raise their labor costs, but this may not occur in the relevant future. The affected employers could be helped to change to a more profitable line of production; or they could be compensated by the government; or they could participate in the public service employment program.[74]

---

72. See Arthur Pearl, "The Human Service Society—An Ecological Perspective," in Gartner, Nixon, and Riessman, *Public Service Employment*, pp. 57–58; Frank Riessman, "Public Service Employment: Potential Dangers and Possible Directions," in ibid., p. 217.

73. See Harvey, *Securing the Right to Employment*, pp. 43–44.

74. See ibid., pp. 72–74. Harvey also deals in detail with other economic, administrative, and political problems raised by full employment (chaps. 4–6).

Another potential cost of a full employment policy is the creation of a vast governmental bureaucracy, with all its potentials for burdensome inefficiency, tyrannical interference with individual initiative, pettifogging regulations, and so forth. This problem must be taken seriously. But an important part of it can be obviated or at least greatly decreased by instituting appropriate democratic controls, ultimately deriving from the workers themselves as well as the wider public. Consideration of these matters falls appropriately under the rubrics of economic and political democracy, to be taken up in the next two chapters.[75]

6.8. FULL EMPLOYMENT AND SHIRKING

A perennial objection against full employment is that it will encourage workers to "shirk" (defined as not "performing at the customary level of effort for his job"). For, on the assumption that all workers are alike in that they "dislike putting forth effort, but enjoy consuming goods," a worker will not fear being penalized for shirking, for (given governmentally guaranteed employment at the going wage), if he is fired he can always get another job at the same wage. Hence, it is contended that some unemployment is needed as an "incentive device" to dissuade workers from shirking.[76]

To deal with this objection, we must keep in mind that "shirking" is a more complex phenomenon than is suggested by the simplistic assumption that all workers "dislike putting forth effort." The phenomenon is affected not only by the kinds of work in question but also by the economic, social-psychological, and quasi-political context in which the work occurs. Three contexts may be distinguished. First, where work is scarce and is needed for livelihood, would-be workers, far from shunning effort, put forth stren-

75. It may be relevant to compare here the experience of the Public Works Administration that was established as part of President F. D. Roosevelt's New Deal in June 1933: "Between 1933 and 1939 PWA helped in the construction of about 70 per cent of the nation's new educational buildings; 65 per cent of courthouses and the city halls and the sewage disposal plants; 35 per cent of the hospitals and public health facilities; and 10 per cent of all the roads, bridges, subways, and similar engineering structures. It spent about $6 billion, created about a billion and three-quarters man-hours of labor on the site of construction, and generated another three billion man-hours of employment in the production of materials, fabrication, and transportation. No one ever convincingly accused the PWA of boondoggling or of fraud. It was a prodigious accomplishment" (Arthur M. Schlesinger, Jr., *The Coming of the New Deal* (Boston: Houghton Mifflin, 1958), p. 288.

76. Carl Shapiro and Joseph E. Stiglitz, "Equilibrium Unemployment as a Worker Discipline Device," *American Economic Review* 74, no. 3 (June 1984): 435; and see Layard, Mickell, and Jackman, *Unemployment*, pp. 161–63.

uous efforts to obtain employment. For example, "In periods of depression, the search for jobs became more aggressive. During the summers of 1907 and 1908, small gangs of immigrants marched about upstate New York carrying their own shovels or other tools to beg (or demand) jobs from local farmers and municipal authorities. In Detroit during the 1890's, troops of unemployed workers had chased road-repair crews away from their jobs and demanded a turn for themselves."[77]

A second context is where work is readily available but the customary level of effort required for a given job goes beyond certain limits. Here, "shirking" is a rational and morally justified response. For example, "Ferocious bouts of toil were possible for laborers, but no one could sustain such a pace indefinitely. Asked how he had survived sixty-five years of heavy toil, the Welsh-born miner Tom Benyan replied: 'Oh, they can't kill you with work if you have sense enough to go slow.'"[78] Here it is a matter not of a general dislike for putting forth effort but rather of taking care to diminish effort when this is needed to avoid physical damage to oneself. In both these first two contexts the mutuality of rights operates to protect workers' employment-related interests.

A third context, most directly relevant to the connection between full employment and shirking, is where workers and employers cooperate with mutual understanding and concern for one another's needs and objectives. The most obvious case of such a relation is found in producer cooperatives that are owned by their workers. Here, employers and workers are identical; hence, "members show lower absenteeism, a greater work effort, greater work flexibility, and better maintenance of the plant and equipment than do workers in capitalist organizations."[79] But similar levels of work effort may also be found in capitalist enterprises where both economic and psychological incentives through mutuality of rights are provided for loyalty to one's company. This has been the case, for example, in contemporary Japan, where, partly because of government backing, companies can and do guarantee long-term and indeed permanent employment until retirement at close to sixty years of age. "The firm is committed to the employee and provides a sense of belonging, personal support, welfare and retirement benefits, and increased salary and rank with age. Barring serious long-term depression, the employee expects that he will never be laid off, and even if the company were to disband or be absorbed by another

77. David Montgomery, *The Fall of the House of Labor* (Cambridge: Cambridge University Press, 1987), p. 88.

78. Ibid., p. 90.

79. Henry M. Levin, "Employment and Productivity of Producer Cooperatives," in Robert Jackall and Levin, eds., *Worker Cooperatives in America* (Berkeley and Los Angeles: University of California Press, 1984), p. 26.

company, he expects that a new job elsewhere will be arranged."[80] In return, employees take pride in their work and work at a higher level both qualitatively and quantitatively.[81] Thus, given the appropriate context of mutual consideration, there is no necessary incompatibility between full, assured employment and nonshirking.[82]

A governmentally guaranteed right to employment is not antithetical to the enforcement of worker discipline. A worker who shirks can be demoted from one job to another that pays less or that is otherwise less attractive than the one he previously had.[83] Given good working conditions, one's fellow workers can also exert a disciplining influence in calling attention to one who does less than his fair share.[84] To have a right to employment does not necessarily mean having a right to retain a particular job. The range of jobs can be made to parallel the range both of abilities and of efforts.

A more complex version of the objection about shirking bears directly on private sector rather than public sector workers. It is held that if a public sector firm offers the same wages as a private sector firm, then workers in the latter will have an incentive to shirk, because if found out and dismissed they can always get a job at comparable wages in a public sector firm. To

80.   Ezra Vogel, *Japan as Number One* (Cambridge, Mass.: Harvard University Press, 1979), p. 137. See also Andrew Gordon, "The Right to Work in Japan: Labor and the State in the Depression," *Social Research* 54 (1987): 247–72.

81.   See Vogel, *Japan as Number One,* chap. 6.

82.   Subsequent developments in Japan have modified but not substantially altered this pattern. See Andrew Pollack, "Japanese Starting to Link Pay to Performance, Not Tenure," *New York Times,* Oct. 2, 1993, national edition, p. 1; and Pollack, "How Japan Hews to Tradition of Lifetime Jobs," *New York Times,* Apr. 26, 1993, p. 1: When Nippon Steel closed its factory in Kamaishi, it "kept the factory operating long after it became unprofitable and closed it only gradually, transferring workers to other plants. When it could no longer transfer workers, the company scrambled to create almost any business it could to employ the former steelworkers here, including an ill-fated attempt at growing mushrooms." This policy of considerateness stands in sharp contrast to the speculative financial manipulations of Japanese banks, abetted by the government. See, e.g., Christopher Wood, *The Bubble Economy: Japan's Extraordinary Speculative Boom of the 80's and the Dramatic Bust of the 90's* (New York: Atlantic Monthly Press, 1993). On Japanese work and production patterns, see also J. Schonberger, *Japanese Manufacturing Techniques* (New York: Free Press, 1982); K. Doshe, U. Jurgens, and T. Malsch, "From 'Fordism' to 'Toyotaism'? The Social Organization of the Labor Process in the Japanese Automobile Industry," *Politics and Society* 16 (1988): 121–58; Stephen Wood, "The Japanization of Fordism," *Economic and Industrial Democracy* 14 (Nov. 1993): 535–54. For a different but not unrelated perspective, see Anne Allison, *Nightwork: Sexuality, Pleasure, and Corporate Masculinity in a Tokyo Hostess Club* (Chicago: University of Chicago Press, 1994).

83.   See Harvey, *Securing the Right to Employment,* pp. 97–98.

84.   See Alchian and Demsetz, "Production, Information Costs, and Economic Organization," pp. 780–83.

avoid losing needed workers and to provide an incentive for not shirking, the private sector firm will raise wages. But then, the objection continues, to avoid wage inequality the public sector firm will also raise wages. Once again, to avoid shirking the private sector firm will raise wages. But this would reduce private sector demand for labor, and the unemployed workers would go into the always available public sector. This process would continue until private sector firms, because of constantly increasing labor costs, would be driven out of business. Hence, there is a dilemma: "Either some workers are unemployed or some workers are paid less than other workers doing the same job."[85]

Proposed solutions to this dilemma include acceptance of lower wages for public sector workers and improved monitoring of workers by private sector employers so that shirk-prone workers are not hired.[86] But it can be argued that the whole scenario is also weakened in its initial step. Private sector firms can have ways of retaining nonshirking workers without engaging in a continuous spiral of increasing wages. Especially important is provision of good working conditions, which include positive consideration for important factors ranging from health and safety to mutual consultation about work processes and standards. This would require significant modifications of the class-war assumptions that underlie the model. Such modifications need not be viewed as departures from a market system, unless employers in that system are regarded as inveterately myopic. If more and better work can be gotten when workers are treated with respect and civility rather than as instruments to be exploited for maximum short-term profits, the requirements of efficiency as well as of human rights can be fulfilled. More generally, in the workplace as elsewhere the moral requirement of the mutuality of rights can and should be made effective. In chapter 7 I shall examine how economic democracy in the form of worker control can help to obtain this objective.

6.9. EMPLOYMENT AT WILL AND PROPERTY RIGHTS IN JOBS

The preceding sections of this chapter have viewed workers as being either in the private sector or in the public sector, and as moving from the former to the latter when, among other reasons, they are dismissed by private employers and cannot obtain other private sector jobs. It was noted that such dismissals reflect large inequalities of power between employers and

---

85. Elster, "Is There (or Should There Be) a Right to Work?" pp. 73–74. Cf. Shapiro and Stiglitz, "Equilibrium Unemployment," p. 433.

86. See Richard J. Arneson, "Is Work Special? Justice and the Distribution of Employment," *American Political Science Review* 84, no. 4 (Dec. 1990): 1137–40.

workers (6.1). We must now examine whether the specific inequalities in this context are morally justified.

A prime alleged basis of the power to dismiss is the doctrine of "employment at will," according to which all employers "may dismiss their employees at will . . . for good cause, for no cause, or even for cause morally wrong, without thereby being guilty of legal wrong."[87] This sweeping doctrine has undergone restrictions both through collective bargaining agreements whereby workers can be fired only for "just cause" and through legal provisions which prohibit employers from firing workers on grounds of union membership or because of racial, religious, or sex discrimination.[88] But there persists the more general thesis that the unrestricted right to dismiss employees is justified because it reflects the "contract at will" which characterizes all market relations. Thus, although the restrictions previously noted have led American courts "to view the employment-at-will doctrine, strictly applied, as an anachronism,"[89] the contractualist thesis underlying it still merits attention.

The general idea of the contract-at-will thesis is held to be "mutuality": each contractor voluntarily agrees that the other has certain rights against him, and, because the contract is voluntary, each can terminate it at will, that is, by his or her unilateral decision. Thus, on the one hand, the employer has the right to receive specified work from the worker, and the worker has the right to receive specified pay from the employer. And, on the other hand, just as the worker has the right to terminate her employment temporarily by striking or permanently by quitting, so the employer has the right to terminate the worker's employment by firing her. In this way, then, "the right of the employé to quit the service of the employer, for whatever reason, is the same as the right of the employer, for whatever reason, to dispense with the service of such employé. . . . In all such particulars the employer and the employé have equality of right."[90]

This purely formal conception of equality and mutuality ignores the substantive inequalities of need and power between the individual em-

---

87. *Payne v Western and Atlantic Railway,* 81 Tenn. 507, 519–20 (1884).

88. See Frederic Meyers, *Ownership of Jobs: A Comparative Study* (Los Angeles: Institute of Industrial Relations, UCLA, 1964), pp. 3–10; Laurence E. Blades, "Employment at Will vs. Individual Freedom: On Limiting the Abusive Exercise of Employer Power," *Columbia Law Review* 67 (1967): 1404–35, at pp. 1410–13.

89. Alfred G. Feliu, *Primer on Individual Employee Rights* (Washington, D.C.: Bureau of National Affairs, Inc., 1992), p. 5.

90. *Adair v United States,* 208 U.S. 161 (1908). See, to the same effect, Richard A. Epstein, "In Defense of the Contract at Will," *University of Chicago Law Review* 51, no. 4 (fall 1984): 947–82, at p. 957: "The rights under the contract at will are fully bilateral, so that the employee can use the contract as a means to control the firm, just as the firm uses it to control the worker"; see also pp. 955, 966.

ployer and the individual worker (5.2; 6.1). To secure his livelihood the worker needs this particular job far more than the employer needs this particular worker. The employer usually has a far greater pool of willing workers to draw upon than the worker has of willing employers, so that the employer can replace this particular worker far more readily than the worker can replace this particular employer. It follows that the employer's right to dismiss at will any particular worker has far more deleterious consequences for the latter's freedom and well-being than does the worker's right to "dismiss" his employer by quitting his job.[91] The worker's right to quit his job for a better one is hence not parallel to the employer's right to fire a worker at will.[92]

The equality and mutuality of rights upheld by the PGC thus require a substantive as well as a formal consideration (see 3.2).[93] The doctrine of employment-at-will should be rejected because its formal equality of rights does not take account, as the principle of human rights requires, of the substantive inequalities between employers and workers with regard to effective freedom and consequences for well-being. Because of these inequalities, special protection must be provided for the freedom and well-being of workers with regard to their retention of employment. This rejection of the unqualified thesis of "contract at will" does not, as such, remove the prerogatives of management. To reject that there are no limits on the employer's right of dismissal does not entail that the employer has no right either to set appropriate work standards whose violation might, after due process, justify dismissal[94] or to react to market or technological developments that may require reductions of the workforce.[95]

The rejection of the employment-at-will doctrine entails a recognition that workers have certain property rights in their jobs.[96] The justified limits

91. See Blades, "Employment at Will," pp. 1425–26; Patricia H. Werhane, *Persons, Rights, and Corporations* (Englewood Cliffs, N.J.: Prentice-Hall, 1985), pp. 90–91. Compare F. A. Hayek, *The Constitution of Liberty* (Chicago: University of Chicago Press, 1960), p. 121: "In a normally operating competitive society, alternative employment will be available, even though it may often be less remunerative."

92. See Clyde W. Summers, "Individual Protection against Unjust Dismissal: Time for a Statute," *Virginia Law Review* 62 (1976): 481–532, at pp. 491–92.

93. See Blades, "Employment at Will," p. 1419; Summers, "Individual Protection," p. 491.

94. See Summers, "Individual Protection," pp. 501–8; Philip J. Levine, "Towards a Property Right in Employment," *Buffalo Law Review* 22 (1975): 1081–110, at pp. 1082–83, n. 10.

95. See Meyers, *Ownership of Jobs*, p. 10.

96. See William Gomberg, "Featherbedding: An Assertion of Property Rights," *Annals of the American Academy of Political and Social Science* 333 (Jan. 1961): 119–29; Meyers, *Ownership of Jobs*; Levine, "Towards a Property Right in Employment'; James H. Looney, "Expected Continued Employment as a Protected Property Right," *Loyola Law Review* 22

on discharge from employment are at the same time justified protections of workers' interests in retaining their jobs. The recognition of such property rights is especially important because it emphasizes that when persons are employed in factories, offices, or other establishments, property rights are had not only by the employers who own those establishments but also by the employees by virtue of their working in them. The realm of property in the area of productive employment is thus not confined to employer-owners; it extends also to workers.

This property right in one's job is an application of both the consequentialist and the antecedentalist justifications of property rights (5.2, 3); thus it ultimately stems from the human rights to freedom and basic well-being. Nevertheless, in the present context the property right in one's job is a weak right, in two respects. First, it is weaker than the right to employment as this has been upheld in the present chapter. For the former right is a negative right of job retention, so it is contingent on one's having been given employment in the first place. The latter, positive right, on the other hand, requires that employment indeed be given; it is not contingent on prior receipt of employment. Second, the property right in one's job lacks many of the "incidents" of full liberal ownership (5.1); for example, it cannot be "transmitted" or transferred. The right is contingent on employers' decisions about the economic viability or profitability of retaining workers. The "just cause" for which workers may be dismissed, as it has been interpreted in capitalist societies, may include budgetary and related constraints from which workers have no appeal. Thus, the property right in one's job leaves untouched great inequalities of power between workers and employers (5.2; 6.1).

The property right in one's job hence raises more general questions about the whole scope of rights bearing on employment. They include questions not only about the rights of workers to participate in decisions about the conditions of their work but also about the rights of ownership and control of industrial and postindustrial establishments, including the ownership structure of the entire economy. Some of these questions have been touched on in connection with the theses of social contribution and world ownership (3.4; 5.5) and in the discussion of the contribution principle especially as it bears on the rewards due to capitalists (5.7). The questions are further dealt with in the next chapter. But in the present chapter I

(1976): 884–92. For the general background, see Charles A. Reich, "The New Property," *Yale Law Journal* 73 (Apr. 1964): 733–87. See also Munzer, *Theory of Property*, pp. 347–48. For a negative view, which argues from analogies between workers and employers and from costs imposed on other persons, see Simon Rottenberg, "Property in Work," *Industrial and Labor Relations Review* 15 (Apr. 1962): 402–5.

have tried to show that the state as the community of rights has the obligation of providing paid employment for persons who cannot obtain work by their own efforts. In this way the rights to freedom and well-being are brought together with the community whose policies help to fulfill them. The communal solidarity is addressed to the vital needs of its vulnerable members.

SEVEN

THE RIGHT TO ECONOMIC
DEMOCRACY

7.1. ECONOMIC DEMOCRACY AS WORKERS' CONTROL

T he preceding three chapters have traced a sequence of economic biography and a concomitant economic constitution whose phases have
included, first, the development of abilities of productive agency for all persons; second, their acquisition of private property in the earning of income;
third, the assurance of paid employment for all. Each of these phases has
derived from the community of rights, both in its institutional embodiment
in the supportive state and in the recognition by individuals and groups of
the mutual rights of persons. Each phase has involved a modification or
restriction of market relations: the community, acting through the state,
has intervened to provide the welfare income, the education, the legal
structure, and the employment opportunities that are required by persons'
equal rights to freedom and well-being. The legitimacy of these interventions still leaves it open that other operations of the market are justifiable as
uses of freedom in buying and selling. But success in the market on the part
of the persons who are helped by these interventions is not to be a necessary
condition of having or obtaining goods that are objects of human rights:
goods that are necessary either for the very possibility of action or for general chances of success in achieving one's purposes.

Amid these justified interventions, the economy, as so far considered,
may still be capitalist in that capitalists own and control the major means
of production. Thus in North America and in western Europe, elements of
the tax-supported welfare state have existed side by side with capitalist
market economies. What is often called "social democracy" in its varying
degrees is an embodiment of this combination. The development of the
social democratic welfare state has been a major advance toward the fulfillment of the human rights to freedom and well-being. The unbridled
market capitalism that so enraged Marx and saddened Mill and other re-
formers, which left the poor and the working class unable to compete for
adequate wages and work conditions (3.7), has given way to a more hu-

mane society in which the operation of market relations has been restricted by communal institutional provision for basic needs and certain elemental opportunities for all persons. Such provisions have been central illustrations of the conciliation of rights and community to which my first three chapters were addressed, for they have shown how the economic and social rights, as human rights, have required institutions of mutual support and solidarity. Important foundations of the community of rights have thereby been established. These foundations are buttressed and amplified by the gigantic outputs generated by the capitalist market economy with its strong incentives for entrepreneurial innovation and risk-taking and accompanying vast increases in productive efficiency.

Most actually existing capitalist societies, even with their welfare-state components, are nevertheless far from embodying the community of rights as so far presented. Millions of persons still have to rely on welfare payments with even their basic needs barely accommodated; public education in the United States and other countries fails to develop the productive agency of millions of children; vast expanses of poverty and unemployment are found in these societies. There remain, then, two further areas of concern for the community of rights. One is to bring closer to reality those of its phases presented above in education, employment, and other areas that have not yet been fulfilled. The accomplishment of this task requires, among other things, consideration of the capacities of political democracy, which will be taken up in chapter 8.

The other remaining area of concern is to augment the previous phases by calling attention to human economic and social rights that may still be violated even if the previous phases are fulfilled. These violations bear in general on the vast inequalities of wealth and power, with resulting enmity and discord, that disfigure many societies. Significant limitations on these inequalities have been presented above in the theses of social contribution, economic redistribution, and world ownership (3.4; 5.2, 5), which require that property rights not be absolute but be shared for certain purposes with the wider society. A segment of these purposes that must now receive attention can be initially depicted within the specific context of paid work or employment whose guarantee was the subject of chapter 6.

Even if persons develop their abilities of productive agency and obtain employment for those abilities, there may remain serious moral problems about their conditions of work. Despite the mutuality of consideration between workers and employers found in some of the more exemplary capitalist firms (6.8), a main charge against large components of the capitalist system may be put in terms of its undermining the generic rights of workers as prescribed by the PGC. The workers' equal rights to freedom are violated because they are subjected in the workplace to hierarchic controls whereby managers or employers tell them what to do and how to do it, so that the workers are at the bottom end of an authoritarian chain of command in which they are required to execute orders given from above, with no participation or control on their part. The workers' equal rights to well-being are violated because their conditions of work may be unhealthful, dangerous, degrading, and accompanied by feelings of meaninglessness and dissatisfaction, and because, having to work primarily for their employers' interests rather than their own, they are paid less than the full value of what they produce. So the workers are exploited and alienated from both the process and the product of their work. These negative impacts of capitalism operate in some cases by directly removing constituent conditions of freedom or well-being and in other cases by having consequences that effect such removal. The augmentative concern of the community of rights is, in part, to show how the rights previously presented are to be expanded in order to take account of, and if possible to remedy, these violations of rights.

Among the many remedies that have been proposed for these problems, we may distinguish, apart from centrally planned economies with their well-known difficulties, three kinds of political-economic system, each of which uses competitive markets to allocate certain resources. One kind preserves the distinction between capitalists and workers but gives the latter or their representatives fuller, and in some respects equal, authority over the conditions of work and management of firms. The system of "co-determination" in the German Federal Republic after World War II is one of many examples.[1] A second kind gives all the authority to control the conditions of work to the workers or their representatives, but only within single firms, not in the economy as a whole. The producer cooperatives in Mondragon, Spain, and the plywood cooperatives in the Pacific Northwest are examples.[2] A third kind provides that in a whole national economy the control is to be by the workers or their representatives. The "self-managed" economy of the former Yugoslavia is a main example.[3] All three

---

1. See Svetozar Pejovich, ed., *The Codetermination Movement in the West* (Lexington, Mass.: D. C. Heath, 1978).

2. See Henk Thomas and Chris Logan, *Mondragon: An Economic Analysis* (London: Allen and Unwin, 1982); William Foote Whyte and Kathleen King Whyte, *Making Mondragon: The Growth and Dynamics of the Worker Cooperative Complex* (Ithaca, N.Y.: ILR Press, 1988); Christopher E. Gunn, *Workers' Self-Management in the United States* (Ithaca, N.Y.: Cornell University Press, 1984); Edward S. Greenberg, *Workplace Democracy: The Political Effects of Participation* (Ithaca, N.Y.: Cornell University Press, 1986).

3. See Hans Dieter Seibel and Ukandi G. Damachi, *Self-Management in Yugoslavia and the Developing World* (New York: St. Martin's Press, 1982); Ellen Turkish Comisso, *Workers' Control under Plan and Market: Implications of Yugoslav Self-Management* (New Haven, Conn.: Yale University Press, 1979).

of these kinds of market systems, despite their differences, may be called, in a broad sense, "participatory'; and they have also been called systems of "industrial" or "economic democracy." Other phrases that have been applied to them include "workers' control," "workers' self-management," "producers' cooperatives," and "market socialism," although the last refers primarily to whole economic systems. These phrases are not entirely synonymous with one another, and each has been given different meanings.[4] I shall here mainly use "economic democracy" to refer to these market systems, both in individual firms and in a whole society, insofar as they provide for worker control of the productive process. But I shall use the other expressions as well when they seem appropriate. As I shall deal with it here, economic democracy builds upon the egalitarian emphases of the theses of social contribution, economic redistribution, and world ownership presented above. It consists in institutions that develop the implications of these theses for economic and social institutions as they bear on the ownership and control of organizations of economic production.

Let us now examine whether, or how, economic democracy can help to fulfill the requirements of human rights indicated above. Economic democracy has been defined as a system in which products are put out to be sold in competitive markets and the workers themselves control the productive organization and process. This control in some cases also includes aspects of ownership either by the workers themselves or by the state. More specifically, what is controlled may run the gamut from the everyday operations of the firm to broader matters of the rate and kind of investment, financial planning, production goals and methods, the taking on of workers, sales and marketing, supervision and evaluation of management, distribution of income, and so forth. In these and other matters the workers cooperate with one another in running their joint enterprise, with corresponding mutual rights and duties. They are therefore not hired laborers working for wages; instead, they are joint members and partners in their firm, who finance their cooperatives by contributions and entry fees set with their approval. Profits are shared by the members in proportion to hours worked and pay level. Equal rights of control are had by all the workers in a firm or enterprise. They may exercise these rights directly, as in a general assembly, or they may delegate these rights to workers' councils or other elected representatives or managers. But in all cases final authority rests with the

---

4. For a taxonomy of types of productive organizations, with emphasis on varieties of worker control and ownership, see Jaroslav Vanek, ed., *Self-Management: Economic Liberation of Man* (Harmondsworth, England: Penguin, 1975), introduction, pp. 13–16. A distinction of "five steps in the development of the idea of market socialism" is presented in Pranab E. Bardhan and John E. Roemer, eds., *Market Socialism: The Current Debate* (New York: Oxford University Press, 1993), pp. 3–9.

workers, who may remove, correct, and instruct the managers. All workers have equal votes, not contingent on any ownership of capital, and decisions are reached by majority vote.[5]

Underpinning this equality of control are certain important aspects of ownership, especially in producer cooperatives. Thus in Mondragon "each worker has a strong stake in the [sic] own cooperative"; as one worker said, "I feel that this machine in part is mine." And in the plywood cooperative of the Pacific Northwest, "I don't work for nobody else; I work for myself."[6] These points stand in contrast to the capitalist system in which it is the owners of capital or the managers hired by and responsible to them who control the operations of the firm and have the prerogatives of ownership, including the residual claims to its profits. In capitalist systems, capital hires workers; in economic democracy, workers hire capital.

Before taking up the complex task of inquiring whether economic democracy can help to fulfill the requirements of human rights, we must note an initial difference between the right that will be here upheld to economic democracy and the rights discussed in the preceding chapters. All these rights are either constitutive of or instrumental toward the generic human rights to freedom and well-being. But the preceding rights differ in an important respect from the economic democracy which is the object of the right now under consideration. The objects of the preceding rights, such as

5.   The literature on economic democracy, market socialism, and workers' control is vast. In addition to the books cited in nn. 1–4 above, some other representative works are Jaroslav Vanek, *The General Theory of Labor-Managed Market Economies* (Ithaca, N.Y.: Cornell University Press, 1970); Martin Carnoy and Derek Shearer, *Economic Democracy: The Challenge of the 1980's* (White Plains, N.Y.: M. E. Sharpe, 1980); Gerry Hunnius, G. David Garson, and John Case, *Workers' Control* (New York: Vintage Books, 1973); Paul Blumberg, *Industrial Democracy: The Sociology of Participation* (New York: Schocken Books, 1969); Frank H. Stephen, ed., *The Performance of Labour-Managed Firms* (New York: St. Martin's Press, 1982); Derek C. Jones and Jan Svejnar, eds., *Participatory and Self-Managed Firms: Evaluating Economic Performance* (Lexington, Mass.: D. C. Heath and Co., 1982); Robert A. Dahl, *A Preface to Economic Democracy* (Berkeley and Los Angeles: University of California Press, 1985); David Montgomery, *Workers' Control in America* (Cambridge: Cambridge University Press, 1979); David Schweickart, *Against Capitalism* (Cambridge: Cambridge University Press, 1993); David Miller, *Market, State, and Community: Theoretical Foundations of Market Socialism* (Oxford: Clarendon Press, 1989); Nelson Lichtenstein and Howell J. Harris, eds., *Industrial Democracy in America: The Ambiguous Promise* (Cambridge, UK: Cambridge University Press, 1993); David Ellerman, *The Democratic Worker-Owned Firm* (Boston: Unwin Hyman, 1990); Julian LeGrand and Saul Estrin, eds., *Market Socialism* (Oxford: Clarendon Press, 1989); Samuel Bowles, Herbert Gintis, and Bo Gustafsson, eds., *Markets and Democracy: Participation, Accountability and Efficiency* (Cambridge: Cambridge University Press, 1993); N. Scott Arnold, *The Philosophy and Economics of Market Socialism* (Oxford: Oxford University Press, 1994).

6.   The first quotation is from Thomas and Logan, *Mondragon*, p. 160; the second from Greenberg, *Workplace Democracy,*p. 75.

education and employment, are all distributively available, in that each person can receive and have them individually. (This is distinct from the point that the effectuation of these rights requires social provision and enforcement.) Economic democracy, on the other hand, is only collectively available; it cannot be the personal property of a given individual, because it is a social condition, a system of organizing production and distribution. Nevertheless, individual persons can still be held to have a right to economic democracy, in that, as I shall try to show, the system can and should be made available and beneficial to each person. The collective good of economic democracy will be seen to be for the good of each person as a worker in a productive enterprise, in that the system is needed to fulfill the individual's rights to freedom and well-being. The pattern of the argument, then, is that since each individual has rights to freedom and well-being, and since the system of economic democracy is needed to fulfill these rights, it follows that each individual has a right to economic democracy as the system that enables this fulfillment (see 3.8). In this way the ethical individualism of the community of rights is maintained. So insofar as economic democracy is a collective good, the right to economic democracy is a collective right; but insofar as this good is beneficial to the individuals who participate in it, it is also an individual right (see 2.4; 8.1). The system of economic democracy fits into the community of rights in a double way. First, it itself exemplifies a community of rights insofar as the system exemplifies and maintains a solidaristic organization that protects the mutual and equal rights of its members. Second, the system is protected by the state insofar as it is a right of persons. But it still remains to determine the more precise way in which the state as the community of rights is the respondent of the right to economic democracy.

One of the many conditions for the success or adequacy of the argument for the right to economic democracy is that the system of economic democracy must not itself violate any other rights. It may be contended that the capitalist's right of ownership is violated when the ownership and control of his firm are taken over by the workers. There are several interrelated replies. First, the capitalists may be compensated by the workers; or, if this is not possible, the workers may pool their assets, as in pension funds, to buy the firm. This is a promising line of approach, but it also carries the dangers that the workers' stock ownership may be used not to give them control of the firm's operations but to provide a secure financial base for the firm and to forestall independent labor action while solidifying control in a small group of managers.[7] Second, as we saw earlier, rights of own-

---

7. See Raymond Russell, "Using Ownership to Control: Making Workers Owners in the United States," *Politics and Society* 13, no. 3 (1984): 253–94; Joseph R. Blasi, *Employee*

ership are limited or canceled when they result in harm or are put to harmful use (5.2). An egregious case of such harmful use is found when the workers' rights to freedom and well-being are violated. These rights take precedence over the capitalists' ownership rights because of the criterion of degrees of needfulness for action (2.4). Third, capitalists' rights of ownership are in any case limited by the antecedentalist conditions set forth in the theses of social contribution and world ownership (3.4; 5.5). Limitation does not, of course, mean abrogation; but it serves further to indicate the nonabsoluteness of property rights in major means of production. Fourth, the workers may set up their own firms as cooperatives; this indeed is the main pattern, with its attendant problems, that will be followed below.

If the right to economic democracy, like the rights previously discussed, is a claim right, then there remain two further questions: Who is the respondent, the person or group that has the correlative duty? And is it a mandatory or a discretionary right (see 6.4): Is it like the right to education, so that workers have a duty to accept economic democracy for themselves, or is it rather like the right to vote, so that workers should be free to reject exercising the relevant controls if they so desire? To an important extent these questions go together. The duty to establish economic democracy belongs ultimately to constitution makers who could arrange that workers' control be an operative requirement within the whole economy. But such establishment should not be imposed by fiat; it should be the result of a democratic process of discussion, deliberation, and negotiation in which arguments pro and con are carefully considered by the electorate of political democracy (see 8.2).[8] The right to economic democracy is at least a negative claim-right in that obstacles should not be put in the way of its

Ownership: Revolution or Ripoff? (New York: Ballinger Publishing Co., 1988), chaps. 5, 6, 9. See also David Ellerman, "The Democratic Firm: A Cooperative ESOP Model," in J. D. Wisman, ed., *Worker Empowerment: The Struggle for Workplace Democracy* (New York: Bootstrap Press, 1991), pp. 83–100; Niels Mygind, "The Choice of Ownership Structure," *Economic and Industrial Democracy* 13, no. 3 (Aug. 1992): 359–99; Niels Mygard and Charles P. Rock, "Financial Participation and the Democratization of Work," *Economic and Industrial Democracy* 14, no. 2 (May 1993): 163–83; Darryl D'Art, *Economic Democracy and Financial Participation: A Comparative Study* (London: Routledge, 1992).

8. See the rejection of "mandated self-management" in favor of "evolutionary movement towards more practice of self-management and towards a consensus on its desirability," in Louis Putterman, "After the Employment Revolution: Problems on the Road to Enterprise Democracy," in Bowles, Gintis, and Gustafsson, *Markets and Democracy*, pp. 144–45. See also J. E. Meade, "The Theory of Labour-Managed Firms and of Profit-Sharing," in Vanek, *Self-Management*, p. 421: "It may well be the case that the merits of participation should be so highly prized as to make the encouragement of such institutions a major objective of governmental policy." For other discussions of the transition to economic democracy or socialism, see Alec Nove, *The Economics of Feasible Socialism Revisited* (London: Harper Collins, 1991), pt. 4, pp. 163–208; David Schweickart, *Against Capitalism*, chap. 7.

effectuation if the electorate so decides. But even if the workers themselves recognize the affirmative bearing of economic democracy on their generic human rights to freedom and well-being, they should be free to reject it if they so desire. Nevertheless, this strong affirmative bearing supports a set of arguments for making economic democracy a constitutional provision. Persons who are aware of these arguments have duties to advocate the constitutionalization of economic democracy.[9]

A prime ground of opposition to economic democracy as here defined is that the combination of market and workers' control (or "socialism") is self-contradictory. The basis of the contradiction has been put in various ways: workers' control (or socialism) sets a certain kind of egalitarian end at which social policy should aim, but the market concerns only means which may lead to quite different ends;[10] market signaling is individualistic while workers' control is collectivist;[11] in workers' control a firm is run in the interests of its workers, while markets are sensitive rather to the interests of consumers,[12] and so forth.

Now it must be noted that the market operations here envisaged as functioning in economic democracy or workers' control all proceed within the context of the nonmarket institutional arrangements previously analyzed as falling within the community of rights. The equal rights to welfare, education, employment, and so forth have been established independently of market considerations. When persons enter the market in the system of market socialism, then, they are to do so on the basis of these previous egalitarian protections. To this extent, the socialist ends are kept impervious to the variety of outcomes that may be subsequently promoted by market means, so that there is no inconsistency in the combination of markets and socialism. But, as we shall see, the market context does pose

---

9. These considerations about establishing economic democracy are complicated by historical and other variables. It is one thing for a group of persons voluntarily to form a cooperative enterprise; it is another for a group of already employed workers to seize control of a firm's decisional procedures. Negotiation and compensation would be required in the latter kind of case. Questions of firm size also enter here. Should an electrician who hires three persons to work for him at an agreed-upon wage have to share his profits with them in the same way that a giant firm should have to share its capital? See Alec Nove's distinction of five types of producing unit: centralized state corporations; socialized enterprises; cooperatives; private enterprise; and individual entrepreneurs, each with different arrangements concerning workers' control (*Economics of Feasible Socialism Revisited*, pp. 212–20).

10. See Raymond Plant, "Socialism, Markets, and End States," in LeGrand and Estrin, *Market Socialism*, pp. 50–77. The solution I present to this objection owes much to Plant's discussion.

11. Norman Barry, "The Social Market Economy," *Social Philosophy and Policy* 10, no. 2 (summer 1993): 4–5.

12. F. A. Hayek, *The Constitution of Liberty* (Chicago: University of Chicago Press, 1960), p. 277.

problems for the relations between firms each of which practices economic democracy (7.5, 6). As for the "individualism" of market signaling, groups of workers, including collective entrepreneurs, can also respond to market signals. The antithesis between the interests of workers and of consumers may pose some more serious problems. At one level, there is no special difficulty: for cooperative workers, as for individuals, responding to the effective demands of consumers may be in the interests of the providers as well as of the consumers. At a more general level, however, there is the problem of reconciling the economic objectives of workers' cooperatives with those of the wider society. This will be discussed below (7.5).

The following examination of the bearing of economic democracy on the fulfillment of human rights will be in two stages, which may be called "particularist" and "universalist." The particularist stage looks at each economically democratic firm separately; the firm is considered mainly from the inside, with regard to how it affects its own workers' rights to freedom and well-being. The universalist stage, on the other hand, looks at the firm from the outside, through its relations to other firms and to society at large; it considers how the fulfillment of the rights to freedom and well-being on the part of one firm affects the rights of other persons. In this stage, then, the more extensive social and communal aims of socialism receive central attention. These two stages cannot always be kept separate. Insofar, for example, as a firm's efficiency bears on its members' well-being, the well-being of other persons may also be affected. Nevertheless, the division of emphasis in the two stages can be largely maintained.

The first stage will proceed in large part by comparing the impacts of economic democracy and of capitalism on workers' rights to freedom and well-being. An obvious danger in such comparisons is what I have elsewhere called the "fallacy of disparateness,"[13] where the items compared are viewed on different levels or using different criteria. In the present case, the fallacy would consist in depicting capitalism in terms of its most brutal actual manifestations while economic democracy is described in terms of its loftiest moral ideals. It is not easy to avoid this fallacy when there is such a vast range of phenomena available for selection in making the comparisons. Nevertheless, so long as one is aware of the fallacy, its main danger can be largely avoided if the components of each of the items compared are securely anchored in empirical reports of the workings of actual institutions.

This point also serves to emphasize, however, that the phenomena both of economic democracy and of capitalism cover a wide range. In some

13. See my "Positive 'Ethics' and Normative 'Science,'" *Philosophical Review* 69 (July 1960): 311–30.

of its manifestations, especially in its particularist stage, economic democracy's impact on human rights may come close to that of capitalism, and capitalism, in turn, may come close to economic democracy in some of its morally wiser provisions for workers' participation in decision making. Not all capitalists are as benighted as the kinds I shall single out for special attention in the next two sections. Nevertheless, these kinds are sufficiently typical (because of exhibiting what may be called the underlying logic of capitalist profit-maximizing) that they may be cited in the contrasts with economic democracy without incurring the fallacy of disparateness.

7.2. ECONOMIC DEMOCRACY AND THE RIGHT TO FREEDOM

Let us now examine how economic democracy bears on human rights, and first on the right to freedom. As we have seen, all persons have a generic right to freedom, which consists in controlling one's behavior by one's unforced choice while having knowledge of relevant circumstances (1.4). A main charge against one pervasive kind of capitalism as an economic system is that it violates this right in the case of workers. The violation stems in large part from the conflict of interests between employers and workers, since, according to standard market economics, the former aim to maximize their profits, which requires minimizing their costs, including the wages they pay. As a result, in conventional capitalist firms the relation between employers and workers is an adversarial one of hierarchy, in that the employers set out to control the work situations of their employees: "Firms exist as large, hierarchical organizations with capitalists and their managers on top, and layers of workers on the bottom."[14] The employer has power over the workers since he determines whether they will have work in the first place; he gives orders and the workers must carry them out, on pain of dismissal; these orders pertain to what the workers are to do, how they are to do it, and so forth (see 6.1). In this regard, the very fact that the workers are hired or rented by an employer to do his bidding removes from them a certain kind of autonomy or responsibility; even if they have voluntarily agreed to this, they are his instruments, required to do his bidding.[15] Thus the situation of workers in a widespread kind of capitalist economy is marked by a serious curtailment of their freedom. As one writer puts it rather starkly: "Along with his increasing technical responsibility, the worker gains no correspondingly greater mastery over the conditions to which he is subjected and which determine the manner of his work (nor, of

14. Michael Reich and James Devine, "The Microeconomics of Conflict and Hierarchy in Capitalist Production," *Review of Radical Political Economics* 12, no. 4 (winter 1981): 27.
15. See Ellerman, *Democratic Worker-Owned Firm*, pp. 39–43.

course, is there a greater mastery over the product). . . . On the margin of civil society with its formal liberties, there thus persists behind the gates of factories, a despotic, authoritarian society with a military discipline and hierarchy which demands of the workers both unconditional obedience and active participation in their own oppression."[16]

In contrast, a main claim for economic democracy is that it wards off such hierarchic control by having the workers themselves control the conditions of their employment. Their right to freedom is thereby secured in a vitally important part of their lives. As one worker in a U.S. plywood cooperative put it, "Everybody gets together, pools their money, decides to make a particular product, and markets it . . . and with no outside interference, nobody telling them what they have to do."[17] In Mondragon, workers said, "You aren't pushed around here in the way that happens elsewhere."[18]

This contrast between capitalism and economic democracy with regard to hierarchic control has been contested in at least two ways. First, that capitalism involves such a hierarchy of power and thus a diminution of workers' freedom has been denied. It has been held that the relation between employers and workers is simply a case of "ordinary market contracting," similar to the relation between a customer and his grocer: "To speak of managing, directing, or assigning workers to various tasks is a deceptive way of noting that the employer continually is involved in renegotiation of contracts on terms that must be acceptable to both parties."[19] So the relation between employers and workers under capitalism is contractually free and egalitarian after all.

While this thesis is correct in its ascription of a certain contractual freedom to workers, it ignores the more general context wherein there is an asymmetry rather than a symmetry of power, bearing on the divergent abil-

16. André Gorz, *Strategy for Labor*, trans. M. A. Nicolaus and V. Ortiz (Boston: Beacon Press, 1967), p. 36. For empirical instantiations of this sweeping charge, see not only Karl Marx, *Capital* (New York: International Publishers, 1967), vol. 1, esp. chap. 10 ("The Working Day"), pp. 231–302, and John Stuart Mill, *Principles of Political Economy*, 2.1.3, ed. W. J. Ashley (London: Longmans, Green, 1915), p. 210, quoted above (5.2), but also such more recent reports as those by Robert Blauner, Studs Terkel, and *Work in America*, cited above, chap. 4, nn. 34, 36. See also Charles Hampden-Turner, "The Factory as an Oppressive and Non-Emancipatory Environment," in Hunnius, Garson, and Case, *Workers' Control*, pp. 30–45.

17. Greenberg, *Workplace Democracy*, pp. 74–75.

18. R. Oakeshott, "Mondragon: Spain's Oasis of Democracy," in Vanek, *Self-Management*, p. 293. In Yugoslavia, on the other hand, workers "saw management as monopolizing decision making" and complained of "managerial domination" (Comisso, *Workers' Control under Plan and Market*, p. 113).

19. Armen Alchian and Harold Demsetz, "Production, Information Costs, and Economic Organization," *American Economic Review* 62, no. 5 (Dec. 1972): 777–95, at p. 777.

ities to control the consequences of breaking or modifying the contract. As was noted above (6.9), if workers refuse to do as the employer directs, they may be fired. But if the employer refuses to do as the workers ask, they are hardly in a position to fire the employer; instead, they may quit their jobs, but thereby they usually suffer far more than does the employer. Thus the worker has far fewer available options than does the employer. To be sure, "the replacement of the specific skills embodied in, say, a striking labor force will involve major costs" for the employer.[20] But short of a whole labor force, the individual worker or small groups of workers are much less often in a position to inflict "major costs" on employers. Both in their direct conditions of work and in the more general economic background, workers therefore suffer from the forced choices that are antithetical to freedom: they are compelled to choose between severely undesirable alternatives set by employers who have superior bargaining power (6.5). It is for these reasons that the relation between employer and workers is different from the "ordinary market contracting" referred to above. What workers find "acceptable" in their conditions of work is limited by the far fewer alternatives that are open to them and by the compulsoriness, undesirableness, and inequality of power that characterize these alternatives. Thus the workers are far less free than are the employers regarding their conditions of work.[21] The relation of employers to workers, then, is one of hierarchic control, not of contracting between persons who have equal bargaining power.

A prime justification of economic democracy is that it removes this asymmetry of power and freedom. It secures the workers' right to freedom in that they control their own conditions of work, so that it substitutes an equality of freedom for the capitalist hierarchy. Because of this control, the workers' choices do not have the features of compulsoriness, undesirableness, and unequal power that characterize capitalist work relations.

This point is also relevant to the question of the employer's own right to freedom. If workers' control prevents the employer from exercising control over the workers, doesn't this interfere with the employer's freedom, that is, with his control of his own behavior toward "his" workers? The answer cannot refer merely to the "paradox of freedom" whereby the freedom of one person logically or causally requires the unfreedom of other

---

20.   John R. Cable and Felix R. Fitzroy, "Productive Efficiency, Incentives and Employee Participation," *Kyklos* 33 (1980): 102.

21.   Cf. J. E. Meade, "The Theory of Labour-Managed Firms and of Profit Sharing," in Vanek, *Self-Management*, p. 420: "While property owners can spread their risks by putting small bits of their property into a large number of concerns, a worker cannot easily put small bits of his effort into a large number of different jobs. This presumably is a main reason why we find risk-bearing capital hiring labour rather than risk-bearing labour hiring capital."

persons (5.2), for there remains the question of which freedom is justified. Nor can the answer be simply that interferences with freedom are justified when they remove other interferences with freedom, since workers' control interferes with the employer's freedom just as the employer's control inter- feres with the workers' freedom. Moreover, insofar as workers' control is legally enforced, it provides the governmental coercion whose absence has been one of the main grounds for the familiar claim that free-market cap- italism is a realm of freedom as opposed to coercion.[22] Thus there is a sharp opposition between the present thesis that economic democracy is needed for workers' freedom and the older thesis that capitalism is needed for freedom.

The answer to this opposition of freedoms can be put in two ways. One is to point out that, because their great inequalities of power involve that the large-scale employer is in a position to do far more harm to the workers' well-being than they can do to him, the principle of human rights justifies that the capitalist's freedom be restricted rather than that of the workers. So in order to maintain the workers' freedom in controlling their condi- tions of work, the employer's freedom to prevent that control must be curbed. Another way to put this point is that there is no right to freedom where freedom is used to inflict serious harms on other persons, such as workers suffer when they are subjected to the kinds of draconian controls referred to above. This is not necessarily to say that the freedom of capital- ist entrepreneurs must be completely rejected, but short of a system of eco- nomic democracy, it must at least be curbed or moderated, as is done in social-democratic countries by labor unions or codetermination.

Let us now consider a second response to the contrast between capital- ism and economic democracy with regard to hierarchic control. It is held that such control is not unique to capitalism, for economic democracy also involves and, indeed, must involve a hierarchy of power. The need for hier- archy stems from the need, within individual firms, to initiate production objectives, including the coordination and supervision of the various means whereby these objectives are to be achieved. These tasks, especially in large firms, require not only great expertise but also the "functional ne- cessities of subordination," comprising the authority to make decisions that are binding on the workers who must carry them out.[23] It is also held

22. Hayek, *Constitution of Liberty*, chap. 9; Milton Friedman, *Capitalism and Freedom* (Chicago: University of Chicago Press, 1962), chap. 1.

23. Nove, *Economics of Feasible Socialism Revisited*, p. 230; see also pp. 51–53, 213. On the need for hierarchy, see also Oliver E. Williamson, *Markets and Hierarchies* (New York: Free Press, 1975); Williamson, "The Organization of Work: A Comparative Institu- tional Assessment," *Journal of Economic Behavior and Organization* 1 (1980): 5–38; Louis Putterman, "The Organization of Work: Comment," *Journal of Economic Behavior and Or-*

that hierarchic power is needed for greater productivity, so that workers even welcome supervisory compulsion which reduces or eliminates shirking on the job and thereby enables the firm to pay higher wages.[24] In a similar vein, it is noted that many workers do not want the kind of responsibility that goes with labor-managed firms. They would much rather follow orders than have to take initiatives on their own.[25] It is even maintained that "the concept of labor-management is self-contradictory": "Unless the prospective members 'follow' the entrepreneurial leadership and allow themselves to be organized and directed a labor-managed firm will not come into being let alone survive. Yet if they do, the firm is not labor-managed."[26] Thus entrepreneurial leadership is both necessary for and incompatible with labor-management.

These theoretic contentions have been supported by empirical facts about developments in self-managed firms and worker cooperatives. Thus in the former Yugoslavia there were "growing pressures for hierarchy to correct the workings of the market"; this led to "inequalities in influence and power," "oligarchic power structures," and a "gap between workers' control in theory and managerial domination in practice," such that "managerial and technical personnel had a much greater influence than blue-collar workers on the decisions made by self-management organs, regardless of the former's numerical inferiority and regardless of whether they were actually elected members of the authorized bodies."[27] Hence it may be concluded that the workers' rights to freedom in the control of their conditions of employment are as much restricted in economic democracy as in capitalism.

---

ganization 2 (1982): 273–79; Williamson, "The Organization of Work: Reply," *Journal of Economic Behavior and Organization* 2 (1982): 281–83. See also Harvey Leibenstein, *Inside the Firm: The Inefficiencies of Hierarchy* (Cambridge, Mass.: Harvard University Press, 1987), esp. chap. 11.

24. Joseph E. Stiglitz, "Incentives, Risk, and Information: Notes toward a Theory of Hierarchy," *Bell Journal of Economics* 6, no. 2 (autumn 1975): 552–79, at p. 571.

25. See Frank L. Wilson, "Democracy in the Workplace: The French Experience," *Politics and Society* 19, no. 4 (1991): 439–62. Cf. Richard J. Arneson, "Meaningful Work and Market Socialism," *Ethics* 97, no. 3 (Apr. 1987): 517–45, at pp. 527–30.

26. David O'Mahony, "Labour Management and the Market Economy," *Irish Journal of Business and Administrative Research* 1 (1979): 36.

27. Comisso, *Workers' Control under Plan and Market*, pp. 85, 110, 115, 124. Comisso (p. 265, n. 47) lists a large number of studies "that found oligarchic power structures in Yugoslav enterprises." See also Jones and Svejnar, *Participatory and Self-Managed Firms*, p. 86. It has been suggested that similar developments may occur in the Mondragon cooperatives. See Thomas and Logan, *Mondragon*, pp. 183–84; see also Greenberg, *Workplace Democracy*, pp. 103–5.

Despite these serious objections, there are several important respects in which the hierarchies just mentioned differ from the hierarchies found in capitalist firms. First, the former are hierarchies of authority, while the latter are hierarchies of power. What this distinction means is not only that the hierarchies in economic democracy stem from rules that are consented to by the participants, but also, and especially, that the persons at the top of the hierarchy owe their superior positions to election by those below, so that they can be dismissed in subsequent elections. Thus the hierarchies of economic democracy have a fluidity and consensual basis not found in the capitalist hierarchies of power. In this regard there is a parallel between political and economic democracy.[28] In the United States there is a hierarchy of authority, from the president and the congressional majority leaders on down. But this differs sharply from the hierarchy of power found in totalitarian and authoritarian states, whose leaders are not subject to election and possible dismissal by their "subordinate" electorate.

Two further interrelated distinctions should also be noted. First, we must distinguish between two different kinds of control: occurrent and dispositional. Occurrent control consists in the direct exercise of decision making. Dispositional control consists in having the longer-range background ability to exercise occurrent control without actually exercising it. Dispositional control is had by persons or groups who have the final authority over binding decisions, without necessarily making those decisions themselves. But in having dispositional control they are in an institutionally authorized position to check on the contents of occurrently made decisions, and to change or veto them if they so desire. Thus, although managers may have occurrent control, this control may not be finally authoritative if it is subject to the dispositional control of the workers. By and large, in direct participatory democracy the workers exercise occurrent control, but in representative democracy, which is usually far more feasible, they exercise dispositional control by electing representatives who carry out managerial and other tasks.

A second distinction bears on the objects of control. These may be first-order or second-order. First-order controls are decisions made directly about matters like work conditions, wages, marketing arrangements, and so forth. Second-order controls are decisions about first-order decisions, concerning who is to make them, what matters they are to deal with, what are the procedures by which they are to be made, and so forth. Thus workers may effect second-order controls even if they may not be competent to effect first-order controls.[29] And when they become aware of

28. See Greenberg, *Workplace Democracy,* pp. 76, 104.
29. Cf. Dahl, *Preface to Economic Democracy,* p. 118.

the beneficial impact of their having such control on their conditions of work, they are far more likely to welcome it than to reject it.

Concomitantly with these distinctions the hierarchies of authority are marked by a mutualist community of interests, as against the conflict of interests found in capitalism's hierarchies of power. In economic democracy the managers do not stand to lose in profits if the workers gain in wages; instead, both workers and managers gain increased shares as the firm's total revenue increases.

It has also been contended, however, that worker-controlled systems have a strong tendency to "degenerate into capitalism, i.e. a system in which the workers do not control the means of production." This would happen because the vital managerial and entrepreneurial functions needed for competitive market operations require a high degree of expertise which relatively few persons have, so that "manager-entrepreneurs will effectively control the means of production." It is precisely because the managerial elite will have final, real authority (as against the nominal or intermediate authority had by workers) that the "manager-entrepreneurs would begin to function more and more like old-fashioned capitalists and workers would be virtually indistinguishable from proletarians."[30]

To this argument it has been replied that managerial and entrepreneurial abilities are not as scarce as the argument assumes and that competitive pressures are less intense in market socialist systems than in capitalist systems.[31] It must also be noted that worker control need not be merely nominal, especially insofar as the managers themselves are elected by and answerable to all the workers. The analogy to political democracy is again relevant: even though "all the people" do not actually govern, the fact that government officials, both executive and legislative, must run for periodic election gives the people a kind of final authority which is markedly different from the subordinate, passive role which the mass of nongovernmental people have in authoritarian and totalitarian regimes.

It may still be contended, however, that a fallacy of division is committed when one argues from the consensual basis of a whole system or institution to the freedom of its individual members. Institutional or societal freedom does not entail individual freedom: even if the system provides for or rests on consensual procedures, many individuals may find themselves

---

30. N. Scott Arnold, "Marx and Disequilibrium in Market Socialist Relations of Production," *Economics and Philosophy* 3 (Apr. 1987): 23–48, at pp. 33, 35, 38.

31. David Schweickart, "Market Socialist Capitalist Roaders," *Economics and Philosophy* 3 (Oct. 1987): 308–19. See also the further exchange between Arnold and Schweickart, *Economics and Philosophy* 3 (Oct. 1987): 320–38.

bound by decisions or policies from which they dissent or which they have had no part in establishing.[32]

This long-recognized difficulty of democratic theory and practice does not, however, remove the soundness of justifying economic democracy through the right to individual freedom. It is indeed true that, short of unanimity, decision making in groups of various sizes may require that some individuals' preferences be overridden by those of others. The fact remains, nevertheless, that in economic democracy individuals have an equal right to participate in decision making, if not at the occurrent or first-order level then at the dispositional or second-order level. Such right of participation differentiates economic democracy from standard capitalist firms, and it helps to maintain that control over one's behavior that is the essential feature of freedom. There are, then, strong grounds for holding that workers' rights to freedom are secured in economic democracy in a way that stands in significant contrast to the hierarchic controls under which they are placed by capitalism. To this extent, economic democracy itself functions as a kind of community of rights with mutuality of rights and duties among its members, in contrast to the kinds of nonmutuality found in capitalist firms.

7.3. ANALOGIES BETWEEN ECONOMIC AND POLITICAL DEMOCRACY

It will be helpful to connect the points just made about freedom with some broader institutional questions. Economic democracy has thus far been given a consequentialist justification in terms of its fulfilling the freedom rights of workers. But there is also an antecedentalist question about the establishment of the system of economic democracy in the first place. This bears on the general institutional framework of economic democracy as a system of governance. Here the frequently cited analogy between economic democracy and political democracy comes into play. By considering this analogy, we shall be able to present some further, related insights into the bearing of economic democracy on the right to freedom. But this consideration will also set the stage for the very serious disanalogies between economic and political democracy that will be taken up in a later section

---

32. Cf. Gunn, *Workers' Self-Management in the United States*, p. 18: "The *self* in *workers' self-management* does not refer to the individual within the organization. The expression should not be taken as referring to a vehicle for maximizing personal individual freedom of action. Self-management refers to the relative autonomy of the organization to conduct its affairs, to determine its course of action" (emphasis in original). But see below, n. 62 to this chapter.

(7.5), and that serve to bring out both certain severe moral difficulties of economic democracy and the institutional arrangements whereby these difficulties can be resolved.

Economic democracy is often held to be justified on the same grounds as justify political democracy. The following statements are typical: "The very same arguments that for two centuries supported the ceding of political choice to the mass of people rather than its retention by a single individual or a small group, also provide the rationale for production and investment decision making by workers and consumers, not by individual capital owners or their managers."[33] "*If* democracy is justified in governing the state, then it must *also* be justified in governing economic enterprises."[34] I shall call this the *general democratic thesis*.

The central idea behind this thesis is that economic as well as political institutions or associations involve relations of authority whereby decisions are made that are binding on all the members of the respective associations. The general democratic thesis holds that these relations should be not hierarchic but rather egalitarian: "The rule for determining outcomes at the decisive stage must take into account, and take equally into account, the expressed preferences of each citizen as to the outcome; that is, votes must be allocated equally among citizens." "Binding collective decisions ought to be made only by persons who are subject to the decisions—that is, by members of the association."[35] Thus in the economic firm as well as in the political state, the authority over binding decisions should pertain not to a small group of capitalists or governmental officials but to all the members of the respective associations. Just as in political democracy rulers derive their authority through election by all adult members of the society, each having an equal vote (so that in this way the policies of government are ultimately controlled by the citizens), so in economic democracy the firm's officials get their authority through election by all the workers in the firm, each having an equal vote (so that in this way the firm's working conditions and policies are ultimately controlled by the workers). Equality replaces hierarchy and election replaces domination.

The general democratic thesis, in its application to economic enterprises, can be interpreted in two different ways, in terms of the distinction between those who are "affected" by the enterprise and those who are

33. Carnoy and Shearer, *Economic Democracy*, p. 3.

34. Dahl, *Preface to Economic Democracy*, p. 111; emphasis in original. See ibid., pp. 94, 134–35. See, to the same effect, Vanek, *General Theory*, p. 244; A. Corbon, quoted in Vanek, *Self-Management*, p. 46; Carol C. Gould, *Rethinking Democracy* (Cambridge: Cambridge University Press, 1988), pp. 143–44.

35. Dahl, *Preface to Economic Democracy*, pp. 59, 57.

"governed" by its management.[36] Taken in the first way, the general democratic thesis can be traced back at least to the Roman and medieval maxim
that "what affects all should be approved by all."[37] We may here consider
two objections that have been raised against this maxim. One is that the
object or "what" that "affects all" may be something over which some individual or group already has a prior right. For that right would exempt the
affecting object from having to be approved by the persons affected. If, for
example, a woman decides to marry one of her many suitors, then, even
though her decision deeply affects all the other suitors, it should not be subject to their approval because, by virtue of her autonomy, she has a prior
right to decide whom to marry. Or if a great orchestra conductor decides to
retire, then, even though his decision affects the musicians' careers, it
should not be subject to their approval because, again by virtue of his autonomy, he has a prior right to make the decision.[38]

These counterexamples do not, however, invalidate the general democratic thesis and the maxim about "affecting." For in the political context
to which the thesis and maxim are standardly applied, the rulers or legislators whose decisions "affect all" the citizens do not have a prior right to
control those decisions. For there is no "natural right" to rule. In the absence of such a prior right, the equality of human rights (especially the right
to freedom) entails that the citizens have rights over the rulers' authority
that are prior to and determinative of the rulers' rights to govern. This will
be discussed more fully in chapter 8.

This still leaves open the question of the capitalist's ownership rights.
Don't these give the capitalist a prior right over decisions affecting the firm
he owns? Relevant to this question are the primordialist considerations discussed above about self-ownership and world ownership (5.4, 5), as well as
the social contribution thesis (3.4). The capitalist's relation to his firm is
not the same as the self-ownership that figures in the woman's and the orchestra conductor's respective autonomies; their decisions about whom to
marry and how to use musical abilities bear on factors that are far more
intrinsically connected with their respective selves than are decisions or ac-

36. For this distinction and its application to economic democracy, see Ellerman, *Democratic Worker-Owned Firm*, pp. 44–50.

37. *Quod omnes tangit ab omnibus approbetur.* On the history of this maxim, see
Gaines Post, "A Roman-Canonical Maxim, 'Quod omnes tangit' in Bracton," *Traditio* 4
(1946): 197–251. On some undemocratic uses to which the maxim was put in the later middle ages, see Alan Gewirth, *Marsilius of Padua and Medieval Political Philosophy* (New York:
Columbia University Press, 1951), p. 254.

38. These examples are from Robert Nozick, *Anarchy, State, and Utopia* (New York:
Basic Books, 1974), pp. 268–71. See also William N. Nelson, *On Justifying Democracy* (London: Routledge and Kegan Paul, 1980), pp. 45–47.

tions bearing on the external things one owns. If, moreover, the theses of social contribution and world ownership set justified limits on the capitalist's ownership rights, then these also do not invalidate the general democratic thesis.

A second objection against the thesis and maxim, however, invokes an assumption that has some similarities to the "natural right" objection: hierarchic decisions by persons who have relevant expertise are appropriate and indeed mandatory where the success of a justified enterprise requires such expertise. For example, in such associations as a professional football team or a symphony orchestra, binding decisions are, and should be, made not by all members of the association equally but rather by one person: the head coach or the conductor. The reason for this is that for such associations to fulfill their purposes most effectively, the efforts of their respective members must be adequately coordinated, and for such coordination the decision-making authority must ultimately be hierarchically centralized in one person (or perhaps a small group of persons).

This hierarchic point can be reconciled with the general democratic thesis by considerations similar to the distinctions adduced above between occurrent and dispositional control and between first-order and second-order objects of control (7.2). The hierarchic unification of authority itself emerges in accordance with the general democratic thesis in that the unification is decided upon by all the members of the respective voluntary associations collectively. The football players and the orchestra players all agree that the head coach and the conductor, respectively, will make the binding decisions about what plays will be called, how the music shall be played, and so forth. In this way the decisional freedom of political and economic democracy operates as a second-order authority, in that the hierarchic rules that directly govern the relevant actions or policies are themselves decided upon democratically.

Let us now turn to a second interpretation of the general democratic thesis, where the emphasis falls not on those who are "affected" by an enterprise but rather on those who are "governed" by its management. It must be admitted that the "affected" version has certain difficulties with regard to the justification of economic democracy. Since, for example, shareholders are "affected by" the functioning of the enterprise in which they own stock, they would be entitled to participate in the firm's governance as much as would the workers.[39] Hence, the distinction between workers' control and capitalist owners' control would be lost. If, however, the general democratic thesis is interpreted to mean that the persons who should govern an organization should be those who are governed by the

39. See Ellerman, *Democratic Worker-Owned Firm*, pp. 45–50.

organization's authoritative personnel or who take orders from them, then this would confine the proximate or ultimate governing authority in a firm to its workers rather than its owners or managers.

It is this latter, "governed" interpretation that most directly captures the general democratic thesis's traditional application to political democracy: those persons must rule who are ruled, so that there is a more or less direct equation between rulers and ruled, between the people and their government. And it is this version that most directly applies to economic democracy. I shall briefly discuss the justification of the general democratic thesis here; but more will be said on it in the next chapter (8.1).

The rights to both political and economic democracy derive from the generic right to freedom; but, as we have seen (7.1), there is an important difference in the way this right operates in individual action and in political and economic institutions. When it is said that all persons have a generic right to freedom, this freedom is in the first instance an individualist property; it should belong to each individual agent, actual or prospective, with regard to each particular action or transaction in which she is engaged either as actual agent or as recipient (but see 2.4). She is free in that she controls her behavior by her unforced choice in those actions or transactions. But when we come to political and to economic democracy, this individualized context of freedom is broadened in two ways that may seem to remove its salient aspects as a condition of freedom. First, the control in question is to be exercised not by each individual agent but through collective electoral processes by a collectivity comprising all the citizens in a given state or all the workers in a given firm. Second, the object of control is not each particular action but rather a broader set of political or economic conditions and operations, social rules and institutions such as are found in states or in large-scale industrial enterprises, involving the subordination of individual purpose-fulfillment to standardized modes of conduct or work performance. Thus in political and economic democracy an individual may be free even if his behavior is controlled in a way from which he dissents: he may, for example, have voted against a legislator or a representative who in turn votes for a law or a work requirement of which he disapproves. Nevertheless, the individual in question has political and economic freedom in that the legislators or representatives have derived their authority through an electoral process in which he has had an equal vote.

This broadening of the context of freedom in political and economic democracy can be partially reconciled with the requirements of individual freedom in two ways (see also 8.1). First, it may be said that the individual worker is free to join or not join a particular firm or to belong or not belong to a particular country or nation-state. But just as it is usually extraordinarily difficult, for a variety of reasons, to emigrate from one's country of residence, so too, although perhaps less extremely, it is often very difficult for a worker to leave the firm for which he works when he has little or no assurance of finding work elsewhere. I shall soon have more to say about this parallel. Second, the collective freedom that political and economic democracy require has several components that link it closely to individual freedom. These include the civil liberties: each citizen and each worker must be free to advocate various rules or policies and to join with others in that advocacy.[40] But since the context is a collective one, there must be criteria for deciding between conflicting advocacies. As rational, each person recognizes the need for such criteria and for the rules that are determined on their basis. In this way, each freely binds herself to accept the rules that are collectively determined on the basis of decision-criteria that are themselves freely accepted by each person.

7.4. ECONOMIC DEMOCRACY AND THE RIGHT TO WELL-BEING

Let us now examine the bearing of economic democracy on the right to well-being. As we have seen (1.4), well-being consists in having the resources, the abilities and conditions, that are needed both for the very possibility of action and for generally successful action, whereby persons have general chances of success in achieving their purposes. Such well-being falls into three different levels: basic, nonsubtractive, and additive.

An economic arrangement or system impacts on well-being at each of these levels. With regard to basic well-being, the key question is whether the arrangement enables prospective agents to live and to have health and safety. The system must provide for certain minimal levels of productivity, and it must do so in ways that do not endanger persons' lives. Its workers must be able to make a living with an appropriate degree of physical and economic security. With regard to nonsubtractive well-being, the main question for persons in general is whether the arrangement provides a level of productivity which enables them to maintain their standard of living without constant or frequent fears of its being lowered or lost. For workers, nonsubtractive well-being also bears on such questions as whether they remain employed and at least maintain their income level and whether they avoid being subjected to degrading or excessively debilitating work conditions, including "meaningless" work. In one respect, the question of ex-

---

40. According to André Gorz, "Formal recognition of the union organization and of civil liberties on the job remains an abstract demand, incapable of mobilizing the workers as long as it is not organically linked to the demand for concrete workers' powers over the conditions of work" (*Strategy for Labor*, p. 41). As here envisaged, the civil liberties function *within* such "concrete workers' powers."

ploitation also arises here: Do workers, after socially justified deductions, retain all the value that they produce, or is some of it taken away from them by their employers? With regard to additive well-being, the question both for workers and for persons in general is whether an economic system enables them *(a)* to improve their standard of living, including not only their income level but also the satisfactoriness of their conditions of work; *(b)* to develop the self-esteem and the prudential virtues that help them to act effectively for the achievement of their purposes; and *(c)* to foster interpersonal relations of mutual respect and community. Questions of efficiency arise at each of these levels.

It may be contended that the right to economic democracy is sufficiently grounded in what I have called the right to freedom, the right to control the conditions of one's work, so that no further grounding in well-being is needed. Indeed, it may be held that an appeal to well-being departs from the context of rights, because it invokes the *consequences* of economic democracy as against the *right* to economic democracy.[41]

Apart from other difficulties in the separation of rights from consequences (such as when the consequence of exercising one right infringes another right; see 2.2), the above contention overlooks that the consequences of an action or an institution may be wrong because they violate persons' rights. As we have seen, persons have rights to well-being as well as to freedom. Hence, it becomes a relevant issue whether the justification of economic democracy through the right to freedom is compatible with the right to well-being. If, for example, workers' control of their conditions of work were so inefficient that it threatened them with starvation or extremely low income, such a consequence would infringe the well-being to which they also have rights. In such a case, the question would arise not of whether the workers did indeed have rights to freedom, but rather whether these rights should be fulfilled or made effective. There would then be a conflict between the right to freedom and the right to well-being, and rational criteria would have to be provided for resolving the conflict.

It should be noted that this appeal to consequences involves *distributive consequentialism,* which must be distinguished from *aggregative consequentialism* (see 5.2). The latter is the usual version of what is called "consequentialism": according to it what ought to be done is what will maximize good, regardless of how that good is distributed or the varieties of different goods.[42] Distributive consequentialism, on the other hand, im-

---

41. See Dahl, *Preface to Economic Democracy,* pp. 94–110, 152–53; Gould, *Rethinking Democracy,* p. 148.

42. For mainly aggregative versions of consequentialism, see Germain Grisez, "Against Consequentialism," *American Journal of Jurisprudence* 23 (1978): 24 ff.; Samuel Scheffler, *The Rejection of Consequentialism* (Oxford: Clarendon Press, 1982), pp. 1 ff. (Scheffler later

poses two kinds of restrictions on the consequences that serve to determine what ought to be done. The first concerns the subjects, the persons whose interests are to be promoted in the consideration of consequences. These persons are not all individuals or groups indiscriminately but rather some persons as against others. Thus in the present case it is the interests of workers and other deprived groups that are deemed to need special protection. In many cases such distributive consequentialism includes a comparative component, bearing on the proportions or other ways in which goods are to be distributed among persons or groups, especially as regards equality or inequality. John Rawls's difference principle is an example of such distributive consequentialism, for it specifies that economic inequalities are to be justified by their consequences in redounding to the greatest good of those who are "least advantaged," as compared with other groups in the society.[43]

A second restriction imposed by distributive consequentialism concerns the objects, the kinds of goods or interests that are to be promoted in the consideration of consequences. Whereas in aggregative consequentialism these goods are viewed indiscriminately as some sort of maximizable bundle, in distributive consequentialism the goods are dealt with in a more articulated way, so that those that are more needed for action have priority over lesser goods. As we have seen, this conception of degrees of needfulness for action does not have the difficulties sometimes attributed to the "interpersonal comparability of utilities" (2.4).

Before examining how economic democracy impacts on various components of the right to well-being, we must bear in mind the point made earlier, that the impacts in question are, for the most part, matters of empirical, contingent consequences (3.8). As such, they do not exhibit the uniformity and invariability that may be found when (as in the preceding section) we consider the right to freedom by itself—although we saw there too that attempts to implement this right for workers through economic democracy may lead to various justified infringements of the right for employers and other persons.

The impacts of economic democracy on the right to well-being may be divided into two broad groups: psychological and economic. I shall take them up in this order because the former often has a causal influence on the latter. Although the psychological impacts display some broad tendencies,

---

[pp. 29–34] refers to "distribution-sensitive" versions of consequentialism); Shelly Kagan, *The Limits of Morality* (Oxford: Clarendon Press, 1989), pp. xi–xii, 8.

43. John Rawls, *A Theory of Justice* (Cambridge, Mass.: Harvard University Press, 1971), pp. 75–83.

there is far from complete uniformity. In the first instance the impacts in question pertain to the workers themselves in firms that practice economic democracy.

A direct psychological effect of economic democracy is that the workers have stronger feelings of freedom and proprietorship because they are in control of their own work conditions without having to answer to outside owners. This has been discussed in the preceding section.

A second, closely related psychological effect is work satisfaction. In a survey of research findings, Paul Blumberg wrote in 1968: "There is hardly a study in the entire literature which fails to demonstrate that satisfaction in work is enhanced or that other generally acknowledged beneficial consequences accrue from a genuine increase in workers' decision-making power."[44] Subsequent reports have confirmed these findings in the case of the plywood cooperatives and elsewhere.[45] There is not, however, complete uniformity on this point. In Mondragon, while "a high degree of satisfaction" was found with life in general as a result of having the system of producers' cooperatives,[46] the finding with specific regard to work conditions was that "the level of satisfaction was fairly low."[47] In a Yugoslav self-managed firm, work was not viewed as "a source of enjoyment or self-realization" but rather as a necessity for survival;[48] nevertheless, it was found that "participation in workers' councils and/or management boards results in significantly greater general job satisfaction (except among automated workers)."[49] A pervasive complaint in many worker cooperatives was that the work was "monotonous" and "unpleasant."[50] The frequency of absenteeism in Yugoslav firms suggests a similar feeling.[51] A related point is that in the plywood cooperatives the level of workplace safety was very low.[52] In partial contrast, in Mondragon the Social Council elected by

44. Paul Blumberg, *Industrial Democracy*, p. 123.

45. See, e.g., Greenberg, *Workplace Democracy*, p. 93; Robert Jackall and Henry M. Levin, eds., *Worker Cooperatives in America* (Berkeley and Los Angeles: University of California Press, 1984), pp. 7–8.

46. Thomas and Logan, *Mondragon*, p. 189.

47. Ibid., p. 190. See also Greenberg, *Workplace Democracy*, p. 96.

48. Comisso, *Workers' Control under Plan and Market*, p. 169.

49. Gerry Hunnius, "Workers' Self-Management in Yugoslavia," in Hunnius, Garson, and Case, *Workers' Control*, p. 302.

50. Greenberg, *Workplace Democracy*, pp. 40–41, 81 ff., 93, 107, 114; Thomas and Logan, *Mondragon*, p. 70.

51. Comisso, *Workers' Control under Plan and Market*, pp. 144, 159. See, however, Thomas and Logan, *Mondragon*, p. 52, where it is reported, on the basis of specific empirical data, that "absenteeism occurs to a much smaller degree" in cooperative than in noncooperative companies.

52. Greenberg, *Workplace Democracy*, pp. 84–87.

the workers had "work safety" and "work hygiene" among its chief concerns.[53]

Amid the somewhat mixed results concerning work satisfaction, it is important to note a third psychological effect (which may also figure as a motivating cause): the workers experience feelings of group solidarity.[54] The work environment in the plywood cooperatives is "suffused with a strong sense of fellowship."[55] At Mondragon there is "an unusual degree of coherence and of trust between all cooperators," as well as an "ideology" of "cooperativism."[56] In Yugoslavia, "Ideology, which stressed 'productive' labor, the importance of blue-collar workers, and a spirit of collective sacrifice for a better future, also contributed to a sense of solidarity in the plant."[57] Such feelings are important components of well-being for each cooperator because they give him confidence of "collegial support"[58] from his fellows in important phases of his work situation. They therefore contribute to strengthening his capacities for purpose-fulfillment.

In addition, with specific reference to a central theme of this book, the feelings in question are communitarian as well as individualist, and indeed they underlie the way in which economic democracy is an important part of the community of rights. Each worker has rights against the others that they cooperate for the common good of the enterprise, so that each also has positive duties to the others to practice and foster such cooperation. Here again rights and community sustain one another, because the rights both contribute to and are upheld by a cooperative system of mutual support. Although these mutual rights are contractually based, they are also based on the content of the contract, including the values both of cooperation and of economic benefit. This communitarian relationship is different from whatever legal rights the workers may have under capitalism. For the latter rights are not part of a community of rights, since the rights are not had equally in common because of the inequality of power and at least potential conflict of interests between workers and capitalists.

The psychological impacts of economic democracy also contribute importantly to its economic consequences in productivity and efficiency.

53. Thomas and Logan, *Mondragon*, pp. 28–29. For a survey of workers' safety measures, see Jacques Monat and Hedva Sarfati, eds., *Workers' Participation: A Voice in Decisions, 1981–85* (Geneva: International Labour Office, 1986), chap. 4, pp. 164–81.

54. See Jackall and Levin, *Worker Cooperatives*, p. 22. On the relation between solidarity and mutuality, see below, 7.7.

55. Greenberg, *Workplace Democracy*, p. 95; but cf. p. 109.

56. Thomas and Logan, *Mondragon*, pp. 183, 189.

57. Comisso, *Workers' Control under Plan and Market*, p. 64. See also Jackall and Levin, *Worker Cooperatives*, p. 126.

58. See Henry M. Levin, in Jackall and Levin, eds., *Worker Cooperatives*, p. 25.

While these consequences inevitably affect persons in addition to the workers themselves in a cooperative firm, for present purposes the main consideration in the first instance is the consequences for the individual worker, especially as regards income. Indeed, a constant refrain of the workers' control literature is that "The one key operating principle . . . is that of maximization of income per laborer."[59] "The objective function of the [labor-managed] enterprise is to maximize dividend per worker."[60] The maximization of the worker's income is strongly affected by, if it is not identical with, the productivity and efficiency of the firm of which she is a cooperating member. So, with a view to ascertaining the bearing of economic democracy on the well-being of the individual worker, we shall consider the performance of the labor-managed firm.

While productivity as such is a matter of outputs, especially output per worker, efficiency concerns the relation of output to input. There are many different concepts of efficiency, which go by such names as "technical efficiency," "allocative efficiency," "X-efficiency," "Pareto efficiency," and so forth. Without attempting to give precise definitions of each of these, we may note that they involve two main kinds of emphasis. One is on increasing, or, at the extreme, maximizing outputs on the basis of antecedently given inputs. The other is on improving the productive capacities of inputs themselves through the kinds of effort, motivation, and skill that enter into them.[61] Each of these emphases incurs problems of the criteria of "outputs" and "inputs" and of the ways in which these are to be measured. For example, outputs may be conceived along a range from physical products to monetary revenues to various psychic and even moral emoluments, including the value of participating in a cooperative enterprise.[62]

59.   Vanek, *General Theory,* p. 2.

60.   Deborah Duff Milenkovich, "Is Market Socialism Efficient?" in Andrew Zimbalist, ed., *Comparative Economic Systems: Present Views* (Boston: Kluwer-Nijhoff, 1984), p. 72. See, to the same effect, Vanek, *Self-Management,* p. 30; Gunn, *Workers' Self-Management,* p. 17; Thomas and Logan, *Mondragon,* p. 8.

61.   See Harvey Leibenstein, "Allocative Efficiency vs. 'X-Efficiency,'" *American Economic Review* 56 (June 1966): 392–415. For a contention that "this type of inefficiency can usefully be assimilated into the traditional theory of allocative inefficiency," see George J. Stigler, "The Xistence of X-Efficiency," *American Economic Review* 66 (Mar. 1976): 213–16.

62.   "In the case of worker participation at least one of the outputs of the firm will be the value to the workers of participating in the decisions of the firm rather than being objects of compulsion by their managers" (Henry Levin, "Issues in Assessing the Comparative Productivity of Worker-Managed and Participatory Firms in Capitalist Societies," in Jones and Svejnar, *Participatory and Self-Managed Firms,* p. 48). Vanek, *Self-Management,* pp. 30–31, lists five different objectives that have been suggested for labor-managed firms. Cf. the emphasis on "the need for careful definition of efficiency," in Thomas and Logan, *Mondragon,* p. 106.

One of the main ways of examining the efficiency of worker-controlled firms is by comparing them with capitalist firms that make similar products. There are obvious difficulties in deriving conclusions from such comparisons. Even if worker-controlled firms are more efficient on some relevant criterion than capitalist firms, there remains the question of whether this greater efficiency derives from its being a worker-controlled firm or from some other cause, such as its location, its national or ethnic or historical background, or other variables. We might want to hold, at a minimum, that such comparisons prove that worker-controlled firms *can* be efficient, that their being worker-controlled is not a decisive obstacle to their being efficient. But even such a modest conclusion could incur problems about size or scale of operations: if a relatively small worker-controlled firm can be efficient, this could still leave room for doubt about very large worker-controlled firms, or conversely. It could also be argued that economic democracy, either within particular firms or especially as an economic system, cannot be more efficient than capitalism or capitalist firms on the Pareto superior criterion of efficiency, because that criterion is fulfilled only if no one loses; but in economic democracy, as against capitalism, the would-be capitalists lose, since they are less well off than in firms or systems where they can accumulate profits (see 2.4).[63]

Despite these difficulties, many studies using rather straightforward criteria of allocative efficiency have shown worker-controlled firms to be more efficient than their capitalist counterparts in that they have greater outputs on the basis of similar inputs. For example, Melman studied six "managerially controlled" and six "cooperatively controlled" industrial enterprises in Israel matched as to industry and product, and he found that the median sales per production worker man-hours were 26 percent greater for the cooperative than for the managerially controlled enterprises, and that the median profit of the cooperative firms was 12.9 percent of capital investment as against 7.9 percent for the managerially controlled firms.[64] In Mondragon it was found that in 1972 the value added per number of workers and cost of working capital was 7.5 percent greater in cooperatively controlled firms than in the largest Spanish capitalist firms and 40 percent greater than in medium- and small-sized capitalist firms, while the value added per employee was approximately one-third greater in cooperative firms.[65] In the U.S. plywood cooperatives of the Pacific North-

63. See Adam Przeworski, *Capitalism and Social Democracy* (Cambridge: Cambridge University Press, 1985), p. 236.

64. Seymour Melman, "Industrial Efficiency under Managerial vs. Cooperative Decision-Making: A Comparative Study of Manufacturing Enterprises in Israel," *Review of Radical Political Economics* 2, no. 1 (spring 1970): 16–22.

65. Thomas and Logan, *Mondragon*, pp. 106–8.

west the output of plywood per man-hour averaged 115 to 120 square feet in the 1950s and 170 square feet in the 1960s, as against conventional firms' output of 80 to 95 and 130 square feet, respectively.[66] Comparable results have been found for Yugoslav self-managing enterprises by comparison with capitalist firms,[67] as well as in various other contexts.[68]

While there are also correlations in the reverse direction,[69] these results are sufficiently copious to establish as highly plausible that there is a causal connection between economic democracy and increased efficiency. The grounds for this can be found both in the psychological impacts of economic democracy mentioned above and in more specific motivations, both monetary and nonmonetary. Since workers are not hired in order to produce profits for capitalist-owners but are themselves the owners or share directly in the firm's income, they have a direct monetary stake in the firm's success. One consequence of this is that self-managed firms require far fewer supervisory personnel than do conventional firms.[70] Another consequence is that workers' income in self-managed firms tends to be higher than that of workers in comparable conventional firms; the worker-owned plywood firms in the Pacific Northwest are an example of this.[71]

The nonmonetary motivations that make for higher productivity are of two interrelated kinds. One kind, which has been discussed above, is personal, consisting in the greater satisfaction that workers experience when they are their own bosses or at least participate in decision making rather than being subject to stringent rules laid down by others.[72] Greater auton-

66. Katrina V. Berman, *Worker-Owned Plywood Firms: An Economic Analysis* (Pullman: Washington State University Press, 1967), pp. 118–21, 189–90.

67. See Janez Jerovsek and Stane Mozina, "Efficiency and Democracy in Self-Managing Enterprises," in Josip Obradovic and William N. Dunn, eds., *Workers' Self-Management and Organizational Power* (Pittsburgh: University of Pittsburgh Press), pp. 279–95.

68. See Karl Frieden, *Workplace Democracy and Productivity* (Washington, D.C.: National Center for Economic Alternatives, 1980); Frank H. Stephen, ed., *The Performance of Labour-Managed Firms* (New York: St. Martin's Press, 1982).

69. See Jones and Svejnar, *Participatory and Self-Managed Firms*, pp. 11, 51–52.

70. See Jackall and Levin, *Worker Cooperatives*, pp. 27, 192–99; Jones and Svejnar, *Participatory and Self-Managed Firms*, p. 46; Carnoy and Shearer, *Economic Democracy*, pp. 170 ff.; Blumberg, *Industrial Democracy*, p. 223; Greenberg, *Workplace Democracy*, pp. 43–48.

71. See Paul Bernstein, *Workplace Democratization: Its Internal Dynamics* (Kent, Ohio: Kent State University Press, 1976), pp. 20–21. But cf. Henry Levin, "Issues in Assessing the Comparative Productivity of Worker-Managed and Participatory Firms in Capitalist Societies," in Jones and Svejnar, *Participatory and Self-Managed Firms*, p. 62, who refers to the possibility that "workers in the LMF [labor-managed firm] are willing to take lower wages because of a higher level of work satisfaction."

72. See Jones and Svejnar, *Participatory and Self-Managed Firms*, pp. 48–53; Vanek, *Self-Management*, p. 293.

omy as both fact and feeling contributes to greater pride in one's work and greater effort to accomplish it well.[73] A second kind of nonmonetary motivation is social, consisting in the solidarity that workers experience as a group when they are involved in a participatory cooperative enterprise. This is directly related to the third psychological impact discussed above. Thus in workers' cooperatives "the workers tend to reinforce the productivity and work effort of their members through collegial support and peer pressure . . . there is strong social reinforcement and camaraderie for working together and making a contribution."[74] In such ways economic democracy fulfills one of the defining conditions of community discussed above (3.4), and it bears a close relation to aspects of the noneconomic sense of productive agency (4.6, 8).

Let us now consider some of the more important arguments that have been brought against the efficiency of economic democracy. One argument invokes the "free rider" problem. Since "both decision making and profits are widely shared among the workers . . . , no one worker will gain very much from improved productivity."[75] Hence, some workers will shirk while profiting from the work of the rest; the former's shirking will not decrease productivity enough to cause them to lose as much as they gain from their own decreased effort. Nevertheless, total productivity will be lowered in a participatory firm.

This potential effect can be and has been countered by various informal social pressures, including reports of shirking and other modes of surveillance by other workers (see 6.8).[76] Indeed, as was noted above, workers in labor-managed firms need little or no outside supervision. They "have strong incentives to monitor their fellow-workers to make certain they are not shirking."[77] At the same time, "The incentives for shirking in the worker-managed enterprises are reduced because the workers, not the cap-

73. See Blumberg, *Industrial Democracy*, pp. 78 ff. See also Jaroslav Vanek, *The Participatory Economy* (Ithaca, N.Y.: Cornell University Press, 1971), p. 31.

74. Henry M. Levin, "Employment and Productivity of Producer Cooperatives," in Jackall and Levin, *Worker Cooperatives*, p. 25. See also Robert Jackall, "Paradoxes of Collective Work: A Study of the Cheeseboard, Berkeley, California," in ibid., p. 126. Compare the cautionary contrast to "the likely behaviour and attitudes of the real working class" after "the overthrow of landlords and capitalists," in Alec Nove, *The Economics of Feasible Socialism Revisited* (London: HarperCollins, 1991), p. 61.

75. Roger A. McCain, "Empirical Implications of Worker Participation Management," in Jones and Svejnar, *Participatory and Self-Managed Firms*, p. 38.

76. See ibid., p. 39. See also Greenberg, *Workplace Democracy*, p. 49; Levin, "Employment and Productivity," in Jackall and Levin, *Worker Cooperatives*, p. 25.

77. Henry Levin, "Issues in Assessing the Comparative Productivity," in Jones and Svejnar, *Participatory and Self-Managed Firms*, p. 46.

italists, receive the profits."[78] Thus it is significant that when a previously worker-controlled firm is taken over by capitalists, a much larger number of foremen are needed even though the workforce has been considerably reduced.[79]

There are at least two further arguments against the productivity of economic democracy. One, the "additional workers problem," will be taken up in a later section (7.5). The other is the "investment horizon problem." If, as in many worker-controlled firms, the worker does not own any of the firm's assets, his income will not benefit from investment decisions that lead to greater productivity and firm profits after he has left or retired from the firm. Hence the worker in such a firm will veto these decisions and will vote instead only for investments that increase his income during the period of his working connection with them. Thus a worker-controlled firm is less efficient and productive than a capitalist firm whose investments are not bounded by the income horizons of contemporary workers.[80] This problem is held to derive from the self-interested concern of workers in labor-managed firms to maximize their incomes even if this causes them to restrict productivity-increasing employment or investment.[81]

A first answer to the horizon investment problem is that, *mutatis mutandis*, it applies as much to capitalist firms as to worker-controlled firms. Capitalist firms, with their concern for short-term "bottom lines," also frequently seek to maximize immediate profits without regard to long-term productivity.[82] A second answer is that worker-controlled firms can have constitutional restrictions that help to prevent such foreshortening of investment perspectives. This can be done, for example, by having different age groups successively represented in the investment boards, so that the

78. Deborah Duff Milenkovich, "Is Market Socialism Efficient?," in Andrew Zimbalist, ed., *Comparative Economic Systems*, p. 93.

79. See P. Bernstein, *Workplace Democratization*, p. 19: "Under the new [capitalist] owners, 8 more foremen are needed, though there are 100 fewer workers." These considerations, which will be further developed below (7.6, 7), cast doubt on N. Scott Arnold's contention that monitoring will be much less effective in workers' cooperative firms than in classical capitalist firms (*The Philosophy and Economics of Market Socialism*, pp. 187–193).

80. See Eirik G. Furubotn, "The Long-Run Analysis of the Labor-Managed Firm: An Alternative Interpretation," *American Economic Review* 66 (March 1976), pp. 104–123. See also Michael Jensen and William Meckling, "Rights and Production Functions: An Application to Labor-Managed Firms and Codetermination," *Journal of Business* 52 (October 1979): 469–506, esp. pp. 481–84; Arnold, *Philosophy and Economics of Market Socialism*, pp. 200–205, 211–12.

81. Jaroslav Vanek refers to such a phenomenon as the "plundering effect" (*The General Theory of Labor-Managed Market Economies*, p. 291).

82. See Roger McCain, "Empirical Implications of Worker Participation Management," in Jones and Svejnar, *Participatory and Self-Managed Firms*, pp. 33–36.

younger members can exercise some surveillance over investment decisions with a view to assuring that they reflect longer-term as well as shorter-term interests. This would be another example of mixed altruism, where members would look out for others' interests as well as their own.

Since in economic democracy workers are not hired as commodities by capitalists, they do not receive "wages" in the capitalist sense. Nevertheless, we can speak of their work incomes as wages, with the recognition that these are set by the workers themselves. Such a system incurs the danger that workers will expand their wages beyond what is justified by their productivity and beyond the requirements of longer-term investment. This danger, with the resulting inflation, was realized in Yugoslavia.[83] On the other hand, insofar as worker-controlled firms are more efficient than capitalist firms, their higher wage levels are justified according to the general criterion that distribution should be proportional to contribution (see 5.7). Thus, in the plywood cooperatives of the Pacific Northwest, average hourly pay has been at least 25 percent higher than in unionized capitalist firms, and year-end bonuses or division of profits have pushed the workers' earnings even higher.[84] In Mondragon take-home pay in the worker-controlled firms is only slightly higher than in capitalist firms, but the total position in terms of both earnings and wealth is much higher because the surplus is distributed not according to each member's capital stake but rather according to each member's labor contribution as reflected in total earnings plus interest.[85]

The above considerations would seem to justify the conclusion that, in general, economic democracy makes valuable contributions toward fulfilling workers' rights to well-being as well as to freedom.

7.5. DISANALOGIES BETWEEN ECONOMIC AND POLITICAL DEMOCRACY

Thus far in this chapter economic democracy has been mainly discussed in what I have called the "particularist stage": I have considered the internal impact of each particular worker-controlled firm on the human rights of its individual members; only secondarily, through the consideration of efficiency, have I considered its impact on the interests of other persons. We

83. See Ota Sik, "The Economic Crisis in Yugoslavia," *Economic and Industrial Democracy* 7 (1986), pp. 363–65. See, however, Thomas and Logan, *Mondragon*, pp. 103–4.

84. See Paul Bernstein, "Worker-Owned Plywood Companies of the Pacific Northwest," *Working Papers for a New Society* 2 (Summer 1974): 24–36; Katrina V. Berman, "The United States of America: A Comparative Model for Worker Management," in Frank H. Stephen, ed., *The Performance of Labour-Managed Firms*, p. 79.

85. Thomas and Logan, *Mondragon*, pp. 136, 154–55.

must now move to the "universalist stage," which directly examines the external impact of economic democracy on other persons, other firms, and society at large. To get at this broader picture, it will be helpful to look again at the relation between economic and political democracy.

Besides the frequently invoked analogies so far considered between economic and political democracy, we must now note that there are at least three important disanalogies. Two concern membership or citizenship rights in the respective kinds of democracy; the third concerns their respective fields of operation. All three disanalogies involve greater restrictiveness in economic democracy and a consequent diminution of its role in fulfilling human rights. These considerations have an obvious importance for the bearing of economic democracy on the economic biography and economic constitution that are here being traced in relation to the community of rights.

First, in political democracy all native-born or naturalized persons are citizens, with comparatively minor exceptions in the case of criminals or mental incompetents. In economic democracy, on the other hand, citizenship is restricted to the "workers" in a given enterprise; excluded are capitalists, landowners, entrepreneurs, and, at least in the first instance, managers. Thus in the standard arguments based on the analogy between political and economic democracy, there is often a seemingly unconscious slide from unrestricted universality in the political case to a certain restriction in the economic case. A typical example is found in Robert A. Dahl's discussion. First he writes that one of the "criteria for a democratic process" is that "throughout the process of making binding collective decisions, *each citizen* must have an adequate and equal opportunity for expressing a preference as to the final outcome."[86] But when he comes to economic democracy, he describes it as "a system of economic enterprises collectively owned and democratically governed by all the people who *work* there"; "each person *employed* in an enterprise is entitled to one and only one vote." He adds that "the people who *work* in the firm might be called citizens of the enterprise."[87] But this then entails that in his criterion for a "democratic process," the reference to "each citizen" must be restricted to workers, "people who *work* there." He subsequently distinguishes "employees" from "managers and owners."[88]

86. Dahl, *Preface to Economic Democracy*, p. 59 (emphasis added).
87. Ibid., pp. 91, 92 (emphasis added).
88. Ibid., p. 100. Similarly, Herbert Gintis, referring to economic democracy, speaks of "the accountability of managers and technicians to the will of workers," so that "workers" excludes "managers and technicians" ("Welfare Economics and Individual Development: A Reply to Talcott Parsons," *Quarterly Journal of Economics* 89 [May 1975]: 301–2). For similar slides from the comparatively unrestricted citizenship of political democracy to the

There is, then, a much greater restrictiveness of the governing group in economic democracy than in political democracy, a class emphasis that excludes many persons who are citizens in political democracy. To be sure, there are economic classes in political democracy, and they have markedly different degrees of influence in its actual functioning (see 8.4, 5). But these inequalities are not part of the theory or constitution of political democracy, as they are of economic democracy. A moral basis for the latter's class emphasis may be found in two interrelated considerations. First, the excluded groups, especially the capitalists, are precisely those who possess the hierarchic power which economic democracy is designed to abolish. Thus, despite its departure from universality in restricting power to workers, economic democracy may be held to maintain its moral basis in the generic right to freedom. For it excludes from economic power only those whose hierarchic class position is antithetical to the PGC's equality of freedom whereby persons control the conditions under which they live and work. Second, on the familiar Marxist thesis that capitalists contribute nothing essential to the productive process, so that their profits reflect only the exploitation whereby they appropriate the surplus value produced by the workers (5.7), it would follow that capitalists as such deserve no role in the governance of economic enterprises.

There are, nevertheless, difficulties in explicating this departure of economic democracy from the universality of political democracy. They bear especially on the question of what is meant by the "workers" all of whom are to have equal authority in the control of economic enterprises. There is a dilemma here. If "workers" is defined in the traditional Marxist way as persons who sell their labor-power for wages while having no ownership of the enterprise, then "workers" will include not only the industrial proletariat of manual blue-collar laborers, including machine operators and the like, but also clerical workers and various professionals hired by the firm to administer its activities and make and market its products, such as engineers, lawyers, accountants, marketing agents, advertising specialists, and so forth;[89] and indeed many managers and some entrepreneurs also belong to this protean group.[90] But since such professionals are already comparatively better advantaged through superior education (and also possibly tal-

---

worker-restricted citizenship of economic democracy, see Vanek, *The Participatory Economy,* p. 8; Vanek, ed., *Self-Management,* pp. 13–14; also Gould, *Rethinking Democracy,* pp. 143–44.

89.   See Harry Braverman, *Labor and Monopoly Capital,* p. 25; Adam Przeworski, *Capitalism and Social Democracy,* pp. 55–59.

90.   See Alec Nove, *The Economics of Feasible Socialism Revisited,* pp. 4, 51–52, 62–63, 220; Derek C. Jones, "American Producer Cooperatives and Employee-Owned Firms: A Historical Perspective," in Jackall and Levin, *Worker Cooperatives in America,* p. 39.

ent), this serves to dilute the theoretical emphasis of economic democracy on protecting the rights of those who are most vulnerable and deprived and most in need of empowerment in industrial relations. The inclusion of professionals among "workers" also blurs the class character marked by the exclusion of capitalists from the governance of firms.

If, on the other hand, the "workers" who control the firm do not include such professionals, then economic democracy entails an even greater departure from the universality of political democracy. Nevertheless, the exclusion of professionals has been defended on such grounds as that they are not "direct producers," "immediate producers," or "active members."[91] It has also been felt that, because of their higher income, status, and expertise, as well as their more salubrious working conditions, members of such groups have more and better alternatives available to them, so that they do not need the kinds of protections of their freedom and well-being that economic democracy provides for other workers. But to exclude them on such grounds then runs into a slippery slope difficulty. For it fails to take account of the job segmentation whereby, parallel to the distinction noted above between "creative" and "depressive" work (4.5), workers are divided into two sharply different groups, "primary" and "secondary." The former have various relevant skills; they include "technical, professional, managerial, and craft" workers with considerable opportunities for initiative and upward mobility. The secondary workers, on the other hand, have jobs that require few skills; they are paid much less and have no opportunity for advancement.[92] But the argument for excluding professionals from the "workers" who are to control enterprises would then seem to apply to the "primary" workers as well.

These considerations also bear on a second disanalogy between political and economic democracy. In political democracy, as was noted above, citizenship is open to all native-born and naturalized persons; apart from the most elementary cognitive skills there are no tests of "political" competence bearing on specific abilities of effective citizenship, although, as we shall see, restrictions bearing on health, livelihood, and other factors may be imposed on would-be immigrants. In economic democracy, on the other hand, not only is its membership limited to "workers" in given firms, but to become a worker in a firm requires that one have relevant competences of productive agency and human capital. Thus "the labor-managed firms are

---

91. For these exclusions, see respectively Comisso, *Workers' Control Under Plan and Market,* p. 161; Przeworski, *Capitalism and Social Democracy,* p. 46; Vanek, *Self-Management,* p. 14.

92. See Thierry J. Noyelle, *Beyond Industrial Dualism: Market and Job Segmentation in the New Economy* (Boulder, Colo.: Westview Press, 1987), pp. 10–11.

free to hire or not to hire a particular man";[93] "workers are screened as to general suitability";[94] "labour is taken on only when it increases the value of its [i.e. the firm's] marginal product";[95] "after an initial probationary period, it is 'up or out'; a worker is either accepted into membership or let go."[96] In addition, persons taken on as members must often pay an initial financial contribution.[97] Thus economic democracy embodies meritocratic restrictions that are quite different from the egalitarian universalism of political democracy with regard to rights of citizenship.

The basis of this difference is found in a third disanalogy. Political democracy, unlike economic democracy, does not involve its citizens in the production of specific products or exchange values within a context of market competition where only some firms may survive. When it is held that in economic democracy decisions about hiring and firing should be made by a firm's workers or by committees elected by the workers, this comprises an exercise of power which is quite different from that of political democracy. Voter-citizens are not hired or fired in terms of the state's success in fulfilling its purposes (whatever they may be). But when, in economic democracy, would-be workers are not hired, this may be a severe setback to their economic well-being; and this is perhaps still more the case when workers are fired. Yet the firm's economic purposes may require such draconian decisions. In this way the situation of workers in economic democracy may be morally far more onerous than the situation of citizens in political democracy.

A frequently adduced example of the disadvantages that economic democracy may inflict on workers may be called the "additional workers problem." It focuses on situations where there is an increase in the selling price of some product. A capitalist firm, since its objective is to maximize its profits, will respond to such a situation by increasing production through hiring more workers. But a worker-controlled firm will not respond in this way because hiring more workers will mean that the firm's total dividend must be divided among more workers, so that each worker's income will be reduced. Instead, the firm may dismiss some workers

93. Vanek, *Participatory Economy*, p. 12.

94. Thomas and Logan, *Mondragon*, p. 24. See also Keith Bradley and Alan Gelb, "The Mondragon Cooperative: Guidelines for a Cooperative Economy?" in Jones and Svejnar, *Participatory and Self-Managed Firms*, p. 158.

95. Stephen, *Performance of Labour-Managed Firms*, p. 7. See Comisso, *Workers' Control under Plan and Market*, p. 62: "Enterprises competed fiercely to attract and hold educated cadres, causing interskill differentials to widen."

96. Ellerman, *Democratic Worker-Owned Firm*, p. 73.

97. Oakeshott, "Mondragon: Spain's Oasis of Democracy," p. 292.

toward the same objective. Hence, economic democracy will operate to decrease rather than increase productivity and employment.[98]

In this problem, it will be noted, the objection is not that the individual worker's income will be lowered but rather that it will be maintained at the potential expense either of other workers who would have been hired under capitalism or of society at large through the nonincrease in productivity. Moreover, since the worker-controlled firms of economic democracy engage in market competition, whole firms may be thrown into bankruptcy, with severe resulting hardships for their workers, while other firms survive and flourish. Although political democracies may also engage in trade wars (as well as military combat), such competition is not part of their constitutional functioning as it is of market socialist firms.

It is indeed true that just as economic associations are themselves "political" in that they provide in various ways for the exercise of power over their members, so too democratic political associations are "economic" in that candidates for office compete in political markets to win votes from the electorate.[99] But even if we conceptualize the latter context as one in which candidates for office compete in the political marketplace to be "hired" by the voters on the basis of their promised services, this still leaves the analogy as one in which elected officials are assimilated to workers for hire, so that the latter are in turn assimilated not to citizen-voters but to candidates for political office. This is hardly a realistic model; moreover, it does not conform to the analogy whereby workers in economic democracy are assimilated to citizen-voters rather than to elected officials in political democracy.

Economic associations in market socialism or economic democracy differ from political ones like the state (to which political democracy is directly related) in that economic firms, as such, are established for purposes that in certain respects are much more narrowly defined. Let us initially characterize these as the making of certain products (including services) which are to be sold for a profit on the market. The firms compete with one another for shares of the market. Even if firms in economic democracy or market socialism may refrain from expanding their workforce to accommodate increased demand for their products, they still try to make their

98. A classic source for this problem is Benjamin Ward, "The Firm in Illyria: Market Syndicalism," *American Economic Review* 48 (1958), pp. 566–89. See also Furubotn, "Long-Run Analysis"; Saul Estrin, "Workers' Co-operatives: Their Merits and Their Limitations," in LeGrand and Estrin, *Market Socialism*, pp. 175–76.

99. See Joseph A. Schumpeter, *Capitalism, Socialism, and Democracy* (London: George Allen and Unwin, 1950), chap. 22; Anthony Downs, *An Economic Theory of Democracy* (New York: Harper and Row, 1957).

products sufficiently attractive to obtain buyers at profitable prices. In this competition, some firms may fail. This process in economic democracy may be analogized to the political situation before 1989 when the citizens of East Germany and other eastern European countries tried to "vote with their feet" by escaping to the West. But in any case the relevant analogue here is not political democracy. The market aspect of economic democracy, as so far considered, may, then, generate severe hardships for workers in failed firms.

On all these grounds the analogy of economic democracy to political democracy breaks down: the former, unlike the latter, may impose severe restrictions and hardships on its would-be citizens and on other persons. The analogy might still hold if the immigration policies of the United States and other political democracies are considered; for they too impose restrictions as to who will be allowed to immigrate and obtain citizenship. But this would not serve to support the main idea behind the analogy, which concerns the internal, particularist functioning of political democracy as providing for government by the people who are governed.

7.6. THE UNIVERSALIZATION OF ECONOMIC DEMOCRACY

We have now reached the somewhat paradoxical position that while economic democracy in its particularist or internal stage in the particular firm goes far toward securing the equal rights of all its worker-members to freedom and well-being, in its universalist or external stage it may have a quite adverse impact on those rights for nonmembers, including workers in other worker-controlled firms, and for society at large. In their relations to the rest of society, workers' cooperatives that practice economic democracy as so far analyzed may behave like capitalist firms: they engage in market competition, they produce for profit without regard to basic needs, they strive to maximize their profits or incomes, they discriminate against, or at least are indifferent toward, outsiders so far as concerns economic rewards or penalties, they hire and fire on the basis of cost-benefit analysis, they may exhibit, from one firm to another, vast inequalities of wealth and power. This is the basis of the charge that an economy of self-managed firms or workers' cooperatives may embody a form of "workers' capitalism" or "collective egoism" where each firm pursues its own selfish interests at the expense of other potential workers and other firms, with severe inequality as a possible result.[100] The anomalous outcome is that a system justified as

---

100. See, e.g., Gar Alperovitz, "Toward a Pluralist Commonwealth," in Virginia Held, ed., *Property, Profits, and Economic Justice* (Belmont, Calif.: Wadsworth, 1980), p. 162. Referring to "workers' groups" that practice "self-management," he writes: "there is no obvious reason why such (partial) groups will not develop special interests ('workers' capitalism')

fulfilling the principle of human rights may also violate those same rights. The question that remains for economic democracy, then, is whether it can maintain the egalitarian universalism of human rights while also maintaining its economic viability under market conditions. The answer to this question is that if economic democracy is to maintain its justification as fulfilling human rights, its scope must be broadened, and indeed universalized, so that it provides for all persons the same protections of freedom and well-being that it has been seen to provide within the particular firm. I wish to suggest it is only in this way that economic democracy can be fitted into the cooperative solidarity of the community of rights.

An initial sketch of the required universalization may be given as follows. The scope of economic democracy must be broadened so that it encompasses a whole national economy, whose parts are divided into two levels. On the first level are particular firms controlled by their workers and engaged in production of commodities for the market. But just as these firms fulfill—provide for and protect—their individual workers' rights to freedom and well-being in the ways indicated above, so there is a second, more general level of organization whose function is to see to it that the particular firms continue to fulfill their individual workers' rights, and moreover that they do so in ways that do not adversely affect, but rather promote, the freedom and well-being of other persons. Thus, while the particular firms of the first level enter into market competition, their economic relations both with one another and with the rest of society are not left simply to the "anarchy" of the market. When firms are threatened with failure and consequent layoffs of workers, they are not simply permitted to fail. Instead, the general organization of the second level helps them either to improve their efficiency or to convert to some other line of production in which they can successfully compete. Thus at this more general level the relations between particular firms, and between their respective members, are such that they are enabled to maintain their role of fulfilling human rights, so that mutuality is upheld and the two levels together function as a community of rights.[101]

---

which run counter to the interests of the broader community." See also Estrin, "Workers' Co-operatives," p. 185: "There is nothing to stop each of these groups of workers acting selfishly with respect to the broader society. An economy of this sort is workers' capitalism, not socialism, with capitalists replaced by selfish worker-owners." See also Carnoy and Shearer, *Economic Democracy*, pp. 181–82, and the reference to "collective egoism" (stemming from Sidney and Beatrice Webb) in Thomas and Logan, *Mondragon*, p. 3. One aspect of this charge can be traced back to Marx, who writes of "the co-operative factories of the labourers themselves" that "the antithesis between capital and labour is overcome within them, if at first by making the associated laborers into their own capitalist" (*Capital*, vol. 3, chap. 27, p. 440).

101. This second level is similar to what Vanek calls "a shelter organization or institution on the national level (which can be decentralized according to need), whose express

To make this two-level structure of economic democracy more concrete, I shall analyze it by somewhat detailed reference to the system developed in Mondragon, in the Basque region of Spain.[102] I shall cite from that system only the aspects that are directly relevant to the present project.

The Mondragon system, like the universalized system just outlined, comprises two main levels. The first consists of particular cooperative firms, that is, firms that practice the economic democracy so far described. Taken by themselves, as presumably distinct, independent enterprises, they would have both the virtues and the potential vices discussed above. The vices are avoided, however, because there is a second level, an organization which assists and coordinates the firms of the first level in accordance with the norms of economic democracy and human rights. These norms now govern not only the internal workings of each firm taken by itself but also the interrelations of the various firms, including their actual or potential members, so that they are helped to maintain the norms in ways that are both efficient and mutually supportive. This organization is based upon a constitution that requires practical allegiance to the norms of economic democracy and, more generally, of human rights, so that it comprises a community of rights. The particular firms at the first, operational level are all bound to this organization by a contract of association that requires them, in their internal functioning, to abide by these same norms, including workers' control on the basis of one worker—one vote and nondiscrimination on the basis of race, gender, religion, or politics.[103] Membership in the particular firms is at the option both of the members and of candidates for admission. Workers may, if they prefer, belong instead to noncooperative firms, although it is hoped that the cooperatives will be sufficiently benefi-

---

function would be to fund and promote the self-managed sector or economy" (introduction to Vanek, *Self-Management,* p. 35). See also Thomas and Logan, *Mondragon,* pp. 7–8.

102.   The Mondragon system, both in its history and in its detailed working, has been described in many writings. See especially Oakeshott, "Mondragon: Spain's Oasis of Democracy," pp. 290–96; Quintin Garcia, *Les coopératives industrielles de Mondragon* (Paris: Editions Économie et Humanisme, 1970); Thomas and Logan, *Mondragon;* David F. Ellerman, "The Mondragon Cooperative Movement," Harvard Business School, Case No. I-383-270 (Boston, 1984); Hans Wiener and Robert Oakeshott, *Worker-Owners: Mondragon Revisited* (London: Anglo-German Foundation for the Study of Industrial Society, 1987); Whyte and Whyte, *Making Mondragon.* For recent critical discussions, see A. Melissa Moye, "Mondragon: Adapting Co-Operative Structures to Meet the Demands of a Changing Environment," *Economic and Industrial Democracy* 14, no. 2 (May 1993): 251–76; Elizabeth A. Bowman and Bob Stone, "Worker Ownership on the Mondragon Model: Trap or Opportunity for Socialists?" in Justin Schwartz, ed., *Beyond Communism and Capitalism: The Role of Markets in a Third Way* (Atlantic Highlands, N.J.: Humanities Press, 1995).

103.   See Whyte and Whyte, *Making Mondragon,* p. 69; Thomas and Logan, *Mondragon,* pp. 22–26.

cial for freedom and well-being to attract most workers. Thus there is cooperation not only between the members of each firm taken by itself but also among the various firms themselves and their respective actual or potential members, through the guidance of the second-level organization. I shall refer to these two levels, respectively, as the Operational Level and the Supportive Level (or, alternatively, the Supportive Organization).

The Supportive Organization exercises its authority through a general assembly whose members are elected, directly or indirectly, by all the members of the particular cooperatives of the first level.[104] Thus, just as the particular firms of the first level are democratic in that their affairs are managed, directly or indirectly, by the equal votes of the worker-electorate, so the Supportive Organization is also democratic in that its officers and other functions are determined, directly or indirectly, by the equal votes of the workers as a whole. A main component of this second-level organization is the cooperative bank called Caja Laboral Popular (People's Labor Bank).[105] Financed initially by contributions from each firm, the bank concentrates especially on the expansion of employment, in large part by encouraging entrepreneurship among its members, and hence a sense of personal responsibility for profitable innovations.

Another vitally important function of the Supportive Organization is education. Amid the selectivity noted above whereby each firm chooses its members on the basis of competence, the Supportive Organization administers a large educational network, from elementary schools to postgraduate training, whose aim is to develop as fully as possible the productive agency, cultural as well as economic, of all persons who may wish to belong to the cooperative enterprise, as well as an understanding of the moral mutuality of the community of rights.[106] This system, which bears considerable resemblance to the education for productive agency discussed above (4.9, 10), serves to moderate the restrictiveness as to citizenship that was seen to be a meritocratic feature of economic democracy in its particularist stage (7.5). In its universalist stage, economic democracy serves to foster equality of opportunity for all.

Directly in keeping with these objectives is an interventionist function that addresses an important moral issue mentioned at the beginning of this section. We noted that workers' cooperatives engage in market competition that may bankrupt some of them. It is to avoid this danger that the central bank of the Supportive Organization devotes some of its main resources. Rather than letting firms fail, with their harmful consequences for

104. See Whyte and Whyte, *Making Mondragon*, pp. 60, 68.
105. See ibid., pp. 49–52, 68–87; Thomas and Logan, *Mondragon*, chap. 4.
106. See Thomas and Logan, *Mondragon*, pp. 52–65; Whyte and Whyte, *Making Mondragon*, pp. 30–31, 53–54, 200–205.

the workers' rights, the central bank intervenes to help prevent their failure. It does so by making, together with the firm's officers, a careful study of the firm's operations and markets, on the basis of which it may recommend discontinuing production of some items, developing new products, or reducing personnel (some of whom are transferred to other cooperatives).[107] Thus while the firms of the Operational Level all produce for markets, the organization at the Supportive Level intervenes to help them secure market success. This stands in contrast to firms under capitalism which may go under if they cannot survive market competition from their rivals. This interventionist function is not only a contribution to efficiency; it also helps to assure that economic democracy, and with it the protection of human rights, are maintained throughout the economy. In this way the Supportive Organization functions as a community of rights, and the rights it protects are positive ones.

A chief objection to this interventionist policy is that it makes for inefficiency. If firm managers know that when they are threatened with failure they will be bailed out by the government or the Supportive Organization, then what incentive do they have to improve their performance? Such intervention may be held to be a prime example of what has been called the "soft budget constraint," where "the strict relationship between expenditure and earnings has been relaxed, because excess expenditure over earnings will be paid by some other institution, typically by the State."[108] When decision makers come to expect such external financial assistance, they cease to fear the penalties of failure and feel more comfortable about moderating their efforts. In this way passive dependence comes to replace productive agency.

The difficulties of the soft budget constraint cannot, however, be charged to the Mondragon system. The reason is that the central cooperative bank sets stringent conditions for firms threatened with failure; these conditions provide strong incentives for the firm to do all it can to avoid having its earnings fall below its expenditures. The conditions may include reducing members' pay, having members make additional capital contributions to the firm, decreasing the labor force, switching to new product lines, and relocating members; in addition, the firm being assisted must share with the central bank the personnel and other costs of the central bank's intervention, as well as the expenses of relocation and unemployment support. When a firm must have a loan to keep it afloat, the interest rates are made to depend on the needed degrees of intervention, and, ex-

107. See Whyte and Whyte, *Making Mondragon*, pp. 72–73, 158–87; Ellerman, *Democratic Worker-Owned Firm*, pp. 103–4.

108. Janos Kornai, "The Soft Budget Constraint," *Kyklos* 39 (1986): 3–30, at p. 4. See also Arnold, *Philosophy and Economics of Market Socialism*, pp. 222–25.

cept for emergency situations, there are "no concessions on the interest rates on outstanding loans until [the central bank] has approved a five-year business and reorganization plan prepared by the firm with the assistance of the intervenor."[109] These conditions are far from the painless bailing out that the soft budget constraint thesis attributes to cooperative or market socialist firms; on the contrary, "the process of intervention . . . was painful for everyone involved."[110] On the other hand, the emphasis is not on the "punishment" and "fear" generated by the hard budget constraint where deficits "may lead to extremely serious consequences" and "persistent loss is a matter of life and death."[111] The aim is rather to enable firms to maintain their adherence to the norms of economic democracy and human rights while also being efficient.

The Mondragon intervention takes an intermediate position between the draconian measures upheld by the hard budget constraint with its rigorous enforcement of contracts under strict market conditions and the soft constraint where avoidance of sanctions for loss or failure is made painless. The aim is rather the affirmative one of helping firms to remain economically viable under market conditions and persons to retain their jobs while at the same time providing incentives for avoiding the costs of assistance. If the costs arise, they must be paid for by the firms and workers affected, thereby imposing on them requirements of responsibility, while at the same time strenuous efforts are made to obtain successful outcomes. It is noteworthy that at Mondragon from 1956 through 1983, "of 103 cooperatives that were created, only three have had to go out of business."[112] These three were very small firms. "So far, every intervention in larger firms has been successful." This stands in marked contrast to "the frequently noted finding that only 20 percent of all firms founded in the United States survive for five years."[113]

A vital part of the Supportive Organization's function comprises an Entrepreneurial Division which serves to create new firms and hence also

109. See Whyte and Whyte, *Making Mondragon*, pp. 151, 171, 172, 181–82. These and related conditions also serve to answer the contention that "state-owned enterprises" cannot cope with such problems as the subdividing of ownership, "the ultimate discipline of bankruptcy," and "how to deal with firms that are suffering persistent losses" (G. Warren Nutter, "Markets without Property: A Grand Illusion," in Eirik G. Furubotn and Svetozar Pejovich, eds., *The Economics of Property Rights* [Cambridge, Mass.: Ballinger, 1974], pp. 217–24). The Mondragon cooperatives are not "state-owned," but their ownership is collective rather than belonging to private capitalists. See also Nove, *Economics of Feasible Socialism Revisited*, p. 224.

110. Whyte and Whyte, *Making Mondragon*, p. 182.

111. Kornai, "The Soft Budget Constraint," p. 18.

112. Whyte and Whyte, *Making Mondragon*, p. 172.

113. Ibid., p. 3.

new jobs. In the typical view the function of entrepreneurship has been reserved to the imaginative, innovative, risk-taking individual who engages in a special type of cost-benefit analysis and resulting activity: he perceives opportunities for selling some good at a price that is greater than the cost of buying it, and he makes arrangements for producing that good, so that profit results (see 5.7). The process inherently involves risk and competition whereby different enterprises vie with one another in projects for buying and selling various commodities.[114] According to this view, only an individual can be an entrepreneur, because the alertness and initiative that are central traits of entrepreneurship are "highly individualistic characteristics," so that the idea of collective entrepreneurship is "inherently contradictory."[115] Because of the risks involved, workers are averse to take on entrepreneurial roles.[116] On this view, then, successful entrepreneurship is incompatible with economic democracy.

There is, however, an opposed view according to which the idea of the "heroic individual entrepreneur" is an anachronism, analogous to "the garage inventor or basement tinkerer." Instead, entrepreneurship, like technological invention, has become a process that requires the cooperative, organized efforts of many individuals, so that some form of "socialized entrepreneurship" is the norm.[117]

While each of these extreme views may incur difficulties, the actualization of the latter view in the Mondragon cooperatives shows that a flourishing kind of socialized entrepreneurship can be supported by economic democracy. The credit cooperative bank of the Supportive Organization has an "Entrepreneurial Division" which assists in the formation of new workers' cooperatives. A group of workers who have an initially plausible new product idea select a "manager" who is given expert technical help by

114. See Israel M. Kirzner, *Competition and Entrepreneurship* (Chicago: University of Chicago Press, 1973), pp. 14–16. See also Joseph A. Schumpeter, *Capitalism, Socialism, and Democracy*, who refers to the "supernormal intelligence and energy" of past entrepreneurs (p. 16).

115. O'Mahony, "Labour Management," pp. 31, 37. Kirzner refers, in an imaginary example, to "a group of outsiders" as entrepreneurs (*Competition and Entrepreneurship*, p. 14).

116. On workers as averse to entrepreneurial risks, see J. Zuparov, "The Producer and Risk," *Eastern European Economics* 7 (1969): 12–28; R. Carson, "A Theory of Cooperatives," *Canadian Journal of Economics* 10 (1977): 565–89, at p. 584.

117. David Ellerman, "Entrepreneurship in the Mondragon Cooperative," *Review of Social Economy* 42, no. 3 (Dec. 1984): 272–93, at pp. 274, 275. For a similar view, see Schumpeter, *Capitalism, Socialism, and Democracy*, chap. 12. Schumpeter's view is rejected by Janos Kornai, "Market Socialism Revisited," in Bardhan and Roemer, *Market Socialism: The Current Debate*, p. 59. See also Arthur M. Okun, *Equality and Efficiency: The Big Trade-off* (Washington, D.C.: Brookings Institution, 1975), pp. 59–60. See above, 5.7, and n. 85 to chap. 5.

the bank to develop a "feasibility study" which deals with the production process, marketing, and other relevant aspects of the proposed product. After the completion of the feasibility study, which takes about eighteen months, the bank's Operations Committee decides whether or not to back the proposed cooperative. Because of the intensive studies already completed, the decision is usually affirmative. Financing is then arranged and the cooperative is launched, with due provision for start-up costs and about three years of losses before the break-even point is reached.[118] As was noted above, nearly all these firms have been successful.

An important part of this social entrepreneurial function deals with the "additional workers problem" cited above (7.5), where profitable workers' cooperatives refuse to take on additional worker-members because this will require dividing the firm's profits among more persons. In such situations the entrepreneurial division of the central bank helps to organize new firms to take advantage of the product's increased selling price. In this way what would otherwise be a case of "collective selfishness"[119] is so channeled that the benefits of market development are extended to persons other than those of the original cooperative firm. This does not involve a financial or other sacrifice by the latter but rather a further promotion of additive well-being. In a parallel way, workers threatened with loss of their jobs are helped to obtain retraining and to find jobs in existing or new firms.[120] So again human rights are maintained, and the entire enterprise functions as a community of rights.

7.7. COMPETITION AND SOLIDARITY

The account given in the preceding section comprises a double universalization. One is from the particular worker-controlled firm to all firms within a given economy: the economic and ethical arrangements that economic democracy provides for particular firms taken separately are extended to a

---

118. See Ellerman, "Entrepreneurship in the Mondragon Cooperative'; also Ellerman, "The Mondragon Cooperative Movement'; Whyte and Whyte, *Making Mondragon*, pp. 71–75, 80–81. According to N. Scott Arnold, the successful entrepreneur in a workers' cooperative is "exploited" by the other members in that he "does not get the value of his contribution," because he "must share whatever pure profits he earns with everyone else in the firm" (*The Philosophy and Economics of Market Socialism*, p. 197). But the entrepreneur may receive an income that is at the upper end of the pay scale. See also below (7.7) on "income solidarity."

119. Whyte and Whyte, *Making Mondragon*, p. 273.

120. See Whyte and Whyte, *Making Mondragon*, pp. 72–75, 81–82, 151; Thomas and Logan, *Mondragon*, pp. 430–49; J. E. Meade, "The Theory of Labour-managed Firms and of Profit-Sharing," in Vanek, *Self-Management*, pp. 403, 409; Robert A. Dahl, *A Preface to Economic Democracy*, p. 122; Nove, *Economics of Feasible Socialism Revisited*, pp. 234–35.

comprehensive cooperative system, that of Mondragon, wherein all firms in the economy are enabled to maintain such arrangements through a Supportive Organization which is itself based on economic democracy. The other universalization is from one comprehensive system of economic democracy to all economies: the former universalization of economic democracy, as instantiated in the particular empirically ascertainable case of the Mondragon system, is extended to all economic systems.

This latter universalization may be attacked on the ground that the Mondragon case is unique, so that neither its first-level nor its second-level arrangements can be soundly extended to other firms, societies, or national economies. This is an important objection. It casts doubt on the present thesis that the community of rights can be actualized in the kind of two-level system of economic democracy that has been described above. I shall now examine some of the main grounds of this objection.

One ground is relatively slight. Mondragon is not a whole national economy or society but only a section within the Basque region which is itself a part of Spain; hence it may be thought unsound to assimilate Mondragon to what I have called the supportive organization of a whole economy. This objection presents no reason why the Mondragon system cannot be thus extended. Questions of size are undoubtedly important, and the Mondragon experience has shown that its values and efficiency are best promoted in relatively small units.[121] But this does not prevent the total number of units being quite large; in 1986 Mondragon had more than one hundred worker cooperatives.[122] So the system could, in principle, be extended to a whole national economy and could indeed be given international scope.

A more serious objection is that the Mondragon system is the result of special, indeed unique circumstances that cannot be generalized or duplicated. They include the genius of its founder, Don José Maria Arizmendi, and the unity of its people's ethnicity and culture. These circumstances can to some extent be combined on the ground that the founder took advantage of the cultural values he found within Basque society.[123]

It would be idle to deny that the ethnic and cultural homogeneity of the Basque people had something to do with Mondragon's success.[124] "They manifest strong ethnic pride and commitment to egalitarian values and

121. See Thomas and Logan, *Mondragon*, pp. 35, 92, 117–19; Whyte and Whyte, *Making Mondragon*, p. 261.

122. Whyte and Whyte, *Making Mondragon*, p. 3.

123. See ibid., pp. 4, 254 ff.

124. There is a dispiriting contrast here to the fate that befell the vaunted "self-management" economy of the former Yugoslavia under the impact of the murderous ethnic nationalist hatreds that tore the country apart in the 1990s.

democratic government." But these features are not sufficient conditions of the kind of system that developed in Mondragon, for "they occur elsewhere where no such movement has arisen."[125] Moreover, to the extent that past or present workers' cooperatives have approximated significant aspects of Mondragon's structure of economic democracy,[126] it can be argued that the Basques' ethnic and cultural homogeneity is not a necessary condition of Mondragon's development.

Nevertheless, amid the economic factors that have been adduced to account for the frequent failures of worker cooperatives,[127] the Mondragon system embodies certain cultural and moral values that can plausibly be held to have made a significant contribution to its success. These values are especially relevant to the attempt to generalize from the Mondragon experience to the wider extension and universalization of economic democracy. This consideration is perhaps made more explicit when the reference is to "market socialism." We have seen that the moral lapses of workers' cooperatives result in important part from the challenges that the market system poses for the egalitarian values of socialism, including its commitment to solidarity in the effectuation of human rights. The broader question here is whether the market aspect is compatible with the socialist aspect, whether the competitiveness intrinsic to market relations is compatible with the cooperativeness and solidarity upheld by socialism, including the structure of rights which has been attributed to economic democracy.

A negative answer is reflected in the contention that to appeal to workers' sense of solidarity to ward off the effects of competitive market relations is to assume "a bifurcation in the workers' motivation which, unless properly explained, may seem to border on the schizophrenic." For the workers under market socialism are depicted, as marketeers, as having "competitive, non-altruistic motivation," while, as maintaining socialist relations, they have "a diametrically opposed sort of motivation." Hence it is concluded that "a successful defense of market socialism depends upon

125. Whyte and Whyte, *Making Mondragon*, p. 255.

126. See, e.g., Vanek, ed., *Self-Management*, Part 2, entitled "Actual Cases," where nine examples of economic democracy are discussed. See also David Montgomery, *Workers' Control in America*; Nelson Lichtenstein and Howell John Harris, eds., *Industrial Democracy in America: The Ambiguous Promise* (Cambridge, UK: Cambridge University Press, 1993). For specific arguments against "ethnicity as the determining factor of Mondragon's success," see Keith Bradley and Alan Gelb, "The Mondragon Cooperatives: Guidelines for a Cooperative Economy?" in Jones and Svejnar, *Participatory and Self-Managed Firms*, p. 157.

127. See David Miller, "Market Neutrality and the Failure of Cooperatives," *British Journal of Political Science* 11 (1981): 309–29; Jon Elster, "From Here to There; or, If Cooperative Ownership Is So Desirable, Why Are There So Few Cooperatives?" *Social Philosophy and Policy* 6, no. 2 (spring 1989): 93–111; Estrin, "Workers' Co-operatives: Their Merits and Their Limitations," pp. 165–92.

the development of a more adequate account of motivation."[128] This requirement also poses an important challenge to the attempt to generalize from the Mondragon system to all economic systems.

The question of motivation arises at each of the two levels we have distinguished. At the operational level of the particular firms, the question arises when the interests of the members may conflict with the interests either of nonmembers or of future members, in accordance with such issues as the "additional worker" and "investment horizon" problems discussed above (7.5, 6). Here, as we have seen, the self-interested, competitive motivations of the members are brought into line with the solidaristic, cooperative goals of economic democracy through the Supportive Organization which intervenes to promote and enforce those goals.

This, however, may seem simply to push the problem back a step. Who will monitor the supporters? Won't they have the self-interested motivations of the market system that will lead them to favor their own interests over those of the operative members?[129]

A salient part of the answer is that the question of motivation is not only or mainly personal; it involves various institutions that build solidarity into the Mondragon system and direct its officials' conduct in a cooperative direction. For one thing, when the Supportive Organization intervenes in the particular firms to promote and enforce the cooperative goals of economic democracy, this is not solely or even mainly a matter of force majeure. The Supportive Organization has as one of its functions an educational mission whereby the moral necessity of respecting equal human rights is comprehensively taught. This education proceeds not by propaganda but by rational and institutionalized argument whose understanding is within the competence of all the members. In this way the Supportive Organization is itself monitored by the operative workers whose performance it in turn monitors. In this two-way street each level is checked by the other on the basis of the cooperative moral values that they publicly acknowledge, endorse, and collectively need. This process helps to bring it about that each participant is a reasonable self in the sense distinguished above (3.6). In this way, also, the Supportive Organization's authority is not antithetical to the workers' self-determination upheld in economic democracy.

In this regard it will be helpful to consider the relation between the solidarity here envisaged as an indispensable part of the culture of economic

128. Allen Buchanan, *Ethics, Efficiency, and the Market* (Totowa, N.J.: Rowman and Allanheld, 1985), p. 116.

129. See Louis Putterman, "Incentive Problems Favoring Noncentralized Investment Fund Ownership," in Bardhan and Roemer, *Market Socialism: The Current Debate*, pp. 156–58.

democracy and the mutuality that was discussed earlier as an essential part of the concept of human rights (1.2; 3.2). As we have seen, the mutuality of human rights is a stringent kind of symmetrical relation whereby each person has rights to freedom and well-being against all other persons and all other persons have these rights against him or her. In this way mutuality is a distributive relation: it bears on the rights of persons against each other. The enforcement of this mutuality helps to promote social solidarity; but the two values are not identical. Solidarity is a collective rather than a distributive relation. In it persons are brought closer together so that their common interests are promoted and differences between them are narrowed, and the persons accept and appreciate this kind of closeness. Such solidarity is especially promoted when equal human rights are secured, but it need not be confined to the sphere of rights; it may also concern other human emoluments. But in all such cases the solidarity is a feature of the community of rights in both of the ways distinguished above (3.4).

In the Mondragon system such solidarity is maintained in several institutional ways. There is income solidarity, whereby income differentials among members are kept within narrow limits of the ratio 4.5:1, and "the starting rate for unskilled workers was fixed at approximately the prevailing rate for similar jobs in the private sector."[130] This solidarity is also expressed in the pooling of profits and losses of all the firms in the inclusive cooperative, with the members' compensation derived from this pooling.[131] There is also community solidarity, especially with the surrounding Basque community, which takes such forms as creating Basque-language cooperative schools and refraining from placing new cooperative firms where they might compete with already existing Basque firms.[132] More generally, solidarity takes the form of assuring common, institutionalized outcomes: "Members of a given cooperative should rise and fall together; individuals should not gain while others lose."[133] This also applies to relations among the cooperatives, so that the structure is not to be that of a zero-sum game.[134] By the same token, there is an avowed "need for the more privileged to help those less fortunate."[135]

130. See Whyte and Whyte, *Making Mondragon*, pp. 44–45; Thomas and Logan, *Mondragon*, pp. 24–25. This point, including the idea that solidarity is itself among the members' "values," casts some doubt on N. Scott Arnold's assertion that an egalitarian income structure would involve an "exploitation" of the more skilled workers by the less skilled (*Philosophy and Economics of Market Socialism*, pp. 176–79). See Arnold, *Philosophy and Economics of Market Socialism*, pp. 180–81. See also above, n. 62, this chapter.
131. Whyte and Whyte, *Making Mondragon*, p. 61.
132. Ibid., p. 86.
133. Ibid., p. 258.
134. Ibid., p. 259.
135. Oakeshott, "Mondragon: Spain's Oasis of Democracy," p. 295.

These solidarist emphases all occur within a context of market competition; they are institutionalized ways in which the supportive organization modifies the competitive relations of the market. We have already seen that this moderation does not occur at the expense of efficiency (7.3, 6). It is further buttressed by other aspects of the strong cooperative culture that has been developed in Mondragon. There is no conclusive reason why such a culture cannot be developed elsewhere, in ways that exemplify the communitarian aspects of the community of rights. The invocation and practice of "mutual support" by workers during many phases of the promotion of labor union solidarity in the United States provide a suggestive example of such development.[136] This cooperative motivation is further strengthened by some more specifically moral and rational considerations. When persons become aware of the general human rights of other persons, this can provide a powerful counterbalance to the force of self-interest.[137]

While this moral consideration is of first importance in the context of justification, it is important not to exaggerate its influence in the context of motivation. As Nove has said, "let us not build an economic system on the assumption of high-minded altruism."[138] That such "altruism" cannot be attributed to the Mondragon workers is attested by the vehement strike that was called in 1974 by a large number of members who were dissatisfied with the new job evaluation program that would have a major impact on their rates of pay.[139]

It would nevertheless be a great oversimplification to ignore the institutionalized moral and cultural values that serve to buttress cooperative motivations in an economic democracy like that of Mondragon and in market socialism more generally. In such a truncated view, market socialism would be like the "worker's capitalism" referred to above (7.6), so that its only difference from capitalism would be in its "top management."[140] The motivational structure, both personal and institutional, that is required for universalized economic democracy (and that is exhibited in the

136. See the discussion of "mutual support," "sympathetic strikes," and "class solidarity" in Montgomery, *Workers' Control in America*, pp. 18–27.

137. See above, chap. 1, nn. 5, 27.

138. Nove, *Economics of Feasible Socialism Revisited*, p. 218.

139. Whyte and Whyte, *Making Mondragon*, pp. 93–102. See also the report (following the strike) that "The desire to share in the profits appeared to be the main reason members were attached to their cooperative" (p. 105).

140. See Charles E. Lindblom, *Politics and Markets* (New York: Basic Books, 1977), pp. 95–96: "As an alternative to private enterprise, market socialism is, in principle at least, easy to establish. Merely remove top management from all existing corporations and put government officials in their places. Or put the same managers back in their jobs, but make them government officials. Instruct them to carry on as before: produce and sell whatever customers will buy, pay for whatever inputs are necessary, avoid losses, cover costs."

Mondragon system) can perhaps be best characterized as one of mixed altruism. This structure is the same as that presented in the PGC as the principle of human rights: "Act in accord with the generic rights of your recipients as well as of yourself" (1.5). This principle does not require the kind of complete altruism that would negate one's own self-interest. It requires rather that, when moral rights are at stake, one be a reasonable self (3.6): that one respect the equal rights of other persons as well as one's own. Conversely, the kinds of important interests that are the objects of human rights must be protected for oneself as well as for others. Persons can become aware of the inherent rationality of this principle and can guide their behavior accordingly. Such seems to have happened to a considerable extent at Mondragon, and it may be applicable to the economic objects of human rights elsewhere as well. In these ways there are some strong grounds for holding that economic democracy can help to develop the solidarity that is a distinctive feature of genuine community within the context of human rights. Economic democracy thus serves to augment in a mutualist direction the phases of the fulfillment of economic and social rights that were developed in chapters 4 to 6.

In addition to the considerations so far discussed, critics have cited two further features of the Mondragon cooperatives that do not characterize other economies and that are hence held to be obstacles to "replicating" Mondragon's successes in a wider economic system. One feature bears on labor mobility, which is far lower in Mondragon than in most other modern industrial regions. Low mobility contributes to strong "community-cooperative links," which in turn cement "cooperative solidarity . . . through social network contact, generating familiarity and high trust relationships among cooperateurs." As a result, capital mobility is decreased, because workers are less likely to want to withdraw their capital while working for their firm. In addition, the linkages with the local communities "partially insulate the cooperatives from competitive pressures of the external labor market, permitting a more compressed payments scale."[141] Because other industrial societies have far greater labor mobility, it is held that these stabilizing aspects of the Mondragon system, which markedly contribute to its success, would not apply to these others. A second feature is the screening that we have seen to move Mondragon and other cooperatives in a meritocratic direction (7.5). This screening is concerned not only with the competence of individual applicants for employment but also with their "social acceptability," including their attitudes toward the local community, as well as with their monetary contribution in

---

141. Keith Bradley and Alan Gelb, "The Mondragon Cooperatives: Guidelines for a Cooperative Economy," in Jones and Svejnar, *Participatory and Self-Managed Firms*, pp. 157, 168. See also N. Scott Arnold, *Philosophy and Economics of Market Socialism*, p. 239.

giving the required down payment.[142] Such a screening process is said to yield "an unrepresentative sample of workers. . . . This type of cooperative might be hard pressed if it had to take in the highly heterogeneous and mobile labor force (not to mention some of the charmers from capitalism's underclass) that exists in the rest of the world."[143] So on both these grounds it is contended that the universalization I have upheld from Mondragon to other economies is untenable.

These arguments may have considerable plausibility insofar as they contrast the Mondragon system with existing capitalist industrial societies characterized by vast labor mobility and heterogeneity. The arguments are less cogent, however, when a whole economic system is envisaged on the Mondragon two-level model. In that model, community attachments serve markedly to decrease labor mobility. That such decrease is in fact possible in existing industrial societies is shown by the fact that it is closely approximated in Japan and Switzerland, as well as in the plywood cooperatives of the Pacific Northwest.[144] The universalized system of economic democracy would, moreover, build on the previously developed community of rights with its fulfillment of the rights to education, productive agency, income, and employment. This would provide a mutualist basis for the implementation of the system. In this way, the improved efficiency characteristic of economic democracy can serve to enhance its fulfillment of the human rights to freedom and well-being. In addition, the right to employment would be implemented for all persons either within or outside of the system of economic democracy. The two-level model of economic democracy can, then, be viewed as a feasible kind of economic system which has a vital role in the fuller establishment and functioning of the community of rights. In addition, although the screening procedures which give Mondragon its great labor-force solidarity would be maintained in the two-level model, it must be kept in mind that those procedures would not operate simply within existing capitalist societies with all their deprivations. Rather, what is envisaged here is that the selectivity would proceed within the context of the fulfillment of the right to productive agency, including its educational requirements with their equality of self-actualization (4.6–10).

7.8. ECONOMIC DEMOCRACY AND SOCIAL DEMOCRACY

The better to understand these points, we must look somewhat more explicitly at the relation between economic democracy as analyzed in this

142. Bradley and Gelb, "Mondragon Cooperatives," p. 158.
143. Arnold, *Philosophy and Economics of Market Socialism*, p. 168.
144. See Bradley and Gelb, "Mondragon Cooperatives," pp. 168–69.

chapter and the various economic and social rights upheld in chapters 4 to 6. On the one hand, economic democracy does not preclude those rights; although the arguments for them were set forth as moderating and correcting the deprivations found in market capitalism and other systems, they are just as valid in the context of economic democracy. On the other hand, the severe deprivations and inequalities of wealth and power that emphasized the need for fulfilling the rights would not arise in the system of economic democracy outlined above. But it does not follow that the discussions of chapters 4 to 6 can be simply done away with in favor of an exclusive concentration on economic democracy. Such a course would be utopian; we must begin from conditions as they are, and these require a concern for implementing the rights presented in the three preceding chapters. Economic democracy as here discussed can be regarded as culminating the economic biography and constitution developed in the earlier chapters; but so long as the severe deprivations that evoked them persist, they must receive the distinct attention I have given them here.

The same point applies to the various modifications and restrictions of private property rights that have been presented above, which serve to emphasize the nonabsoluteness of those rights, especially when they characterize the great inequalities and deprivations of modern societies. These restrictions have included the doctrines about the degrees of needfulness for action whereby property rights may be infringed to secure welfare and other basic goods (2.4) as well as the theses about social contribution, redistribution, and world ownership (3.4; 5.2, 5). These doctrines remain valid for the system of economic democracy presented here, although they would be moderated because the system would preclude the extreme inequalities of wealth that made their applications especially pressing. A main argument for economic democracy is that it would make far more accessible the economic and social rights to freedom and well-being whose fulfillment is jeopardized in a system of market capitalism characterized by the severe problems emphasized by the deprivation focus.

It must nevertheless be recognized that the arguments of chapters 4 to 6, taken by themselves, can provide a justification for a social-democratic welfare state within a system of market capitalism. Such a state could go far toward fulfilling elemental social and economic rights and thereby removing some of the main wrongs and harms encapsulated in the deprivation focus. This does not mean, however, that in the full normative institution of the community of rights the right to economic democracy may be left unfulfilled. On the contrary, that institution requires for its full realization that its economic system be one of economic democracy in the universalized form presented above. But while there is indeed a right to economic democracy on the grounds upheld in this chapter, that right may be deemed less pressing than the rights upheld earlier, which may be fulfilled in a system of social democracy operating within a capitalist economy. The criterion of degrees of needfulness for action may be invoked here: important as economic democracy is for the rights to freedom and well-being, if circumstances require a choice between economic democracy and the welfare, education, income, and employment that are the objects of the rights upheld in chapters 4 to 6, the latter must be given priority. The choice may be required by the restricted resources available for pressing the claims to the respective rights. Nevertheless, amid the codetermination found in some social-democratic capitalist systems, the fuller self-determination provided in the system of economic democracy is an important right that deserves recognition in the full community of rights. Various combinations of social democracy and economic democracy may also be maintained.[145] In this way the community of rights may be fulfilled in varying degrees that take account of relevant empirical possibilities, while at the same time the mandatoriness of the rights is upheld.

145. For valuable discussions of such combinations, see Nove, *Economics of Feasible Socialism Revisited*, pt. 5. See also n. 9 to this chapter.

EIGHT

THE RIGHT TO POLITICAL DEMOCRACY

8.1. POLITICAL DEMOCRACY AS THE METHOD OF CONSENT

The preceding chapters have presented the community of rights as a solidaristic system dedicated to fulfilling the equal economic and social rights of all persons. In accordance with the deprivation focus, major emphasis has been placed on protecting and promoting the freedom and well-being of the more vulnerable members of society. What has emerged from this discussion is both an economic biography and an economic constitution. The members of the most deprived groups, while being given the protection of welfare payments, have also received, from their earliest years, an education that equips them for productive agency in both the general and economic senses, with attendant autonomy and acceptance of personal responsibility. They have thereby been enabled to earn an adequate income, have been assured of employment, and have received the emoluments of economic democracy. Parallel with this development, the community of rights has been based on an economic constitution that provides, for the whole society, the legally sanctioned policies and institutions that establish these measures of welfare, education, income property, employment, and workers' control. As a result, there has been a marked reduction in the great inequalities of economic and political power that were among the main sources of the need for protection of vulnerable persons' rights.

These outcomes have been presented not as utopian hopes for a better world but as requirements of justice whose moral mandatoriness has been established on the basis of the principle of human rights. These outcomes, moreover, are readily available through resources that are presently within the reach of Western democratic societies. Other societies should also be helped to attain these resources and to move toward such outcomes, as part of the mutuality of obligations that underlies the community of rights. Through this community a greater equalization of economic and political power will be attained.

Among the problems that confront the envisaged outcomes I have just sketched, two must especially be noted here, because they bear on the motivations or incentives that affect the implementation of the indicated policies. One problem concerns the recipients of the policies; the other concerns their agents. What assurance is there that the persons whom the policies are intended to help will be willing to accept them? There is at least a potential gap between the institutional elaboration of policies and the acquiescence of persons and groups who are their intended beneficiaries. Will such persons be willing to undergo the exertions and discipline required for the development of productive agency? May they not opt instead for a permanent life on welfare assistance?

In reply, it must first of all be kept in mind that persons do not have positive rights to be helped to have basic well-being unless they cannot secure it by their own efforts (2.3). Persons may hence be denied such assistance if they can help themselves. By the same token, they have an incentive to acquire the productive agency that enables them to act more successfully in pursuit of their purposes. This incentive is furthered by considerations of self-esteem and self-respect, based on persons' awareness of the mutuality required by the morality grounded in the principle of human rights. Such awareness, and the accompanying motivations, can be especially fostered by the early education, emotional as well as intellectual, that helps to develop the abilities of productive agency (4.9, 10).

Let us now turn to the agents of the policies comprised in the community of rights: the respondents of the rights. I have thus far presented these policies as being institutionally embodied in an economic constitution. But it is not enough to have argued for them on the basis of their being required by the principle of human rights. That they are justified in this way still leaves open the question of how they are to be brought into effect, how they are to be enforced and stabilized in the actual conditions of society. This question sets the problem of the remainder of this chapter.

Our problem in this chapter, then, is an intensely practical one: How, in the existing conditions of society, are to be brought about the various policies of the economic constitution that protect all persons' equal rights? How are existing states to be made into communities of rights? As we have previously recognized, the welfare states of social democracy already encompass some of these institutions to some degree. But, as we have also seen, in the major capitalist states, especially including the United States, there remain very extensive areas of severe economic deprivation and misery, and thus violations of human rights (4.1; 7.1). The analyses of the various policies and institutions upheld in the preceding chapters have tried to show how the principle of human rights can be applied in a fundamental way to remove the causes of these violations. But to make these applications effective requires the use of political means.

I have previously argued that this effectuation of the principle of human rights cannot be left either to markets or to private charity, but must instead be a duty of the state as a community of rights (2.5). But I have also held that the establishment of economic democracy must be effected through a democratic political process (7.1). Accordingly, when it is said that the state as a community of rights must be the effectuating agency of the economic and social rights, an essential addition must be made: the state in question must be democratic. For, besides the economic and social human rights discussed above, there is also a political human right of persons that they be governed by democratic states. This right derives from the generic human right to freedom in a way already sketched in the justification of economic democracy (7.3).

This appeal to political democracy raises many fundamental questions, of which four must receive special attention here. The first two are empirical, the others normative. First, how likely is it that politically democratic states, operating through consensual electoral procedures, will be willing to support the fulfillments of the economic and social human rights to which attention has been called above? These fulfillments will require vast resources of wealth, especially to give both the children of deprived parents and the parents themselves the educations and subsequent employment opportunities they need in order to escape the debilitating and degrading conditions under which they live. A second, closely related question is this: when it is said that "the state," as a community of rights, must be charged with effectuating the human rights, how likely is it that this charge will be fulfilled in view not only of the conflicting interest-group pressures to which democratic politicians are subjected but also of the inefficiencies of political control? Third, because of the enormous importance of fulfilling the economic and social rights, is it justified to subject this fulfillment to the contingencies of democratic consensual decisions, including the strong possibility that middle-class voters will reject the financial sacrifices which the fulfillment would require? In this regard the question of the "overload" prescribed by positive rights (2.5) must again receive attention. Fourth, especially in view of the previous questions, what is the justification of political democracy in the first place? Is there a right to political democracy, such that it should have the preferred position among the varieties of possible political systems?

I shall now deal with these four questions in the reverse order from that in which I have just stated them.

First, then, on the right to political democracy. Is there such a right, and what is its justification? We saw above that the right to economic democracy is a collective right, not directly an individual one, in that its direct object is a collective good, a system of organizing economic production and distribution (7.1). This also applies to the right to political democracy. Its direct object is an institutional procedure for determining the possession and exercise of political authority. But just as economic democracy was also seen to be for the individual worker's good as fulfilling her rights to freedom and well-being, so too, more generally, political democracy is justified because it is a political expression of the equal right to freedom for all persons. This equal right entails a system of mutual obligations whereby citizens are enabled to participate equally in political action. And it is the consensual procedures of political democracy as a community of rights that must be used to effectuate the economic rights discussed above in terms of the economic biography of the gradual relief of deprivation. In this way the rights become incorporated into the economic constitution of the community of rights, with their subsequent judicial and executive enforcement. This is a major illustration of the conciliation of rights and community stressed in chapters 1 to 3 above, for it shows how the economic and political human rights require for their effectuation a consensual institutional system of mutual support.

Two objections to this must be noted at once. First, many of the specific rights justified above, such as the rights to welfare, education, productive agency, and employment can be and have been fulfilled to varying degrees in societies that were not political democracies. Hence, political democracy is not a necessary condition of the effectuation of these rights, so that to this extent the consequentialist argument for political democracy as being instrumental to such effectuation is at best inconclusive. A second objection is that the democratic state, like all states, operates through the actual or implicit exercise of coercive force. Hence, it cannot be justified by the human right to freedom.

To deal with these objections, we must first recall that procedures, methods, or means are morally important in their own right, quite apart from their contribution to the bringing about of consequences, outcomes, or ends. We have seen this from the outset in the fundamental thesis that there is a procedural human right to freedom as well as a substantive human right to well-being, despite the criterion of degrees of needfulness for action that sometimes operates to subordinate particular freedoms (2.4). We have also seen this procedural emphasis in the theses of productivist welfarism and the right to productive agency (4.6), and in the antecedentalist justification of property rights (5.3).

Now the right to political democracy is also a procedural right. For political democracy is a procedure that is used to determine which persons will have political authority in a state, including the legislators who decide the contents of specific laws and the executives who administer them. The essence of this procedure is the method of consent, which may be analyzed as having three main features. First, the civil liberties are mutually and equally available to all adult persons in the society (with such minor exceptions as criminals). Second, these liberties are used to discuss and advocate various social policies and the election of officials who will promote them. Third, these officials' authority is contingent on their winning the election by the required majority or plurality of votes, and elections are held periodically, with continuing use of the civil liberties available to those who have lost as well as those whose side has won the election. (Important qualifications of these norms will be discussed below, 8.4–6.)

As involving the civil liberties, the right to political democracy is an application of the PGC's right to freedom. The PGC's protection of this right requires that each person be left free to engage in any action or transaction according to his unforced choice so long as he does not coerce or harm other persons. These protected actions include speaking, publishing, and associating with others, so that, as a matter of constitutional requirement, each person is able, if he chooses, to discuss, criticize, and vote for or against the government and to work actively with other persons or groups of various sizes to further his political objectives. In these ways an important kind of social pluralism is provided for, in that, within the limits set by human rights (4.11), persons are free to associate with one another in many different ways in pursuit of their own values, thereby forming a kind of "civil society" that is independent of state control but that serves rather to control the state by limiting its spheres of action. So here the community of rights is social as well as political.

The freedoms in question are called 'civil liberties' for three interconnected reasons, bearing on three different relations the freedoms must have to the state. First, the freedoms are passive and negative in that they must not be restricted or interfered with by the state. Second, they are passive and positive in that they must be protected by the state as equal and mutual rights of persons. Third, they are active in that the actions that are their objects operate in the political process to help determine, through a consensual institutional arrangement, who shall govern in the state. In all relations, the PGC requires that the civil liberties pertain equally to each adult prospective purposive agent in the state (except criminals): each person has an equal right to use his freedom noncoercively and nonharmfully (where harm consists in violating the basic, nonsubtractive, or additive rights to well-being), to participate freely and actively in the political process, and to be protected by the state in that participation and in his other actions.[1] Insofar as there are diverse states, this equal right pertains to each citizen, and each person has a right to be a citizen of a state having the civil liberties. These considerations provide a procedural justification of political democracy, in that the procedures involving the equal distribution of the civil liberties, which are justified by the PGC as the principle of human rights, serve in turn to justify the institution of political democracy. Such a politically democratic state, with its mutuality of rights and duties, is a vitally important part of the community of rights.

As was noted above, there may be states that protect economic rights without being politically democratic. Although this protection is itself of great value, such states derogate from the personal autonomy that is an essential part of the human right to freedom (see also 4.2). This point can also be put in terms of the contrast between agency and passive recipience to which attention was called above in my discussions of welfare and of the distinction between antecedentalist and consequentialist justifications of property rights (4.3, 6; 5.3). Persons who are denied the effective use of the civil liberties and hence of political democracy are put into a position of dependence and subservience, of being political recipients of the agency of others, as against being agents on their own behalf. This is a violation of the human right to freedom.

Although the freedom of action to which there is a human right is not identical with the political freedom of political democracy, there is a close connection between them. For freedom of action, like well-being, is a necessary condition not only of action but of generally successful action; and the absence of political freedom may sharply restrict persons' range of successful actions: such is the experience not only of slaves but also of other subjects of repressive regimes. Just as freedom of action consists in controlling one's behavior by one's unforced choice while having knowledge of relevant circumstances, so by political freedom, which includes the civil liberties, one participates in controlling one's rulers, including their impact on one's own behavior. The political freedom involving the use of the civil liberties in political democracy thus has important continuities with the general freedom of action to which all persons have rights.

Political democracy is both a constituent of the community of rights and a means toward effectuating it. As we have seen, insofar as the state is a community of rights it protects the human rights of all its members, while at the same time it embodies the equality and mutuality of human rights themselves (3.4). Political democracy is a part both of that embodi-

1. See RM, 202–22, 230–36, 264–67; also my Human Rights: Essays on Justification and Applications (Chicago: University of Chicago Press, 1982), pp. 56–57.

ment and of the protections it provides. Insofar as the right to political democracy is a collective right, its respondent is the collectivity of persons who support the system of political democracy because, as was noted above, it is a political expression of the right to freedom for all persons. This collectivity, however, is comprised of individuals and, as we shall see (8.2), they give their rational consent to being governed by a democratic regime.

How is the political freedom of democracy compatible with the coercion which is an essential part of political authority? One answer to this question is given by the "paradox of freedom" according to which freedom requires unfreedom (5.2). This involves, among other things, that to protect any one person's freedom requires the constitutionally mandatory restriction, by force if necessary, of the freedom of any others to remove or interfere with that person's freedom. For this reason there must be laws that are coercive, even if not coercing.

A further answer to the question of coercion requires careful attention to several distinctions, which I have tried to spell out in detail elsewhere (RM, 306–7). A main point is that the method of consent operates *within* the state, but not as *grounding* the state. That there is to be a minimal state with coercive laws to protect against criminals is not itself subject to persons' optional consents or choices. (This is one of the errors of contractualist theories of political obligation.) For the existence of such a state is required by the principle of human rights as morally necessary. A main reason for this is that basic well-being, to which all persons have equal rights, is protected by the criminal law embodied in the minimal state. Because basic well-being is a necessary good of action, its protection cannot be left to persons' optional choices or consents. Similarly, that states must be democratic, using the method of consent in designating their officials, is also not subject to persons' optional consents; as we have seen, this is required by the human right to freedom in the way indicated above. But for designating their specific officials and laws the PGC requires that the voluntary consents of the persons subject to them must be invoked as fully as possible through the effective use of the civil liberties in an electoral system. In this way as much freedom is preserved as is compatible with the moral necessity of having states and democratically enacted laws. So the problem of how political freedom is compatible with political coercion is solved through combining the constitutional mandatoriness of having coercive or binding laws with the procedural consensualness of using the method of consent, including the civil liberties, to determine the contents of specific laws and officials. The minimal state and the democratic state comprise two distinct phases or parts of the community of rights. Community and rights, far from being antithetical to one another, are brought together because the human rights to freedom and well-being are both protected by and exemplified in political systems of mutual support.

8.2. SHOULD ECONOMIC RIGHTS BE SUBJECT TO POLITICAL DEMOCRACY?

The human rights that figure in the political democracy of the community of rights include not only the political rights of the civil liberties but also the economic and social rights that were upheld in the preceding four chapters. We have seen that none of these rights should be left for their effectuation to the vicissitudes of the market or to the voluntary efforts of private charity, although the latter can be a valuable supplement. But now the following problem arises: Should the economic and social rights be subject for their effectuation to the consensual procedures of political democracy? There is a dilemma here: If the answer is negative, then political democracy is in effect made irrelevant to vitally important segments of human social life, since it is, or at least may be, excluded from dealing with the economic institutional bases of the necessary goods of freedom and well-being; instead, decisions about those bases may be made contingent upon persons' optional choices or may be undemocratically imposed on the members of the society regardless of their own wishes. On the other hand, if the answer is affirmative, then the economic and social rights that we have seen to be essential for the necessary goods of action are left to the variable and shifting decisions of democratic majorities, so that there is no guarantee that the rights will be fulfilled. So by the negative answer the political rights of democracy may be infringed, while by the affirmative answer the economic and social rights may be infringed.[2]

This conflict reflects familiar problems of democratic political theory, bearing as they do on the relations between democratic methods and libertarian-egalitarian outcomes. Ultimately the problems may be traced

---

2. This dilemma is not the same as the more general "underlying dilemma" that Robert A. Dahl attributes to pluralist democracy: "Organizations ought to possess autonomy, and at the same time they should also be controlled" (*Dilemmas of Pluralist Democracy* [New Haven, Conn.: Yale University Press, 1982], p. 1). The political rights might be assimilated to "autonomy" and the economic rights to "control," but this would require considerable stretching. Although the political democracy horn of the political democracy–economic rights dilemma may be construed as involving an aggregation of a social ordering out of individual orderings, the dilemma in its central point does not involve such aggregation, so that it is not subject to the famous "impossibility theorem" set forth by Kenneth Arrow, *Social Choice and Individual Values,* 2d ed. (New York: John Wiley and Sons, 1963). The political democracy–economic rights dilemma would remain even if the aggregation discussed by Arrow were entirely possible, because the dilemma bears on values—economic rights—that are distinct from such aggregation.

back to the relation between freedom and well-being as, respectively, the procedural and the substantive necessary goods of action; for these may conflict in various ways, including when agents use their freedom in opposition even to their own well-being (*RM*, 260–67, 319–22).

While recognizing the difficulties of each horn of the dilemma just stated, I shall here argue for the affirmative answer, but only within certain important limits. To begin with, both political and economic rights stem from the constitution of the community of rights, whose contents are determined by the principle of human rights. This determination involves that both sets of rights have rational justifications as being constitutive of or instrumental to the necessary goods of action and generally successful action. To this extent, there is no conflict between the two sets of rights. Insofar as the common foundation of the rights is effectively recognized, the procedural political rights will lead to or support the substantive economic rights. This means that the economic rights are subject to the procedures of political democracy only in a secondary sense. In the primary sense, the economic rights, like the political rights, are subject to the universal principle of equal human rights which provides their rational justification. The economic rights are subject to political democracy only in the secondary sense that the procedures for establishing and effectuating the economic rights are to be democratic ones; but, insofar as these procedures are maintained in their status of being rationally justified by the principle of human rights, they do not depart from but rather uphold the economic rights. Each set of rights is in this way kept inviolate, and each supports the other by virtue of their common rational foundation.

Another way to put this point is by the distinction between rational and empirical consent (see *RM*, 302–9). Rational consent is consent that is based on rational recognition of the arguments for the principle of human rights and its various implications. Such consent, then, is necessary insofar as persons recognize that they logically must accept the argument justifying the human rights (1.5). Empirical consent, on the other hand, is optional and contingent; it can vary from one person to another depending on her variable opinions and interests. Insofar as persons rationally consent to the principle of human rights, they will also rationally consent to both the political and the economic rights as providing justified procedural and substantive grounds, respectively, for the social institutions of the community of rights.

This thesis raises the following question: If the economic rights are rationally justified by the principle of human rights, then why do we have to use the democratic political rights at all as validating or legitimating the economic rights? Within the rational context just indicated, the answer is that social institutions include procedures for determining their contents.

Since, as we have seen, the democratic method of consent is the rationally justified procedure, it must be the one that is invoked for incorporating the economic rights into the effective constitution of the community of rights.

We must next recognize again, however, that there are potential conflicts between the economic rights and the political rights of democracy. The method of consent used in political democracy is empirical, that is, it is an empirical phenomenon; whether, as actually implemented, it is also rational in the sense indicated above depends on various circumstances. As empirical, the democratic method of consent is confronted by the fact that there are many conflicts of opinions and interests concerning the economic rights. Even if the general principle of human rights is accepted, there may be many disagreements over the question of whether, or to what extent, the economic rights are indeed specifications of this general principle (see 3.8). These disagreements provide an important basis for appealing to democratic decision procedures. More generally, while emphasis must still be laid on the rational arguments for the economic rights, careful attention must also be paid to how—by what procedures—the rights are to be effectuated and incorporated into the ongoing constitution of the state. This is the question of how the normative structure of the community of rights is to be made effective in states as they are. This question is itself in one respect normative, in another respect empirical.

The normative question is our previous one of whether rights, including economic ones, should be made contingent for their effectuation on decisions arrived at by political processes. Doesn't their being rights give them a moral justification that should exempt them from being subject to the potential risks and vicissitudes of democratic majoritarian debates and sanctions? In particular, since governments as representing their individual citizens are the respondents of the rights (2.5), doesn't this fact of itself require that governments help the holders of the rights to have the economic goods to which they are entitled? Hence, far from being contingent on the outcomes of democratic electoral processes, isn't the effectuation of the economic rights logically required by the fact of their being morally justified rights?

This question rests in part on a logically prior question about the appropriate sphere of political decision making: When should an issue be regarded as a political one subject to resolution by democratic procedures? This question is partly a conceptual one about the meaning of "political." But it is also a moral question, for it bears on whether, or to what extent, moral rights and other important values should be left vulnerable to the empirical, optional decision-procedures of democratic electorates. In view of its relevance to our present project, we must look more closely at this joint conceptual-moral question.

We may distinguish three different answers that have been given to this question. One answer bears on the grounds for choices or outcomes. It holds that an issue is a political one, and thus subject to the variable choices made in democratic electoral politics, only if there is disagreement on the issue, some practical choice has to be made concerning it, and the choosers are "without independent grounds for making the choice . . . without guiding standards or determining norms."[3] A related way of putting this point is that an issue is not a political one, not subject to democratic decision making, in cases "where there is an independent standard for the correctness of an outcome," such as where a minority's rights must not be violated by a majority's decision. For in such cases the outcome of itself determines whether a policy is justified; the fairness or rightness of the political procedure whereby the outcome is attained is held to carry no independent moral justificatory weight.[4]

On this view, the issues of economic rights would not be "political" issues subject to the electoral procedures of political democracy because the recommendations concerning them that have been presented here have rested on "guiding standards," namely, the criteria that ultimately go back to the principle of human rights. To justify their being political issues would hence, on this view, require surrendering the theses that there are indeed rationally and morally grounded rights to welfare, productive agency, employment, and so forth.

This answer is too draconian. It depicts the "political" as resting on an uncharted moral sea, one "where truth is not—or is not *yet*—known."[5] One may, of course, give so austere a definition of "truth" that its ascertainment, or indeed its existence, in any practical context is beyond human reach. But, to take two clear examples, the issues of slavery in the nineteenth century and of civil rights in the twentieth did not cease to be political because there were firm rational grounds for the moral positions that were taken on them. What made them political issues was, at a minimum, that there were sharp conflicts of opinions and interests concerning them and that they figured very prominently in debates concerning governmental policy. But it is a fallacy to infer, from the fact of disagreement over some issue, that there are not rationally definitive grounds for upholding one side of the issue as against other sides. So the fact that the economic rights have

3. Benjamin Barber, *Strong Democracy* (Berkeley and Los Angeles: University of California Press, 1984), pp. 20–21. See also Joseph Schumpeter, *Capitalism, Socialism, and Democracy* (London: George Allen and Unwin, 1950), pp. 251–52; David Miller, *Market, State, and Community* (Oxford: Clarendon Press, 1989), p. 253.

4. See William N. Nelson, *On Justifying Democracy* (London: Routledge and Kegan Paul, 1980), pp. 22–23, 111.

5. Barber, *Strong Democracy*, p. 129; emphasis in original.

a rational justification does not, of itself, debar them from being subject to the procedures of political democracy.

A second possible answer to the question of when an issue should be regarded as a political one would concede that there are indeed moral rights to productive agency and so forth, so that the theses that have here been upheld concerning them are rationally grounded; but nevertheless these economic rights raise political issues because it is not generally known or accepted that they are genuine rights, so that further argument and persuasion are needed. Democratic politics would provide the sphere for such argument and persuasion.

While I think this answer is on the right track, it incurs at least two difficulties. One is elitism: the view that some persons have deeper moral insight or rationality than others, so that the former are in possession of moral truths about which they must patiently try to convince the latter. Nevertheless, this is not an overpowering difficulty if one holds that moral disputes are subject to rational arguments and solutions. The claim is not that some persons have a power of moral intuition not available to other persons; on the contrary, the claim focuses on reasons or grounds that, with sufficient analysis and argument, can be understood by all persons. The antislavery agitators of the nineteenth century and the civil rights advocates of the twentieth can, without distortion, be depicted as upholding rationally grounded moral truths about which they sought to persuade other persons. The need and willingness to persuade are a tribute to the potential rationality of all persons as capable of understanding the reasons that ground the rights. So the rational justifiability of the rights does not debar them from being subject to the procedures of democratic decision making.

A further difficulty of the second answer recurs to the general question raised above: If what is at issue here concerns genuine moral rights, then why should they be subjected to the conflicts and possible compromises of democratic politics? After all, if persons have a moral right to X, then they ought to be protected in their having X as a matter of what is personally owed to them, so that they have a definitive claim to X.

The cogency of this difficulty, with its severe diremption between moral rights and democratic politics, cannot be accepted simply as stated. It overlooks at least two salient points. First, there may be conflicts *between* rights, so that simply being a right is not sufficient to remove the need for political conflict resolution. Second, there may be conflicts *about* rights: Even when strong arguments are given to show that there is a right to X, there may also be strong opposing arguments, so that there is still an important place for the kinds of public rational discussion and deliberation that political democracy makes possible and that are an important part of the community of rights.

A third answer to the question of when an issue should be regarded as appropriately subject to democratic political procedures builds on the one just given in a way that may avoid its difficulties. We recur to the point that there must be public disagreement over the issue. But this is only an initial point, at most a necessary, not a sufficient condition of being appropriately subject to democratic debate. (Is it even a necessary condition? Suppose there were near or complete agreement about the rightness of slavery; would it then not have been an appropriate political issue, one that *should* have been subject to democratic debate?) The more directly salient point is that while the economic rights are derived from the rationally grounded principle of human rights, they are derived as specifications of the human rights. As such, they rest in large part on empirical or factual allegations to the effect that certain institutional arrangements are required for persons' having the freedom and well-being that are the general objects of the human rights. Now, as we noted above, such statements of requirements, either as necessary or as sufficient conditions or both, may leave open alternative possibilities as to means to the given ends (3.8). While there are rational arguments for the economic rights I have upheld, there may also be rational arguments for different and even opposed arrangements, so that the rights have a certain element of normative contingency, as against the generic rights themselves. Thus, quite apart from the undeniable conflicts of interests that exist in this sphere, there are also grounds for rational discussion and debate. It is these grounds that make it appropriate, and indeed mandatory, that the economic rights be subject to the deliberative procedures of political democracy, with its method of consent and use of the civil liberties.

In addition to these factual or empirical considerations, there are also joint conceptual and normatively moral considerations that figure in the ways that the economic rights are specifications of the general human rights and should be subject to democratic political procedures. The very meaning of "freedom" or "well-being" and its applications in complex areas like welfare, education, employment, or workers' control may leave open many possibilities of alternative interpretations and evaluations. These problems are similar to those of interpreting the United States Constitution with its provisions for "freedom of speech" or "equal protection of the laws." But where the Constitution has a Supreme Court that makes decisions on the basis of "original intention" or other criteria, the principle of human rights as embodied in the PGC appeals rather to the rational arguments that have been invoked throughout this book to justify the economic rights upheld here.

It is, then, to these rational arguments that attention must be directed when warnings are issued about the dangers of subjecting human rights to the consensual procedures of political democracy. What is vitally important here is that those procedures themselves are inherently rational in the crucial respect that they make available the public deliberation, debate, and scrutiny of opposing arguments that figure in the democratic method of consent using the civil liberties and that stem from the mutuality of the community of rights. Thus while there is no guarantee that those procedures will have as their outcome the effectuation, in a constitution and accompanying laws, of the economic rights for which I have argued, the practical problem of effectuation comes closest to a rationally justified solution when the democratic procedures are used for that purpose. In this regard, it is important to keep in mind that the state as the community of rights embodies the political rights of democracy as well as the social and economic rights upheld in chapters 4 to 7.

8.3. SHOULD BASIC RIGHTS AND POLITICAL RIGHTS BE SUBJECT TO POLITICAL DEMOCRACY?

The answer I have just given to the question of whether economic rights should be subject to the decision-making procedures of political democracy may be further clarified if a similar question is asked about other parts of the general principle of human rights. We have already seen above that the method of consent does not extend to the grounding either of the minimal state or of the democratic state (8.1). Consider first the personal basic rights to freedom and well-being, which, insofar as they are negative rights, require abstention from murder, enslavement, physical assault, illegal imprisonment, and other crimes that are basic harms. These basic rights should not be subject to the democratic political process for decision about whether they should be fulfilled or not, because they are not specifications of the general human rights; they are not means to the fulfillment of the generic rights to freedom and well-being. Rather, they directly are those rights; they are not instrumental to them but are constitutive of them in their most basic part. For violations of these rights are attacks against the essential preconditions of action (*RM*, 53–54, 211–17). Concerning their relation to the generic rights to freedom and well-being, then, there is no question about whether they will serve or promote or help to effectuate the rights. To infringe these personal rights is directly to infringe the human rights themselves that are the foundations of moral rightness. Hence, while there may be philosophical questions about the rational arguments that justify that there are human rights and that they are rights to freedom and well-being as the necessary conditions of action and generally successful action, there are no valid or legitimate questions about whether the criminal basic harms are violations of human rights and should be prohibited. So it should not be left to the democratic political process, with its possibly varying outcomes, to determine whether these basic human rights should be effectuated (see also *RM*, 301–3).

There are two areas where basic harms like those mentioned above can be legitimate objects of democratic decision making. One is when conflicts of rights and other complications may arise to leave open the question of whether the harms in particular cases are indeed crimes. Killing and assault in self-defense are obvious examples. Here juries and other modes of deliberation are appropriate means of arriving at decisions. Second, there may be questions about what penalties should be imposed for crimes that violate the basic rights of persons. Here democratic debate is also appropriate. I have argued elsewhere that the basis of criminal punishment should be primarily retributive and only secondarily deterrent (*RM*, 294–301). But the relevance of democratic debate to questions of criminal punishment leaves untouched the thesis that the prohibition of basic harms that are crimes should not be left to the democratic political process. Rather, this should be part of the constitution that upholds the human rights of persons. It is the most basic part of the community of rights, and it embodies the conciliation of rights and community at the fundamental level of constitutional solidarity.

Let us now turn to the political rights of the democratic process itself. Should it be left to that process to determine whether persons are to have the civil liberties? These political rights, unlike the economic rights, are constitutive of political democracy. Hence, to make the political rights subject to the democratic political process would be to call into question the core of that process itself. The civil liberties are presuppositions of political democracy, so that they cannot also be regarded as outcomes of political democracy and as possibly subject to abolition by the democracy acting as a democracy.

The case of the Weimar Republic's using the democratic state to abolish its democracy may be a sobering empirical example of this issue. But this shows a deficiency of the Weimar constitution itself, not of the principled relation here upheld. It can also be argued that the situation of Germany in 1933 was so pathological, with its huge economic hardships and other unnerving instabilities, that it cannot be regarded as typical.[6] Our present question, in any case, is normative, not empirical. The tragic out-

---

6. Compare, however, the threat of fascism in the United States during the Depression. See Arthur M. Schlesinger, Jr., *The Politics of Upheaval, 1935–1936* (Boston: Houghton Mifflin, 1960), chap. 5, "The Dream of Fascism," pp. 69–95; also pp. 26–28.

come of the German vote serves, if anything, to reinforce the negative answer to the question of whether the existence of the civil liberties should be left to democratic decision making.

I have thus far argued for a contrast between economic and political rights, in that while the economic rights should be subject for their effectuation to the democratic political process, the political rights should not. There is, however, an important respect in which both kinds of rights can be affirmatively related to the democratic process. This involves that, with regard to the economic rights, there is an intermediate position between holding that they should be completely outside of or impervious to the democratic political process and holding that they should be vulnerable to the variable decisions of shifting democratic majorities. The difficulty with the latter position is that the economic rights, despite what I have called their specificatory relation to the generic human rights, are so important for human freedom and well-being, especially for deprived persons, that, at least in their main outlines, they should be kept inviolate. But this is also the situation with regard to the civil liberties that are the political rights of democracy.

The solution that is called for regarding both kinds of rights is a constitutional one. There should be a constitution that is initially set up by a democratic political process, but which then gives a fixed, firm status to both the political and the economic rights.[7] As parts of the constitution, both sets of rights have a stability and permanence that exempts them from the possibly changing views of shifting majorities. This solution does justice to the joint convictions that, with certain qualifications, social arrangements which affect persons' most vital interests should be subject to their approval (7.3) and that there should be stability and dependability in their protection of those interests.

This constitutional solution could still leave the economic rights more open to democratic deliberation than the political rights, for at least two reasons. First, since, as was already noted, the political rights are constitutive of political democracy while the economic rights are not, continued political deliberation over the economic rights would not call into question the very basis of that deliberation as would a similar process applied to the political rights. Second, although the political rights, like the economic ones, are specifications of the generic rights to freedom and well-being, the political rights leave far fewer alternatives as instrumental to effectuating the generic rights. It has, indeed, been held that, according to the criterion

7.   For this thesis with regard to political rights, see Stephen Holmes, "Precommitment and the Paradox of Democracy," in Jon Elster and Rune Slagstad, eds., *Constitutionalism and Democracy* (Cambridge: Cambridge University Press, 1988), pp. 195–240.

of degrees of needfulness for action, democratic political rights may be detrimental to, or at least are less important than, economic rights to subsistence and other vital needs. But, as we saw above, there are strong reasons for rejecting this ranking (2.4). On the other hand, the democratic political process, while enshrining the economic rights in a constitution that recognizes their role in protecting vital interests of freedom and well-being, must also leave open the possibility of continuing debate over economic systems and policies. This debate should also confront and test further the arguments set forth in this book, which I have presented as being rationally grounded in the principle of human rights, especially as bearing on the relief of suffering and deprivation.

8.4. WILL ECONOMIC RIGHTS BE SUPPORTED BY POLITICAL DEMOCRACY?

In the preceding sections I was largely concerned with the normative question of whether the economic rights, as genuinely human rights, should be subject to the democratic process with its possibly alternative outcomes. I turn now to the empirical question of how effective political democracy can or will be in fulfilling these rights through legally enforced social policies. It is important to take up this empirical question, because the kind of idealization of the rationality of the democratic process to which I appealed above should be counterbalanced by the conflicts of interest that may hinder the realization of that rationality. These conflicts generate crucial difficulties for the project of relieving the sufferings of the masses of persons who figure in the deprivation focus, and whose equal rights to economic and social goods are most directly jeopardized.

In view of these conflicts, we must recognize an important distinction about the meaning of the empirical question of whether political democracy will support fulfillment of the economic rights. One meaning is constitutional and legislative: it bears on whether the consensual processes of political democracy will lead to the enactment of a constitution and accompanying laws that support the fulfillment of the economic and social rights.[8] The other meaning is executive: it asks whether the government itself, even if it is elected by democratic methods, is the best or most efficient way of implementing the economic rights. These two questions are distinct because a democratically elected government that legislates the constitutional fulfillment of the economic rights may decide to leave the implementation of that fulfillment in private hands whose operations may be only loosely controlled by the government. This policy is sometimes

8. On this question, see Miller, *Market, State, and Community*, pp. 236–37.

called "privatization," and it is opposed to policies whereby the government itself, through elected or appointed officials, performs executive functions of entrepreneurship, management, delivery of services, and so forth.

Privatization may take many different forms,[9] and it raises important issues both of efficiency and of justice. In the present context, however, the most important point derives from the thesis presented above that, for reasons both of assurance and of fairness, the state, as a community of rights, must be the primary respondent of the economic and social rights (2.5). The sense of "respondent" here is directly the legislative one: The state through its democratically based laws must require the various institutions and policies of what I have called the "economic constitution" to provide for the fulfillment of the economic and social rights, including welfare, education, employment, and so forth. Whether the constitutional and legislative requirements themselves are to be laid down cannot be left open as a function of privatization: neither the market nor private charity is to be entrusted with decisions concerning whether the requirements are to be set. It is a quite distinct matter, however, whether the legislated requirements are themselves to be carried out by the state; here, questions of efficiency may become especially important.[10] Thus, to take an example from an only partially related sphere, it is one thing to hold that air traffic control may be operated more efficiently by private managers;[11] but it is a quite different thing to hold that whether there should be an air traffic control system at all (or a system performing analogous safety functions) should itself be left to the profit-oriented decisions of private entrepreneurs who may opt not to perform such services if it does not pay them to do so. The decision on the latter question should be a function of the state as the protector of vital social interests and individual rights.[12] Important moral issues may indeed be raised by privatization: the transfer of property rights into private hands may exacerbate economic inequalities, and the subject-

9. See John Vickers and George Yarrow, *Privatization: An Economic Analysis* (Cambridge, Mass.: MIT Press, 1988); Sheila B. Kamerman and Alfred J. Kahn, eds., *Privatization and the Welfare State* (Princeton, N.J.: Princeton University Press, 1989); Robert W. Poole, Jr., "Privatizing Essential Services," in David Boaz and Edward H. Crane, eds., *Market Liberalism: A Paradigm for the Twenty-first Century* (Washington, D.C.: Cato Institute, 1993), pp. 205–23.

10. On the complexities of measuring "efficiency" in the context of market and nonmarket alternatives, and the mixed results of such comparisons, see Charles Wolf, Jr., *Markets or Governments? Choosing between Imperfect Alternatives* (Cambridge, Mass.: MIT Press, 1988), esp. chap. 7.

11. See Poole, "Privatizing Essential Services," pp. 208–10.

12. This point also applies to the debate over the use of vouchers to pay for public school education; see above, chap. 4, n. 80.

ing of public goods to market forces may leave many persons unable to enjoy those goods.[13] Such problems, however, fall in various ways under the issues of economic rights that have been previously discussed.

In the remainder of this chapter, then, in dealing with the relation of political democracy to the effectuation of the economic and social rights, I shall be concerned primarily with the legislative and constitutional sense of "effectuation." The executive sense refers to a means-end relation that, while important, may not involve the issues of principle that bear on whether the end itself—the fulfillment of the economic and social rights— should be made a political and legal requirement.

To begin with, we must recall that the connection between the political rights of democracy and the economic rights is in important respects contingent: there is no logical or factual necessity that the use of democratic methods will eventuate in the institutional effectuation of the economic rights. Nevertheless, as we have seen, it should be by these methods that public decisions are reached about the fulfillment of the economic rights, including their incorporation into a constitution. Our present concern, then, is with the question, partly empirical and partly moral, of what likelihood there is that a democratic electorate will support this fulfillment, and how that support can be most effectively obtained.

An especially complicating factor in dealing with this question arises from a contrast between a certain form of both universalism and particularism. On the one hand, the democratic political rights are universalist in that the civil liberties and the suffrage to which they lead must be equally available to all citizens. On the other hand, as we saw in presenting the deprivation focus (4.1), the economic rights as elucidated here are mainly particularist in that they are designed especially to protect the economic interests of persons whose levels of freedom and well-being are sharply inferior without such protection. (This particularism is not the same as that which is upheld by some communitarians.) But will—or even should— democratic majorities support these interests of the economically deprived classes?

The "should" question has been given an affirmative answer in the argument for positive rights given above, and in many subsequent normative considerations about the mutuality required by human rights. The empirical question that remains concerns how democratic majorities using the method of consent can be led to support the economic rights. To deal with

13. See Vickers and Yarrow, *Privatization*, chap. 2; Kenneth Hoover and Raymond Plant, *Conservative Capitalism in Britain and the United States* (London: Routledge, 1989), chap. 9; Paul Starr, "The Meaning of Privatization," in Kamerman and Kahn, eds., *Privatization and the Welfare State*, pp. 15–48.

this question requires that we look more closely at the nature of the democratic process.

Distinctions have been frequently drawn between two different kinds of democratic procedures. The kinds have been called by various names: "competitive struggle for the people's vote" as against "will of the people for the common good";[14] "adversary" as against "unitary";[15] "thin" as against "strong";[16] "market" as against "forum";[17] "interest-aggregation" as against "dialogue."[18] Although these kinds can be traced back in large part to Rousseau's contrast between the "will of all" and the "general will,"[19] and perhaps to ancient sources, the considerations they embody are not entirely the same. Moreover, in these distinctions (apart from the first) it is not always clear whether the respective authors regard themselves as depicting political democracy as it is or as they would like it to be. While selectivity is inevitable in discussing such a complex institution as political democracy, realism is imperative when what is at stake is the actual possibility or probability of using democracy to effectuate the economic and social rights of the more deprived members of society. At the same time, this normative aim makes it necessary that one seek out the most promising ways in which this effectuation can be accomplished.

To have a common terminology for referring to the kinds of democratic procedures distinguished above, I shall use the words *competitive* and *cooperative*. While these words and the elucidations I shall give of them do not capture all aspects of the respective kinds, I wish to call attention to three main interrelated bases of the present distinction, whose analogues can also be found in some of the other distinctions listed above. One basis concerns the interests of the persons or groups who engage in democratic political procedures. According to the competitive model, their interests are opposed to one another, while according to the cooperative model they share common interests. A second basis concerns the purposes or the spirit of the democratic protagonists. According to the competitive model the aim is to have one's own interests prevail, while according to the cooperative model the aim is to promote impartial justice or the common good. The third basis concerns the components of the democratic process. According to the competitive model these components are the "prefer-

14. Schumpeter, *Capitalism, Socialism, and Democracy*, chaps. 21–22.

15. Jane J. Mansbridge, *Beyond Adversary Democracy* (New York: Basic Books, 1980), chap. 2.

16. Barber, *Strong Democracy*, chaps. 1, 6.

17. Jon Elster, "The Market and the Forum: Three Varieties of Political Theory," in Elster and Aanund Hylland, eds., *Foundations of Social Choice Theory* (Cambridge: Cambridge University Press, 1986), pp. 103–32.

18. Miller, *Market, State, and Community*, chap. 10.

19. J. J. Rousseau, *The Social Contract*, 2.3.

ences" of the protagonists, while according to the cooperative model they are "reasons" that are offered for impartial examination.

Although the distinction between the cooperative and competitive models of democracy corresponds in important part to the distinctions drawn by communitarians between their conceptions and those of their "liberal" adversaries (1.1; 3.4), the distinction involves many unclarities. "Interests" may be taken in a positive or in a normative sense, as consisting either in the goals or purposes one tends to pursue or in goals that one would pursue given full rational knowledge. Within "positive" interests, moreover, there is a distinction between self-interested preferences and preferences one has more generally, at least some of which may favor the well-being of persons other than oneself. Moreover, preferences may themselves be viewed as reasons for action. And the promotion of justice may be held to require that one's own interests prevail.

Let us now focus on this last consideration, in the context of the economic rights for which I have argued in the last four chapters. On the one hand, these arguments have upheld the interests (at once positive and normative) of some persons as against others, namely, the deprived persons, including workers or would-be workers, who are most vulnerable to the exertion of economic as well as political power. On the other hand, the arguments have been presented as upholding rights and justice. It would seem, then, that the pattern I have followed has been at once competitive and cooperative.

There is no inconsistency here, because arguments for justice may uphold outcomes that favor one group over another, when the former group's rights are violated by the latter group or by institutions that favor the latter group. A partial way to put this point is by the distinction between ends and means: the end of equal distribution of resources for freedom and well-being may require, as means, the unequal distribution of those resources in order to remove existing inequalities. This is only a partial way because the above arguments for economic rights have been concerned not to establish an absolute equality but to remove those inequalities that prevent persons from attaining the effective capabilities of successful agency.

Another way to see that there is no inconsistency between the competitive concern to promote some persons' positive interests at the expense of others' and the cooperative concern to attain impartial justice is through the distinction between extension and intension. Extensional diversities and partialities wherein some persons' interests are favored over others' can be justified on the basis of intensional impartialities of rational argument. My above arguments have often favored the interests of workers over the interests of capitalists, but the arguments themselves have been based on reasons, ultimately those of the principle of human rights, that take impar-

tial account of the action-related interests of all persons as prospective purposive agents and that thus reflect the mutuality of the community of
rights.

If these distinctions are not recognized, the cooperative model of political democracy incurs serious dangers, which are in fact incurred by some
communitarians (3.5). By treating the "common good" or the "public interest" as if it were in all respects an already existing condition, it may tend
to blur the ways in which many important goods are not "common," that
is, not equally distributed among the members of a society, so that in these
respects there is not a common good. And by regarding the "common
good" as a universally accepted ideal, it may illegitimately move from genuine public goods on which there is general agreement, such as pure air or
the avoidance of nuclear war, to other goals that are favored only by some
groups as against others. So the appeal to heed or to make sacrifices for the
common good may serve to support goods that are not common either in
possession or in aspiration. In these ways the conceptualization of political
democracy as using procedures of the "forum" as against the "market" or
of "dialogue" as against "interest-aggregation" may give a misleading picture.

These general difficulties are exacerbated when we turn to the specific
context of the economic rights. For between workers and capitalists,
whether as individuals or members of the respective groups, there are conflicts rather than communities of positive interests (see 5.2; 6.1). Given the
goal of maximizing profits, the capitalists' aim is to keep wages as low as
possible consistent with productive efficiency, while the workers' aim is to
have wages as high as possible. It is in the capitalists' interests to have a
large pool of unemployed workers in order to keep wages down, while it is
in the workers' interests that there be full employment. The capitalists' aim
is to have exclusive control over both firms and processes of production,
including the hiring and laying off of workers, while the workers' aim is at
least to share in control and management, and to ensure job security. The
capitalists' aim is to keep as low as possible the costs of protecting the
workers' health and safety, while the workers' aim is to maximize such protection, with cost being a secondary factor. Hence it seems that there is
little or no basis for the assumption of common interests that undergirds
the "forum" or "unitary" conception of political democracy.

It may be contended that these conflicts of interests can be mitigated if
not entirely removed if one takes a normative rather than a positive view of
"interests." The normative view would define 'interests' not as the goals
that persons actually pursue but rather as the goals they would ideally pursue in the light of rational knowledge. This normative view can take two
different forms. In one, instrumental form the ideal goals would ultimately

be instrumental to persons' actual goals or values,[20] while in the other, ideal form the goals would involve a change of character that would aim at quite different values. In the instrumental form, the capitalists would recognize that to achieve their goal of maximizing profits, at least in the long run, they need a contented work force, which requires higher rather than lower wages, worker participation in management rather than exclusive control by a distinct managerial class, and maximal protection of health and safety. Such a more enlightened capitalism would indeed go a long way toward satisfying the requirements of justice (see 6.8). But there remain serious questions about its economic viability in the light of market fluctuations, including the competitive challenges posed by low-wage workforces in underdeveloped or developing countries and other aspects of the national and international movement of capital. These considerations have an important bearing on the universality of human rights so far as concerns their effectuation.

The ideal form of the normative view of "interests" may have different versions. One historically prominent version, found in Plato and Rousseau among others, would involve a surrender of ordinary self-interest with its drive for self-aggrandizement; it would invoke instead an ideal self dedicated to impartial justice.[21] A main difficulty with this conception is that it leaves unexplained just how it would be upheld by rational knowledge, and how the transition from actual persons to the ideal is to be effected. The concept of the reasonable self discussed above (3.6) is an attempt to surmount this difficulty.

Amid these complexities of the distinction between competitive and cooperative models of the democratic process, it must be kept in mind that the community of rights that supports the equal human rights of all persons is a normative conception whose validity is based on the rationally justified principle of human rights in the ways traced above. Our present concern is with how actually existing democratic states can be led as fully as possible to approximate this normative conception. With this end in view, let us recur to the competitive-cooperative distinction and take from it two phases that are crucial to our present problem. From the competitive model we take the idea of conflicts of positive interests between the more deprived members of society and the other classes. From the cooperative model we take the idea of reasoned discourse on justice and rights, discourse that is itself based on the mutuality of the community of rights.

20. See "the principle of self-interest rightly understood," in Alexis de Tocqueville, *Democracy in America*, pt. 2, bk. 2, chap. 8 (New York: P. F. Collier and Son, 1900), vol. 2, pp. 129–132.

21. See Plato, *Republic*, 4.444; Rousseau, *Social Contract*, 2.8. See also Andrew Levine, *Arguing for Socialism* (London: Verso, 1988), pp. 76, 150.

How, amid the conflicts, can reasoned discourse get an adequate opportunity to influence social policies?

I have already touched on the conflicts of interests. Two of their reper-
cussions for political democracy are especially salient. The operations of
political democracy are themselves intensely competitive: different groups
in society try to use the political process to advance their own, opposed
interests. But since the lower classes are far inferior in economic power,
they are also inferior in their ability to marshal the economic resources
needed for influencing the democratic process in support of their interests.
Moreover, whatever may have been the case in crisis eras like the New Deal
of the 1930s and the civil rights movement of the 1960s, the middle and
upper classes largely evince little or no concern with the plight of the lower
classes. The former have "seceded" from the rest of society, and seek only
to be left alone to pursue and enjoy their good fortune or to attend to their
own more special grievances.[22] It would take us too far afield to trace the
history that has led to this outcome, although the conflicts of interests between rich and poor have been a central feature of political thought and
reality in nearly all eras, including, in the West, from the ancient Greeks
through Federalist Paper 10 to Marx and on to the present. But it should be
clear that such "secession" is a serious violation of the mutuality required
by the principle of human rights. The very possibility of a morally justified
functioning of political democracy requires serious consideration of how
this mutuality can be restored. This is in important part the question of
how the competitive model of the democratic process can be turned in a
cooperative direction.

In what follows I shall focus primarily on conditions in the United
States in their bearing on the political effectuation of economic rights. My
reason for this is not the point made by some communitarians, that one's
local or particular context has special moral value in contrast to the purported universalism of human rights. Nor do I claim that conditions in the
United States are fully representative of conditions in other parts of the
world. My point rather is not only that focusing on the United States will

22. See Robert B. Reich, *The Work of Nations* (New York: Alfred A. Knopf, 1991),
chaps. 21–24. See also the analysis of "the rivers of change that have eroded the party's base,"
written before the 1992 Democratic National Convention, including the following: "The
have-nots are still there and still vocal, but there are far more haves now, and many are less and
less prepared to help the have-nots; they are hostile to the old Democratic goal of income
redistribution" (R. W. Apple, Jr., "Is There Room at the Top for Democrats?" *New York
Times*, July 12, 1992, sec. 4, p. 1). For an argument that "democratic control of a capitalist
economy" can be achieved only through "continuous control of the state by a labor movement party," see Andrew Martin, "Is Democratic Control of Capitalist Economies Possible?"
in Leon N. Lindberg et al., eds., *Stress and Contradiction in Modern Capitalism* (Lexington,
Mass.: D. C. Heath, 1975), pp. 13–56.

give my discussion a certain helpful specificity but also that it is relevant to other parts of the world where institutions of political democracy are either present or matters of future development. Because of this relevance, and because the right to political democracy is a universal human right, the focus on American conditions need not detract from the general concern with human rights that motivates this book.

8.5. Civil Liberties as Effective Powers

We have so far reached a largely negative answer to the empirical question of whether democratic procedures, taken as competitive, will lead to the effectuation of economic and social rights. But it is important not to stop here. I shall argue that the civil liberties, viewed both empirically and normatively within the community of rights, can provide the basis for an affirmative answer. The main point is that the state, as a community of rights, must secure for deprived persons and groups their right to participate effectively in the democratic political process. Such participation should aim in important part at using the cooperative conception of the democratic process to bring to persons' attention their mutual obligations with regard to vital needs. To see how this is so, we must first take up some conceptual considerations, bearing on the relation of the civil liberties to freedom and power.

It will be recalled that freedom of action is both negative and positive: negative as consisting in noninterference by other persons; positive as consisting in the power or ability to act (1.4).[23] This power is itself a complex notion. For present purposes we must distinguish between remote, latent, or passive power and proximate, effective, or active power. A person may have only the remote or passive power to do X, in that his doing X is not entirely beyond his capabilities but it requires that other persons act on him in order to activate his power, so that he then and only then has the proximate or effective power to do X. He has the effective or proximate power to do X if his doing X depends on his own choice so that, given his choice to do X, he does X.

In terms of these distinctions, civil liberties are effective powers to perform or engage in a certain range of actions. The members of this range may be gathered from the Bill of Rights of the American Constitution: they include the actions of speaking, publishing, assembling or associating with

23. I have elsewhere dealt in detail with the relations between negative and positive freedom. See my "Civil Liberties as Effective Powers," especially its first part (pp. 311–17), reprinted in Gewirth, *Human Rights: Essays on Justification and Applications* (Chicago: University of Chicago Press, 1982), pp. 310–28. In the present section I repeat, with modifications, some of the last two parts of this essay. See also above, 1.4, n. 14.

others, and so forth. For present purposes it is not important to distinguish between "speech" and "action," since we are not here concerned with the problem of the justifiable limits on speech. In the generic sense, speaking is itself a kind of action. As we have seen (8.1), the freedoms to perform or engage in speaking and other kinds of action just mentioned are rights constitutionally guaranteed by democratic government. The crucial initial question concerns the nature of this guarantee.

The First Amendment to the Constitution provides that "Congress shall make no law . . . abridging" the freedoms of speech, press, and assembly. From this it has sometimes been inferred both that the freedoms in question consist simply in governmental noninterference (or nonabridgment) and that the government's guarantee of them consists solely in this pledge of noninterference. The former inference, however, is unsound. For since freedom is positive as well as negative, a person is not free to speak, for example, unless he has the effective power to speak; mere noninterference by other persons is not logically sufficient to constitute this freedom, although, of course, for every normal person noninterference from other persons is as a matter of fact a sufficient condition of his having the effective power to speak. As we shall see, however, in the complex political circumstances in which the civil liberties have one of their main fields of application, it cannot be granted that the effective power to speak requires only noninterference on the part of government.

Let us now turn to the other inference drawn from the language of the First Amendment, that the government's guarantee of civil liberties consists only in its pledge or obligation not to interfere with their exercise. Doubt may be cast on this inference by the fact that when civil liberties are threatened or interfered with by private persons, as when someone making a speech is attacked by persons who disapprove of what he is saying, the law intervenes to protect the speaker's right to talk. Thus the role of government in relation to civil liberties is not only the negative one of noninterference but also the positive one of protecting them from interference on the part of other persons. This active role of government, however, may still leave the civil liberties as negative rights, in that the government's aim, so far, is simply to prevent or remove interferences with persons' use of their effective powers of speaking, assembling, and so forth (see 2.2).

The question we have to consider is whether the civil liberties in relation to government are positive as well as negative rights, that is, whether democratic governments have not only duties not to interfere with them and to prevent interferences by others, but also duties to assist persons to make use of their civil liberties in certain ways that can achieve certain ends. This question has an obvious bearing on the democratic effectuation of economic rights. To deal with it, we must recall that the relation of the civil liberties to democracy is at least a double one (8.1). On the one hand, the civil liberties are "active" in that they consist in forms of action or effective powers which function to determine who shall govern; on the other hand, they are "passive and positive" in that they receive protection from those who govern. In both relations, moreover, political democracy as justified by the principle of human rights requires that the civil liberties pertain equally to every citizen: each citizen has an equal right to participate actively in the democratic process and to be protected by government in that participation. Before going more fully into what ought to be the passive relations of civil liberties to government, we must examine more carefully the conceptual structure of civil liberties in their active relations. For in this latter respect, as kinds of action which operate in the context of the democratic process, the civil liberties involve some important qualifications in the general concept of freedom as analyzed above. And these qualifications have an important bearing on the democratic effectuation of economic rights.

As so far presented, the positive freedom to do X has been defined as the effective power to do X, and "effective power" has been equated with active or proximate power as distinguished from passive, remote, or latent power. A person has the effective power to do X if his doing (or not doing) X depends on his own unforced choice, in that, given his unforced choice to do X, his doing X then occurs, so that he is not prevented from doing X or from not doing X by obstacles either internal or external to himself.

When we try to apply these definitions to civil liberties as they actively operate in the context of the democratic process, it appears that they must be sharply qualified in several respects, especially with regard to the concepts of "doing X" (or action) and of "effective power." Take, for example, freedom of speech, which according to the above account consists in having the effective power to speak. In the context of the democratic political process, speaking is not, like walking, a potentially private act. It is public and social, for it is addressed to other persons, and potentially to large multitudes. It is also teleological, in that it aims at an end other than the mere performance of the action. It is tendentious, in that, both on the competitive and on the cooperative conceptions of the democratic process, its aim is to influence other persons as to how they shall think and act with respect to issues of social policy. And to have any realistic hope of succeeding in this aim in the conditions of modern society, political speaking requires abundant economic resources: to hire a hall or at least a sound truck, to buy time on television or radio and space in newspapers or at least leaflets, and so forth. It is true that picketing, marching, demonstrating, sitting-in, and similar activities have at various times been judicially upheld as forms of speech protected by the First Amendment; and these, while of course social in nature and sharing the other characteristics of political speech just noted, may not require such elaborate economic resources. But such activities are essentially localized and hence may have only a limited impact when wider sociopolitical issues are at stake.

If, then, the effective powers to speak and to publish in which the civil liberties consist have the social, teleological, and tendentious features just noted, and if in the political process the exercise of these powers requires such abundant economic resources if it is to have any chance of success,[24] to what extent do the masses of the poor in our society, or even the bulk of ordinary citizens, have these civil liberties? In answer to this question, it may be held that it is important to distinguish between the concepts of effective *powers* and effective *actions*. According to the definition given above, a person has the effective power to speak if his speaking depends on his own choice, so that, among other things, he is not prevented from speaking by other persons, including the government. On the other hand, even if a person has the effective power to speak, his speaking may not itself be effective in that it does not achieve the goal he intends it to achieve, so that it is not productive in the general sense indicated above (4.6). In other words, we must distinguish between being able to perform an action and succeeding in achieving the aim of that action, where the action is teleological in the sense noted above. To illustrate this difference, we may distinguish between two different groups with regard to their possession of civil liberties. The members of the first group are prevented from speaking, publishing, and assembling in support of their views or interests. The prevention may come from governmental prohibitions and punishments, or from the threats or coercion of antagonistic private groups. The members of this group lack civil liberties in that they lack the effective power to speak, and so forth, in the social-public and tendentious ways we have seen to be essential to civil liberties in their political application. In contrast to this group, the members of a second group are not prevented from speaking and so forth, but they lack the economic resources required to compete on even terms with members of opposed groups; hence, their actions are not successful: the views or interests they seek to promote by their speaking and

24. See the report headlined "Record $678 Million Was Spent by Candidates for Congress in '92," *New York Times,* Mar. 5, 1993, national edition, p. A10. Robert A. Dahl, in *Democracy and Its Critics* (New Haven, Conn.: Yale University Press, 1989), while recognizing the severe challenge that economic inequalities pose for political democracy (pp. 114–15, 326, 332–33), nevertheless holds that "the long-run prospects for democracy are more seriously endangered by inequalities . . . that are derived not from wealth or economic position but from special knowledge," which he equates with "intellectuals" (p. 333). Intellectuals, however, have often sided with oppressed groups; and it seems plausible to say at least that such intellectuals, like the groups they support, have to overcome the severe disadvantages posed by the wealth of their opponents.

writing do not prevail. Of the members of this group we may say that they do indeed have civil liberties, but that these are not effective, in that, while they have the effective *power* to speak, publish and assemble, these *actions* of theirs are not themselves effective.

From this distinction it follows that persons may equally have civil liberties, defined as effective powers to speak and otherwise participate in the democratic political process, even if they do not equally have the economic resources to succeed in the aims of their speech. Moreover, these effective powers are good in themselves even if the persons who exercise them do not attain their tendentious objectives. All one need do to verify this is to consider the many groups in totalitarian societies and elsewhere who are legally or otherwise prevented from exercising these powers.

While this distinction is defensible and indeed important, it does not alter the fact that insofar as the actions which comprise the civil liberties are teleological and tendentious, effectively to have these liberties requires not merely the power to speak, publish, and so forth but also the power to succeed in the aims of one's speaking and publishing. I shall refer to the former of these powers as *conative* and to the latter as *achievemental*. They specify two different senses in which the civil liberties may be had as effective powers. The achievemental powers are comparative in a way which the conative powers may not be; for to be able to succeed in one's efforts requires not only the exertion of effort but also a certain relation to possible obstacles or competitors, such that one is able to marshal relevant resources that are superior to those which would otherwise prevent one's success. Although, for a group to have effective achievemental powers, it need not always triumph over its opponents, it is safe to say that if the group never triumphs in relevant respects, then it lacks the effective achievemental powers which are approximately required for success. There may be many reasons for such lack. The aims or contentions of many unsuccessful groups may lack rational merit, and hence may fail to be convincing to the democratic electorate. Here, however, I wish to focus on those deprived groups whose contentions do have rational merit because what they claim are the economic and social rights whose justification has been developed in the preceding chapters. The crucial question is how we can move from the competitive model, where the preferences of some groups triumph over those of other groups, to the cooperative model of the community of rights, where the reasons in support of the economic and social rights of deprived groups are given effective positive consideration.

In the achievemental sense, the exercise of the civil liberties by various groups is aimed directly at influencing governmental policy in the direction of their views and interests. Here it is the competitive conception of the democratic process that is central. The stake of the deprived groups in such exercise is especially obvious because of their great and unfulfilled needs in such areas as health, food, education, child-care, housing, and other objects of economic and social rights. There are wide inequalities between the poor and the rich in respect of the distribution of such vital resources. These inequalities are unjust, and according to the principle of human rights with its criterion of degrees of needfulness for action and concomitant deprivation focus, the highest priority should be given to removing such inequalities (2.4; 4.1).

These substantive ends, however, are at once confronted by procedural questions—questions of means. How, by what methods, should the goal of a greater approach to equal justice be realized, especially in the face of widespread indifference on the part of the more affluent groups? The traditional answer of political democracy is that the democratic process itself provides the means or methods in question, for this process allows every citizen to press her views and interests in the public forum and to unite with other, like-minded persons in free competition for votes to elect persons who will support the policies advocated by the respective groups. In other words, it is alleged that in a democratic society the universal availability of the civil liberties, in what has been called their active relation to government, provides a sufficient basis for confidence that the democratic process will be able to rectify the substantive injustices referred to above and thus to effectuate the economic and social rights.

This answer, however, incurs the difficulty that the democratic process, as competitive, is itself characterized by the same inequalities as characterize the other, substantive aspects of society. Just as the poor are at the low end of the distribution of other resources, so, largely for that very reason, the poor are at the low end of the distribution of political power, that is, the effective achievemental ability to participate in the political process in such fashion as to influence the outcome of that process in the direction of their own views and interests.[25] For to have this effective achievemental ability in the democratic process requires the use of such means of communication as the press, radio, and television, and to command these means of communication to the degree required for success requires superior economic resources. But the poor, lacking these resources, are at a great disadvantage in the political process, despite the fact that their basic needs are the greatest of all.

In view of these inequalities, what is the status of the claim just mentioned, that the civil liberties provide a sufficient basis for confidence that

25. For a recent empirical analysis of the relevant correlations, see Sidney Verba and Norman H. Nie, *Participation in America: Political Democracy and Social Equality* (New York: Harper and Row, 1972), esp. chap. 20.

the democratic process will operate to rectify the injustices of the unequal fulfillment of basic needs caused by the unequal distribution of wealth? It now appears that the civil liberties, as effective achievemental powers, are caught in the same pattern of inequality and injustice as the substantive problems they were supposed to resolve. Hence, to appeal to the civil liberties to remedy the injustices of society by way of the competitive democratic process is to seek to lift oneself up by one's bootstraps.

8.6. CIVIL LIBERTIES AS POSITIVE RIGHTS

The question, then, is whether and how this methodological injustice within the democratic process can be remedied. Here I suggest, as one important possibility, that we turn from the "active" to the "passive and positive" relation of the civil liberties to democratic government. In the latter relation, the various liberties are protected and fostered by government. As we have seen, there is a widespread theory, derived in part from the language of the First Amendment and more generally from a traditional conception of freedom, that this passive relation of the civil liberties to government should be only negative, in that government, while preventing other persons from interfering with persons' speaking, publishing, and so forth, should itself also simply refrain from interfering. This hands-off policy, however, serves to permit the existing distribution of economic resources in the society to work itself out in the political sphere: the political effectiveness of the civil liberties is itself distributed largely in accordance with the existing distribution of economic resources. I suggest, then, that the passive relation of civil liberties to government should also be positive, in that government should affirmatively intervene to remove not only occurrent but also dispositional or institutional obstacles to poor persons' exercising their civil liberties in the democratic process with an effectiveness equal to that of the affluent. Thereby government will positively assist the poor to make effective use of their civil liberties, so that the civil liberties are positive rights. In this way, the state would be a community of rights in the vitally important sphere where it would protect and support the civil liberties as positive and effective rights, by bringing to emphatic attention the mutual obligations required by the principle of human rights. Because these obligations are objects of rational argument that can be understood and accepted by all persons, the democratic process would now be a cooperative one.

The precise scope and method of such intervention involve, of course, many detailed problems. But one relevant possibility is that the government, recognizing how the inequalities in respect of the effective use of civil liberties mar the procedural justice of political democracy, would make radio and television time, newspaper space, and the like freely available to groups of the poor, designated by certain methods to be spelled out. These groups would then have at their disposal more regularized methods of public rational communication than the sit-ins, marches, demonstrations, and near or actual riots that have hitherto been the only means effectively available to them to press their claims of justice in the public forum.[26] What is sought is not an unattainable absolute equality of effective influence for each person in the informal political processes leading to the casting of the vote, but rather a closer approach to equality in this area on the part of the economically disadvantaged groups in the society. The aim is to make far more available to such groups the effective ability to press their rationally grounded claims in public communication as matters of the mutuality of moral obligations, and hence to make their civil liberties more nearly equal to those of richer groups as effective achievemental powers toward fulfilling their morally justified goals.

At this point, however, we seem to recur to the bootstrap problem that I mentioned before. The sequence of my argument has been, first, that to rectify the substantive injustices of American and other societies it is not enough to appeal to the equal availability of the civil liberties as active procedural determinants in the democratic political process, for those liberties when properly viewed as effective achievemental powers are themselves unjustly distributed. But now, secondly, I have appealed to a positive functioning of government to rectify those procedural injustices. The obvious question that arises here is that in pushing the situation back to this step, aren't we confronted with the same difficulty all over again? Since it is the operations of the civil liberties that are held to determine the policies and personnel of government, will not those policies and personnel in turn reflect the very injustices of those operations or procedures? It is this question that leads many inquirers to hold that some nondemocratic method, such as revolution or violence, must be used to break this circle of injustices, just as Rousseau, to cite an earlier example, appealed to what he called a *législateur* and what we would call a moral-political élite to effect the required transformation.[27]

While this problem of circularity or of the bootstrap is indeed very serious, I want to suggest that the analysis sketched above indicates ways of

26. For a discussion of legislative and judicial problems of making such communication available, see Thomas I. Emerson, *The System of Freedom of Expression* (New York: Vintage Books, 1971), chap. 17, "Affirmative Promotion of Freedom of Expression." See also Jerome A. Barron, "Access to the Press—A New First Amendment Right," *Harvard Law Review* 80 (1967): 1630–78; and Barron, "An Emerging First Amendment Right of Access to the Media?" *George Washington Law Review* 37 (1969): 486–509.

27. See Rousseau, *Social Contract*, 2.7. See also above, n. 21.

resolving it. We must now move from the competitive to the cooperative conception of the democratic process, with its emphasis on deliberative rationality and mutuality. Two main points are especially important. One bears on a suggestion just made in citing Rousseau. There are many reasonable selves in American society (3.6), and they comprise moral forces that can be used to help effect the needed procedural and structural changes. I refer in particular not only to components of major and minor political parties but also to various public interest groups, like the American Civil Liberties Union, Public Citizen, Common Cause, Center for Responsive Politics, and other organizations of civil society that act, in part, as advocates of the poor. There are also precedents in recent American history, such as the Community Action Programs which had as their purported aims to bring about "maximal feasible participation of . . . the groups served" in coping with their substantive problems of poverty.[28] The failure of these programs provides instructive lessons for future efforts at increasing for the poor their effective use of civil liberties.[29] But they were important anticipatory movements toward what I have here called the community of rights in its relation to the cooperative democratic process.

A second main point of the above analysis that bears importantly on the bootstrap problem is the central place of the concepts of rights and justice. The bootstrap problem arises when the democratic political process is viewed with the competitive conception, as a battle of opposed forces each of which seeks to promote its respective positive interests. On such a view, there is no way of breaking out of the circle whereby the stronger force—which usually means the economically dominant force—carries the day in a zero-sum game, regardless of the level at which one tries to break the circle. This is, indeed, an eminently realistic view of a part of the political process. Nevertheless, moral considerations of rights and justice may themselves carry great weight in the political process, and thereby help to break the circle wherein economic power is decisive. What is crucially important here is that the claims in question be given adequate means of cooperative public elucidation and advocacy as claims of justice, of equal rights, of mutual obligations, of truth, and not of force. Such moral elucidation was strongly influential in bringing about the far-reaching Voting Rights Act of 1965, an act whereby the government took important steps

28. *Economic Opportunity Act of 1964,* Title II (U.S. Government Printing Office, Washington, D.C.).

29. For two views on this failure, see David Stoloff, "The Short Unhappy History of Community Action Programs," in M. E. Gettleman and D. Mermelstein, ed., *The Failure of American Liberalism: After the Great Society* (New York: Vintage Books, 1971), pp. 232–39; Daniel P. Moynihan, *Maximum Feasible Misunderstanding; Community Action in the War on Poverty* (New York: Free Press, 1969).

toward equalizing civil liberties insofar as they are directly reflected in the electoral process. Further progress can be made by calling explicit attention to the unfinished business of rights and justice in respect of the civil liberties and as effective achievemental powers in the political process. In this regard the equal rights of all persons to the civil liberties would be complemented by the rights of the poor to an equalization of their effective liberties, with correlative obligations of government and the owners of public means of communication. What can be especially helpful here is if the poor and their representatives ally themselves with other segments of the population who also stand to benefit from an effectuating of mutual obligations through a greater democratization of the political process (see 4.1, including n. 7 to chap. 4).

As was noted above, governmental action may serve to expand as well as to restrict freedom, by interfering with interferences with men's actions. Since interferences with or obstacles to persons' equally effective use of their civil liberties derive largely from their economic inequalities, taxation which reduces the inequality of individuals' economic resources would help to make less unequal the effectiveness of their use of the civil liberties (see 3.4; 5.2, 5). There are, however, several more direct ways of effecting such civil-libertarian equalization. One, already mentioned, is by making available to groups of the poor, without charge, sufficient newspaper space and television and radio time to enable them to press their views and interests in public forums to a far greater extent than is available to them at present. Another way is to cut down the effectiveness of superior wealth in political communication by sharply restricting the amount of money that can be spent by candidates for office.[30] These and other methods would interfere with the freedom of the rich to maximize the effectiveness of their use of their civil liberties; but by the same token they would increase the freedom or effective power of the poor in this respect.

These methods of equalizing the effective political use of civil liberties may be approached either legislatively or judicially. The legislative approach would be continuous with the attempt made to protect the right to vote on the part of blacks and other minorities in the Civil Rights Acts of 1957, 1960, and 1964 and the Voting Rights Act of 1965. These laws, by prohibiting not only violence but also literacy tests, poll taxes, and other means that had been used to deny the vote to blacks, sought through the community of rights to assure effective equality of voting rights for all citi-

30. A step has been taken in this direction by the Federal Election Campaign Act Amendments of 1974 (Public Law 93-443). For a critical discussion, see Marc F. Plattner, "Campaign Financing: The Dilemmas of Reform," *The Public Interest*, no. 37 (fall, 1974): 112–30. See also above, n. 24.

zens by the cooperative invocation of moral reasons. Without disputing the enormous importance of these provisions, a case can be made that the equal right to vote presupposes the equal right to make effective use of one's civil liberties in support of the objects of one's vote, that is, the candidates whose policies one favors. Voting may in this regard be viewed as the culminating act of the political process so far as this involves participation by the ordinary citizen, and the earlier phases of the process, including the use of various methods of communication to influence the voters' views, may exert a strong influence on the direction of that culminating act. The civil liberties are the means, equally guaranteed to all citizens in accordance with the principle of human rights, for using these methods of communication. But if, as is in fact the case, economic inequalities produce drastic inequalities in the ability to make effective use of one's civil liberties for this purpose, the result is that the effectiveness of the equal right to vote is sharply reduced. Hence, the logic of the various legislative enactments for assuring equality in the right to vote provides a ground for supporting further legislative enactments for assuring equality in the right to make effective use of one's civil liberties in the political process. In this way the civil liberties would be positive rights.

There are also grounds for supporting a judicial approach to equalizing the effective use of civil liberties in the political process. The Fourteenth Amendment's provision for equal protection of the laws has been used by the United States Supreme Court to declare unconstitutional a state's requiring payment of a poll tax as a prerequisite to voting.[31] Citizens are denied the equal protection of the laws if persons with low economic resources are denied equal access to the ballot box with those of higher incomes. It could be argued with some plausibility that citizens are also denied the equal protection of the laws if persons with higher incomes are allowed to have stronger influence in the political process which culminates in the ballot box. Another, although perhaps less direct, analogue of the judicial intervention here proposed in the political process is found in the various reapportionment cases where the Supreme Court has held that the equal protection of the laws requires that each person's vote count equally with each other person's, so that congressional and state legislative districts must contain numerically equal populations so far as possible.[32] Again, there is justification in arguing that the right to an equally counting vote implies the right to an equally effective use of the legally available influence-producing preliminaries to voting.

31. *Harper v Virginia Board of Elections,* 383 U.S. 663.
32. *Baker v Carr,* 369 U.S. 186 (1962); *Reynolds v Sims,* 377 U.S. (1964).

The poverty that afflicts sizable groups in society and drastically reduces the effective achievemental power of their civil liberties in the political process derives from a set of humanly caused institutions that constitute dispositional obstacles to the ability to act successfully on the part of the poor. The positive governmental policies just suggested should be viewed, then, as attempts to expand the freedom of the poor at a crucial point, for their aim is to remove the impact of these obstacles on such groups' effective ability to participate more equally in the democratic process and to use that process to effectuate their social and economic rights. The state would thereby become a community of rights in the dynamic sphere of helping persons to fulfill their political and civil rights. Community and rights are here interconnected because the state becomes a community through its mutualist concern for securing the equal rights of political democracy.

In this section and the preceding one I have been considering the question of whether the consensual procedures of political democracy can or will be used to effectuate the economic and social rights of the deprived members of society. It may be objected that the route I have taken to answering this question is unduly circuitous. If the aim is to secure persons' economic and social rights, then why not appeal to the electorate directly to enact those rights legislatively or constitutionally, as against the indirect route of appealing instead to equalization of the procedures or methods whereby such enactment would be achieved? Why shouldn't the appeal be directly substantive rather than procedural? And if the richer groups are at best indifferent to the substantive claims and needs of the poor, then why won't they be equally indifferent to their procedural claims? Moreover, the procedural route may be held to threaten an infinite regress. For to successfully advocate Procedure P_1 would require using Procedure P_2, which would in turn require successful advocacy through Procedure P_3, and so forth.

There are four replies to this objection. First, while the substantive arguments presented in this book must indeed be adduced in the democratic debate with a view to their acceptance and enactment, the fact remains that procedures are so intrinsically connected with political democracy that it may be easier to make evident their unfairness than the unfairness of the substantive outcomes to which they presently lead. To focus on the procedures is to take democracy seriously in the most direct way.[33] Hence, the democratic electorate, amid its many conflicts of interests, may be brought more readily, through its awareness of the cooperative model's mutual obli-

33. This can be seen from the persistent and widely accepted attempts to attain "campaign reform" whereby the influence of large financial contributions to persons running for office can be minimized or at least controlled. See above, nn. 24, 30.

gations, to vote for equalizing the procedures than for the substantive measures. Second, emphasis on the procedures accords more readily with the autonomy to which all persons have rights of agency. Through the procedures the deprived persons are enabled to participate as political agents, as shapers of their own destinies, as against being passive recipients of the agency of others. In this way the securing of economic and social rights through democratic methods obtained and used by the poor themselves is directly in accord with the principle of human rights as dedicated to securing for all persons the rights of agency, with their accompanying dignity, self-esteem, and self-respect. Third, it must be kept in mind that the substantive economic and social rights whose fulfillment is advocated are themselves in important part procedural. The rights are primarily active rather than passive, in that what they require is not simply the provision of welfare or other goods but rather that deprived persons have the means to develop their own abilities of productive agency and to participate in the productive process. These rights are continuous with the procedural democratic rights, in that in each case persons take an active role in controlling their own lives. There is evidence that the democratic electorate looks far more favorably on persons' being given the opportunity to work than on their being given welfare payments;[34] in each case there is greater support for enabling persons to act for themselves. Being helped to attain effective political procedures is continuous with such action. Fourth, there is no infinite regress of procedural justifications because the cooperative conception of democratic procedure, to which appeal was made to equalize the civil liberties as effective powers, is based on the principle of human rights, which has its own independent justification.

What emerges from these considerations is that the democratic effectuation of the economic and social rights can be achieved when the civil liberties that are used in that effectuation are equalized as effective powers and positive rights. The equalizing of the procedures can strongly assist toward the equalization of the fulfillment of the economic and social rights.

In this context the democratic political rights are positive rights whose respondents are democratic governments and the citizens who participate in and benefit from them. There is mutuality in this relation because, while the more affluent citizens act for the rights of the poor by voting to equalize their effective civil liberties, the poor concomitantly contribute by promoting the justice of the whole political system, including the equal rights of all its members. In this way the community of rights is reinforced.

34. See Philip Harvey, *Securing the Right to Employment* (Princeton, N.J.: Princeton University Press, 1989), p. 2.

8.7. SOME CONCLUDING REFLECTIONS

Two normative themes have figured centrally in this book. One is the requirement to develop qualities of autonomy and personal responsibility on the part of each individual in meeting his or her fundamental needs of agency. This theme underlies my emphasis on productive agency as a means of avoiding welfare dependence and on the rights to private property, employment, and the two kinds of democracy: rights that derive from the principle of human rights. The other theme is the mutual obligations of persons and of their society to contribute to such development by, among other things, supporting governmental policies that uphold these human rights. This has been the point of my emphasis on the state as a community of rights.

The two themes are in potential conflict: just as rights were initially held to be in conflict with community (1.1), so individualism may conflict with mutuality and autonomy with obligation. I have argued that each of these conflicts is resolved in essentially the same way, by showing how their various parts follow from and are fitted into the rational and moral principle of human rights. In upholding for all persons their rights to freedom and well-being, the principle supports a rational autonomy whereby persons not only set for themselves the morally justified rules of their action but also cooperatively help one another to achieve such autonomy (4.2, 6; RM, 138–39). Insofar as persons can understand the justification of this principle, they can also understand, and be motivated to exert, their corresponding rights and obligations whereby they mutually help one another to develop as autonomous and cooperative persons through the policies and institutions of the community of rights. In this way the principle of human rights lays the groundwork for a decent society in which all persons are treated with the respect that accords with their dignity as rationally autonomous and mutually cooperative purposive agents.

In this concluding section I want to take up some considerations that bear on the interpretation of my whole enterprise. To begin with, it is to be noted that in contemporary political polemics, especially in the West, "human rights" are almost entirely confined to political and civil rights, especially as they concern democratic institutions and the avoidance of torture and other serious wrongs. While fully agreeing with these concerns, my emphasis in this book has been mainly on economic and social rights. Despite the inclusion of the latter in the Universal Declaration of Human Rights promulgated by the United Nations in 1948, economic and social rights figure only slightly in contemporary political discourse (including political philosophy) in the West, whether national or international. I have focused on them in this book for several reasons. One is that the political and civil rights are less in need of elucidation and defense because they are much more widely and effectively recognized in the West, although there are also some serious shortcomings. But another, major reason is that the deprivations represented by poverty, dependence, lack of education, unemployment, economic insecurity, and other economic and social ills have especially harmful effects on the possibility of successful action; and indeed, if not remedied, they may threaten the continued stability of the political and civil rights themselves. The latter rights have, however, been implicit throughout my discussion and have been made explicit in the present chapter both as essential components of the rights to freedom and well-being and as procedurally required for effectuating the economic and social rights through the community of rights. But the economic and social rights require special attention on their own account; their violations pose severe problems throughout the world, including the West, and, in some important respects, especially in the United States.

The solutions I have proposed for these problems, based on the principle of human rights, have included an espousal of a positive role for the state as the community of rights in effectuating economic and social rights. This espousal raises controversial issues of the proper function of government. Libertarians, conservatives, and others condemn the positive role upheld here both on moral grounds as a violation of the right to individual freedom and on empirical causal grounds as being counterproductive in relation to its avowed aims. I have tried at various points to show how these criticisms are to be answered. Especially important in the answers have been the theses about the degrees of needfulness for action and the limitations of markets in the allocation of resources. I have tried to emphasize that the moral necessities of effectuating the economic and social rights cannot rightly be subjected to the contingencies of market arrangements and outcomes, including the economic inequalities they reflect and foster. More generally, because the human rights, economic and social as well as political and economic, are required for the freedom and well-being that are the necessary conditions of action and generally successful action, the effectuation of the rights should not be left to optional private arrangements but rather must be guaranteed by the state as the community of rights insofar as deprived persons cannot fulfill them by their own efforts (2.5). Within the limits set by these guarantees, market transactions and other modes of voluntary arrangements, including charity, are to be given free rein.

An important moral criticism of such a positive role for the state is that it fosters dependence and lack of personal responsibility on the part of the persons helped, with correspondingly deleterious effects on both freedom and well-being. What must be stressed in reply is that the aim of the welfare and other economic and social rights should be to help their recipients to develop their own abilities of productive agency, with concomitant positive effects on their autonomy and sense of personal responsibility. This is the point of what I have called "productivist welfarism" (4.6), and it marks a major difference from most philosophical theories of social justice, which view persons as passive recipients of institutional arrangements, not as active contributors to their own economic well-being. Thus what emerge from the development traced in this book, not as a distant utopian future but as a directly envisaged and feasible outcome, are persons whose autonomy and sense of personal responsibility are fostered by their acquisition of skills of productive agency that enable them to produce exchange values adequate for achieving a decent standard of living within a largely market economy. It must be stressed here that the development itself must not be subject to market operations, although its outcomes will usually proceed within such operations, with, however, the qualifications required by the limitations of property rights (3.4; 5.5), the right to employment (6.1, 2), and the protections provided by a universalist system of economic democracy (7.6, 7).

Confronted by the important powers I have here attributed to the state, some libertarian and conservative thinkers may still be tempted to charge that the community of rights as delineated above is an all-powerful monolith that subjugates persons to its ironclad laws and leaves them dependent on the unappealable decisions of political bureaucrats. While the dangers of bureaucracy must be taken seriously, there are two main further bases for rejecting the charge. One is that the community of rights is, and functions as, a political democracy in which officeholders are subject to effective evaluation by the electorate. The other is that persons are helped by the community of rights to develop and exercise their own abilities of productive agency and thereby to attain an autonomy that removes them from both economic and political dependence.

An important outcome of the community of rights as thus conceived is that it provides for a "civil society" independent of the state. Civil society consists in a large variety of voluntary associations and institutions that are independent of the central governing apparatus of the state (see *RM*, 282–90), except where the state embodies the minimal, democratic, and supportive states that protect human rights. Within the limits set by these protections, persons are left free to develop their own groupings, including their centers of authority that are independent of state control.[35] The mandatoriness of the laws protecting the human rights thus leaves open a large

35. For a good recent discussion, see Ernest Gellner, *Conditions of Liberty: Civil Society and Its Rivals* (New York: Allen Lane, Penguin Press, 1994).

area of freedom of action and association. At the same time, such groups can both be parts of and make their own contributions to the community of rights. But it must also be stressed that civil society as thus conceived presupposes and requires the protection of rights provided by the community of rights. Community and rights are brought together here because persons' vital interests in freedom and well-being are protected through an institutionalized framework of mutual assistance whereby persons are helped to develop their abilities of productive agency and to find suitable employment for those abilities. The freedom and voluntariness of civil society are thereby given a stable grounding.

Various phases of this development of productive agency and its outcomes have been referred to above as parts of an "economic biography." This notion is paralleled in part by what may be called the "political biography" that has figured in modern political philosophies, where persons are depicted as beginning from a nonpolitical "state of nature" and more or less gradually attaining the conditions of political society with its legal order and civilizing emoluments (4.1). Even more extensive kinds of political biography have figured in ancient and modern political philosophies that begin from the family and then trace a sequence through neighborhoods, villages, towns, and so forth to states.[36] So far as concerns economic biography, familiar examples may be found in works of literature ranging from the "rags to riches" stories of Horatio Alger to the more sober novels about economic careers by such writers as William Dean Howells, Frank Norris, Theodore Dreiser, and Abraham Cahan. Biographies of tycoons like Carnegie and Rockefeller have been factual counterparts of this literature, as have been, on a more massive social scale, works of economic history.

The economic biography presented in this book differs from the kinds just mentioned in several respects. It is neither literarily fictional nor empirically historical, nor are its prototypes taken from business careers. Instead, it reflects the deprivation focus where persons are regarded as beginning from poverty and gradually attaining the abilities and conditions needed for successful agency, where "success" is viewed in terms of productive agency in both the general and the economic senses of "productive" (4.6). It is this envisaged sequence, whereby fundamental human rights are fulfilled, that poses the greatest challenge to economic and social justice. This sequence as presented here is normative in that it analyzes and argues for the successive economic steps that are required for fulfilling the human rights to freedom and well-being. The persons who emerge from this sequence have left poverty and "welfare" behind; apart from those

36. See, e.g., Aristotle, *Politics*, bk. 1.

who are incapacitated by age, illness, or mental deficiency they have attained education, productive skills, and private property at least in sufficient earned income; they have been guaranteed adequately paid employment if they cannot find work by their own efforts, and they have achieved a certain important degree of autonomy in controlling their conditions of work together with the economic rewards derived from their work. These outcomes have enabled persons to maintain a kind of economic independence that generates self-esteem and self-respect; they have been relieved from the fears generated by poverty, unemployment, unsafe and unhealthy working conditions, and the uncontrolled operations of the market. Such persons can participate more confidently and effectively in market transactions precisely because they have been brought, through the nonmarket provisions of the state as a community of rights, to the levels of freedom and well-being to which they have rights. In these ways, in contrast to being passive dependents on the actions of others, persons are helped to become effective agents who, as reasonable selves, respect the rights of other persons as well as their own (3.6). They are also enabled thereby to live lives that attain ethical, spiritual, and other cultural values and virtues of additive well-being. The resulting community of rights is a much healthier and far more decent society than those which are found in most parts of the world, with their inveterate poverty, unemployment, and economic insecurity as these derive either from unfettered operations of the market or from tyrannical political regimes.

The steps through which the state as the community of rights has enabled persons to achieve this economic biography are embodied in what I have called an "economic constitution." This constitution provides, in a stable institutionalized way, for the effectuation of the human rights to welfare, education, private property, employment, and so forth. As has been frequently noted above, the moral necessity of these rights requires that the state help to effectuate them through its laws, whose outcome is the fulfillment for all persons of their rights to freedom and well-being. These laws will, of course, encounter various contingencies concerning the specification and implementation of the general rights. This leaves an important place for democratic consensual procedures (3.8; 8.2). Nevertheless, the central aim is to fulfill for all persons, especially for those who are deprived in the ways indicated above, their human rights to freedom and well-being. Through the economic constitution, the economic biography summarized above is securely anchored in institutional arrangements that are both feasible and, in their general outlines, morally obligatory as fulfilling human rights.

The constitutionalization provided by the economic constitution supplies an answer to an important objection that has sometimes been raised against the economic and social rights as they have been presented in this book. It has been held that they are not genuine rights or "valid claims" but are at most only rights in "a special 'manifesto sense,'" because, even though their objects are goods that are greatly needed by persons, "in conditions of scarcity there may be no determinate individuals who can plausibly be said to have a duty to provide the missing goods to those in need.'[37] Another version of this criticism is that the positive rights to assistance that have been upheld here have as their correlatives duties that "are in the first instance *unallocated* obligations. . . . That they are *imperfect* obligations follows from the fact that the argument fails to establish who owes whom which sorts of help.'[38] From this it is held to follow that the rights in question do not have either the stringency or the priority over duties that have been maintained here (see 1.3).

This criticism bears in major part on the respondents of economic and social rights. If there are no determinate individuals who have the positive duty to fulfill these rights, either because their objects or the means of their fulfillment are not available or because who the respondents are is left vague or unspecified, then the rights upheld here are merely "manifesto rights" that embody deeply felt needs or aspirations, but are not legally enforceable (see also 2.5, 6). The principle that 'ought' implies 'can' may also be adduced here; for if the rights cannot be fulfilled, then it is not the case that they ought to be fulfilled, where 'ought' connotes a certain stringency and determinate responsibility. And if no assignable persons have the duty to fulfill the rights, then, however emotively poignant be the needs on which the rights are based, the rights are left indeterminate and ineffectual.

The constitutionalization of the economic and social rights helps to provide an answer to these criticisms. For it lays on courts and governments the responsibility for fulfilling the rights, by making legally determinate provisions for fulfilling them. In these ways, as we have seen, the society whose government makes such provisions is a community of rights. Where governments do not have the will or the resources to fulfill the rights, they must be helped by other governments, especially through facilitating processes of democratization and developing in their own members the abilities of productive agency whereby they can provide the needed resources for themselves (2.5, 6), and also by making international trade less subject

37. Joel Feinberg, *Social Philosophy* (Englewood Cliffs, N.J.: Prentice-Hall, 1973), pp. 66–67. See also above, 2.6(c). See J. E. S. Fawcett on "programme rights" in "The International Protection of Human Rights," in D. D. Raphael, ed., *Political Theory and the Rights of Man* (London: Macmillan, 1967), pp. 119–33, at pp. 128–29.
38. Onora O'Neill, *Constructions of Reason: Explorations of Kant's Moral Philosophy* (Cambridge: Cambridge University Press, 1989), pp. 230–31; emphasis in original.

to domination by richer nations. The citizens of political societies that can provide such resources directly or indirectly have obligations to participate actively in the democratic processes that lead to the legal enactment of the economic and social rights. These obligations derive from the mutuality which is an essential feature of the human rights.

It is indeed true that the obligations are not legally enforceable; there are no legal sanctions for nonparticipation. Nevertheless, such participation is morally required of persons; and insofar as they become rationally aware of the principle of human rights, with the compassion that can both help lead to and accompany such awareness, they will have strong bases for advocating for deprived persons fulfillment of their positive rights to freedom and well-being. But the direct responsibility for effectuating such fulfillment rests with governments implementing the mutuality of the community of rights. Thus rights and community are brought together.

A related objection to the constitutionalization of the economic and social rights bears on their relation to judicial enforcement and legislative enactment. If the rights are part of a constitution, then they must be enforced by the courts. But just as with other so-called "positive rights" (such as the right to "a favorable living environment" or to "the highest possible level of physical health," which figure in some East European constitutions), it may be contended that the economic and social rights upheld in this book are too diffuse or too demanding of specific supervision to lend themselves to the kind of enforcement available to courts. Hence, either the rights will not be enforced (as with "manifesto" rights) or, if they are, the courts will be usurping that which is properly a task for legislatures elected by the people and subject to their possibly varying specific preferences.[39]

In reply, it must be said that the positive social and economic rights upheld in this book have determinate contents that exempt them from the charge of diffuseness. Their enforcement is in varying ways both a political and a legal matter. It will be recalled that whether they are put into a constitution and thus potentially made legally enforceable depends on their being voted upon in a democratic political process (8.2); the officials elected through this process are to make the relevant constitutional provisions establishing the economic and social rights as mandatory legal requirements. Their subsequent enforcement is to be not only judicial but also legislative: It is to be judicial in that courts would make decisions concerning whether their requirements are being met. But it is also to be legislative in that laws would be made concerning the specific ways in which the rights are to be implemented. The government in its executive branch would enforce the

39. For this objection, see Cass Sunstein, "Against Positive Rights," *East European Constitutional Review* 2 (winter 1993), pp. 35–38. The examples of "positive rights" in some East European constitutions are from this article.

decisions and laws. It must also be recognized, however, that if the process of constitutionalization were deemed too arduous, an important part of the relevant mandatoriness could be achieved by making the economic and social rights the more direct objects of democratic legislation.

Many of the specific normative recommendations that I have presented in this book are not original with me; they have been the contents of various liberal and socialist programs for more than a century. A main contribution of this book has been to set these recommendations in a justificatory framework of human rights whereby their connection with the necessary goods of human agency has been brought out. I have tried to develop the recommendations in a systematic way so that their main interconnections have been clarified. In particular, the relation of the human rights to what I have called the community of rights has been of central importance in showing the imperative connection of the rights with the mutuality both of personal obligations and of institutional protections. In such ways, I have tried to bring a certain normative coherence and comprehensiveness to the various policies and institutions for which I have argued here as being mandatory requirements of a just society.

This endeavor raises many more general philosophical questions. One concerns ethical pluralism. To what extent, if any, can these requirements be derived from moral premises other than the principle of human rights as interpreted here? I have already briefly indicated my reservations about intuitionism, utilitarianism, Rawls's ideal contractualism, natural law, and some other general moral principles (1.3, 7; preface, n. 4). It is no part of my intention, however, to claim exclusive pride of place for the deontological principle of human rights, including the way in which I have derived it by the dialectically necessary method from the necessary conditions of human action. Especially as a practical matter of advocacy in the public forum, other moral-political principles can be welcomed insofar as they serve to support this book's mandatory recommendations for public policy. In this way a certain kind of political pluralism can be accepted and even encouraged. But doubts may remain about the intellectual cogency of other proffered principles, and these doubts, in the sifting dialectic of reasoned public debate, may spill over to the normative conclusions about economic and social rights for which I have argued here. For these and many other reasons the sequence of argument I have presented in this book should, I believe, receive the special consideration I have claimed for it.

The endeavor of this book has also raised many logical questions, not only about my argument for the principle of human rights (1.5, 6) but also about the whole sequence of the set of discussions that have been developed here. A main such question concerns "foundationalism." This book and its predecessor have been presented as resting on certain firm foundations—

human action and its necessary conditions—and arguing from them in a unilinear sequence to the PGC, the principle of human rights as the supreme principle of morality, and from it in turn to conclusions about the morally mandatory policies of governments with regard to the fulfillment of economic and social rights. Such a sequence may be subject to certain standard objections that have been raised against foundationalism in general epistemology. Two of the main objections have dealt with the alleged independence and the alleged fecundity of purported "foundations" for knowledge. The independence objection is that the foundations that have been put forth, such as sense data or intellectual intuitions, are not absolute starting-points for knowledge, because they presuppose a whole panoply of assumptions about knowledge and the world. The fecundity objection is that the purported foundations do not suffice by themselves to derive or generate the remainder of our knowledge.[40]

While these objections have considerable merit in general epistemology, I do not think they apply against the kind of foundationalism I have presented in this book and its predecessor. An important reason for this is that my claims are more modest. I have tried to begin from a premise that is independent not absolutely but only in relation to moral considerations. Such is the statement labeled (1) above, "I do X for end or purpose E" (1.5). This is a statement-form that, given certain minimal assumptions about rationality, no agent can rationally deny about himself, so that it has a certain necessity within the sphere of human action (*RM*, 25–26, 42–43, 48). Such a premise is needed if the moral principle to which it leads is to be categorically obligatory. At the same time, statement (1) does not presuppose any moral principle, so that the independence objection does not apply. Moreover, I argue from this premise, in the ways indicated above, to the PGC as the supreme principle of morality, and from it to the economic and social rights delineated above. In this way I have held that the fecundity objection is also met.[41]

My main emphasis in this book has been on the vast unfulfilled needs

40.   See, e.g., Bruce Aune, *Knowledge, Mind, and Nature* (New York: Random House, 1967), chap. 2. See also Nicholas L. Sturgeon, "Metaphysics and Epistemology," in Lawrence C. Becker and Charlotte B. Becker, eds., *Encyclopedia of Ethics* (New York: Garland, 1992), vol. 2, pp. 801–4. For a defense of foundationalism in epistemology, see Roderick M. Chisholm, *The Foundations of Knowing* (Minneapolis: University of Minnesota Press, 1982), chap. 1.

41.   In an incisive criticism of my "foundationalism," Renford Bambrough has held that there is no need for foundations in moral philosophy because morality is a "going concern" which is already available to us; what is needed is only to describe it, not to justify it on the basis of first principles. See his essay, "The Roots of Moral Reason," in Edward Regis Jr., *Gewirth's Ethical Rationalism* (Chicago: University of Chicago Press, 1984), pp. 39–51. I have replied to Bambrough in ibid., pp. 192–97. See also above, 1.3.

for freedom and well-being on the part of masses of persons in the United States and throughout the world. What to do about these needs poses, in my opinion, the major challenge that confronts moral and political philosophy. If the needs are left unfulfilled, dire consequences may well follow for both West and East, both North and South. These consequences bear not only on the fates of millions of deprived persons throughout the world but also on the endurance of democratic institutions. I have tried to show that fulfillment of these needs is a matter of the human rights of the persons concerned. The mandatoriness of the needs makes mandatory the fulfillment of the rights.

Democratic institutions to be viable must show that they can cope with such needs in ways that are both just and effective. In taking such steps they must be communities of rights that secure the economic and social rights of persons, especially those who cannot fulfill them by their own efforts. By the mutuality of human rights, all persons have obligations to help see to it that their societies function as such communities through appropriate governmental policies and institutions. The persons who contribute such help will not only exercise their own rational autonomy but also further their dignity as rational and cooperative agents who fulfill their rights within a community that protects and fosters them. What is required here is the opposite of the "secession" that has characterized the attitudes and actions of many members of the more fortunate classes (see above, 8.4). On the part of governments, what is needed is positive intervention whereby persons are enabled to develop and fulfill their rights of productive agency. In these ways the solidaristic characteristics of community are shown to be not only compatible with but required by the mutuality of human rights.

INDEX

Aaron, Henry J., 205n
Abilities: of successful agency, 59,
331; of productive agency, 137,
140, 141, 182, 183, 217, 350; of
effective citizenship, 291. *See also*
Productive agency
Ackerman, Bruce, 162n
Action: as basis of human rights, xiv,
13–20, 39; necessary goods of, 6,
17, 108; generic features of, 13–
14; and production, 132; agent-
cause theory of, 193. *See also*
Agency; Generic features of action
Adair v. United States, 208 U.S.
(1908), 253n
Additive well-being, 14, 23, 43, 51,
91, 132, 149, 279; synonymous
with general achievemental sense
of productive agency, 132–33,
137; subsumes human capital,
140; object of productive labor,
147; contributed to by cultural
and other values, 149–50, 151,
164–65; includes self-esteem, 224;
values and virtues of, 352. *See also*
Well-being
Adeonticist, 10, 18, 23–24
Adversarial conception of relation
between rights and community, 2,
7, 31; replies to, 19–20, 87–91
Agency, needs of, 58, 135; success-

ful, 59, 331; rights of, 59, 105,
201, 347; proximate capacity to
engage in action, 132; contrasted
with passive recipience, 135, 201,
316, 347. *See also* Action; Produc-
tive agency
Agent-cause theory of action, 193
Aiken, William, 58n
Akerlof, George A., 241n
Alchian, Armen A., 212n, 251n,
267n
Alger, Horatio, 351
Alienation, 2, 32, 259
Allison, Anne, 251n
Alperovitz, Gar, 294n
Alston, Philip, 102n
Altruism, 126; moderate, 25, 61–62;
mixed, 288, 307; "high-minded,"
306
Amoralist, 10, 18, 23–24
Anderson, Lucille W., 155n
Apartheid, 3, 90, 92, 95
Apple, Michael W., 139n
Apple, R. W., Jr., 334n
Aquinas, Thomas, 89n
Aristotle, xiv, 15, 28, 69, 87, 92, 95,
132n, 158n, 160n, 161n, 172n,
182, 193n, 204n, 351n
Arizmendi, Don José Maria, 302
Arneson, Richard J., 85n, 252n,
270n

Arnold, N. Scott, 206n, 211n, 261n, 272n, 287n, 298n, 301n, 305n, 307n, 308n
Aronowitz, Stanley, 227n
Arrow, Kenneth, 318n
Attfield, Robin, 224n
Aune, Bruce, 356n
Austin, J. L., 89n
Autonomy, 15; not opposed to community, 95–96, 117; right to, 111, 117, 347; and welfare system, 115–19; belongs to same family as freedom, 115–16; desire- and behavior-, 116n; differs from freedom, 117; a necessary good, 117; rational, 52, 92, 117, 135, 163, 348, 357; lacked by welfare recipient, 117; protected by property rights, 171; secured by productive agency, 201; greater, in self-managed firms, 283–84; derogated from, in nondemocratic states, 316; and democratic procedures, 347; conflict of, with obligation, 348; in controlling conditions of work, 352. *See also* Freedom

Baier, Annette, 33n
Baker v. Carr, 345n
Balogh, Thomas, 139n
Bambrough, Renford, 356n
Bane, Mary Jo, 158n
Banfield, Edward C., 92n, 115n
Bankruptcy, 215, 222; in economic democracy, 293, 297–98, 299n
Baran, Paul, 142n, 145n, 146n
Barber, Benjamin, 321n, 330n
Barron, Jerome A., 342n
Barry, Brian, 80n, 81n, 85n, 109n
Barry, Norman, 264n
Basic rights, 197; not subject to democratic process, 324–25. *See also* Rights
Bauer, P. T., 180n
Bauhn, Per, 93n

Becker, Charlotte B., 356n
Becker, Dismas, 109n
Becker, Gary S., 138n, 153n, 154n, 237n
Becker, Lawrence C., 76n, 85n, 166n, 167n, 173n, 175n, 184n, 194n, 232n, 356n
Beechey, Veronica, 149
Benn, S. I., 174n
Bentham, Jeremy, 50n, 174n
Berle, Adolf A., 166n, 208n
Berlin, Isaiah, 15n, 174n
Berman, Katrina V., 285n, 288n
Bernays, Edward L., 216n
Bernstein, Paul, 285n, 287n, 288n
Beveridge, William, 215n
Beyleveld, Deryck, xi, 20, 23n, 28n, 41n, 45n, 102n
Birdsall, Nancy, 202n
Blades, Laurence E., 253n, 254n
Blasi, Joseph R., 262n
Blaug, Mark, 136n, 142n, 211n, 213n, 237n
Blauner, Robert, 130n, 267n
Block, Fred, 229n
Blumberg, Paul, 261n, 281n, 285n, 286n
Böhm-Bawerk, E., 136n
Bond, E. J., 24n
Bonner, Deanna, 124n
Bootstrap problem, 341, 342, 343
Bowles, Samuel, 139n, 153n, 161n, 246n, 261n
Bowman, Elizabeth A., 296n
Bradley, Harriet, 149n
Bradley, Keith, 292n, 303n, 307n, 308n
Brandt, Richard B., 12n, 27–28, 50n
Braverman, Harry, 130n, 145n, 146n, 290n
Braybrooke, David, 21n, 112n
Brison, Susan J., 102n
Brown, Peter G., 112n
Browning, Edward K., 179n
Brownsword, Roger, 102n
Brunner, Karl, 242n

Buchanan, Allen, 77n, 8on, 9on, 205n, 304n
Bureaucracy, 120, 249, 350

Cable, John R., 268n
Cahan, Abraham, 351
Caja Laboral Popular, 297
Callahan, Daniel, 66n
Campbell, T. D., 8on, 232n, 234n
Capital, 136, 207; necessary for production, 210. *See also* Human capital
Capitalism: provides context of productive labor, 143; criteria of, 145; and educational equality, 153, 161–62; harmful effects of, 153, 176–78, 258–59; and slavery, 176–77; forms of, 207; definition of, 207–8; and outpouring of consumer goods, 212; afflicted by unemployment, 214; mutualist and enlightened, 250, 333; and social democracy, 257, 309–10; violates workers' rights, 266–67; and freedom, 268–69; workers', 294–95, 306; deprivations in, 309
Capitalist: his receipt of surplus value makes labor productive, 143; classed as unproductive, 146; "abstinence" of, 210–12; distinguished from worker, 207; contribution to productive process, differing views of, 210–13; limits of ownership rights of, 263; hierarchic power of, 266–68, 290
Carlyle, R. W. and A. J., 188n
Carnegie, Andrew, 351
Carnoy, Martin, 162n, 261n, 274n, 285n, 295n
Carson, R., 300n
Categoricalness of moral 'ought,' 12, 16, 17, 24, 27, 356
Catholic Bishops, 110n
Chamberlain, Neil W., 138n, 139n
Champernowne, D. G., 240n

Chandler, Alfred D., 195n, 208n, 209n
Chapman, John W., 2n, 23n, 33n, 65n
Charity, 38n; not to be relied on to fulfill positive rights, 59, 79–80, 100, 313, 318, 328
Charvet, John, 2n
Chisholm, Roderick M., 193n, 356n
Choice: forced and unforced, 13, 116, 237–40, 268; and work, 134; and effective power, 337
Christman, John, 116n
Citizen: requires economic and social as well as political and legal rights, 68–69; in political and economic democracy, 289–92; meritocratic restrictions concerning, 292, 307; right to be, of democratic state, 316
Civil disobedience, 122
Civil liberties, 53; in political democracy, 315; three different relations of to the state, 315, 336–37; equal right to, 315–16, 337; not subject to democratic political process, 326–26; as effective powers, 335–41; as negative and positive rights, 336; qualifications in general concept of freedom, 337; social, teleological, and tendentious features of, 337–38; active, 337–41; passive-positive, 337, 341–47; passive-negative, 337, 341; inequalities of, 340–41; as positive rights, 341–47; equalization of, 342, 343–44, 347. *See also* Freedom; Political democracy
Civil rights, subsumed under human rights, 68–69. *See also* Human rights; Rights
Civil Rights Acts of 1957, 1960, and 1964, 344
Civil society, 315, 350–51
Class structure: of society, 41, 110, 204, 252, 290, 291, 306n, 333,

Class structure (*continued*)
334, 357; in economic democracy,
290, 291
Cloward, Richard A., 122n
Codetermination, 259, 269, 310
Coercion, 4; mere, not in community
of rights, 60; exercise of, in democratic state, 314; compatible with
political freedom, 317; by laws,
317. *See also* Choice; Laws
Cohen, G. A., 84n, 112n, 174n, 188,
196n, 210n
Cohen, Morris, 174n
Cohen, Roger, 220n
Cole, G. D. H., 99n
Coleman, James S., 154n, 155n
Collective rights, 2, 3, 52, 83, 201,
262, 314, 317; contrasted with
utilitarian benefits, 48–49. *See
also* Rights
Comisso, Ellen T., 146n, 259n,
267n, 270n, 281n, 291n, 292n
Common good: distributive and collective meanings of, 94–95;
dangers of concept of, 94–95,
332; system of rights as, 97–98
Common interests, 87–88, 196; as
basis of reflexive rights, 234–35;
in economic democracy, 272, 305;
in cooperative model of political
democracy, 330. *See also* Conflicts
Communitarianism: ties to socialism,
98–99; and shared goods, 163;
solidaristic culture of, 306
Communitarians, 32–33, 36; ignore
rights, 86–87; invoke families,
87–88; absolutism of, 88; assimilate rights to Hobbesian view, 91;
constitutiveness doctrine of, 91;
difficulties of, concerning "common good," 94–95, 332; diverse
doctrines of, 96; distinction between models of democracy, 331
Community: as antithetical to rights,
1–5, 348; as essential background
of rights, 2–3; as having rights,

2–3; initial conciliation of, with
rights, 6–8; as component of well-
being, 15–16; conciliation of, with
rights, 15–16, 19–20, 32, 41, 69,
70, 73, 79, 87, 96–97, 108, 117,
127, 132, 147, 150, 162, 165,
179, 197, 198, 201, 213, 226,
234, 258, 282, 314, 317–18, 325,
346, 351, 354; as honorific, 81–
82; harmony and solidarity of, 82;
as institutionalized social bond,
88; requires rights, 88–89; and
slavery, 92; distributive, adjectival
meaning of, 94, 234; not opposed
to autonomy, 95–96
Community of rights: as oxymoron,
1–2; as fulfilling needs, 5, 59,
147, 150, 152; the state as, 59–
60, 79, 341, 346; two bases of
PGC's society as, 82–84; departs
from egoism and individualism,
83; mutuality in, 83; psychological
attitudes in, 83, 85–86, 93, 98,
197; adjectival sense of, 94–95,
234; means to protect individual
rights, 97; both means and end,
100–101; embodies three kinds of
state, 103; largely identical with
the supportive state, 104; two
lines of policy of, 127; not neutral
on conceptions of good, 162–65,
231–33; and privacy of property,
173; provides employment, 219–
23; relations of, to economic democracy, 262, 282; economic
democracy functions as, 298; social as well as political, 315;
includes political democracy, 316–
17; public rational discussion in,
322; embodies political and economic rights, 324; supports civil
liberties as positive rights, 341; as
monolith, 350; a decent society,
352. *See also* State
Comparable worth, 205
Competition, 204; in economic de-

mocracy, 293–94, 295, 297–98; in political democracy, 293; modified by economic democracy, 306

Conflicts: of rights, 44–46, 78; of justifications, 53; of interest, 282, 327, 330, 333, 334; in economic democracy, 304; between capitalists and workers, 244, 266, 282, 332; may hinder realization of rationality of democratic process, 327; in competitive model of political democracy, 330

Consent: voluntary, 51, 317; in voluntary associations, 78; method of, 315; operates within state but not as grounding state, 317, 324; optional, 317; rational and empirical, 317, 319–20; inherently rational procedures of, 324; does not extend to basic rights or democratic political rights, 324–26. See also Civil liberties; Contract; Freedom; Political democracy

Consequences: and rights, 37–38, 279–80; as benefits to individuals, 170; as products of work, 185

Consequentialism: and justification of property rights, 170–81; distributive, 189; contrasted with aggregative, 279–80

Conservatives, xiii, 4, 5, 349, 350

Consistency in ethics, 24–25. See also Generic Consistency, Principle of

Constitution, 152, 263, 287, 290, 293, 296, 320, 324, 329; basis of political and economic rights, 319; upholds basic rights, 325; set up by democratic political process, 326; gives firm status to political and economic rights, 326–27; diffuseness of rights in some East European constitutions, 354. See also Economic constitution

Contract: rational-choice, 11–12n; and reciprocity, 77; social, 25,

106, 195; and mutual relations, 119–20; at will, 253–54; market, 267–68; of association among firms in economic democracy, 296; state not based on, 317. See also Consent

Contribution, 183; disentangling of, 185, 206; principle, 204–14, 288, 301n

Control: hierarchic in capitalism, 266–67; in economic democracy, 269–70, 276; occurrent and dispositional, 271; first-order and second-order, 271–72

Cook, Rebecca J., 33n

Cook, Robert F., 227n

Cooperatives, worker, 250, 260, 263, 302, 303; may behave like capitalist firms, 294–95; success rate in Mondragon, 299; failures of, 303. See also Economic democracy; Market socialism

Copp, David, 75n

Cost-benefit analysis, 45n, 144, 294; human capital and, 139

Cox, Harold, 226n, 247n

Cranston, Maurice, 62n

Criterion-based obligations, 235. See also Duties; Obligations

Crosson, Pierre R., 57n

Cullen, Bernard, 221n

Cultures, diversities of and universality of human rights, 66–68

Cunningham, Frank, 112n

Dahl, Robert A., 261n, 271n, 274n, 279n, 289, 301n, 318n, 338n

D'Art, Darryl, 263n

Datta, Lois-Ellin, 156n

Davidson, Donald, 50n

Declaration of the Rights of Man and the Citizen, 68–69

DeGeorge, Richard T., 215n

Degrees of needfulness for action, 45–54, 60, 78, 81, 104, 175, 182–83, 188, 242, 246, 247, 248,

Degrees of needfulness for action (*continued*)
263, 280, 309, 310, 314, 326–27, 340, 349. *See also* Interpersonal comparison of utilities

Democracy, 58; general democratic thesis, 274; two interpretations of, 274–78. *See also* Economic democracy; Participation; Political democracy

Demsetz, Harold, 167n, 176n, 212n, 251n, 267n

Den Uyl, Douglas, 44n, 63n, 215n

Dependence, and welfare, 118–23; upheld in theories of social justice, 135; held to be fostered by positive role for the state, 349; removed by development of productive agency, 350. *See also* Welfare

Deprivation, 106, 309, 312; focus, 110, 141, 152, 165, 171, 192, 206, 207, 309, 311, 327, 329, 331, 340, 349, 351. *See also* Needs; Poverty

Descartes, René, 190

Desert, 160–61, 188–94

Determinacy of rights-principle, 12, 105

Determinism, 190–91

Dewey, John, 29n, 193n

Dialectical arguments, 26–29; dialectically contingent argument, 27

Dialectically necessary method and argument, 16, 21, 29, 39, 44, 66, 73, 89n

Dignity, human, 19, 21, 29, 53, 66, 69, 73, 113, 117, 125, 148, 164, 201, 347, 348, 357; agency as basis of, 135; and human capital, 138

Dobb, Maurice, 204n, 205n

Donagan, Alan, 104n, 124n, 193n, 224n

Donaldson, Thomas, 53n

Donnelly, Jack, 3n, 35n

Doshe, K., 251n

Downing, A. B., 66n

Downs, Anthony, 168n, 293n

Doyal, Len, 107n

Drèze, Jean, 57n

DuBoff, Richard B., 195n, 242n

Dunlop, John T., 204n, 244n

Duties, as correlative to rights, 6–7, 9, 16, 33–36, 59, 77; overload of, 54–62. *See also* Criterion-based obligations; Obligations

Dworkin, Gerald, 116n

Dworkin, Ronald, 47n, 72n, 84n, 162n, 187n

Economic biography, xiii, 20, 99–100, 108, 114, 137, 142, 149, 160, 167, 170, 171, 179–80, 214, 217, 257, 289, 309, 311, 314, 351–52

Economic constitution, xiii, 20, 100, 214, 257, 263–64, 287, 289, 290, 309, 311, 312, 314, 319, 324, 327, 328, 352; in Mondragon, 296; democratic political enactment and effectuation of, 312, 329, 354; legislative and executive fulfillments of, 327–28; required by the state, 328; provides for effectuation of economic and social rights, 352; and enforcement by courts, 354. *See also* Constitution

Economic democracy, 127, 178, 261–310; contrasted with capitalism, 261; fits into community of rights in two ways, 262; establishment of, 263–64, 313, 314; particularist and universalist stages of, 265, 288–89, 301–2; and right to freedom, 266–73; community of interests in, 272; may ""degenerate into capitalism," 272; analogies to political democracy, 271, 272, 273–78; disanalogies to political democracy, 273–74, 289–

94; and right to well-being, 278–88; psychological effects of, 281–82; economic effects of, 282–88; part of community of rights, 273, 282, 286, 296; meritocratic restrictions in, 291–92, 307; moderate meritocratic restrictions, 297; decreases employment, 292–93; solidarity in, 286, 303, 305–6; inequalities of wealth and power in, 294; universalization of, 295–301, 302–3, 307–8; expansion of employment in, 297. See also Cooperatives; Democracy; Market socialism; Mondragon

Economic growth: and human capital, 138, 141; and two justifications of property rights, 201–2; and worker motivation, 245–46

Economic justice, 135. See also Economic rights; Justice

Economic Opportunity Act of 1964, 155, 343n

Economic rights, 29, 99–100, 135, 309, 313; relative importance of, 53–54; and participation in productive process, 135; subject to principle of human rights, 319; of the economic constitution, to be established by democratic procedures, 319; conflicts with political rights, 319, 320; normative contingency of, 323. See also Human rights; Justice; Political rights; Rights

Edel, Abraham, 67n

Education: civic, 60; right to, 36, 137, 150, 152; and human capital, 139, 149; for productive agency, 149–55, 245, 342; as not developing productive agency, 153–55; voucher system, 150n; vocational and cultural, 151; and democratic participation, 151–52; Marxist criticism of, 153, 161–62; and

social-scientific findings, 153–55; and self-actualization, 158–62; legally obligatory, 162–63; as laying conditions for autonomous action, 192; in economic democracy, 297, 304. See also Head Start

Efficiency: and productivity, 144; efficiency wage, 221, 241, 252; kinds of, 283; in economic democracy, 283–88; and state effectuation of rights, 328; distinguished from ""efficient cause," 182n

Efficient cause: of action, 15; of property rights, 53, 169, 182, 202, 212; of profits, 145; distinguished from efficiency, 182n

Efforts, 39, 40, 42–44, 191–92, 193–94, 205, 249–51, 312

Egoism: of rights, 2, 9–10; as universal feature of humans, 7; contrasted with community of rights, 82–83, 85–86; not necessarily connected with rights, 90; ethical, 97; "collective," 294, 301. See also Self-interest

Ehrenreich, Barbara, 107n

Eisner, Robert, 220n

Elitism, 28, 95, 322, 342

Elkin, Stephen L., 100n

Ellerman, David, 212n, 261n, 263n, 266n, 275n, 276n, 292n, 298n, 300n, 301n

Ellwood, David T., 115n, 219n

Elster, Jon, 21n, 50n, 158n, 206n, 224n, 227n, 252n, 303n, 330n

Emerson, Thomas I., 342n

Employment: right to, 134, 213–56; a negative right, 217–19; a positive right, 219–23; full, 127, 219, 242–49; and shirking, 249–52; at will, 217n, 252–54. See also Unemployment; Work

Engels, Friedrich, 99n

Engerman, Stanley, 138n

Entitlements, 56, 194

Entrepreneurs, 140, 209; and risks, 209, 300; and unemployment, 215, 221–23; socialized, in Mondragon, 299–301; individual, opposed views on, 300
Epps, Frances M. J., 157n
Epstein, Richard A., 253n
Equality, of rights, 24, 65; economic, 50–51, 52, 56, 175; not part of rights as such, 72–73; indispensable contribution of, 72–73; protects freedom, 73–74; of opportunity and of outcomes, 74–75, 158–59, 191, 197; contrasted with rights to equal goods, 74–75, 175; of self-actualization, 75, 158–62, 308; moral, 112; proportional, 159–60; of opportunity in economic democracy, 297; may require unequal distribution, 331; of effective liberties, 344. See also Inequality
Equal protection of the laws, 345
Estlund, David M., 78n
Estrin, Saul, 293n, 295n, 303n
Ethical individualism. See Individualism
Ewin, R. E., 2n
Exchange-value, 120, 133–34, 140, 141, 167, 183, 185–86, 206; and unemployment, 215–16, 225–26. See also Markets
Exdel, John, 188n
Exploitation, 205, 209, 259, 278–79, 290, 301n, 305n

Fallacy: rationalistic, 24; of composition, 94; of division, 115, 272–73; of disparateness, 265, 266
Family: and community, 86, 87–88; may be antisocial, 92; and organicist relations, 125–26; needs rights, 125; conflict between family autonomy and equal opportunity, 153, 157–58; and educational achievement, 154; and parental involvement in Head Start, 157–58; may facilitate efforts, 192
Family Support Act of 1988, 128n
Famine, 56–59. See also Starvation
Farber, Henry S., 219n
Fathers, 107, 111, 124, 125. See also Parents
Fawcett, J. E. S., 353n
Federal Election Campaign Amendments of 1974, 344n
Federalist Paper 10, 334
Feinberg, Joel, 45n, 72n, 176n, 192n, 231n, 234n, 238n, 353n
Feliu, Alfred G., 253n
Feminism, 32–33, 36, 89n, 117, 205. See also Mothers; Women
Final cause, 171n; of action, 15; of property rights, 53, 169, 171, 183, 202
Fisher, Irving, 146n
Fishkin, James S., 55n, 153n, 158n
Fisk, Milton, 158n
Flathman, Richard E., 2n
Fogel, R. W., 138n
Fogelson, Robert M., 122n
Foldes, Lucien, 179n
Foundationalism, 10, 355–56
Flew, Antony, 150n
Fraser, Nancy, 118n
Freedom, 6; as generic feature of action, 13, 66; as procedural feature of action, 14–15, 115–16; negative and positive, 15, 335, 336; occurrent and dispositional, 46, 49; different objects of, 46, 49; general right to, 47–48; paradoxes of, 174–75, 268–69, 317; workers' rights to, violated, 258; and economic democracy, 266–73; individual and collective, 277–78; generic right to, 277; right to, applied in political democracy, 315; of action, relation to political freedom, 316; as effective power to act, 335; qualifications of, by civil liberties, 337–38. See also Civil liberties

Freeman, Richard, 219n
Free riders, 59, 93–94, 230; in economic democracy, 286–87
Frey, R. G., 101n
Fried, Charles, 47n
Frieden, Karl, 285n
Friedman, Marilyn, 33n
Friedman, Milton, 150n, 152n, 243n, 246, 247n, 269n
Friedrich, Carl J., 38n
Furubotn, E. G., 167n, 287n, 293n

Galbraith, John K., 148, 180n
Galston, William A., 164n
Garcia, Quintin, 296n
Gauthier, David, 11–12n
Gay-Williams, J., 66n
Gellner, Ernest, 135n, 350n
Generic Consistency, Principle of, xi, 19, 62; as principle of human rights, 19, 39, 63, 307; as principle of justice, 71–72, 81; as principle of universal and equal rights, 73; direct and indirect applications of, 103–4; and mixed altruism, 307; right to political democracy as application of, 315; as supreme principle of morality, 356. See also Human Rights
Generic features of action, 13–14, 18, 19, 27, 28, 29, 96. See also Action; Necessary goods of action
Generic rights, 18–19, 183, 258; are human rights, 29, 63, 96; ultimate purpose of, 135. See also Human Rights; Rights
Geohegan, Thomas, 219n
Gibbard, Allan, 12n, 50n
Gibson, Mary, 112n, 218n
Gierke, Otto von, 125n
Gilder, George, 115n
Gill, Colin, 229n
Gilligan, Carol, 33n, 117n
Ginsburg, Helen, 220n
Gintis, Herbert, 139n, 153n, 161n, 289n

Glendon, Mary Ann, 2n
Goal-based, humanity value as, 81
Golding, Martin P., 2n, 23n, 231n
Gomberg, William, 254n
Good: ascribed to purposes, 17; conceptions of, not shared, 95; alternative conceptions of, 162–65. See also Necessary goods of action
Goodin, Robert E., 90n, 109n, 115n, 119n, 120n
Good Samaritan paradox, 114n
Gordon, Andrew, 251n
Gordon, David M., 245n, 246n
Gordon, Linda, 118n
Gordon, R. A., 245n, 246n
Gorz, André, 112n, 229n, 267n, 278n
Gough, Ian, 107n, 145n
Gould, Carol C., 33n, 274n, 279n, 289n
Government: role of, xiii, 55–56; as respondent of rights, 29, 64, 67, 217, 320. See also State
Gramsci, Antonio, 146n
Gray, John, 174n
Greenberg, Edward S., 259n, 261n, 267n, 270n, 271n, 281n, 285n, 286n
Griffin, James, 50n
Grisez, Germain, 279n
Grunebaum, James O., 196n
Gunn, Christopher E., 259n, 273n, 283n
Gutmann, Amy, 21n, 95n, 150n, 151n, 152n, 160n

Haavelmo, Trygve, 237n
Habermas, Jürgen, 28–29
Hacker, L. M., 195n
Hampden-Turner, Charles, 267n
Handler, Joel F., 111n, 115n, 129n
Hardin, Russell, 12n, 50n
Hardwig, John, 33n
Hare, R. M., 21n, 102n
Harm, 47–48, 175–76, 263; basic, 51; and unemployment, 218; consists in violating rights, 315

Harmful use of property, 175–78, 218, 242, 263

Harper v. Virginia Board of Elections, 345n

Harrington, Michael, 228n

Harris, John, 50n, 55n

Harris, Patricia R., 122n

Harrison, Bennett, 228n

Hart, H. L. A., 11n, 85n, 199n

Harvey, David, 207n

Harvey, Philip, 220n, 221n, 227n, 248n, 251n, 347n

Hasenfeld, Yeheskel, 111n, 115n, 129n

Hawkesworth, Mary E., 129n

Hayek, Friedrich A., 110n, 148, 180n, 194n, 195n, 164n, 169n

Head Start, 129, 150n, 155–62. *See also* Education

Hegel, 125n

Held, Virginia, 33n, 149n, 172n, 294n

Henkin, Louis, 53n

Herman, Edward S., 195n

Herrnstein, Richard, 153n

Herskovits, Melville J., 172n

Hierarchy, in capitalism, 266–68, 290; in economic democracy, 269–70; different kinds of, 271–73; opposed by general democratic thesis, 274; justified by expertise, 276. *See also* Equality; Inequality

Hilgert, Raymond L., 219n

Himmelfarb, Gertrude, 99n

Hines, A. G., 240n

Hobbes, Thomas, 25, 91, 106

Holmes, Stephen, 151n, 326n

Holocaust, 60

Holt, Charles C., 245n

Honoré, A. M., 166n, 172n, 175n

Hook, Sidney, 174n

Horvat, Branco, 146n

Housewife, 148–49. *See also* Feminism; Mothers; Women

Howard, Rhoda, 53n

Howells, William Dean, 351

Hudson, W. D., 21n

Human capital, 136–41; and productive agency, 137; and ethical individualism, 137, 139, 140; right to development of, 137; and economic growth, 138, 141; criticism of, 138–41; and education, 139, 153–55; two meanings of, 140. *See also* Capital

Humanity as value, 80

Human rights, 6, 9; existence of, 8–13, 23, 38; personal as well as social, 29–30; universality of, 62–70; include civil rights, 69; and development of productive abilities, 131; include economic and social as well as political and civil rights, 348–49. *See also* Generic rights; Rights

Hume, David, 7n, 50, 126, 182, 194, 229

Hunnius, Gerry, 261n, 281n

Hunt, E. K., 144n

Husak, Douglas N., 23n, 45n, 65n

Incentives, 52, 131, 184, 189, 258; in mutualist capitalist enterprises, 250–51; in economic democracy, 286–87, 298, 299; to acquire productive agency, 312. *See also* Motivation

Income: should be separated from work, 229; basic, 229–31; workers', higher in self-managed firms, 285; reduction of, 292–93; solidarity, 305. *See also* Wages

Individualism: of rights, 2; contrasted with community of rights, 83, 86; ethical, 97–98, 125, 137, 139, 152, 167, 170, 173, 199, 262; reconciled with communitarianism, 98; "possessive," 185; and market socialism, 264–65

Inegalitarian harm thesis, 176

Inequality, 56, 110, 198–99; of power, 12n, 73–74, 177, 216–17, 218, 222–23, 252–53, 253–54,

267–69, 282, 309, 340; economic, 168, 198, 203–13, 339–40; in economic democracy, 294; reduction of, 311; of political power, 340–41. *See also* Equality; Hierarchy

Inflation, and full employment, 242–49

Institutions, as basis of rights, 11, 13; effects of, 43; as helping, 43–44, 82–83; justification of political, 64–65; as grounds of particular transactions, 70; rights and obligations embodied in, 93, 234–35; build motivations of solidarity into Mondragon system, 304; maintain solidarity, 305–6

Interests, as basis of rights, 9, 11; and necessary conditions of action, 25; harmony of, 234; conflicts of, between workers and capitalists, 244, 266, 282, 332; positive and normative, 331–34

Interpersonal comparison of utilities, 51, 280. *See also* Degrees of needfulness

Intuitionism, 10–11, 102, 105, 355

Investment horizon problem, 287–88

Irwin, Terence, 172n

Jackall, Robert, 281n, 285n, 286n

Jacoby, Neil H., 217n

Jacques, Elliott, 212n

Jaggar, Alison M., 149n

Jahoda, Marie, 224n

Japan, 250–51

Jencks, Christopher, 14n, 107n, 109n, 115n, 124n, 125n, 128n, 154n

Jenkins, Clive, 227n, 228n, 229n

Jensen, A. R., 153n

Jensen, Michael, 287n

Jerovsek, Janez, 285n

Jones, Derek C., 261n, 270n, 285n

Josephson, Matthew, 194n

Jouvenel, Bertrand de, 180n

Justice, material and formal, 71–73; PGC as principle of, 71–73; contrasted with charity and humanity, 79–81; philosophical theories of, view persons as passive recipients, 135, 350; moral virtue of, 136; distributive, criterion of, 204; requirements of, 311; aim of cooperative mode of democratic process, 330, 333; and widely unequal distribution of vital resources, 340; substantive and procedural, 340–41, 342–43. *See also* Rights

Justifying basis of rights, 9, 11–20; two kinds of, 10

Kagan, Shelly, 55n, 180n

Kaldor, Nicholas, 202n

Kamerman, Sheila B., 328n

Kant, 7, 24, 123

Katz, Michael B., 111n, 115n, 125n, 128n

Katznelson, Ira, 82n

Kerr, Clark, 204n

Keyfitz, Nathan, 154n

Keynes, John M., 237n, 240, 245

Keyserling, Leon, 220n, 221n

King, Seth S., 57n

Kipnis, Kenneth, 55n, 72n

Kirzner, Israel, 134n, 209n, 300n

Knight, Frank H., 131n, 177, 186n, 212n

Kochan, Thomas A., 219n

Kolakowski, Leszak, 99n

Koontz, Sidney H., 142n

Kornai, Janos, 209n, 298n, 299n, 300n

Kotlowitz, Alex, 156n

Kozol, Jonathan, 156n

Kuttner, Bob, 220

Kuznets, Simon, 202n

Kymlicka, Will, 92n, 95n

Labor, as absorbed into capital, 138–39; as justifying property rights, 183; as application of rights to freedom and well-being, 183; as dynamic, 197. *See also* Productive and unproductive labor; Work

Labor unions: role of, 218–19, 269; solidarity among, 306
La Follette, Hugh, 58n
Lash, Scott M., 145n
Laws, 21, 352; need for, 94, 317. *See also* Government; State
Layard, Richard, 237n, 241n
LeGrand, Julian, 109n, 138n, 150n, 261n
Leibenstein, Harvey, 270n, 283n
Lekachman, Robert, 227n
Lerner, Abba P., 240n
Levin, Henry M., 162n, 250n, 283n, 285n, 286n
Levine, Andrew, 117n, 333n
Levitan, Sar A., 108n, 156n
Levy, Leonard, 102n
Lewis, H. Gregg, 219n
Liberals, xiii, 5, 32, 91, 94, 162n, 331, 355
Libertarians, xiii, 4, 5, 43, 44, 88, 187, 349, 350
Lichtenberg, Judith, 34n
Lichtenstein, Nelson, 261n, 303n
Lindbeck, Asser, 216n
Lindblom, Charles E., 177n, 212n, 216n, 306n
Livernash, E. Robert, 244n
Locke, John, 15n, 38n, 161n, 170n, 177, 186, 188n; "proviso" of, 175, 197–98
Lomasky, Loren E., 22n, 102n
Lopate, Carol, 149n
Love, xv, 21–22, 83, 149
Lucas, J. R., 174n
Lucas, Robert E., Jr., 237n, 238n, 240n
Lukes, Steven, 89n, 97n
Lyons, David, 72n

MacCallum, Gerald C., Jr., 15n
Macfarlane, L. J., 235n
Machan, Tibor, 44n, 63n, 150n
MacIntyre, Alasdair, 2n, 21n, 91n
Mack, Eric, 35n
Malinvaud, Edmond, 216n

Mansbridge, Jane J., 7n, 330n
Maoism, 92
Managers, 209
Marginal product, difficulties of measuring, 206
Margolis, Howard, 7n
Marie, Jean-Bernard, 3n
Markets, 4; insufficient for fulfilling positive rights, 59, 312, 328, 349; interfered with by community of rights, 127–28, 257–58, 350; inequalities of, 150; and objections on unemployment, 215; and risks, 215; and governmental intervention for employment, 221–22; incapable of providing for needs and public goods, 228; imperfection of, 239; and contract-at-will, 253; justifiable operations of, 128, 148, 232, 257, 349, 350, 352; contracting, 267–68; may generate hardships in economic democracy, 294; challenges of, to egalitarian values, 303; modified by economic democracy, 306; effective participation in, 352. *See also* Capitalism; Exchange value
Market socialism, 260; varieties of, 260n; a contradictory notion, 264–65, 270, 300, 303–4; competition in, 293; compatibility of market and socialist aspects, 303–4. *See also* Economic democracy
Marmor, Theodore R., 108n, 115n
Marshall, Alfred, 146n, 207n, 211n
Martin, Andrew, 334n
Martin, Rex, 64n, 189n, 190n, 221n
Marx, Karl, 14, 87, 98n, 99n, 112, 130, 131, 139n, 140n, 143, 144, 168n, 176n, 182n, 194n, 203n, 204n, 205, 207n, 209n, 212n, 229, 232n, 244n, 257, 267n, 295n, 334
Maslow, A. H., 158n
May, Larry, 61n
McBride, William L., 149n
McCain, Roger A., 286n, 287n

McGuire, Martin C., 55n
McMahon, Christopher, 22n
Mead, Lawrence, 115n, 124n, 128n, 129n
Meade, J. E., 263n, 268n, 301n
Means, Gardiner, 166n, 208n
Mecca, Andrew W., 225n
Medical care, right to, 36, 42, 65–66, 67, 73, 108, 109, 147, 230. *See also* Needs
Meiksins, Peter, 145n
Melman, Seymour, 284
Melnyk, Andrew, 63n
Meritocracy, 292, 297, 307
Meyer, Michael J., 66n
Meyers, Diana T., 55n, 72n
Meyers, Frederic, 253n
Milenkovich, Deborah D., 283n, 287n
Mill, J. S., 112, 143–44, 148, 176, 182n, 194n, 196n, 208, 209, 211n, 257, 267n
Miller, David, 92n, 99n, 20cn, 261n, 303n, 321n, 327n, 330n
Milne, A. J. M., 3n, 67n
Milton, John, 131
Minford, Patrick, 240n
Mises, Ludwig von, 134n, 211n, 236n, 240n
Modality, in relations of reciprocity and mutuality, 77–78. *See also* Necessity
Mondragon, 100n, 259, 261, 270n, 281, 284, 288, 296–308; two levels in, 296–97. *See also* Economic democracy
Monroe, Kristen R., 41n
Montgomery, David, 250n, 261n, 303n, 306n
Moon, J. Donald, 226n
Moral: rights, 10–12, 16, 39; rights, conditions of justification of, 12–13, 16, 39; precepts, 13; judgments, as categorically obligatory, 24, 27; necessity, 27, 304, 317, 349, 352; rightness, 28; considerations

and self-respect, 79, 223; requirements, 79; virtue of justice, 136; reasons, 343, 345. *See also* Justice; Rights
Morality, rational foundation of, xi; range of, 13; PGC as supreme principle of, 19, 356. *See also* Generic Consistency, Principle of
Morgan, Richard E., 101n
Morris, Arval A., 24n, 65n
Mothers, 107, 123–24, 149, 157. *See also* Feminism; Parents; Women
Motivation: to accept concept of human rights, 7, 25–26, 126–27; of self-interest and of reasonableness, 94; not exclusively self-interested, 126; children's, to take advantage of opportunities, 156; of workers, 245–46, 252; in economic democracy, 285–86, 303–4; in institutions, 304; of recipients of policies of productive agency, 312. *See also* Incentives
Moye, A. Melissa, 296n
Moynihan, Daniel P., 343n
Mulgan, R. G., 102n
Munson, Ronald, 66n
Munzer, Stephen R., 166n, 167n, 178n, 187n, 224n, 255n
Murray, Charles, 115n, 129n, 153n
Mutual assured destruction (MAD), 75
Mutuality, 6, 19–20, 41, 44, 47, 62–64, 127, 136, 168, 223, 252, 311; contrasted with reciprocity, 75–79; material and formal components of, 75, 253–54; in community of rights, 83, 98, 117, 232; and social contribution thesis, 85; of interdependence and exchange, 120–22, 186; and welfare, 120–22; an interpersonal relation, 123; and productive agency, 141, 142; different interpretations of, 146; and private property, 168; in labor justification of property rights, 183,

Mutuality (continued)
184, 194; violation of, 184, 202–3;
and property rights, 200; and contribution principle, 205, 209, 223;
and governmental provision of
work, 219; and loafing, 231; and
duty to work, 231–32; and mandatory rights, 233–35; in some
capitalist firms, 258; in economic
democracy, 282; difference of, from
solidarity, 304–5; among labor
unions, 306; violated by secession,
334; in democratic effectuation of
economic rights, 347, 348
Myers, Gustavus, 194n
Mygard, Niels, 263n
Mygind, Niels, 263n
Myint, Hla, 143n
Myrdal, Gunnar, 57n

Narveson, Jan, 174n
Nathan, Richard, 128n
Nature, as ontological context of politics, xiv, 15
Nature of rights, 8–9, 15, 37–38, 73,
89
Nazism, 60, 92, 122
Necessary goods of action, 6, 17, 108,
147; procedural and substantive,
14–15, 319; autonomy as, 117;
productive agency as, 132. See also
Action; Generic features of action
Necessary projects, 84–85
Necessity, normative, of rights, 12, 13,
16, 18, 24–25, 77–78, 79–80, 102,
108; moral, 27, 304, 317, 349,
352; of statement about action,
356. See also Categoricalness
Needs, 11, 14n, 21, 55, 104, 111,
148, 170, 196; for agency, 51, 201;
for productive work, 226; for goods
without effective demand, 226–27;
fulfillment of, and employment,
227–28; fulfillment of, without
work, 229; for services, 230; for

freedom and well-being, 356–57;
basic, 340, 341; mandatory, 356–
57
Nehamas, Alexander, 161n
Nelson, William N., 78n, 275n, 321n
Neumann, Franz, 100n
Neutrality, about conceptions of the
good, and the community of rights,
162–64
Nevile, John W., 243n
Nicholas, Ted, 222n
Nickel, James W., 39n, 64n, 67n, 68n,
112n, 221n
Nie, Norman, 340n
Nietzsche, F., 28, 161
Nino, Carlos Santiago, 35n, 95n
Norris, Frank, 351
Nove, Alec, 99n, 146n, 148n, 179n,
210n, 163n, 164n, 269n, 286n,
290n, 299n, 301n, 306, 310n
Noyelle, Thierry J., 291n
Nozick, Robert, 36n, 44n, 46n, 49n,
84n, 170n, 180, 186n, 187n, 190n,
275n
Nutter, G. Warren, 299n

Oakeshott, R., 267n, 292n, 296n,
305n
Objects of rights, 6, 8–9, 38, 81, 101–
2, 280; as necessary goods, 78, 79.
See also Rights
Obligations: on behalf of the needy,
47; to help toward democratization,
58; criterion-based, 235; imperfect,
353; to participate in democratic
processes, 354, 357. See also Du-
ties; 'Ought'
O'Connor, James C., 145n
Offe, Claus, 229n
Okun, Arthur M., 206n, 300n
Oliner, Pearl M., 60n
Oliner, Samuel P., 60n
O'Mahony, David, 270n, 300n
O'Neill, Onora, 40n, 58n, 80n, 353n
Ontological: problem of relation be-

tween rights and community, 1–2; conceptions of the self, 91; questions about human relationships, 125–26
Organicism, 125–26
'Ought': and 'is', 16, correlative with rights, 17, 22, 39; utilitarian grounds of, 22–23; self-interested and other-directed, 24; and 'can', 56, 67, 200, 353; strict, 17, 80; and legal enforcement, 80; need not be explicitly invoked against respondents of rights, 90. See also Duties; Obligations
Overload of duties, 55–62, 313
Ownership, common, 172–73, 196–97; divided, 196–97; public, 208; residual claims of, 261. See also Property rights
Oxfam, 57–58

Paine, Thomas, 38n, 220
Palmer, Francis H., 155n
Parent, William, 66n
Parents, involved in Head Start programs, 157–58. See also Fathers; Mothers
Pareto optimality, 46, 122, 284
Parijs, Philippe van, 229n
Participation, 260, 314, 335, 337, 343, 354; equal right of effective, in political process, 314–15, 335, 337. See also Economic democracy; Democracy; Political democracy
Particularism, 165, 199; justified by universal principle, 86; in communitarian doctrines, 92, 334; focus on the poor, 110; of economic rights, 329. See also Universalism
Passell, Peter, 181n
Paternalism, 164
Payne v. Western and Atlantic Railway, 81 Tenn. (1884), 253n
Pearl, Arthur, 248n

Pejovich, Svetozar, 259n
Pence, Gregory E., 66n, 130n
Pennock, J. Roland, 2n, 23n, 65n
Perfectionism, 164. See also Neutrality
Perlman, Helen H., 193n
Perlman, Richard, 204n, 237n
Perry, Charles R., 151n
Peters, R. S., 174n
Petro, Sylvester, 219n
PGC. See Generic Consistency, Principle of
Phillips, A. W., 242n
Phillips, Derek L., 27n, 28n, 82n, 190n, 206n
Phillips curve, 242–46
Pigou, A. C., 205n
Piore, Michael J., 244n
Piven, Frances Fox, 107n, 122n
Plant, Raymond, 82n, 112n, 150n, 264n, 329n
Plato, 24, 25, 87, 92, 125n, 160n, 333
Platt, Harlan D., 222n
Platt, Stephen, 215n
Plattner, Marc F., 344n
Pluralism, social, 315; ethical, 355; political, 355
Pocklington, Thomas C., 101n
Poleman, Thomas T., 57n
Political democracy: right to, 313, 314; must be used to effectuate economic democracy, 314; a procedural right, 314–15; an application of PGC's right to freedom, 315; procedural justification of, 315–16; constituent of community of rights, 316; rational procedures in, 324; two kinds of procedures of, 330–31; competitive and cooperative models of, 330–35, 339–41, 343; operations of, intensely competitive, 334; weight of moral reasons in, 343; procedural vs. substantive arguments in, 346–47. See also Civil liberties; Democracy

Political issues, criterion of, 320–24, 324–27
Political rights, 29, 64, 313, 314; conflicts with economic rights, 53, 319, 320; not subject to democratic political process, 325–26. *See also* Human rights; Rights
Pollack, Andrew, 251n
Pollack, Ervin H., 67n
Pollis, Adamantia, 67n
Poole, Robert W., Jr., 328n
Popper, Karl R., 174n
Positive rights, 4, 20, 31–70; importance of, 31–32; distinction of, from negative rights, 33–38, 45; argument for, 38–44; property rights as, 166, 200; civil liberties as, 341–47; too diffuse, in some East European constitutions, 354–55. *See also* Human rights; Rights
Poverty, 106–10, 152; absolute and relative, 107n; "feminization of," 107; prima facie violation of human rights, 108, 109. *See also* Deprivation; Needs
Post, Gaines, 275n
Power: in welfare dependence, 118; active and passive, 161; property relations as asymmetrical relations of, 174, 178; inequalities of, in property rights, 177–78; four dimensions of capitalists', 177–78; and determination of wages, 204; and extraction of profits, 212; remote and effective, 335, 337; civil liberties as effective, 335–41; qualifications of, in political process, 337–38; conative and achievemental, 339
Power, Marilyn, 124n
Primordialist questions about justification of property rights, 169, 188–89. *See also* Property rights
Primorack, Igor, 148n
Prior, A. N., 114n
Prisoner's Dilemma, 94

Privacy of property rights, 172–73. *See also* Property rights
Privatization, 150n, 327–29; limits of, 328
Productive agency: positive right to development of, 132; analysis of, 132–36; and action, 132; and additive well-being, 132–33; a necessary good, 133; general and economic, 132–33, 338, 351; education for, 149–55, 245; and property rights, 153–55, 167–70; two senses of economic, 210–11. *See also* Employment; Work
Productive and unproductive labor, 141–49; normative assumptions of distinction between, 142; criteria of, 143–49, 206, 210–13; a barren distinction, 146; relative to context of human rights, 147–49, 227; primary kind of productive, 147–48, 227; more fundamental than the two senses of productive agency, 147. *See also* Labor; Work
Productivist welfarism, 134–35, 136, 314, 350. *See also* Productive agency; Welfare
Promise-keeping, 11, 69–70, 233, 234–35
Property rights, 53, 56, 166–213; and productive agency, 153–55; not absolute, 46, 173, 175, 184, 198, 258, 263; may conflict with welfare rights, 104; as claim-rights, 166, 166n; negative and positive, 166, 200–201; utilitarian justifications of, 167; "personal" and "private", 168–69; consequentialist justification of, 169, 170–81; antecedentalist justification of, 169, 181–88, 188–98; primordialist objections to justification of, 169, 188–98; conditions of action, 171; and privacy, 171–72; priority of, 175, 181; harmful use of, 175–78, 218, 242, 263; labor justification

of, 183; purposive-labor thesis of, 184–98; and mutuality, 184, 186; and self-ownership, 186–87, 188–94; and world ownership, 194–98; conflicts between justifications of, 199–200; as positive rights, 200; two justifications of, needed, 201; and inflation, 242; in jobs, 254–55. *See also* Ownership; Rights

Proportionality, Principle of, 24, 65, 77, 101; proportional equality, 159–60

Prostitute, 144, 145, 148

Przeworski, Adam, 284n, 290n, 291n

Public goods, 48, 173, 197, 201

Puritans, 95

Purposive-labor thesis of property rights, 184–98, 206; primordialist objections to, 188–98. *See also* Property rights

Purposiveness, as generic feature of action, 13, 17; as basis of property rights, 183–84

Putterman, Louis, 263n, 269n, 302n

Quinn, Michelle, 222n

Quod omnes tangit, 275n

Rabossi, Eduardo, 11n

Race, 33n, 68, 73, 91, 92, 93, 100, 107, 139, 154–55, 158, 204n, 217, 253, 296, 344

Rachels, James, 66n

Rae, Douglas, 160n

Raphael, D. D., 38n, 62n, 63n, 69n

Rational choice, 11, 25, 41; not exclusively self-interested, 19; minimal conditions of, 22

Rawls, John, 26–27, 85n, 96, 151n, 152n, 163n, 188–92, 206, 224n, 280, 355; on ""least advantaged," 112–14, 189; determinism of, 190–91

Raz, Joseph, 3n, 47n, 48n, 89n, 134n, 164n

Reason: fundamental principle of, 19; use of in action, 26, 66; correct use of, 117

Reasonable self, 93–94, 96, 127, 136, 235, 304, 307, 333, 343, 342. *See also* Self

Reasons, in moral disputes, 322; as components of cooperative model of democratic process, 331–32, 333–34, 339; for mutual obligations, 341; moral, may carry weight in political process, 343, 345

Reciprocity, 41; contrasted with mutuality, 75–79

Redistribution, 52, 94, 179–81, 213, 214, 309, 334n. *See also* Economic rights

Regis, Edward, Jr., xi n, 21n, 23n, 356n

Reich, Charles A., 255n

Reich, Michael, 266n

Reich, Robert B., 131n, 179, 334n

Reiman, Jeffrey, 24n

Rein, Mildred, 128n, 129n

Religion, 67, 68, 91, 158, 163–64, 217, 253, 296

Rescher, Nicholas, 112n

Rescue, duty to, 45, 56, 60–61, 62–63, 103, 126

Respondents of rights, 8–9, 11–12, 22, 29–30; the state as, 29, 59–60, 64, 108; courts and governments as, of economic and social rights, 353–54. *See also* Rights

Responsibility, individual, 36, 61

Reutlinger, S., 57n

Reynolds v. Sims, 345n

Richards, Janet R., 148n

Riessman, Frank, 248n

Rifkin, Jeremy, 229n

Rights, as antithetical to community, 1–5, 348; and correlative duties, 6–7, 9; and self-interest, 6–7, 9, 90; as entailing community, 6–8; structure of, 8–9; nature of, 8–9, 15, 37–38, 73, 89; prior to duties, 9; legal, 10, 21, 23, 59, 86, 232; moral, 10, 21, 23, 59, 86, 232; gen-

Rights (*continued*)
    eral and special, 11, 69–70, 199;
    procedural and substantive, 14–15,
    314–15, 319; conciliation of, with
    community, 15–16, 19–20, 32–41,
    69, 70, 73, 79, 87, 96–97, 108,
    117, 128, 132, 150, 162, 165, 179,
    197, 198, 201, 213, 226, 234, 258,
    314, 325, 346, 351, 354; transition
    from prudential to moral, 18–19;
    generic, 18–19, 29; negative and
    positive, 35–36, 336–37; mixed,
    36, 41; as side-constraints, 36–37;
    mandatory and discretionary, 38,
    163n, 231–35, 263; few absolute,
    47, 51; political as against eco-
    nomic, 53; of agency, 59;
    universality of, across cultures, 66–
    69; civil, 68–69; needed even in
    ideal community, 88–89; distinc-
    tion between contents and claiming
    of, 89; may lead to mutual respect,
    90; application of, in productive la-
    bor, 183; diversity relations
    between duties and, 233; reflexivity
    of duties and, 234–35; and
    criterion-based obligations, 235;
    and claims, 236; nonsubtractive,
    242; weak, 255; distributive and
    collective, 261–62, 277–78; ques-
    tion of their being subject to
    political procedures, 319–27; con-
    flicts between and about, 322;
    "manifesto," 353, 354. *See also*
    Duties; Economic rights; Generic
    rights; Human rights; Political
    rights; Positive rights
Rights-inflation, 80, 101–4
Right-to-work laws, 217–18
Riley, Clara M. D., 157n
Risks, of entrepreneurship, 209, 300;
    in market economy, 215, 238;
    workers averse to, 300. *See also* En-
    trepreneurs
Ritchie, David G., 69n
Robbins, Lionel, 50n, 239

Rockefeller, John D., 351
Roemer, John E., 50n, 196n, 205n,
    260n
Roosevelt, Franklin D., 220, 249n
Rorty, Richard, 10n
Rosen, Sumner N., 218n
Rosenblum, Nancy L., 2n
Ross, Susan Deller, 33n
Rottenberg, Simon, 255n
Rousseau, J. J., 176, 330, 333, 342,
    343
Runciman, W. C., 73n
Russell, Raymond, 262n
Rustin, Michael, 221n

Sachs, David, 224n
Samuels, Warren J., 212n
Sandel, Michael J., 2n, 91n, 92n, 94n
Santomero, Anthony M., 243n
Sarvasy, Wendy, 123n
Say's law, 237
Scheffler, Samuel, 279n
Scherer, Donald, 45n
Scheuermann, James, 22n
Schlesinger, Arthur M., Jr., 249n,
    325n
Schmidtz, David, 197n
Schonberger, J., 251n
Schorr, Lisbeth, 115n
Schultz, Theodore W., 58n, 136n,
    138n, 153n, 202n
Schumpeter, Joseph, 136n, 147n,
    209n, 293n, 300n, 321n, 330n
Schwab, Peter, 67n
Schweickart, David, 112n, 168n,
    210n, 212n, 238n, 261n, 263n,
    272n
Seccombe, W., 149n
Secession, of upper classes from soci-
    ety, 334, 357
Seibel, Hans D., 259n
Self, constitutiveness doctrine of, 91–
    96, 125; abstractness of concep-
    tions of, 96; organicist conception
    of, 125–26. *See also* Reasonable
    self

Self-actualization, 75, 131, 158–62
Self-determination, 193n
Self-esteem, 79, 130; of welfare recipients, 130; and unemployment, 215; and employment, 223–28; distinguished from self-respect, 223–24; tied to productive agency, 224; objections to tying to positive right to employment, 225–27; variability of causal factors of, 225
Self-fulfillment, xv, 5, 159, 160, 168
Self-interest, and rights, 7–8, 9–10, 12, 17, 18, 26, 333; may be counterbalanced by awareness of rights, 26, 306; Rawls's basis in, 113–14. See also Egoism
Self-management, 259n; the "self" in, 273n
Self-ownership, 140, 186–94, 275
Self-respect, 79; and productive agency, 201; and employment, 223–28; distinguished from self-esteem, 223–24
Selowsky, M., 57n
Sen, Amartya, 7n, 14n, 26n, 35n, 57n, 107n, 134n
Shaffer, Henry W., 139n
Shapiro, Carl, 237n, 241n, 249n
Shapiro, I., 33n
Sher, George, 192n
Shirking, 241, 270; and full employment, 249–52; in economic democracy, 286–87
Shue, Henry, 34n, 35n, 45n, 55n, 58n, 112n
Sidgwick, Henry, 40, 50n
Sidorsky, David, 53n, 67n
Siegel, Richard L., 221n
Sieghart, Paul, 57n
Sik, Ota, 288n
Sinclair, Peter, 227n, 238n, 241n
Singer, Marcus G., 40n
Singer, Peter, 55n
Sinnott-Armstrong, Walter, 102n
Skocpol, Theda, 111n, 129n
Slavery, 11, 90, 92, 176

Slichter, Sumner H., 219n
Smith, Adam, 14n, 119, 143, 144, 148
Smoker, Barbara, 66n
Social contribution thesis, 83–85, 91–92, 152, 173, 175, 197, 275, 276
Social democracy, 111, 177, 257–58, 269, 309–10, 312
Socialism, 43–44, 198, 265, 355; varying definitions of, 98; ties to communitarianism, 98–99; upholds solidarity, 303
Social science, and educational development, 153–55
Södersten, B., 224n
Soft budget constraint, 298–99
Solidarity, 219, 282; entailed by human rights, 6; in economic democracy, 286, 303, 305–6; upheld by socialism, 303; difference of, from mutuality, 304–5; types of, 305
Soltan, Karol E., 100n
Soviet Union, xii, 75, 232
Sparer, Edward V., 108n
Specification, 68, 85; problem of, 104–5, 280, 320, 323, 324, 326, 352
Spirituality, xv, 21, 22, 352
Stalinism, 92
Stanley, David T., 222n
Stark, Evan, 157n
Starr, Paul, 329n
Starvation, 30, 42, 53, 54, 72, 107, 200. See also Famine
State, the, as respondent of rights, 59, 94, 108, 152, 328, 349; justification of, 60; as community of rights, 59–60, 79, 341, 346; existence of, required by principle of human rights, 317; inefficiencies of, 323
Stearns, Marian S., 156n
Steigleder, Klaus, xi n
Steinbock, Bonnie, 34n
Steiner, Hillel, 179n
Stephen, Frank H., 261n, 292n

Stigler, George J., 283n
Stiglitz, Joseph E., 237n, 241n, 249n, 270n
Stoloff, David, 343n
Stone, Bob, 296n
Streeten, Paul P., 139n
Sturgeon, Nicholas, 356n
Subjects of rights, 8–9, 101, 280. See also Rights
Sufrin, Sidney C., 219n
Summers, Clyde W., 254n
Summers, Lawrence M., 216n
Sunstein, Cass, 354n
Supportive Organization, 297–306; functions as community of rights, 298
Surplus value, produced by productive labor, 143, 290
System of human rights, 52, 93, 97–98

Tarantino, T. H., 109n
Taylor, Charles, 2n, 32, 91n, 182n
Taylor, Frederick, 138
Taylor, Michael, 82n
Taylor, Richard, 193n
Technological developments, render work unnecessary, 229–31. See also Work
Terkel, Studs, 131n, 267n
Thalberg, Irving, 193n
Thomas, Henk, 259n, 261n, 270n, 281n, 283n, 288n, 292n, 295n, 296n, 297n, 301n, 302n
Thomson, Judith J., 2n, 54n
Thurow, Lester C., 159n, 206n
Tierney, Brian, 38n
Tiffin, Susan, 123n
Titmuss, Richard, 126
Tobin, James, 221n, 244n
Tocqueville, Alexis de, 333n
Townsend, Peter, 107n, 110n, 215n
Treiman, Donald, 205n

Uchitelle, Louis, 178n, 216n
Ulmer, Melville J., 226n
Unemployment: effects of on well-being, 214–15; voluntary and involuntary, 221, 236–42; "natural rate of," 243n; as incentive device, 249. See also Employment
Universal Declaration of Human Rights, xii–xiii, 29–30, 64, 68, 205n, 220, 348
Universalism, of human rights principle, 92, 110, 165, 199, 334; of political rights, 329. See also Particularism
Universality: of human rights, 6, 17; of positive rights, 62–70; of rights across cultures, 66–68; and focus on poverty, 110-11. See also Human rights; Positive rights
Universalizability, 18, 72
Use-values, 133, 144, 183, 185, 223
Utilitarianism, 11–12, 47, 167, 355; contrasted with collective rights, 48–49; of rights, 49–52; cannot do normative work of rights, 80; and property rights, 167; and unemployment, 243

Valentine, Jeanette, 157n
Van Dyke, Vernon, 2n
Vanek, Jaroslav, 260n, 261n, 274n, 283n, 285n, 286n, 287n, 290n, 291n, 292n, 295n, 296n, 303n
Veatch, Henry B., 14n
Veblen, Thorstein, 134
Vedder, Richard K., 216n, 237n
Verba, Sidney, 340n
Vickers, John, 328n, 329n
Viner, Jacob, 240n
Virtues, 13, 103, 136, 137, 150, 151, 162; intellectual and cultural, 164, 352. See also Justice; Moral
Vogel, Ezra, 251n
Voluntariness: as generic feature of action, 13; and character development, 193n; of unemployment, 236–37; and unforced choice, 237–39. See also Action; Freedom; Generic features of action

Voluntary associations, 78, 103
Voting Rights Act of 1965, 343
Vouchers, 110n, 328n

Wages, determination of, 204; effi-
    ciency, 221, 241; contours, 244–
    45; and manpower policies, 245;
    increases in, 245–46; costs of full
    employment, 246–48; in economic
    democracy, 288. See also Income
Waldron, Jeremy, 3n, 40n, 47n, 49n,
    168n, 175n, 187n, 199n
Wallace, James D., 40n
Walters, Harry T., 57n
Walzer, Michael, 2n
Ward, Benjamin, 293n
Warnock, John W., 57n
Warr, P., 215n
Wasserstrom, Richard, 72n
Webb, Sidney and Beatrice, 295n
Weimar Republic, 325–26
Weisbrod, Burton A., 159n
Weiss, Andrew, 241n
Welfare, 59, 108–10; positive right to,
    108, 114, 127, 200, 233, 350; sys-
    tem, 114–14, 118; antithetical to
    autonomy, 117–18; dependence,
    118-25, 312; state, 82, 88, 103,
    108–9, 135, 138, 177, 257, 310,
    312; state as abolishing welfare,
    135
Welfarism, productivist, 134–35, 136,
    314, 350
Well-being, 6; as generic feature of ac-
    tion, 13–14; as substantive feature
    of action, 15; hierarchy of levels of,
    14, 23, 46, 147, 278–79; basic, 14,
    23, 42, 51, 278; nonsubtractive, 14,
    23, 29, 278–79; additive, 14, 23,
    43, 51, 91, 132, 149, 279; vari-
    ability of, 14; right to, 17; and
    productive agency, 132–33, 147;
    workers' rights to, violated, 259;
    and economic democracy, 278–88.
    See also Action; Additive well-
    being; Generic features of action

Wellman, Carl, 55n, 112n
Werhane, Patricia H., 254n
Westen, Peter, 160n
Westinghouse Report, 155–56n
Wheeler, David, 243n
White, Stephen K., 28n
Whyte, W. F. and K. K., 100n,
    259n, 296n, 297n, 298n, 299n,
    301n, 302n, 303n, 305n,
    306n
Wiener, Hans, 296n
Will, use of in action, 66
Williams, Patricia J., 33n
Williamson, Oliver E., 269n, 270n
Willis, Paul, 161n
Wilson, Frank L., 270n
Wilson, William Julius, 111n, 115n,
    128n, 129n
Wolf, Charles, Jr., 328n
Wolf, Susan, 61n
Women: as having human rights, 100;
    and welfare, 111; workers, 205. See
    also Feminism; Mothers
Wood, Christopher, 251n
Wood, Stephen, 251n
Work: may generate self-esteem and
    self-respect, 130; depressive and
    creative, 130–31, 160, 224, 291;
    contrasted with action, 133; general
    concept of, 133; converted into em-
    ployment, 133; reduction of
    depressive, 151; and wages, 204;
    not needed, 229–31; duty to, 231–
    35; conditions of, 258–59. See also
    Employment; Labor
Workers: dependent on employers,
    118; distinguished from capitalists,
    207, 289–90; from managers and
    technicians, 289n; from profes-
    sionals, 290–91; motivation of,
    245–46, 252; control by, 260;
    types of control by, 260n; primary
    and secondary, 291; additional
    workers problem, 292–93, 301;
    sense of solidarity, 303–6; as averse
    to risks, 308

Workfare, 128–31
Work in America, 128n, 131n, 145n, 267n
World ownership, 188, 194–98
Wuthnow, Robert, 89n

Yellen, Janet L., 241n
Yugoslavia, 60, 259, 281, 288, 302n

Zigler, Edward, 155n
Zuparov, J., 300n